JN418371

GLOBAL BUSINESS ENGLISH

무역영어 스토리

김민호 · 한방울

도서출판 두남

Preface

무역 업무를 수행하려면 상대방과 효과적인 커뮤니케이션이 필수적이다. 특히 각 상황에 맞는 분명하고 효과적인 표현을 읽히는 것이 중요하다. 이것은 글을 쓰는 사람 혹은 소속 회사의 능력과 전문성을 나타내 줄 수 있기 때문이다.

대학에서 무역영어를 강의하면서 아쉬웠던 것은 기존의 교과서들이 주제별로 별개의 사례로 된 예문만을 열거하여 놓아서 수강생들이 각 주제 간의 흐름을 잘 이해하지 못하였다는 점이다.

이 책은 이런 점을 염두에 두고 쓰여졌다. 즉 전반적인 무역의 흐름을 이해하면서 각 상황에 맞는 효과적인 표현을 학습할 수 있도록 하는 것이 이 책의 목표이다. 이를 위해 이 책은 먼저 실제 무역현장에서 일어날 수 있는 상황을 가정한 2개의 Story가 전개된다. 각 Story는 무역의 진행 상황에 따른 여러 개의 Situation들로 구성되어 있어서 각 Story를 다 학습하고 나면 무역의 전반적 흐름을 파악함과 동시에 이에 따른 표현들을 배울 수 있도록 하였다.

Story I에서는 한국의 Qtopia System의 Jennifer Kim과 미국 LA의 EveryImport사의 Paul Frederic이 등장해서 Qtopia System사가 개발한 휴대전화용 무선 레이저 포인터인 Qtopia II에 대한 수출입 상담이 진행된다.

Story II에서는 한국의 전문 무역업체인 Global gTrading의 Eugine Park과 인도의 Allgarment Enterprises사의 Javv Gupta 사이에 전개되는 의류 수출입 상담이 수록되어 있다.

위와 같은 Story의 각 Situation 내용은 다음과 같이 구성되어 있다.

첫째, 각 Story내의 Situation은 일어난 순서대로 배열되어 있다. 예를 들면 Situation 2는 Situation 1에 대한 대답인 식이다. Situation들은 현장감을 살리기 위하여 e-mail, letter, fax 등의 형식을 그대로 옮겨 실었다.

둘째, Situation의 다음에는 Synopsis가 있다. Synopsis는 본문의 내용을 일일이 해석하기보다는 전반적인 내용을 파악할 수 있도록 Situation에 대한 대략적 설명 수록하였다.

셋째, Situation의 내용을 좀 더 구체적으로 파악하고, 상황에 맞는 영문 표현을 학습할 수 있도록 본문의 내용 중 중요한 부분을 밑줄로 표시하고 이에 대한 설명을 덧붙였다. 설명은 크게 무역실무와 관련된 내용과 그러한 내용을 영어로 표현하는 방법에 대한 설명으로 나뉘어져 있다.

넷째, Situation에 대한 설명 후, Practice Tests를 제공하였다. 여기에는 TOEIC 식으로 본문의 내용에 대하여 질문하는 형식과 적절한 영어 표현을 고르는 문제를 수록하여 학습한 내용에 대한 점검을 할 수 있도록 하였다. 이와 함께 무영영어 검정시험, 국제무역사, 관세사 등 무역 관련 자격시험에서 출제된 문제 중 본문의 내용과 관련된 문제를 수록하여 추후 시험 준비과정에 도움이 될 수 있게 하였다.

이 책에 수록한 2개의 Story를 통하여 실제 무역현장에서 일어날 수 있는 각종 상황에 맞는 영어문장을 구사할 수 있는 능력을 키울 수 있을 것이다. 무역 활동은 매우 다양한 상황에서 전개되기 때문에 한 권의 책으로 모든 실무를 다룰 수는 없었다. 그러나 이 책의 내용을 충실이 학습하고 나면 다양한 무역 활동에 적응할 수 있는 응용력이 생길 수 있을 것이다.

마지막으로 이 책이 무역현장에서 뛰고 있는 실무자들과 무역을 배우고 있는 학생들에게 경쟁력 있는 커뮤니케이션 향상에 도움이 되었으면 하는 바람이다.

2019년 8월
저자 씀

Contents

Story I

Qtopia vs. EveryImport

Story II

Global gTrade vs. Allgarment Enterprises

Business Letter의 구성요소

모든 공식적 문서가 그렇듯이 공식 business letter에도 일정한 형식이 있다. 내용을 전달하는 방법은 시대에 따라 letter, fax, e-mail 등으로 바뀌었지만 그 형식은 크게 변하지 않고 쓰이고 있다. 물론 전달하려는 내용을 정확히 쓰는 것이 중요하지만 그 내용을 담을 형식 역시 professional한 business person에게는 매우 중요하다. 다음 페이지의 편지는 일반적 business letter가 가질 수 있는 요소를 담은 sample이다. 편지의 형식이지만 e-mail이나 fax에서도 같이 적용된다.

Sample Business Letter

①

Qtopia Systems

134 Seocho-dong, Seocho-ku, Seoul 130-070, Republic of Korea
Phone: +82-2-2374-4785
Fax: +82-2-2374-4788
E-mail: systems@Qtopia.com

⑧ Reference No. 2006-0451

② September 1, 2015

③ EveryImport Co., Inc., 3434
Sunset Boulevard, Los Angeles,
CA 90832 USA

⑨ Attention of Mr. Paul Frederick

④ Dear Mr. Frederick:

⑩ Reply to your inquiry

⑤

Thank you for the mail expressing your interest in our Q-pointer II. In the attached catalog you will find more information about the Q-pointer. We look forward to serving you in near future, and thank you again for your interest in our Qtopia systems.

⑥ Yours sincerely,

⑦ Jennifer Kim

Jennifer Kim (Ms.)
Director, Export
Department Qtopia
Systems

⑪ JAA/hr
⑫ Encls: Our Catalog
⑬ C.C.: The Korea Exchange Bank
⑭ P.S.: Thank you again for your inquiry.

1 Business Letter의 중요 요소들

① Letterhead

회사의 독특한 로고나 주소, 전화번호, 팩스번호, e-mail, web주소 등이 인쇄된 부분을 Letterhead라고 한다. 보통 편지지의 맨 윗 부분을 차지하고 있다. Letterhead는 수신자에게 발신자의 상호, 주소, 영업종목 등을 효과적으로 알리고 또 수신자가 쉽게 회신할 수 있도록 개성 있고 간결하게 인쇄하는 것이 좋다. e-mail을 보낼 때에는 미리 회사의 로고나 주소 등을 자동으로 입력하게 하는 회사가 많다.

② Date Line

통신문의 발신일자는 letterhead 바로 밑에 온다. 편지지의 왼쪽 혹은 오른쪽에 올 수 있다. 미국식은 September 1, 2015로, 영국식은 1st September, 2015로 쓴다. 연도 앞에 쉼표를 붙이는 것이 일반적이고 영국식의 경우 서수표시 -th, -st, -nd, rd는 있어도 되고 없어도 된다. [그러나 읽을 때는 미국식, 영국식 모두 서수를 넣어서 읽는다. 즉, September first two thousand fifteen으로 읽는다.] 어느 것을 쓰든지 상관없지만 하나의 형식으로 일관성 있게 써야 한다. 우리나라 기업의 경우 거래 상대방의 국적(미국 혹은 유럽)에 따라 유연하게 바꿔 쓸 필요는 있다. 어떤 경우에도 숫자만으로 표시하는 것은 피해야 한다. 9/1/14와 같이 쓰는 것은 일상생활에서는 쓸 수 있지만 특히 국제무역에 있어서는 혼란을 야기할 수 있기 때문이다. 미국식과 영국식의 표기형태가 다르기 때문에 미국식을 쓰는 나라에서는 9월 1일로 이해하지만, 영국식을 쓰는 곳에서는 1월 9일로 받아들인다. 또 미국에서도 공식문서에서 영국식처럼 일-월-년 순으로 쓰는 경우가 있기 때문에 반드시 확인을 해야 한다. e-mail에서는 날짜가 자동으로 입력되므로 생략하고 쓰기도 한다.

③ Inside Address

및 국명 등을 쓴다. 이 sample에서처럼 attention line(⑨에서 설명함)에는 받는 사람의 이름이 생략된다. 주소를 쓰는 원칙은 나라마다 다르므로 상대방이 쓴 형식으로 쓰는 것이 가장 무난하다. 일반적으로 영어를 쓰는 나라는 회사명-건물번호-길 명칭-도시 이름-주 이름-우편번호-나라이름 순으로 쓴다.

④ Salutation

주로 Dear ...로 시작되는 본문의 시작을 알리는 부분을 salutation(인사)이라고 한다.

상대방의 이름을 모르는 경우, Dear Sir가 가장 일반적으로 쓰인다. Dear Sirs는 특정 한 사람보다는 회사의 관계자에 보내는 경우 쓰인다. 이 경우 미국에서는 Gentlemen이 일반적이다. Dear Madam은 상대방 이름은 모르지만 여성일 경우 사용된다. 첫 편지의 경우 상대방에 이름이나 성별을 전혀 모르는 경우가 대부분일 것이기 때문에 Dear Sir or Madam(혹은 Dear Sir/Madam)로 쓰는 것이 가장 안전하다.

상대방의 이름은 알지만 잘 알지 못하는 경우에는 Mr., Miss, Mrs., Ms. 등의 존칭(이것을 courtesy title이라 부른다)를 쓰고 상대방의 성(last name)을 Dear Mr. Smith와 같이 쓴다. 이름(first name)은 쓰지 않는 것이 일반적이지만, 이름까지 안다면 써도 된다. 단, 이 경우 Dear John과 같이 first name만 써서는 안 된다. 이것은 거래가 이루어지고 어느 정도 상대방을 알게 되거나, 개인적 친분이 있는 경우에 쓴다. Courtesy title은 남자는 Mr., 여자의 경우 미혼인 경우 Miss, 기혼인 경우 Mrs.를 써왔다. 그러나 사회가 발달하고 여성의 사회진출이 활발한 오늘날에는 이런 구별을 하는 것이 무의미해졌고 현실적으로도 본인이 밝히지 않는 한 결혼 여부를 알기 힘들다. 따라서 요즘은 여성의 경우 결혼 여부에 상관없이 Ms. [miz]를 쓰는 것이 권장된다. Miss를 제외한 courtesy title 다음에 period를 찍는 것이 일반적 이지만 없이도 쓰인다.

이름은 모르지만 상대방의 직책을 안다면 직책명을 사용하여 Dear Director of Personnel, Dear Accounting Manager 등으로 쓴다. 또 의사나 박사학위가 있는 사람은 Doctor(Dr.), 교수는 Professor(Prof.), 군대의 계급 중 장군은 General(Gen.), 대령은 Colonel(Col.), 소령 Major(Maj.), 대위 Captain(Capt.) 등을 Dear Dr. Kim, Dear Professor Kim, Dear General McArthur와 같이 쓴다. 상대방을 잘 모르고 공식적인 경우 Salutation의 뒤에는 colon(:)을 쓰고, 서로 친분이 있거나 개인적인 편지의 경우 comma(,)를 쓰는 것이 권장된다. 그러나 실제로는 정확히 지켜지지 않고 아예 colon이나 comma을 쓰지 않기도 한다. 어느 것을 쓰건 항상 일관성이 있어야 한다.

⑤ Body of Letter

본문의 행 사이는 single space로 하고 절 사이는 double space로 한다. 서신의 내용이 2장 이상일 경우에는 다음 용지는 레터헤드가 없는 용지를 사용한다. 본문의 내용은 간결, 명확(simplicity and clarity)하고 정확(accuracy)하며 거래를 성사시킬 수 있도록 설득력(persuasive) 있게 그러면서도 정중(courtesy)하게 써야 한다. 특히 상대방으로부터 호감을 살 수 있게 하기 위하여서는 you-attitude(상대방 우선)를 항상 염두에 두고 쓰는 태도가 필요하다. 예를 들면

We shipped your order today.보다는
Your order will arrive on Thursday. 혹은
You will receive your order on Thursday.로 쓰는 것이 바람직하고,

We will process your order as soon as possible.보다는
Your order will be processed as soon as possible.이 바람직하다.

⑥ Complimentary Close

본문 끝머리에 붙여 끝맺음을 하는 인사를 말하며 첫 글자는 대문자로 시작한다. Sincerely yours, Sincerely가 가장 일반적인 맺음말이다. 미국에서는 Truly yours, Yours truly도 흔히 쓰이지만 영국에서는 공식적 business letter에서 잘 쓰지 않고 Your faithfully, Faithfully yours가 선호된다. 친구 사이나 상대방을 어느 정도 알면 Best wishes, Best regards, Regard 등을 쓰기도 한다. complimentary close의 끝에 comma를 쓰는 것이 일반적이지만 없어도 무방하다. 단, 어느 것 하나를 일관성 있게 써야 한다.

⑦ Signature

자필서명을 해야 하며 그 서한의 책임소재를 분명히 하기 위함이다. 서명 다음에는 서명한 사람의 이름과 직책을 typing하는 것이 일반적이다. 자기 자신의 이름에 Mr. Ms. 등의 courtesy title을 쓰는 사람도 있지만 권위적으로 보이므로 피하는 것이 좋다. 그러나 여성의 경우 자신이 선호하는 courtesy title을 이름 다음에 뒤 괄호 안에 쓰는 것이 좋다. 이는 자신의 성별이 뒤바뀌는 것을 미연에 방지하고 상대방에게 제대로 쓸 수 있게 하는 배려이다. 여성은 Nara Jang(Ms.), 남성은 Eugine Park(Mr.)과 같이 쓰면 된다. e-mail에서 는 미리 서명을 scan하여 이미지가 자동으로 입력되게 할 수 있다. 가끔 편지의 공식적 발송자는 상급자이지만 비서 혹은 아래 직급을 가진 사람이 상급자를 대신해서 서명할 때가 있다. 상급자가 장기간 부재 중이거나 간단한 연락내용을 처리할 때 사용되기도 한다. 이럴 때는 자필서명한 사람과 타이핑한 사람의 이름이 다르게 되므로 상급자의 이름 앞에 p.p.(per pro: for and on behalf of)를 붙여서 쓴다.

2 그 밖의 요소들

⑧ Reference Number

통신문의 참조번호로 문서의 분류 등 관리를 용이하게 하기 위하여 붙이는 문서번호(File No.)이다. Date Line 위에 기재하는 것이 일반적이다. Our Ref. No. 456, Your Ref. No. 789 등으로 표시한다.

⑨ Attention Line

특정수신인은 Inside Address의 첫줄이 회사나 단체명일 때에 사용하는 것으로 수신회사 내의 특정인에게 보내기를 원할 때 사용한다. Attention(Attn): Mr. James, Sales Manager 혹은 Attention of Mr. James 등으로 표시한다.

⑩ Subject

서신 전체의 내용을 일목요연하게 한 줄로 간추린 말로서 밑줄 표시 등을 하는 것이 좋다. 간혹 Subject:이나 Re:를 붙이고 제목을 쓰기도 한다. 다만 Re:의 경우 with regard to의 준말이지만 e-mail의 reply와 혼돈을 줄 수 있으므로 요즘은 피하는 것이 좋다.

⑪ Identification Marks

서신 작성과 관련하여 그 책임소재를 식별하기 위하여 서명자와 typist의 성명 첫 글자를 서명란 아래 좌측 여백선부터 기재한다. 보통 서명자의 initial은 대문자로 typist의 initial은 소문자로 하여 KSM/sk, DJ-hh 등으로 쓴다.

⑫ Enclosures

동봉물이 있을 경우에 그 명칭 및 통수를 표시하는 것을 말한다. 동봉물이 한 개일 경우 Enclosure(Encl, Enc.): L/C와 같이 사용하고 두 개 이상인 경우는 Enclosures (Encls, Encs): ① L/C ② B/L 등으로 표시한다.

⑬ Carbon Copy Notation

서신의 사본이 수신인 이외 다른 관련자에게 보내졌음을 나타내는 것으로 C.C.: Mr. Johnson 혹은 Copy to Mr. Johnson 등으로 표시한다. 또 같은 편지 사본을 다른 사람

에게도 보냈지만 상대방에게는 알리고 싶지 않은 경우 B.C.C.: Mr Johnson과 같이 편지 사본에 써둔다. B.C.C.는 Blind Carbon Copy의 약자이다. 물론 상대방이 받아보는 편지에는 아무런 표시 없이 보내야 한다. 이런 기능은 e-mail에서 더 유용하게 쓰인다.

⑭ Postscript

computer 이전 typewriter를 쓰던 시절에는 중간에 빠진 내용을 삽입하는 것이 어려웠다. 그래서 P.S.: 표시를 하고 본문에서 빠진 내용을 썼다. 그러나 요즘은 그럴 필요가 없어졌고 P.S.는 특별히 본문의 요점을 강조하기 위하여 사용하는 경우가 더 많다.

Story 1

Qtopia vs. EveryImport

등장인물

Jennifer Kim: Director, Export Department, Qtopia Systems
Paul Frederick: Manager, Purchasing Department, EveryImport
Kevin K. Smith: Credit Information Department, Bank of America

줄거리

Qtopia Systems의 수출사업부 Director인 Jennifer는 최근 자사가 개발한 Smartphone을 이용한 laser pointer인 Q-pointer II를 전 세계에 수출하기 위하여 여러 곳의 portal site에 제품을 올렸다. EC21에 올린 제품을 보고 LA 소재 EveryImport의 Purchasing Manager인 Paul이 Jennifer에게 e-mail을 보내서 Q-pointer II에 대하여 inquiry를 했다. 이에 대해 Jennifer는 가격이나 거래조건에 대한 답장을 보내면서 신용조사를 위하여 EveryImport의 은행과 거래처 중 한 곳을 알려달라고 했다. 신용조사가 끝난 후 구체적 거래조건을 Jennifer가 Paul에게 보냈는데, Paul은 가격이 너무 높다라며 깎아 줄 것을 요구했다. 이에 Jennifer는 여러 가지 상황 상 깎아 줄 수는 없고 약간 성능이 떨어지는 Q-pointer IIe를 권하였다. 이 조건에 대하여 Paul은....

Situation 1

Smartphone용 wireless laser pointer Q-pointer II를 EC21에 광고하다.

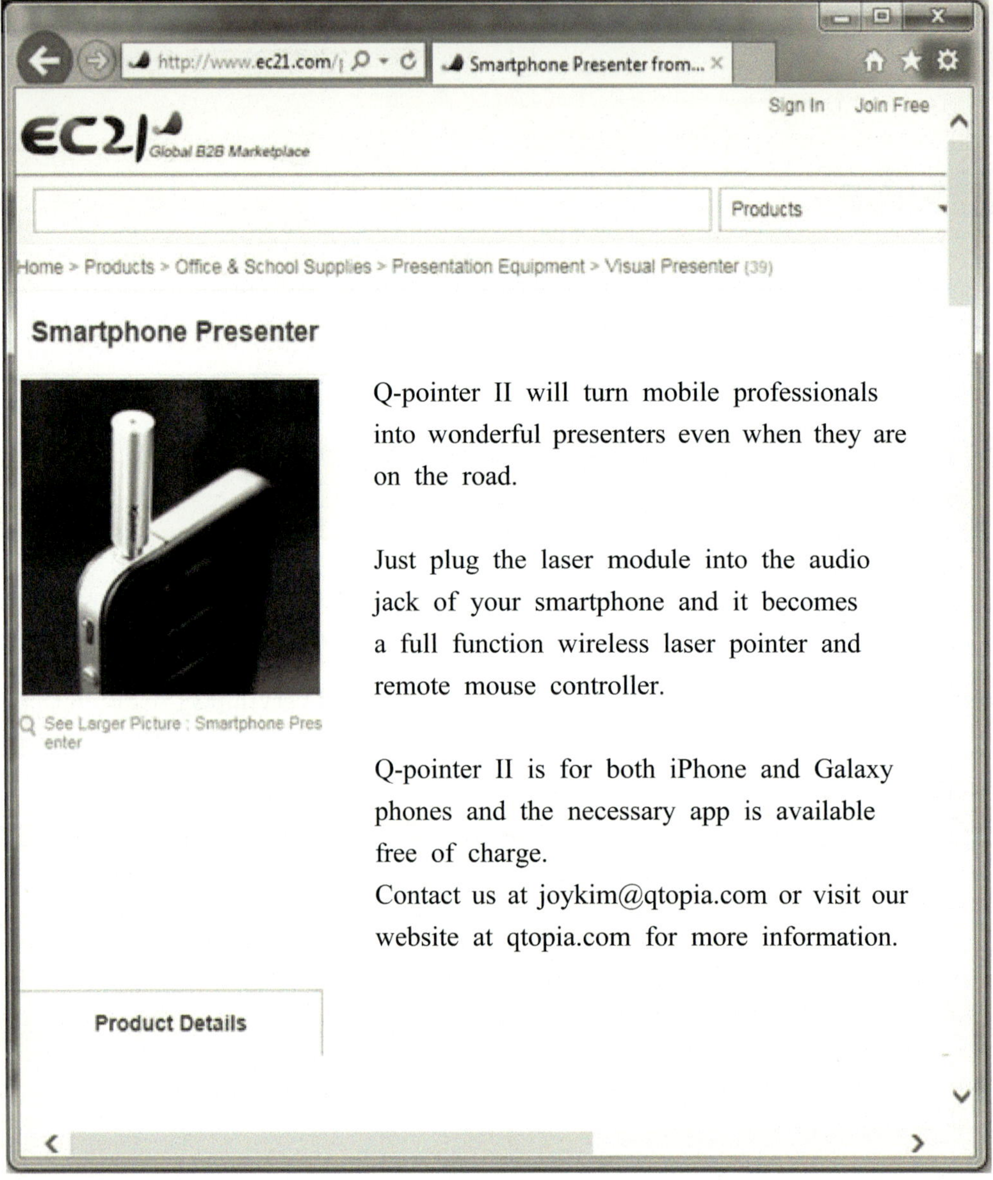

Synopsis

한국의 Qtopia systems은 스마트폰을 이용한 laser pointer인 Q-pointer II를 개발하였다. 이 제품은 스마트폰의 audio jack에 꽂아서 쓸 수 있는 획기적인 제품이어서 많은 수요가 예상되고 있다. 이 회사의 Export Department의 Director인 Jennifer Kim은 Q-pointer II를 전 세계로 수출하기 위하여 여러 곳에 광고를 냈다. 이것은 portal site인 EC21에 올린 광고문의 일부이다. 여기에서 Jennifer는 Q-pointer II의 특징을 간략하게 요약해서 서술하고 구매를 유도하고 있다.

◈ seeking overseas counterparts

국제간의 거래를 위한 해외 거래처의 발굴은 여러 가지 형태로 이루어진다. 최근에는 본문에서처럼 인터넷을 통하여 발굴하는 방법이 많이 쓰인다. 인터넷상에 광고를 하거나 ECplaza 등의 무역 관련 portal site에 자사의 제품을 올려서 해외 바이어를 발굴하기도 한다. 또한 circular letter라고 부르는 거래 권유편지를 상대방에 직접 보내서 거래를 성사시키기도 한다. 어떤 방법으로 건 상대방 회사나 제품에 대하여 알게 되어 수입할 의사가 있게 되면, 물품에 대한 문의를 하게 되는데 이것을 inquiry라고 부른다. 계약으로 연결될 가능성이 있다고 판단되는 거래선에 대하여서는 신용조사(credit inquiry)를 하게 되는데, 일반적으로 거래은행 혹은 상대국의 거래처나 상공회의소 등을 활용하게 된다. 조회처가 은행인 경우 bank reference라고 하고 거래처인 경우 trade reference라고 한다.

신용상태에 대한 긍정적 판단이 되면 거래조건을 서면으로 작성하여 제시하게 되는 데 이를 offer라고 부른다. offer는 수출상이 수입상에게 제시하는 selling offer와 구매조건을 수입상이 수출상에게 제시하는 buying offer가 있다. offer를 받은 쪽에서 offer의 내용을 일부 수정하여 다시 제의하는 과정을 여러 번 되풀이 하면서 최종 합의에 이르게 되는데, 이런 반대청약을 counter offer라고 부른다. 최종적으로 offer에 대한 승낙, 즉 acceptance가 이루어지면 계약을 성립하자고 하는 의사표시가 된다. acceptance만으로 거래가 이루어지기도 하지만 합의된 모든 조건을 서면으로 작성한 정식의 계약서(contract)가 작성된다. contract에는 일반적으로 품질, 가격, 수량, 포장, 보험, 선적, 지불 그리고 분쟁 발생 시 해결방안 등이 명시된다.

circular letter, 광고, 인터넷포털 등 → inquiry → offer → counter offer → acceptance → sales contract

◈ mobile professionals

Mobile은 사람 또는 물건이 "이동성을 가진, 움직여 다닐 수 있는 혹은 이동할 수 있는" 뜻으로 [móubəl, -biːl/-bail]로 발음된다. Professionals은 일반적으로 전문직 사람들을 말한다. 본문의 광고문은 "자사의 제품을 가진 사람은 모두 전문직이다"라는 암시를 주어서 구매를 유도하고 있다.

- mobile home(이동식으로 지은 집)
- mobile police(이동 경찰)
- mobile troops(이동 군대)

mobile은 또 명사형으로 쓰여서 이동전화, 움직이는 조각을 말하기도 한다.

- A mobile is the same as a mobile phone.
- A mobile is a decoration you hang from the ceiling.

◈ road

☞ on the road : traveling from place to place

- The band has been on the road all summer.
  (그 밴드는 여름 내 연주 여행을 다녔다.)

☞ on the street: having no place to live, homeless, out of job

- He is now on the street. (그는 거리로 나앉았다. 망했다.)

☞ on the way, on one's way: coming, during the journey

- Spring is on the way.
- She got two children, and another one on the way.
- We'll have lunch on our way.

☞ in the way, in one's way: 방해가 되어

- I can't get the car out because those boxes are in the way.
- Please don't stand in my way.

street: 거리 양쪽에 건물이 줄지어 서있는 도로; a shopping street(상점가)
road: 도시와 도시를 연결하는(차의 통행을 위한) 도로; a main road(간선 도로)
avenue: 넓은 street로서 대개는 가로수가 있는 거리
boulevard: 도시의 넓은 가로수길. 중앙안전 지대가 있는 경우도 있음:

- The main street is busy all the times of the year.
- The road out of our village goes up a steep hill.
  (동네 밖은 심한 언덕길 이다. The street out of ~로 쓰면 어색함)
- Fifth Avenue is one of New York City's most famous streets.
- Hollywood Boulevard is lined with palm trees.

contact

'연락을 취하다, 연락해 달라'의 의미의 contact은 동사로 쓰이면 with 등의 전치사 없이 쓰인다.

- Contact us if you are interested in our products.
- Please feel free to contact me whenever you need my help.
- Please do not hesitate to contact me if you have any questions.

그러나 명사형으로 쓰이면 contact with ~로 쓰인다.

- He tried to make contact with her after she had become famous.
- I lost contact with my former clients.

동사형의 발음은 [kəntǽkt], 명사형은 [kɑ́ntækt/kɔ́&ntækt]으로 한다.

The Road not Taken(가지 않은 길)

by Robert Frost(1875~1963)

Two roads diverged in a yellow wood, And sorry I could not travel both And be one traveler, long I stood And looked down one as far as I could To where it bent in the undergrowth:	노랗게 물든 숲 속에 두 갈래 길이 있었습니다. 난 나그네 몸으로 두 길을 다 가볼 수 없어 아쉬운 마음으로 그곳에 서서 한쪽 길이 덤불 속으로 감돌아간 끝까지 한참을 그렇게 바라보았습니다.
Then took the other, as just as fair, And having perhaps the better claim, Because it was grassy and wanted wear: Though as for that the passing there Had worn them really about the same,	그리고는 다른 쪽 길을 택했습니다. 먼저 길에 못지 않게 아름답고 어쩌면 더 나은 듯도 싶었습니다. 사람들이 밟은 흔적은 비슷했지만 풀이 더 무성하고 사람의 발길을 기다리는 듯해서였습니다.
And both that morning equally lay In leaves no step had trodden black. Oh, I kept the first for another day! Yet knowing how way leads on to way, I doubted if I should ever come back.	그날 아침 두 길은 모두 아직, 발자국에 더럽혀지지 않은 낙엽에 덮여 있었습니다. 먼저 길은 다른 날로 미루리라 생각했습니다. 길은 길로 이어지는 것이기에 다시 돌아오기 어려우리라 알고 있었지만.
I shall be telling this with a sigh Somewhere ages and ages hence; Two roads diverged in a wood, and I- I took the one less traveled by, And that has made all the difference.	먼먼 훗날 어디에선가 나는 한숨 쉬며 이야기를 할 것입니다. "숲 속에 두 갈래 길이 있어 나는 사람이 덜 다닌 길을 택했습니다. 그리고 그것이 내 인생을 이처럼 바꿔 놓은 것입니다" 라고

Practice Tests - Situation 1

1. What is for the Q-pointer II?
   (a) presenting pointer (b) audio jack
   (c) touch pen (d) all of the above

2. With a smartphone you access the internet while you are ___________.
   (a) off the street (b) on the street
   (c) on the way (d) on the road

3. We have another shipment ______ its way from South America.
   (a) in (b) on
   (c) to (d) from

4. Choose the one that fills the blank with appropriate words.
   The firm is located in a ______ in lower Manhattan in New York City.
   Two _____ diverged in a yellow wood, And sorry I could not travel both. I could not get the car out because something was in the _______.
   (a) road – streets – way (b) street – roads – way
   (c) road – streets – road (d) street – roads – road

5. For a free price quote, __________ Mr. Smith at smithk@google.com.
   (a) contact (b) contact to
   (c) contact with (d) make contact

6. 다음 중 수출입 계약체결의 일반적 절차로 옳은 것은?
   (a) circular letter ➡ inquiry ➡ firm offer ➡ counter offer ➡ acceptance ➡ sales contract
   (b) inquiry ➡ circular letter ➡ firm offer ➡ counter offer ➡ acceptance ➡ sales contract
   (c) inquiry ➡ circular letter ➡ counter offer ➡ firm offer ➡ acceptance ➡ sales contract
   (d) circular letter ➡ inquiry ➡ counter offer ➡ firm offer ➡ acceptance ➡ sales contract

[7~8] 다음 일정표를 읽고 물음에 답하시오. [무역영어 2급]

21st Annual International Sales Conference Thursday

9 a.m. – 4 p.m.	Registration and badge pick-up
p.m. – 8 p.m.	Informal reception at West Ballroom, New Plaza Hotel
p.m. – 9 p.m.	Opening address by Ted Singer, Vice President for Sales

Friday

7:30 a.m.	Attendees will be bussed to Carleton Ranch
8:30 a.m. – 9 a.m.	Coffee and rolls
a.m. – 12 p.m.	Plenary Session
12 p.m. – 1 p.m.	Lunch
1 p.m. – 3:30 p.m.	Meetings with regional sales managers
4 p.m. – 7 p.m.	Horseback riding and old-fashioned barbecue
7 p.m.	Attendees will be bussed back to their hotels

Saturday

9 a.m. – 12 p.m.	Sales seminars, New Plaza Hotel
12 p.m. – 1:30 p.m.	Lunch, closing ceremony, and "Sales Reps of the Year" awards

Your badge is your "ticket" to all events.
Dress: Business dress for Thursday and Saturday events. Casual western wear(blue jeans, boots, and cowboy hats!) for events at the Carleton Ranch.

All meals not listed on this schedule must be paid for by attendees. Room service bills are the responsibility of attendees. Attendees who stay over Saturday night must pay for accommodations for that night. Taxis, rental cars, and other ground transportation other than shuttle van to and from the airport will not be reimbursed. Keep receipts for hotel bills and airline tickets in order to be reimbursed.

7. On what day should attendees wear casual Western clothing?

(a) Wednesday (b) Thursday
(c) Friday (d) Saturday

8. When will awards be presented?

(a) During the opening address (b) At the plenary session
(c) At the barbecue dinner (d) During the final event

[9~10] 다음 물음에 답하시오. [무역영어 2급]

Dear Mr. Chang

We are considering sending some of our staff on a training course on Customer Services. Do you have a suitable course available within the next few months? If so please let me have the dates and times plus costs.
If there isn't a regular Pioneer course scheduled, can you tailor-make a course specially for our staff? We could hold it in our conference room.
Perhaps we can arrange to meet to discuss this – are you free next Friday 20 August at 11 a.m.? I could come over to you, or you could come over to my office. Please let me know.

Sharon Tad

9. Who is Sharon Tad most likely to be?

(a) HR Manager (b) Customer broker
(c) A lawyer (d) An accountant

10. What is the main subject of the letter?

(a) Contract on Tailor (b) Arrangements for Training
(c) Changing the Schedule (d) Employing New Staffs

Situation 2

Q-pointer II에 대한 Inquiry와 Catalog를 보내달라고 요청하다.

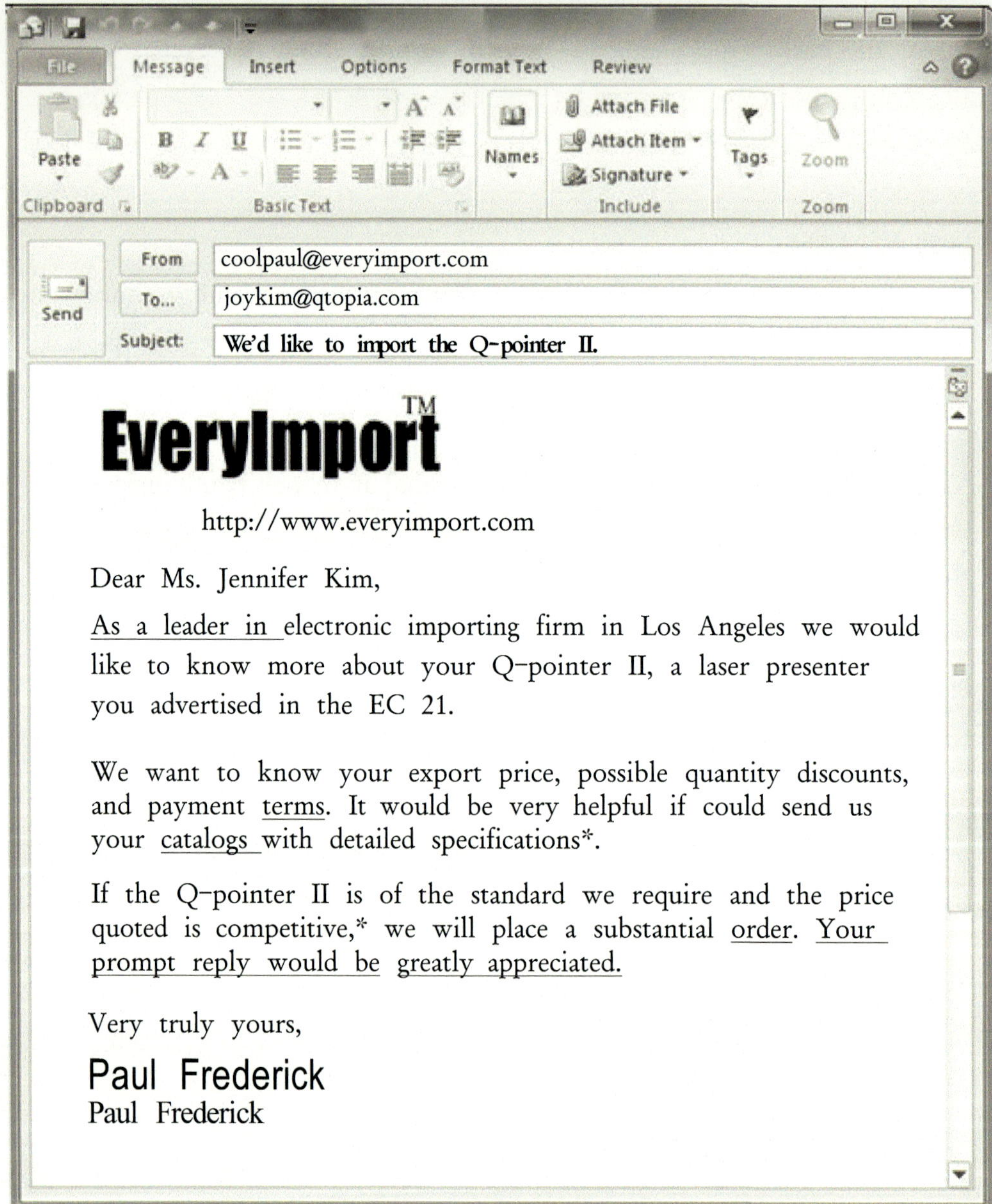

From: coolpaul@everyimport.com

To...: joykim@qtopia.com

Subject: We'd like to import the Q-pointer II.

EveryImport™

http://www.everyimport.com

Dear Ms. Jennifer Kim,

As a leader in electronic importing firm in Los Angeles we would like to know more about your Q-pointer II, a laser presenter you advertised in the EC 21.

We want to know your export price, possible quantity discounts, and payment terms. It would be very helpful if could send us your catalogs with detailed specifications*.

If the Q-pointer II is of the standard we require and the price quoted is competitive,* we will place a substantial order. Your prompt reply would be greatly appreciated.

Very truly yours,

Paul Frederick

Paul Frederick

Synopsis

EC 21에서 Q-pointer II의 광고를 본 LA에 있는 EveryImport사의 Purchasing Manager인 Paul Frederick은 이 제품의 수입에 관심이 있어서 Qtopia의 Jennifer Kim에게 e-mail을 보내고 있다. 그는 수출가격(export price), 대량구매에 따른 할인(possible quantity discount), 지불조건(payment terms) 등에 대하여 질문을 하고, Q-pointer 제원(specification: spec)이 나와 있는 catalog를 보내주면 좋겠다고 얘기하였다. Q-pointer의 품질이 EveryImport이 요구하는 수준이고(of the standard we require) 가격이 경쟁력(competitive)이 있다면 상당량의 주문을 하겠다(place a substantial order)는 뜻도 밝히고 있다.

* specification [spesəfikeiʃ-ən] c. u. 사양; (보통 복수형으로) 명세서, 설계 명세서
specification을 줄여서 spec으로 쓰기도 한다.
· The standard spec includes 1 giga bite memory.
specify: v. 구체적으로 명시하다. specific: a. 구체적인

* competitive [kəmpetətiv] a. 경쟁적인, 경쟁에 의한, 〈제품 · 가격이〉 경쟁력이 있는
competitive market: 경쟁시장 competitive advantage: 경쟁우위
competitive examination: 경쟁시험 competitive spirit: 경쟁심
compete: v. 경쟁하다. competition: n. 경쟁

◈ inquiry

Situation 2는 inquiry letter이다. Inquiry란 거래를 권유받거나 혹은 광고 등을 통하여 상대방과 상대방의 제품에 대하여 알게 된 당사자가 구매할 의사가 있을 경우 문의를 하는 것을 말한다. Inquiry에는 대개 1) 상대방을 알게 된 경위, 2) 자사에 대한 소개, 3) 제품에 대한 문의, 가격 등 거래조건, catalog, sample 등의 요청이 포함된다.

inquire [inkwáiər] v.
① …을 묻다, 알아보다 [of, from, wh.(節), wh. to do]. ▷ASK
② (…에게/…에 관해) 질문을 하다, 묻다 [of/about, after, concerning, on].
③ (일을) 조사하다[into].
④ …의 안부[건강]를 묻다, 병문안을 하다[after].
inquire 다음에 사람이 목적어로 올 때는 항상 of를 쓴다.

- She was inquiring of her friend what she should do. ①
- If you inquire about something, you ask for information about it. ②
- If you inquire into something, you investigate it carefully. ③
- If you inquire after someone, you ask how they are or what they are doing. ④

make an inquiry to: ~에게 조회를 하다.
receive an inquiry from: ~에게서 조회를 받다.
reply to an inquiry: 조회에 대하여 회답을 하다.
in response to an inquiry: 조회에 대한 대답으로

as a leader in ~

'업계에서 선두적인 회사'라는 뜻으로 자기회사를 소개할 때 상대방에게 신뢰감을 주기 위한 표현이다. 자사를 소개할 때 쓸 수 있는 표현으로는,

- We are one of the leading exporting firms of electronic products in Korea.
- We are a large manufacturer of electronic appliances located in New York.
- We have been exporting machinery for more than twenty years.
- We have a proud record as an exporter-importer dealing in general goods.
- Since 1998 we have engaged in the import of consumer goods in Korea.
- We are a first class chain of retailer specializing in cotton products.
- Our company is a subsidiary of LGT and we are interested in the software programs you recently released in the US.

그리고 자사를 소개하기 전에 상황에 따라 다음과 같은 표현을 써서 상대방을 어떻게 알았는지에 대하여 서술할 필요가 있다.

- You were recommended to us by your trade association.
- We were given your name by the Wintel, Inc. in Seoul.
- The US consulate in Seoul has told us that you are looking for an agent.
- We were impressed by the selection of tools in this year's Machine Fair.
- We saw your interesting advertisement in latimes.com.
- We have learned from your homepage that you are offering different variety of chinaware.

◈ catalogs

제품이나 회사를 소개하기 위해서는 이미지나 광고가 실린 인쇄물인 catalog가 필수적이다. catalog는 제품이나 회사의 장점이나 효력을 소비자에게 기억시키기 위해 편집, 디자인, 인쇄, 종이의 질 등 광고효과를 높여주도록 충분히 주의를 기울여서 제작하여야 한다. 요즘은 전자화된 e-catalog도 많이 쓰인다. catalog의 의미로 같이 쓰이는 말은 brochure, pamphlet, booklet 등이 있다. literature는 일반적으로 '문학, 작품'을 의미하지만, '인쇄물'이란 의미로도 쓰인다. 몇 장짜리 가벼운 인쇄물의 의미로 leaflet, flyer 등이 있다. 다음은 catalog나 price list 등을 요구할 때 쓸 수 있는 표현이다.

- Could you please send us your current catalog and export price list?
- We would like to receive your up-to-date brochure for the following goods:
- If you have any booklet about your products, please send us a copy.
- Please send us some literature on the machine.

◈ order

place [give/make/grant] an order: 주문을 하다.

We will place an initial order if your price is competitive.

take [accept/book] an order: 주문을 받다.

Can I take your order now?

process [execute/(ful)fill/carry out/perform] an order: 주문을 처리하다.

Your order will be processed as early as possible.

refuse [decline] an order: 주문을 거부하다.

We have no other choices but to refuse the order due to lack of stock.

cancel an order: 주문을 취소하다.

We regret to inform you that we have to cancel the order.

구어체에서는 동사형을 써서 다음과 같이 표현할 수도 있다.

- I ordered some pasta and a mixed salad.
- There are no shirts left in this size but we could order one for you.

order는 또 something provided 혹은 something ordered(주문품)의 의미도 있다.

- Your order will be shipped by this week.
- If you are not completely satisfied, you may return your order.

initial, opening, first order: 처음 주문
repeat order: 재주문
regular order: 정기주문
additional order: 추가주문
original order: 원주문
advance order: 예약주문
back order: (재고가 없어서) 처리하지 못한 주문, 이월주문
trial, test order: 시험주문: 본격적 주문하기 전에 시험 삼아 하는 주문
sizable, substantial, considerable, large, bulk order: 상당량의 주문, 대량 주문

◈ Your prompt reply would be greatly appreciated.

"답변을 신속히 해주시면 감사하겠습니다"의 의미로, We would appreciate your prompt reply.로 바꿔 말할 수 있다. 문법적으로 두 가지 표현이 다 가능하나 business English에는 상대방 혹은 상대방에 관한 것을 먼저 오게끔 쓰는 것이 상대방에 대한 배려이다. 예를 들면,

- We shipped your order today. 보다는
- Your order will arrive on Thursday. 혹은
- You will receive your order on Thursday.로 쓰는 것이 바람직하고 또,
- We will process your order as soon as possible. 보다는
- Your order will be processed as soon as possible.이 바람직하다.

business English에서 이런 경향을 'you-attitude'라고 한다. 그러나 무조건 I나 We를 피하라는 것은 아니고, You를 먼저 쓰는 것이 부자연스럽거나, 부정적인 내용에서는 오히려 You를 피하는 것이 you-attitude이다.

- Your presentation at the workshop was very enjoyable and valuable.보다는
- I certainly enjoyed your presentation at the workshop. I found it very valuable.이 자연스럽고,

- You misunderstand our monthly statement. 보다는
- Our monthly statement is not clear enough to understand.이 바람직하고,

- We are surprised at your news that you made a delay in shipment. 보다는
- We are sorry to hear that there was a delay in shipment.이 적절하다.

참고로 business letter에서 I와 We도 서로 큰 의미의 차이 없이 쓰이고 개인적 선택의 문제이긴 하지만, 굳이 구별한다면, I, me, my는 'from-me-to-you'의 느낌을 주고, we, us, our는 회사 내 다른 사람과 편지내용을 공유(share)한다는 느낌을 준다. 다음 두 문장을 비교해 보자.

- I very much enjoyed your visit to my office last Monday. Enclosed are the materials I promised to send you.
- Thank you for calling this situation to our attention, Mr. Whang. We appreciate your patience with us.

Practice Tests - Situation 2

1. What is true about the e-mail in Situation 2?

(a) Jennifer is going to place a substantial order.

(b) Jennifer thinks that the quoted price is competitive.

(c) Paul wants to know the export price of Q-pointer II.

(d) Paul is supposed to send the catalog to Jennifer.

2. What type of email is the Situation 2?

(a) Circular letter (b) Inquiry

(d) Firm offer (c) Sales contract

3. If your price is ___________, we will _______ a substantial order.

(a) compensated – place (b) competitive – take

(c) compensated – take (d) competitive – place

4. We want to know your export _________, possible quantity _____, and payment ________.

(a) price – terms – discounts (b) discounts – terms – price

(c) discounts – price – terms (d) price – discounts – terms

5. Enclosed is a list of part ________, and detailed instructions for assembly.

(a) ways (b) systems

(c) methods (d) specifications

6. What is the main purpose of this email? [무역영어 2급]

> From your email of February 25, it appears that there is a misunderstanding of our intention. It was your artificial leathers, not the real leather goods, which our CEO referred to during her visit on February 20. We regret if any misinterpretation here. We are very interested in importing your new colored calf leather goods, since we anticipate that demand for artificial leather goods will decrease. However, feasibility can only be

determined after receiving drawings and specifications from you. Consequently, we would like you to provide this material as soon as possible.

(a) Correcting miscommunications previously made
(b) Exporting artificial leather goods
(c) Informing CEO's visit in February
(d) Complaining of late delivery

7. What does the writer want in the letter below? [무역영어 2급]

We have received your letter of May 2 asking us to cancel your order of March 2 for hand-held mini fans. We are sorry that you find it necessary to make this request, especially at this late stage. To be able to meet our customers' needs promptly, we have to place our orders with manufacturers well in advance of the season. In estimating quantities, we rely upon the orders we have received.
We do not want to refuse requests of any kind from regular customers. However, on this occasion we have no choice but to do so. All orders, including yours, have already been made up and are awaiting delivery. I hope you will understand why we must hold you to your order. If we had received your request earlier we should have been glad to help you.

(a) To confirm the cancellation of the order of March 2.
(b) To refuse the cancel request for the March 2 order.
(c) To apologize for the cancellation of the March 2 order.
(d) To request the buyer to place orders in advance.

8. 밑줄 친 부분과 바꾸어 쓰기에 적절하지 않은 것은? [무역영어 2급]

We are pleased to give a substantial order to you.

(a) send a considerable order with you (b) favor you with a large order
(c) place an initial order with you (d) furnish you with a big order

9. Which of the followings is NOT suitable word as a replacement of 'perform their order'? [무역영어 2급]

(a) excuse their order (b) take up their order
(c) carry out their order (d) fulfill their order

Situation 3

EveryImport의 Inquiry에 대한 답과 신용조회처를 요구하다.

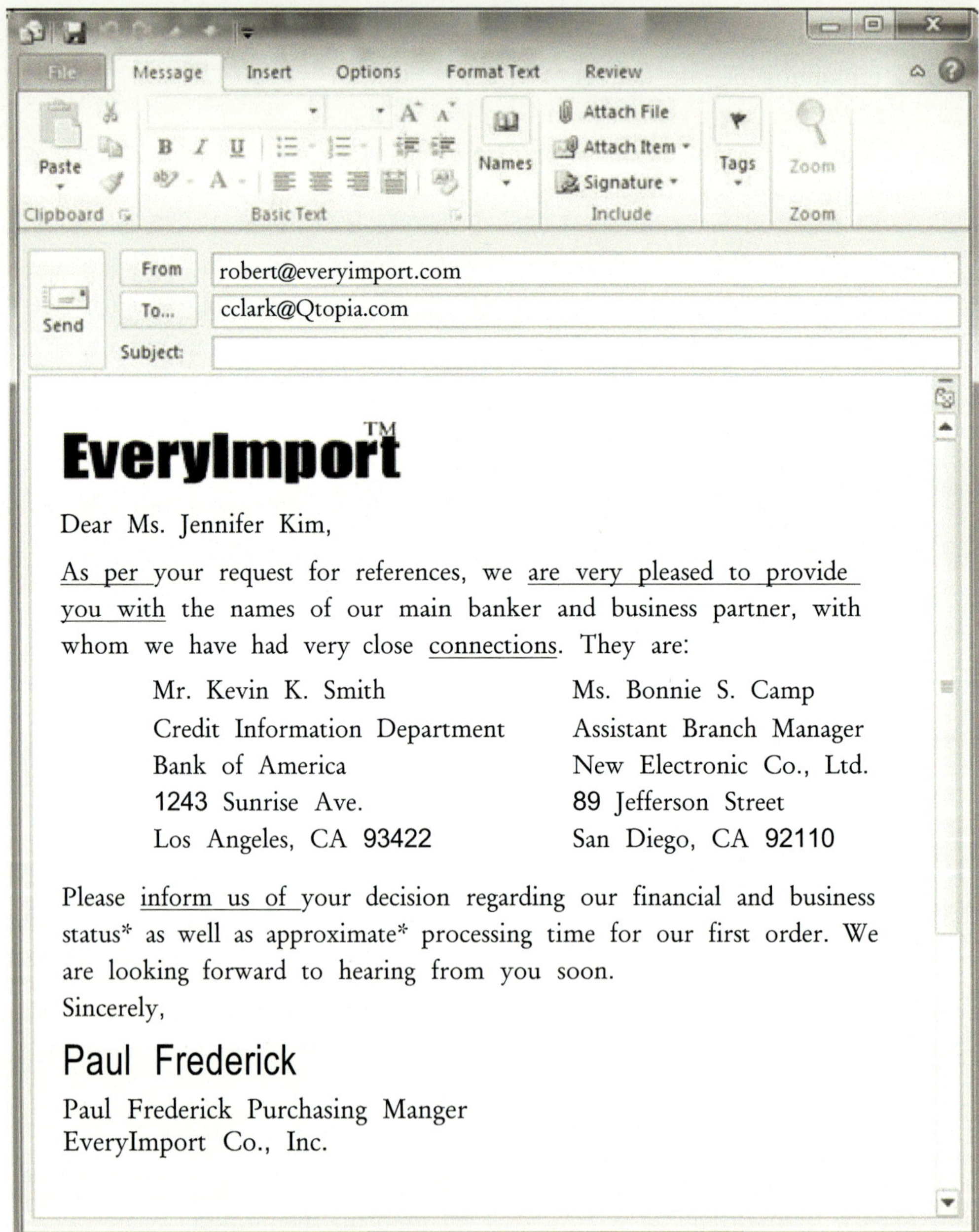

From: robert@everyimport.com
To: cclark@Qtopia.com
Subject:

EveryImport™

Dear Ms. Jennifer Kim,

As per your request for references, we are very pleased to provide you with the names of our main banker and business partner, with whom we have had very close connections. They are:

Mr. Kevin K. Smith	Ms. Bonnie S. Camp
Credit Information Department	Assistant Branch Manager
Bank of America	New Electronic Co., Ltd.
1243 Sunrise Ave.	89 Jefferson Street
Los Angeles, CA 93422	San Diego, CA 92110

Please inform us of your decision regarding our financial and business status* as well as approximate* processing time for our first order. We are looking forward to hearing from you soon.
Sincerely,

Paul Frederick

Paul Frederick Purchasing Manger
EveryImport Co., Inc.

Synopsis

EveryImport의 Paul Frederick으로부터 자사의 Q-pointer II에 대한 문의 메일을 받은 Qtopia의 Jennifer Kim은 상대방이 궁금해 하는 Q-pointer II의 제원(specifications)과 수출가격(export price)을 알려주는 답신 메일을 보내고 있다. 대량 주문에 따른 할인(volume discount)이 있음을 강조하면서, 자세한 가격정보와 재원은 첨부한 catalog를 참조해 달라고 했다. 그리고 첫 주문을 받기 전(before taking first order) 최소한 두 개의 신용조회처(references)를 요구하는 것이 회사의 정책이니까 EveryImport의 거래은행(banker)과 거래처 한 곳(business partner)을 말해달라고 (name) 요구하고 있다.

*reference [ref-ərəns] n. 신용조회처, 추천서, 신용조회장, 참고, 문의.

- References will be provided upon request. (신용조회처는 요구하시면 제공하겠습니다.)
  refer: v. ~을 문의하다, 참조하게 하다.

*name v. 이름을 대다, 정확히 말하다, 지정하다, 임명하다.

- Please name your price. (귀사의 가격을 말해주세요.)
- We are willing to name her as a CEO. (그녀를 기꺼이 대표로 임명하다.)

◈ replies to inquiries

Inquiry에 대한 대답은 먼저 inquiry를 해주어서 고맙다는 말과 함께 질문사항에 대하여 성의 있는 대답을 해야 한다. 제품에 대한 설명이나 수출가격의 제시 등 거래조건에 대한 설명이 필요하며, catalog나 sample 등이 동봉 혹은 첨부가 되는 경우에 대한 언급을 해두어야 한다. 상대방에 대한 정보가 없는 경우에는 신용조회처(reference)를 요구하는 경우도 있다. 서신의 끝 부분에서 주문을 받고 싶다는 의사 표시로 마감하는 것이 일반적이다.

◈ Thank you for~

'감사'의 표현은 Business Letter를 처음 시작할 때 자주 쓰이며 다음과 같이 다양하게 할 수 있다.

- Thank you for [verb+ing]
- We shall(or should) be obliged(or glad/pleased) if you will(or would) [verb] ~
- We shall(or should) be(or feel) obliged by your [verb + ing] ~

- It would be obliged(or indebted/grateful) if you could ~
- I am much obliged for [verb + ing, 명사] ~ [cf] ~ be obliged to [verb]: ~해야만 한다.
- We will(or would, shall, should) appreciate your [verb + ing] ~
- We will(or would) appreciate it if you will [verb] ~
- It would(or should) be appreciated if you could [verb] ~

Thank you for your warm hospitality.
We shall be obliged if you will send us your catalog.
We shall be obliged by your giving us your catalog.
I am greatly indebted to you for valuable advice.
I am grateful to you for the invitation to the party.
I am much obliged to you for your advice.
[cf. I am obliged to(=must) attend the meeting.]
I appreciate your coming here today. [appreciate에 대해서는 Situation 5 참조]

◈ USD30 CIF LA

LA 도착의 CIF 가격조건이 미화로 30불이라는 의미이다. (CIF 등 Incoterms의 가격조건에 대하여서는 Situation 13에서 자세히 설명함.) 달러는 일반적으로 미국(US$)를 말하지만, 미국 이외에도 캐나다(CA$), 호주(AU$), 뉴질랜드(NZ$), 홍콩(HK$), 싱가포르(SG$), 타이완(T$) 등에서도 사용되는 통화 단위이므로 무역거래에 있어서는 분명하게 어떤 달러인지 밝힐 필요가 있다.

◈ discount(할인)의 표현

volume(quantity) discount: 대량주문 할인
trade discount: 동업자간 할인(주로 대량 주문을 유도하기 위한)
special discount: 특별 할인
cash discount: 현금 할인

discount와 함께 allowance도 일반적인 할인을 말할 때 같이 쓰인다. 그러나 allowance는 특히 품질불량이나 수량부족 등 매도인에게 과실이 있는 경우 조정을 하기 위한 할인에 사용되는 경우가 많다.

- We will make you a discount(allowance) of 10% off the list price.
- We will offer 10% allowance(discount) for the damaged goods. 이외에 할인의 의미로 쓰이는 단어들은,

concession: (양보에 의한) 할인
reduction: (양자 합의에 의한) 할인
rebate: (판매 대금 수령 후 일정금액을 돌려주는 형식의) 할인
abatement: (소량의) 할인

◈ attachment(첨부), enclosure(동봉)의 표현

국제간의 거래를 할 때 catalog, pamphlet 혹은 price list 등의 자료를 첨부하거나 동봉할 경우가 많다. 이때 첨부나 동봉을 했으니까 알아서 보겠지 라고 생각하고 아무런 언급이 없이 지나가서는 안 된다. 혹시 첨부나 동봉물을 발견하지 못할 수도 있고, 또 확인을 위해서라도 '첨부한다' 혹은 '동봉한다'라는 말을 본문에 명기하는 것이 필요하다. 이런 경우 가장 일반적으로 사용할 수 있는 표현은, We(I) attach ~, We(I) enclose ~이다. 진행형으로 표시하여, We are attaching, We are enclosing으로 쓰거나 수동형으로 ~ is(are) attached(enclosed)로 쓰기도 한다.

- We attach the specifications of the machine.
- A copy of our Spring catalog is enclosed for you to place an order.

이와 더불어 첨부나 동봉함을 강조하기 위하여,

Attached(Enclosed) is(are) ~
Attached(Enclosed) please find ~
Please find attached(enclosed) ~를 쓰는 경우도 많다.

- Attached please find our plan for the project.
- Enclosed is our plan for the project.

◈ ask for~

ask for: ask somebody to give something(~에게 ~을 요구하다)
ask [for 없이]: ask somebody to tell something(~에게 ~을 묻다.)

- Don't ask me for money.
- Don't ask me my name.
- Ask for the menu.
- Ask the price.

ask는 물건을 사고 팔 때, 가격을 묻고 말할 때는 for 없이 사용된다.

- They are asking $500 a month for renting the room.
- How much is the car? I'm asking fifteen hundred.

◈ look forward to ~

'~을 기대하며 기다린다'의 의미로 commercial correspondence에서 자주 쓰인다. 항상 뒤에 '~ing'나 명사(구) 등이 오는 것에 주의해야 한다.

- We are looking forward to taking(take) your order.
- I look forward to(have) your comments on my proposal.

look forward to와 유사한 의미로 expect, hope 혹은 wait for를 쓸 수도 있으나 미묘한 차이점에 주의하여서 써야 한다.

- I expect to receive a substantial order from your company.
  (귀사에서 상당량의 주문을 받을 것 같은 예감을 하고 있다.)
- I hope to receive a substantial order from your company.
  (귀사에서 상당량의 주문을 받고 싶다.)
- I wait for a substantial order from your company.
  (귀사에서 상당량의 주문해 주길 기다리고 있다. (시간이 지나길 기다린다.))

Practice Tests - Situation 3

1. What is Mr. Frederic supposed to do to make a business relationship with Qtopia systems?
   (a) He needs to ask volume discount.
   (b) He should express his thanks to Ms. Kim for sending the catalog.
   (c) He must find more information about the Q–pointer II.
   (d) He should name two references.

2. What is Qtopia's policy for taking orders from a new customer?
   (a) They send the latest catalog to take the order.
   (b) They let the new customer know the specifications of their product.
   (c) They check the credibility of customer.
   (d) They look forward to serving the customer.

3. 다음 중 그 의미가 나머지 것들과 다른 것은?
   (a) We shall be obliged if you could introduce us to some reliable importers.
   (b) We are obliged to introduce you to some reliable importers.
   (c) We shall be obliged by your introducing us to some reliable importers.
   (d) You will be obliged us by introducing us to some reliable importers.

4. We are willing to offer you a 20% allowance ________ in the goods.
   (a) to compensate the damages　　(b) to rebate for the losses
   (c) to reconsider the defects　　(d) to complain the quality

5. ________ is our summer catalog.
   (a) Attached　　(b) Having attached
   (c) With attached　　(d) Attach

6. They are ________ $500 a month for renting the room.
   (a) asking　　(b) asking for
   (c) ask　　(d) ask for

7. We are looking forward to _______ you in near future.

(a) serve
(b) serving
(c) service
(d) server

8. 다음 문장의 괄호 안에 들어갈 적합한 구를 고르시오. [무역영어 2급]

We are prepared to give you a 10% allowance (   ) in the goods.

(a) to compensate the defects
(b) to complain the quality
(c) to repay the amount
(d) to claim for loss

9. Which of the followings is NOT APPROPRIATE as part of the reply to the letter? [무역영어 2급]

> Dear Sir/Madam
> Please send me details of fax machines which you supply, together with prices. We need a model suitable for sending complex diagrams and printed messages, mostly within the UK.

(a) All the models illustrated can be supplied from stock at competitive prices as shown on the price list inside the catalogue.
(b) May I suggest a visit to our showrooms where you could see demonstrations of the various machines and at the same time view our wide range of office equipment.
(c) Please fax us your wholesale price list along with terms and conditions.
(d) In reply to your inquiry I have pleasure in enclosing a leaflet showing our latest fax machines.

10. Which of the following best completes the letter? [무역영어 1급]

> As requested, we enclose for your attention our (A)___________. You will notice that every single one of our products is made from 100% natural ingredients—we use no (B)___________ at all. This year, for the very first time, we have included samples of our ten most popular aromas. I think you will agree that our range of well over 200 natural flavors and aromas is (C)________ none and is outstanding value for money. If you need more information, please do not hesitate to contact us. I look forward to hearing from you.

(a) commercial invoice – artificial intelligence – the best for
(b) insurance policy and packing list – natural materials – the worst for
(c) irrevocable letter of credit – organic ingredients – first to
(d) price list and catalog – artificial additives – second to

11. Which of the following has a DIFFERENT meaning from others? [무역영어 1급]

(a) As for the inquiry you made, please refer to the Price List No.321 enclosed.
(b) For any information you might have, we will enclose a Price List No.321 within a week.
(c) The prices and other particulars inquired for are shown in the enclosed Price List No.321.
(d) The Price List No.321 enclosed will give you information which you inquired about.

12. Which of the following is most suitable for the blanks in the letter? [무역영어 1급]

> Thank you very much for stopping by our (a)______ at the IFCA Exhibition in Seville last month. As you might have already noticed in Seville, we have established a large customer base in Europe, Asia and North America. We have also been increasing our (b)_________ in the South American market in recent years. Our main strength lies in supplying the highest quality products at the most (c)________. In order for us to better serve you, we would like to know more detailed information about the needs of your esteemed airline.

(a) booth – market share – competitive prices
(b) box – market occupation – cheap prices
(c) columns – market portion – low prices
(d) booth – market share – cheap prices

Situation 4

Q-pointer II의 수입을 위하여 두 곳의 신용 조회처를 제공하다.

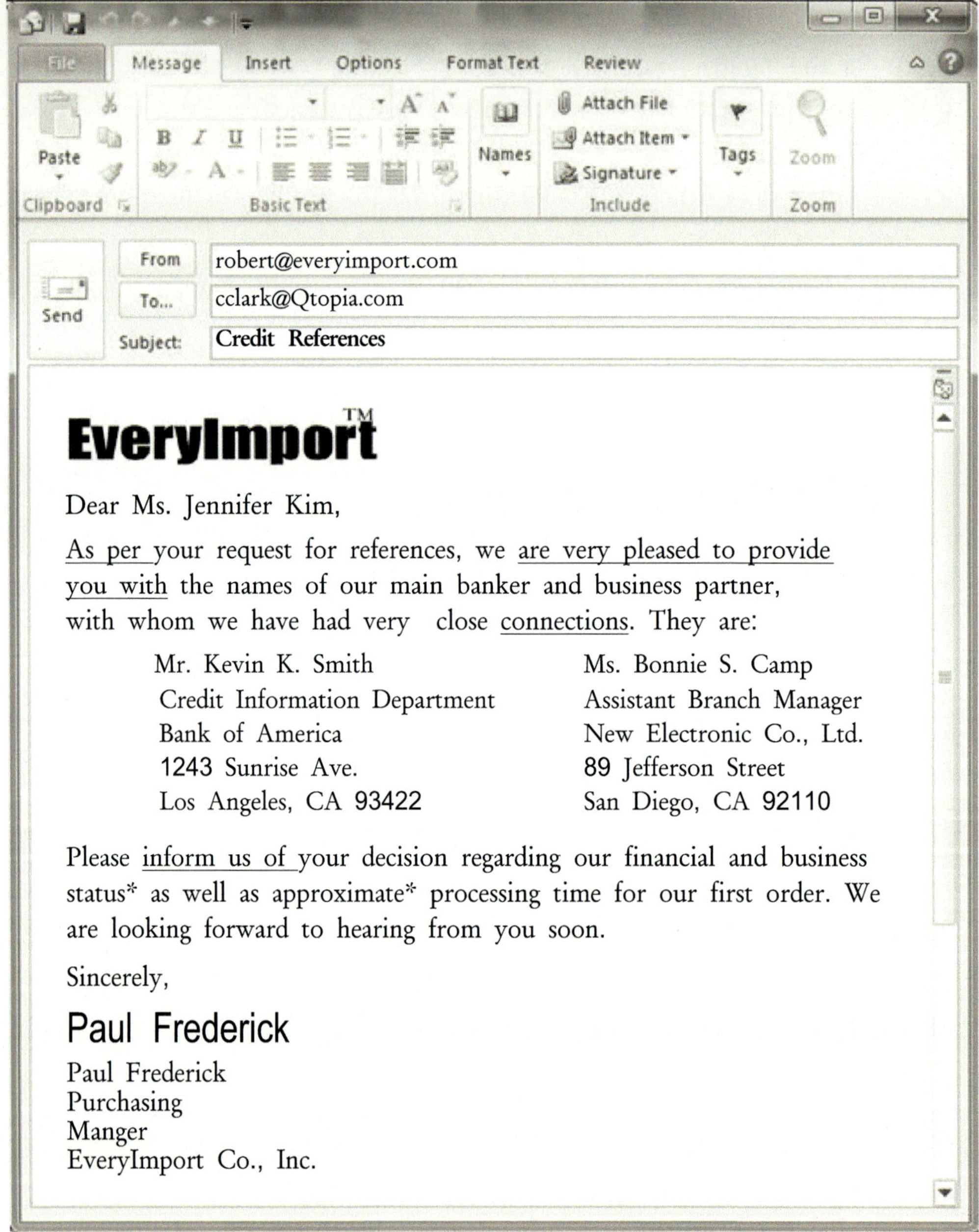

From: robert@everyimport.com
To: cclark@Qtopia.com
Subject: **Credit References**

EveryImport™

Dear Ms. Jennifer Kim,

As per your request for references, we are very pleased to provide you with the names of our main banker and business partner, with whom we have had very close connections. They are:

Mr. Kevin K. Smith	Ms. Bonnie S. Camp
Credit Information Department	Assistant Branch Manager
Bank of America	New Electronic Co., Ltd.
1243 Sunrise Ave.	89 Jefferson Street
Los Angeles, CA 93422	San Diego, CA 92110

Please inform us of your decision regarding our financial and business status* as well as approximate* processing time for our first order. We are looking forward to hearing from you soon.

Sincerely,

Paul Frederick

Paul Frederick
Purchasing
Manger
EveryImport Co., Inc.

Synopsis

reference를 알려줄 것을 요구 받은 EveryImport의 Paul은 자사가 긴밀하게 거래(have had very close connections)하고 있는 Bank of America와 New Electronic의 주소와 담당자 이름을 Qtopia의 Jennifer에게 알려주고 있다. 신용과 영업상태(financial and business status)의 확인이 끝나는 대로 Qtopia 측의 결정에 대하여 알려 달라(inform us of your decision)는 말과 함께 첫 주문을 할 경우 대략 처리기간(approximate processing time)이 얼마나 걸리는지 묻고 있다. 참고로, 신용조회처의 담당자들에게는 미리 신용조회처로 제공하고 싶다는 의사를 표시하고 허락을 얻어야 한다.

* status [steitəs, stætəs] n. 상태; 지위; 자격; [법률] 신분(standing)
  - the present status of affairs: 현재의 상태, 현황
  - social status: 사회적 신분.
  - financial and business status(standing): 재무, 영업상태
* approximate [əprάksəmət] a. 대강의, 근사한 [əprάksəmeit] v. ~에 가까이 가다
  - The approximate cost of construction was $123,000.
  - Her annual income closely approximates to 20,000 dollars.

◈ Credit Inquiry의 내용

국제무역거래는 언어, 상관습, 법률 등이 다른 거래처와의 거래이기 때문에 상대방의 영업상태나 성실성 등에 대한 충분한 정보를 확보하기 힘들고, 잘못 선정된 거래처로 인한 피해를 사후에 보상받기가 어렵다. 따라서 거래를 시작하기 전에 상대방에 대한 철저한 조사가 필수적이다. 신용조사 내용에 필수적으로 강조되는 것은 다음과 같은데 이를 Credit Inquiry의 3C's라고 한다.

① Character(특성): 관련 업계내의 평판(reputation)이나 성실성(integrity), 영업태도(attitude toward business), 계약이행에 대한 열의(willingness to meet obligation)

② Capital(재무상태): 대차대조표, 손익계산서 등 지불능력에 대한 재무상태(financial status)

③ Capacity(생산·영업능력): 영업형태, 연간 생산량 및 매출액 등 영업능력(busi ness ability)

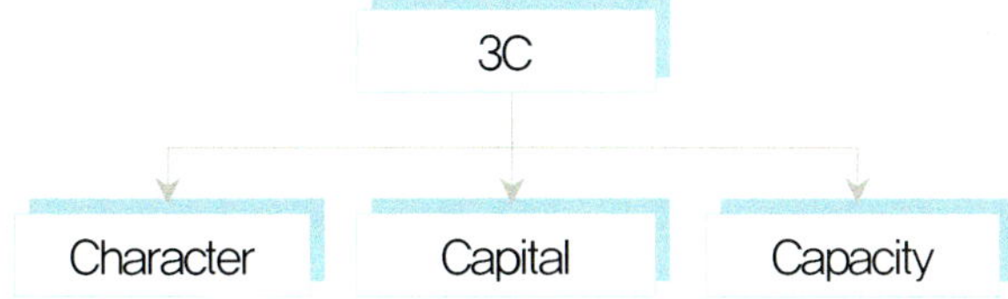

3C's에 거래조건(condition), 담보능력(collateral), 거래통화(currency), 소속국가(country) 가운데 두 가지를 추가시켜서 5C's라고도 한다.

◈ as per your request

"귀사의 요청에 따라"의 의미로 상대방의 요청에 따라 ~을 수행할 때 쓸 수 있는 표현이다. 아래와 같이 다양한 형태로 쓰인다.

귀사의 요청에 따라

as per your request ~
as requested ~
at your request ~
as instructed ~
in accordance with your request ~
according to your request ~
in compliance with your request ~
pursuant to your request ~

as per만으로만 쓰이면 according to ~, in accordance with ~, as indicated (mentioned/shown/listed) in ~ '~와 같이', '~에 따라'의 의미로 쓰인다.

- I faxed you today as per enclosed copy. (동봉한 사본과 같이 팩스를 보냈습니다.)
- Quality is as per sample. (품질은 견본에서와 같습니다.)

◈ be pleased to~

'~ 합니다, ~ 해드립니다'의 격식을 차린 의미로 business letter에서 많이 쓰인다.

- We are pleased to provide you with our latest catalog along with price list. be pleased to와 비슷한 의미이지만 덜 격식이 느껴지는 표현으로는, be glad to ~, be grateful to ~ 등이 있고, 좀 딱딱한 문어체 같은 표현으로는 take(have) pleasure in ~ing를 쓸 수 있다. 반면, 구어체인 표현이지만 be happy to ~를 쓰기도 한다.

- I take pleasure in quoting you our FOB price.
- I am happy to inform you that your proposal has been accepted.

위와 같은 표현은 다음에 긍정적 혹은 부정적이지 않은 내용이 올 때 사용할 수 있다. 반면에 부정적 내용이라면 regret을 사용하여 다음과 같이 쓴다.

- I regret to inform you that we are unable to accept the price at this time.

provide A with B

provide, furnish, supply는 모두 '공급하다, 제공하다'라는 의미로 다음과 같이 같은 용법으로 쓰인다.

'~에게 ~을 제공하다'의 의미로 쓰일 때는(provide+사람+with+사물)으로 쓴다.

- We will provide you with the necessary documents.
  [cf] We will provide the necessary documents.는 가능

거꾸로 '~을 ~에게 제공하다'로 쓰일 때는(provide+사물+to, for+사람)으로 쓴다.

- We will provide the necessary documents to you.
- We must furnish food for our children.

connections

국제 무역을 하다 보면 많은 거래처를 만들기 위하여 노력해야 하는 데 '거래처', '거래관계'를 말할 때 connection 혹은 tie-up이라고 한다.

- They have very good connections in textiles. (섬유업계에 좋은 거래처를 가지고 있다.)
- We have an excellent tie-up with them. (우리는 그 회사와 좋은 관계를 가지고 있다.)
- We have large connections in New York. (우리는 뉴욕에 많은 거래처를 가지고 있다.)
- What's the number of your connections in US?(미국에 거래처가 얼마나 되나요?)

일상 대화에도 두 사람과의 관계 역시 connection을 사용하는 데 We have a connection.이라고 말하면 두 사람이기 때문에 생기는 단순한 관계가 아니고 뭔가 잘 통하는 관계라는 뜻으로 쓰인다. 또 전화 통화할 때 잡음이 많거나 소리가 잘 안 들리는 등 전화선 연결이 좋지 않을 때에는 bad connection이라고 말한다.

◈ inform A of B

'A(사람)에게 B(사물)를 통보하다'의 의미로 쓰일 때 inform ~ of ~형태를 취한다.

- My daughter informs me of her pregnancy.
  = My daughter informs me that she is pregnant.

'통보하다'의 의미로 advise, notify, apprise 역시 같은 형식으로 쓰인다.

- The bank advised us of the arrival of an L/C.
- You must apprise them of the danger that may be involved.

수동형 be ~ed of의 형태로 쓰이면 '~을 통보받다'의 뜻이다.

- He was informed of the facts.
- We are advised of the dispatch of the goods.
- The police was notified of the accident.
- If you are apprised of something, someone tells you about it.

Practice Tests - Situation 4

1. What can you learn from the e-mail in Situation 4?
   (a) New Electronics and Qtopia are business partners.
   (b) EveryImport and New Electronics have accounts with Bank of America.
   (c) Paul Frederic is going to writing two reference letters.
   (d) Ms. Jennifer Kim will check the financial status of EveryImport.

2. What relationship does the EveryImport have with New Electronic?
   (a) They are business partners.
   (b) They have a parent-subsidiary relationship
   (c) They are trying to make business relationship in near future.
   (d) They have no relationship at this time.

3. 밑줄 부분에 들어갈 수 있는 말로 어색한 것은?
   ________ your request your account has been set to expire at the end of your billing period and your most previous invoice refunded.
   (a) As per (b) According to
   (c) Pursuant to (d) Regarding

4. 다음 중 표현이 어색한 것은?
   (a) We are pleased to provide you with our latest catalog.
   (b) We take pleasure in providing our latest catalog.
   (c) We are happy to inform you that your paper has been accepted.
   (d) We regret to inform you that we can supply the goods on time.

5. A paving company wouldn't be able to charge individual drivers for the roads it creates. A hospital can't collect from people who can't afford to pay. Our governments, at all levels, provide us ______ goods and services that are sometimes more difficult for companies or individuals to provide.
   (a) with (b) of
   (c) necessary (d) all

6. There is further evidence that FBI was informed ______ 9/11 terror attacks.

(a) with (b) of
(c) about (d) regarding

7. 다음 문장은 무엇을 위한 것인가?

Would you please allow us to provide Qtopia systems of Korea with your name and address as a credit reference?

(a) asking credit status (b) requesting a permission
(c) circulating a letter (d) providing information

8. You can visit our internet homepage for further information on our sales organization, and we wish you to refer to The Industrial Bank of Korea in Paris regarding our ( )

(a) credit standing (b) company history
(c) shipping schedule (d) business partner

9. ( ) credit and financial ( ) of our firm, the Seoul Bank of Korea, Seoul, will supply you ( ) necessary information.

(a) Regarding – standing – of (b) Concerning – conditions – to
(c) As to – status – with (d) About – situation – for

10. Which of the following is grammatically INCORRECT? [무역영어 2급]

The firms (a) <u>print</u> in the heading of this letter are those for whom we (b) <u>have</u> been serving as the Sole Selling Agents in the Far East for many years and who (c) <u>are</u> showing us their full satisfaction with our service. Our bankers, the Woori Bank, Seoul, (d) <u>will</u> give you any information you may desire as to our financial stability or character.

11. Which of the following are the proper titles of 1~3? [무역영어 1급]

A proposal is a sales pitch for an idea. Its purpose is to persuade someone to accept your idea and put it into action.

1. ______. Early in the proposal you must state CLEARLY your actual idea. You must define its purpose, as well as its scope and limitations.

2. ________. Offer specific reasons for your idea, including the benefits or advantages to be gained from it. Present these reasons logically, not just as a list, but as an organized progression.

3. ______. Provide answers to questions before they occur. This may include credentials of people involved, justification of costs or expenditures, or arguments against alternative ideas.

(a) Make your limitation – Be reasonable – Delete alternatives
(b) Define the idea – Be persuasive – Anticipate objections
(c) Clear away your idea – Make reasons – Provide questions
(d) Prepare your presentation – Offer reasonable things – Explain your doubts

12. Which of the following is NOT appropriately rewritten to have the same meaning? [무역영어 1급]

(a) It's not the document that we asked for. → The document you sent us does not correspond to our request.
(b) I would like to be informed of your scheduled arrival time beforehand. → Please advise us of your scheduled arrival time in advance.
(c) I regret that the delivery will be postponed. → I am sorry to tell you that the dispatch is behind schedule.
(d) Let us give the issue a second thought. → There is no room for reconsideration.

Situation 5

EveryImport의 신용상태를 거래은행에 문의하다.

Qtopia Systems

134 Seocho-dong, Seocho-ku, Seoul 130-070, Republic of Korea
Phone: +82-2-2374-4785
Fax: +82-2-2374-4788
E-mail: systems@Qtopia.com

October 4, 2014

Dear Mr. Kevin Smith,

EveryImport Co., Inc., 3434 Sunset Boulevard, Los Angeles, has been trying to make a business relationship with us and listed you as a credit reference.

We would appreciate it if you would kindly let us have your opinion regarding their financial standing. We precisely want to know how long EveryImport has had accounts with you and the promptness* in paying bills.

We assure you that any information you may supply will be kept in the strictest confidence*, and that you will have no responsibility for the information provided.

Thank you in advance for your kind considerations. Sincerely yours,

Jennifer Kim

Jennifer Kim,
Director, Export Department
Qtopia systems

Synopsis

Qtopia의 Jennifer는 EveryImport의 Paul로부터 받은 신용조회처의 한곳인 Bank of America의 Kevin Smith에게 편지를 써서 EveryImport의 신용상태(financial standing)에 대하여 문의하고 있다. 특히 EveryImport가 Bank of America과 얼마나 오래 계정을 가지고 있어왔고, 각종 대금의 청구(bill)에 대한 지불이 신속히(promptness) 이루어지는지를 묻고 있다. 그리고 알려준 정보에 대해서는 절대 비밀(strictest confidence)로 할 것이며 Bank of America에 어떤 책임(responsibility)도 없음을 강조하고 있다. 귀사의 배려(considerations)에 미리(in advance) 감사한다는 말로 마무리하고 있다.

* promptness [prάmptnis] n. 신속함 a. prompt: 신속한, 즉시불[즉시 인도]의
To Insure Promptness(tip) 은 18세기 영국의 Lloyd's Coffee House에서 "신속한 서비스를 받고자하는 고객들이 자발적으로 베풀던 선심"이 유래되었다는 설이 있다. 호텔이나 레스토랑의 tip을 gratuity 혹은 gratitude라고 부른다.

* confidence [kάnfədəns]
① (남에 대한) 신용, 신뢰. [동의어] trust, belief confident: a. 믿을 만한
② 속내 말; 비밀, 내밀한 일. [동의어] secret confidential: a. 비밀의

◈ Credit Inquiry의 방법

신용조사 방법으로는 상대방의 거래은행에 조사를 의뢰하는 은행조회(bank reference)가 가장 많이 쓰인다. 또 상대방과 거래경험이 있는 국내외의 다른 거래처나 상업회의소 등을 통한 업계조회(trade reference)를 이용할 수도 있다. 거래금액이 큰 경우에는 비용이 들기는 하지만 거래처의 신용을 보다 확실하게 파악하기 위하여 전문적인 신용조사기관(credit agency)을 이용하기도 한다. 국제적으로 유명한 신용조사기관으로는 미국의 Dun & Bradstreet International, 영국의 Bradstreet British Ltd., 독일의 Ausktnfe Burgel Centrale Gmbh, 일본의 Tokyo Shoko Japan International Co., Ltd. 등이 있다. 국내에서는 신용보증기금(Korea Credit Guarantee Fund)이 외국의 관련기관과 제휴를 맺고 조사를 대행해 주고 있다. 이 밖에 대한무역진흥공사, 한국수출보험공사, 수출입은행 등에서도 해 외의 거래처에 대한 신용정보를 얻을 수 있다.

◈ appreciate

'~해 주시면 감사하겠습니다'. 의미로 쓰이는 표현으로 appreciate 다음에 쓰인 it는 if

이하의 내용을 받으므로 if가 수반되면 반드시 it가 쓰이는 점에 주의할 필요가 있다. 이 경우 would appreciate 혹은 will appreciate 등으로 쓴다. 수동형으로 it을 주어로 It would be appreciated if ~와 같이도 쓰인다. 또한 if 대신 ~ing나 명사가 올 수 있으나 to 부정사는 쓰지 않는다.

- We would appreciate it if you would send us your reply early.
- It would be appreciated if you would send us your reply early.
- We would appreciate receiving your early reply.
  (~~to receive~~)

'~에 대하여 고맙다'의 의미로 사용할 때에는 현재형을 쓴다. 또한 이러한 의미로 쓰일 때는 appreciate의 목적어는 어떠한 '사항'이나 '물건'이 오고 '사람'은 오지 않는다. 그리고 appreciate는 전치사(for)와 같이 쓰지 않고 항상 앞에 대명사(I, we, you)가 온다.

- We appreciate your warm hospitality.
  (~~you for~~)
- We appreciate your letter dated May 25.
  (~~for~~)
- We appreciate what you said.
  (~~Appreciate what you said.~~)

Thank you for ~는 appreciate과 달리 소유대명사(my, your, his, her 등)와 같이 ~ing형으로 쓰지 않는 점에 주의할 것.

- Thank you for your help.
  (~~helping me~~)
- Thank you for teaching us.
  (~~your teaching us~~)

appreciate의 명사형 appreciation은 express나 show와 같이 쓰인다.

- I wish to express my appreciation to Mr. Paris for his support.
- Looking for ways to show appreciation to your coworkers and employees?

또한 appreciate은 to be fully aware of; understand; realize; value somebody or something highly의 의미로도 쓰인다:

- We appreciate that you are unable to ship the goods as scheduled.
- I really appreciate you.

(나는 당신을 소중히 여기고 있습니다. 이때는 사람이 목적어로 오는 것에 주의)
이외에도 appreciate은 gain in value의 의미가 있다.

appreciation: 통화의 평가 절상
[cf] depreciation: 통화의 평가 절하

- It is not possible to allow a discount at this time due to the recent appreciation of Korean won against US dollar.
- US dollar has been depreciated against all currencies in these days.

let

'~를 하게 하다'의 의미로 쓰이는 let 다음에는 to가 없이 동사의 원형이 온다.

- We let the children stay up late on Saturdays.
- She didn't let me see what she was doing.

make 역시 비슷하지만 '강제로 ~하게 하다'의 느낌이 있으므로 구별할 필요가 있다.

- I let her go. (=그녀가 바라고 있기 때문에 가게 했다. I allow her to go.)
- I make her go. (=그녀는 원하지 않았지만 가게 했다. I force her to go.)

* allow, permit, force 등은 to 부정사가 온다.

또한 let은
let.... know(=tell, inform)
let... have(=send, give)의 의미로 사용된다.

- Please let us know your decision. (=Please tell us your decision.)
- Please let me have your comments on this. (=Please give me your comments on this.)

◈ keep in the strictest confidence

'~을 극비에 부친다'는 의미로 credit inquiry에 많이 쓰이는 표현이다. keep 대신 treat나 regard를 써서,

keep(treat, regard) strictly confidential keep(treat, regard) in strict confidence keep(treat, regard) as a top secret

- The information will be kept strictly confidential.
- The information will be kept in strict confidence.
- This information will be treated as a top secret.

confidence는 일반적인 의미는 '신뢰', '믿음'(trust, belief)이고 여기에 해당하는 형용사는 confident이다. confidence의 다른 의미는 '비밀'(secret)이고 이런 의미의 형용사는 confidential이다.

- Thank you for your confidence and support. (신뢰와 지원에 감사드립니다.)
- I am confident about our taking their orders. (주문을 받을 것으로 확신합니다.)

- All information we provide is in confidence.
- All information we provide is confidential. (저희가 제공하는 모든 정보는 비밀입니다.)

confidential과 같은 의미로 쓰이는 단어에는 classified가 있다. classified는 일반적으로 '분류된'의 뜻이지만, 비밀의 의미로도 쓰인다.

classified advertising (신문의) 구인 · 구직 등의 항목별로 분류된 소(小) 광고
classified information (특히 군사적인) 비밀 정보

Let it be

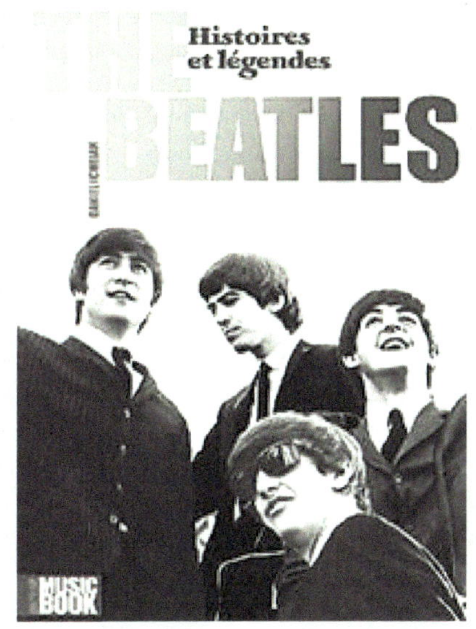

When I find myself in times of trouble
Mother Mary comes to me
Speaking words of wisdom, let it be.

And in my hour of darkness
She is standing right in front of me
Speaking words of wisdom, let it be.

Let it be, let it be.
Whisper words of wisdom, let it be.

And when the broken hearted people
Living in the world agree,
There will be an answer, let it be.

For though they may be parted there
is still a chance that they will see
There will be an answer, let it be.

Let it be, let it be. Yeah
There will be an answer, let it be.

And when the night is cloudy,
There is still a light that shines on me,
Shine on until tomorrow, let it be.

I wake up to the sound of music Mother
Mary comes to me
Speaking words of wisdom, let it be.

Let it be, let it be.
There will be an answer,
let it be. Let it be, let it be,

Whisper words of wisdom, let it be.

Practice Tests - Situation 5

1. What is true statement regarding the letter in Situation 5?
   (a) The information Qtopia obtained from Mr. Smith will be released.
   (b) Mr. Smith is responsible for the information provided.
   (c) Mr. Smith's company has had a business relationship with EveryImport.
   (d) Qtopia and EveryImport already had a business relationship.

2. What is the letter in situation 5 for?
   (a) Jennifer is seeking information about EveryImport.
   (b) Jennifer is trying to persuade Kevin Smith for the secret.
   (c) Jennifer wants to thank Kevin Smith for the information provided.
   (d) Jennifer lets Kevin Smith know that he is not responsible for the information provided.

3. We would appreciate ________ if you could send your sample as soon as possible.
   (a) nothing is necessary (b) you (c) even (d) it

4. We <u>appreciate</u> that you are not able to ship the goods on time.
   (a) thank (b) value highly
   (c) gain in value (d) understand

5. Mary really <u>appreciates</u> Tommy.
   (a) thanks Tommy (b) values Tommy highly
   (c) realizes Tommy (d) understands Tommy

6. We assure you that the information you provided will be ________ in the strictest confidence.
   (a) sold (b) told (c) kept (d) gotten

7. 다음은 어떤 종류의 통신문에 사용하는 문장인가?

We shall be obliged if you kindly give us detailed information on their general business reputation, business conduct and financial rating for reference in our decision-making.

(a) credit inquiry (b) business proposal
(c) counter offer (d) business inquire

8. Below is a credit inquiry. Which of the following has a different reply from others? [무역영어 2급]

We would appreciate it if you would inform us of their financial standing and reputation. Any information provided by you will be treated as strictly confidential, and expenses will be paid by us upon receipt of your bill. Your prompt reply will be much appreciated.

(a) The Company is respected through the industry for highest integrity and reliability.
(b) The amounts involved have been small compared with the sum mentioned in your letter, and even so, accounts were always settled overdue.
(c) As far our information goes it is punctually meeting its commitments and a credit in the sum you mentioned would seem to be safe.
(d) They have maintained a current account with us for more than ten years.

9. Which of the following is grammatically or semantically INCORRECT? [무역영어 2급]

(a) We will keep your letter in our file and will contact you again as soon as they resume production.
(b) We will get in touch with you as soon as we are in a position to supply this line again.
(c) We should appreciate your letting us know if there is any further information we could give you.
(d) Any further information you may give us will pay our careful attention.

Situation 6

EveryImport의 신용상태에 대한 Bank of America의 긍정적 회신

Bank of America Higher Standards

1243 Sunrise Ave. LA, CA 93422 Tel. 923-234-3928 Fax. 923-234-3929

October 8, 2014

Dear Ms. Jennifer Kim,

We are pleased to send the credit information you requested concerning EveryImport Co., Inc.

EveryImport has had a corporate checking account with us for more than 10 years. They have maintained their account with adequate funds to cover all checks drawn, and any settlements* to us have always been prompt. To the best of our knowledge they have no outstanding* financial liabilities*.

In sum, we can say that EveryImport is creditworthy*, and we have no reservation* in extending credit to them. Please understand that this information represents our opinion and we take no responsibility for it. If you need any further information about EveryImport, please do not hesitate to contact us.

Thank you
very much.
Truly yours,

Kevin K.Smith

Kevin K. Smith
Credit Information
Department Bank Of America

Synopsis

EveryImport의 신용에 대한 Qtopia측의 문의를 받은 Bank of America의 Kevin Smith가 EveryImport과의 거래관계에 대한 긍정적 의견을 보내고 있다. EveryImport과는 10년 이상 거래를 해오고 있고, 항상 발행한 수표를 처리하기(cover)에 충분한 자금을 계정에 유지해왔으며, 지불해야 할 것들(any settlement)을 늦은 적이 없다는 점을 밝히고 있다. 그리고 Bank of America가 아는 한(to our best knowledge) 현재 EveryImport가 가지고 있는 금전적 채무(outstanding financial liabilities)는 없다는 점도 밝히고 있다. 이런 점들로 봐서 EveryImport은 신용할 만하고 신용대출 한도를 늘려주는데 주저함이 없지만(no reservation in extending credit) 이것은 단순히 Bank of America측의 의견이며 이에 대한 책임은 없다는 점을 강조하면서 편지를 마무리하고 있다.

*settlement [sétlmənt] n.
① u 정착, 정주(定住); c 정주지. ② u, c 청산, 결산; 지불

*outstanding [àutstǽndiŋ] a.
① 걸출한, 눈에 띄는, 현저한, an outstanding view
② 미결제의(unpaid, past due, overdue), an outstanding debt of $500

*liability [làiəbíləti] n.
① ~의 경향이 있음, [걸리기]쉬움(to), liability to disease: 병에 걸리기 쉬운 체질
② 책임, 부담, 의무(채권의), limited liability: 유한 책임
③ (pl.) 빚(debt), 채무. [opp.] assets.

*creditworthy [kréditwə̀:rði] a. 신용있는, 지불능력이 있는.
creditworthiness: n. 신용할 수 있음.

*reservation [rèzə:rvéiʃ–ən] n.
① c 예약; 예약석[실], 지정석. make a reservation 예약을 하다(for)
② u 조건, 제한, 이런 의미로 쓰일 때는 in ~ing 혹은 about ~ing형으로 쓴다.
· I recommend him to you without reservation or hesitation.
· I have no reservation in extending credit to them.

◈ credit

n. 신용, 외상판매, (은행의) 대출금, 명예
vt. 신용으로 판매하다. 대변(신용장부)에 기재하다.
[opp.] debit: 돈을 계좌에서 인출하다.

- credit card(신용카드): 은행이 카드 사용자의 신용을 믿고 외상거래를 할 수 있게 한 카드
- debit card(직불카드): 은행이 카드 사용자의 신용을 믿을 수 없어서 잔고가 있어야 거래할 수 있는 카드

- Interest is calculated daily and credited to your account. (예금이자가 지급됨)
- Interest is calculated daily and debited from your account. (대출이자가 인출됨)
- As our apology we will credit you for the full amount including the freight. (사과를 드리며 모든 금액을 환불(혹은 추후 사용할 수 있는 금액)하겠습니다.)
- We will confirm the revised amount to you before debiting your account. (귀하의 계좌에서 돈이 인출되기 전에 변경된 잔고를 항상 확인받겠습니다.)

◈ checking account

Business English에서의 check는 주로 기업에서 대금의 지급수단으로 발행하는 수표인 corporate check을 말한다. 반면 개인이 발행하는 수표를 personal check이라고 한다.

~ a check for one million won: 100만원권 수표

~ a check pay to the order of [in favor of] Mr. M: M 앞으로 발행한 수표

- draw [issue, write out, make out] a check: 수표를 발행하다.
- pay by check: 수표로 지불하다.
- cash a check: 수표를 현금으로 바꾸다.

- certified check; cashier's check: 은행이 대금의 지급을 보증하는 수표.
- dishonored [bad] check; rubber check: 잔고의 부족으로 부도 처리된 수표
- cancelled check: 정상적으로 처리되어 발행인에게 되돌아온 수표(대금의 지급영수증으로 활용할 수 있음)
- checking account: 수표를 발행할 수 있는 계좌
- savings account: 일정기간 저축을 위한 계좌

cover

원래의 '~을 덮다'의 의미 이외에 다른 여러 가지 뜻으로 쓰인다.

1. pay for ~; to be sufficient to pay for ~
   - We have ordered to open an L/C to cover this order.
   - They have sufficient fund to cover the project.

2. insure; to provide insurance protection to somebody
   - We cover the item against loss and/or damage for $5,000.
   - You need to obtain full coverage during the entire transit of the goods.

3. extend over
   - The agent covers all the New England area.
   - The local police cover the whole city.

Please do not hesitate to contact us.

"~에 연락하다"의 의미로 가장 많이 쓸 수 있는 단어는 contact이다.

- Please contact me at any time.
- I'll contact you as soon as I receive your letter of reference.

  * contact 다음에 with 혹은 to와 같은 전치사 없이 바로 목적어가 온다.

주저 없이 연락을 해달라고 할 때는 without hesitation 나 feel free를 써서,

- Please contact us without hesitation if you need any further information.
- Please feel free to contact me when you have any questions.

같은 의미로 get in touch with ~를 쓸 수도 있고 "~와 지속적으로 연락 해오고 있다"의 의미로는 keep in touch with ~을 쓴다.

- I need to get in touch with you immediately.
- I will keep in touch with our main office to updated information right away.

Practice Tests - Situation 6

1. What kind of letter is it?
   (a) suggest for extending credit
   (b) request for the business reference
   (c) ask for confidential information
   (d) answer to the credit reference

2. What is the overall evaluation of Bank of America for the EveryImport?
   (a) They believe EveryImport has no outstanding debts.
   (b) They are positive about the financial standing of EveryImport.
   (c) EveryImport is fully responsible for the information provided.
   (d) EveryImport has maintained enough funds to cover the checks drawn.

3. We can use check as a receipt.
   (a) certified (b) dishonored
   (c) cancelled (d) cashier's

4. To the order we have a check for USD5,000.00.
   (a) place – issued (b) cover – issued
   (c) process – drawn (d) pay – cashed

5. We cannot recommend TJ Trading Co. for credit, they have an outstanding account with us that is 90 days overdue.
   (a) unless (b) before
   (c) because (d) although

6. We can get the discount only if we purchase the tickets by credit card, at least 21 days.
   (a) by advance (b) to advance
   (c) in advance (d) with advance

7. Many small businesses, unable to obtain credit from traditional banks, have been __________ to turn to non-bank financial institutions.

(a) forced (b) credited
(c) obtained (d) deposited

8. 다음은 거래은행 앞 신용조회장에 대한 회신의 일부이다. 아래 문장의 공란에 들어갈 단어를 알맞게 배열한 것은?

The company you mentioned is a private company running as a family concern by three brothers and was founded fifteen years ago. It ( ) a good reputation. As far as our information goes it is punctually ( ) its commitments and a credit in the sum you mentioned would seem to be safe. This information is strictly ( ) and given without any responsibility ( ).

(a) enjoys – meeting – confidential – on our part
(b) plays – meeting – confidential – on our part
(c) enjoys – satisfying – coincident – on your part
(d) plays – satisfying – confidential – on your part

9. Fill in with right words. [무역영어 2급]

We would appreciate your sending us information ( ) the company's credit standing. We would especially like to know how long the company has had( ) with you and whether or not any of their debts are( ).

(a) for – loan – paid (b) on – borrowing – paid
(c) about – loan – outstanding (d) regarding – account – past due

10. 다음 밑줄 친 부분과 바꾸어 쓸 때 적절하지 않은 것을 고르시오. [무역영어 2급]

Since Janoski Company has never failed to (a) meet their obligations with satisfaction and their bills have always been (b) settled promptly. We believe that the company is (c) reliable. This company is (d) famous throughout the industry.

(a) (a) –satisfy (b) (b) –solid
(c) (c) –creditworthy (d) (d) –well-known

Situation 7

EveryImport측에 Q-pointer II에 대한 확정오퍼를 보내다.

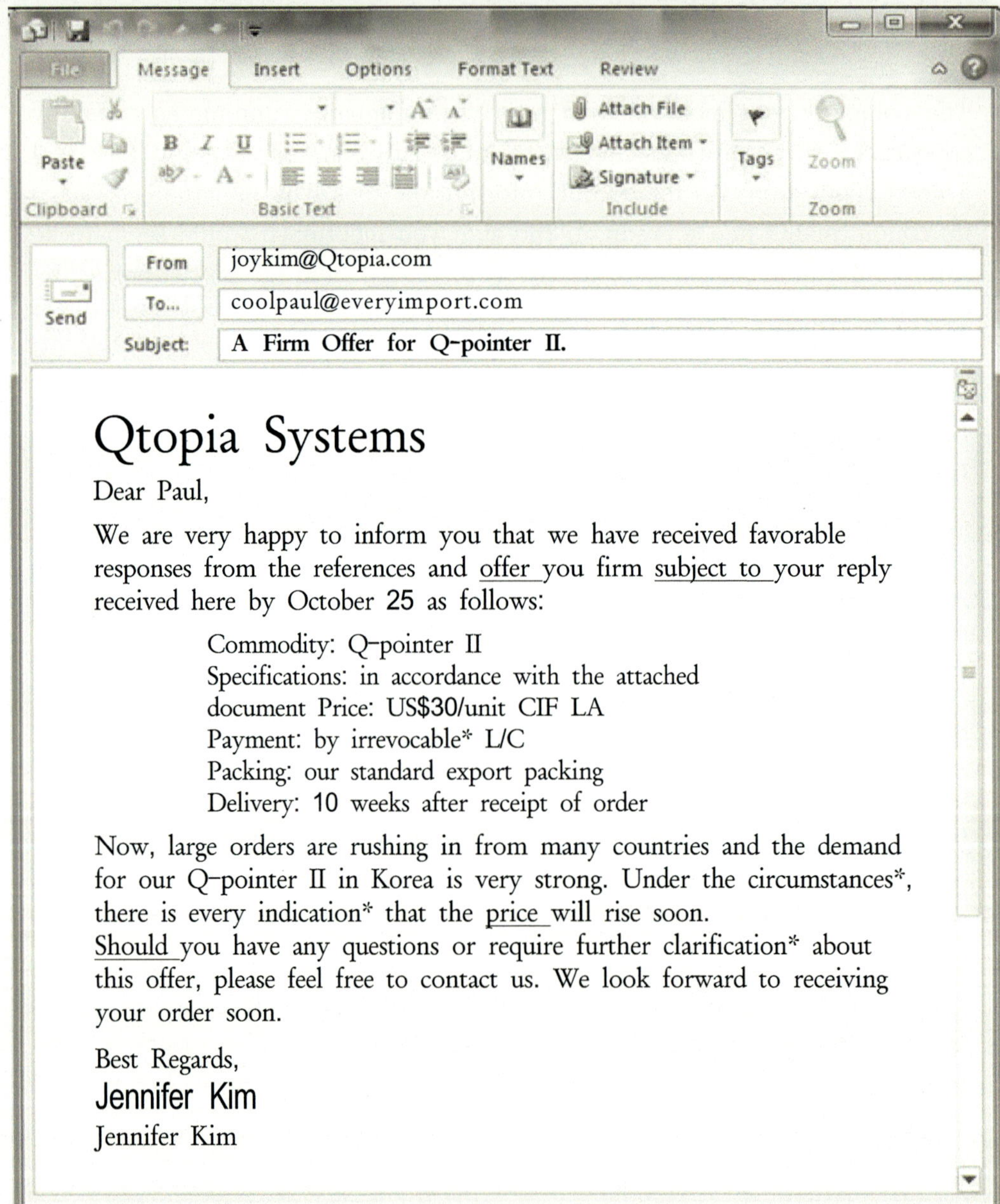

From: joykim@Qtopia.com

To: coolpaul@everyimport.com

Subject: **A Firm Offer for Q-pointer II.**

Qtopia Systems

Dear Paul,

We are very happy to inform you that we have received favorable responses from the references and offer you firm subject to your reply received here by October 25 as follows:

Commodity: Q-pointer II
Specifications: in accordance with the attached
document Price: US$30/unit CIF LA
Payment: by irrevocable* L/C
Packing: our standard export packing
Delivery: 10 weeks after receipt of order

Now, large orders are rushing in from many countries and the demand for our Q-pointer II in Korea is very strong. Under the circumstances*, there is every indication* that the price will rise soon.
Should you have any questions or require further clarification* about this offer, please feel free to contact us. We look forward to receiving your order soon.

Best Regards,

Jennifer Kim

Jennifer Kim

Synopsis

신용조회 결과 EveryImport은 믿을만한 회사라는 판단이 되어서 거래를 시작하기로 한 Qtopia의 Jennifer는 위와 같은 offer를 EveryImport 측에 보냈다. 위는 October 25일까지 회신을 전제로(subject to your reply)한 확정오퍼(firm offer)이다. 이 물품에 대한 주문이 많은 나라에서 쇄도하고 있고(large orders are rushing in), 한국에서도 수요가 많다는 것을 밝히고 있다. 이런 점을 감안하면(under the circumstance) 조만간 가격 인상이 있을 수도 있다는 점을 강조하면서 구매를 유도하고 있다.

*irrevocable [irevəkəbəl] a. 취소불가능 한
  revoke [rivóuk] v. 취소하다. revocable [revəkəbl] a. 취소가능 한
*circumstance [sə:rkəmstǽns / –stəns] n. (보통 pl.) 상황, 환경; 주위의 사정
  · under the(such) circumstances: 이런 상황에서
*indication n. 조짐, 지적, 암시
  · there is every indication that ~: ~할 것 같은 조짐이 많다.
*clarification [klærəfikeiʃən] n. 설명, 해명. clarify: v. 명확히 하다.
  · if you need further clarification ~: 더 자세한 설명이 필요하시면

◈ offer란?

거래제의에 대하여 상대방이 긍정적인 반응을 보이면 구체적인 거래조건을 제시하면서 계약을 체결하고 싶다는 의사표시를 하게 되는데 이를 offer라고 한다. 즉, offer란 offer를 내는 사람(offerer)이 오퍼를 받는 사람(offeree)에게 특정한 물품을 특정한 조건으로 매 도 혹은 매입하겠다는 의사표시를 말한다.

무역거래에 있어서 가장 중요한 오퍼는 확정오퍼(firm offer)라고 할 수 있다. 이는 offerer가 오퍼를 통하여 거래조건을 제시하면서 유효기간(validity)을 지정하여 그 기간 내에 offeree가 승낙(acceptance)할 것을 조건으로 하는 오퍼를 말한다. 유효기간 내에 offeree의 acceptance가 offerer에게 도착되면 매매계약은 확정적으로 성립된다. 반면에 validity가 지나면 그 offer는 자동적으로 무효가 된다. 또한 유효기간 내에는 offerer가 마음대로 오퍼의 내용을 변경하거나 취소할 수 없다. firm offer에는 보통 다음과 같은 문구가 들어 있다.

- We offer you firm subject to your reply being received here by April 15.
- We have made a firm offer for your acceptance reaching us by April 10.

이와 반대로 이러한 유효기간을 명시하지 않은 오퍼를 불확정오퍼(free offer)라고 한다. free offer는 offerer가 수시로 오퍼의 내용을 변경 또는 취소할 수 있으며, offeree의 거래조건을 수락하여도 거래가 성립되기 위해서는 offerer의 최종확인이 필요하다. 또한 일정한 조건이 붙어 있는 오퍼를 조건부오퍼(conditional offer)라고 한다. 이는 offeree의 승낙만으로는 거래가 성립되지 않고 일정한 조건이 충족되어야만 거래가 성립된다. 자주 사용되는 조건문에는 다음과 같은 것들이 있다.

Offer subject to being unsold(재고잔류 조건부 오퍼): 오퍼에 대한 승낙의 의사가 오퍼 수신자로부터 발행자에게 도착했다 하더라도 바로 계약이 성립되는 것이 아니고 그 시점에 당해 물품의 재고가 남아 있는 경우에 한하여 계약이 성립된다는 조건의 오퍼이다. 이를 Offer subject to prior sale(선착순매매 조건부 오퍼)라고도 부른다.

Offer on sale or return(반품허용 조건부 오퍼): 오퍼와 함께 물품을 대량으로 송부하여 오퍼 수신자가 이를 판매하게 하고 팔리지 않은 잔품은 반납하도록 하는 조건의 오퍼로 잡화류 등의 위탁판매에 주로 사용된다. Sale-or-Return을 줄여서 SOR이라고도 한다.

Offer without engagement(무확약 오퍼): 오퍼에 제시된 가격이 확정되지 않아 시가변동(market fluctuation)에 따라 변경할 수 있다는 조건의 오퍼이다.

Sub-con offer(확인 조건부 오퍼): 오퍼 발행자가 오퍼를 발행할 때 계약의 성립에는 발행자의 최종확인이 필요하다는 조건이 붙은 오퍼이다. 이는 형식적으로는 offer이지만, 상대방에 대한 오퍼의 유인(invitation to offer)에 지나지 않는다.

- We offer you the above model subject to being unsold.
- We are offering the goods based on SOR basis.
- We are pleased to offer you subject to market fluctuation.
- We offer you the following goods subject to our final confirmation.

subject to

① 지배를 받는, 복종하는, 종속하는(to).

② 받기 쉬운,(…을) 입기[걸리기] 쉬운(to).

③ … 조건으로 하는, (…을) 받지 않으면 안 되는, (…을) 필요로 하는(to).

④ ~ to …을 (얻는 것을) 조건으로 하여, …을 가정하여, …에 복종하여

- We are subject to our country's laws. (우리는 국법에 복종해야 한다.) ①
- Infants are subject to colds. (유아는 감기에 걸리기 쉽다.) ②
- This treaty is subject to ratification. (이 조약은 비준을 받아야 한다.) ③
- Subject to your consent, I will try again. (승낙해주시면 다시 해보겠습니다) ④

price(I)

1. 가격이 오르다. (자동사)

   rise, increase, advance, go up, gain

   cf. jump, surge, skyrocket, soar spiral: 가격이 급격히 오르다.

   · The prices of everyday items have gone up.

   · The Dow Jones has gained much today.

2. 가격을 올리다. (타동사)

   raise(increase/boost/hike up) the price

   · Due to recent rise in the prices of raw materials, we must raise our price.

   · We need to increase the price of this due to the appreciation of Won.

3. 가격이 내리다. (자동사)

   come down, drop, colla pse, decline, fall, go down, dip, decrease cf. plunge, plummet: 가격이 급락하다.

   · Commodity prices has gone down considerably.

   · The US dollar has plunged to the record low level today.

4. 가격을 내리다. (타동사)

   cut(lower/reduce/shade) the price

   · The store has cut all the prices in half. 가격의 종류에는,

cash price: 현금 가격	gross price: 총가격
net price: 순가격	current price: 시가
list price: 정가표 가격	contract price: 계약가
retail price: 소매가격	wholesale price: 도매가격
buying price: 매입가	selling price: 매도가

competitive price: 경쟁가 introductory price: 보급가 가격을 수식하는 단어들,
bullish, strong, advancing, stiff price: 상승하는, 강세의, 오름세의 가격
bearish, weak, declining, depressed price: 하락하는, 약세의, 내림세의 가격
brisk, active, feverish, excited price: 활발한, 활황세의 가격
flat, inactive, sluggish, dull, dead price: 침체한, 활기 없는 가격

◈ should ~

가정법에 if를 생략할 경우에 주어와 동사의 위치가 바뀌어서 had, were, should, would, could, might 등의 동사가 주어 앞으로 나간다. 따라서 본문의 문장은 If you should have any questions ~(질문이 있으시면 ~)의 의미이다.

- If you should see Fred, give him my regards.
  = Should you see Fred, give him my regards. (Fred를 보거든 안부를 전해줘.)

- If I were not ill, I could go there. (내가 아프지 않았으면 갔을 텐데.)
  = Were I not ill, I could go there.

- If I had know Tim, I would have hired her. (내가 팀을 알았더라면 고용했을 텐데.)
  = Had I known Mary, I would have hired her.

Practice Tests - Situation 7

1. What did Jennifer do to persuade Paul to accept her offer?
   (a) She gave detailed specifications about the Q-pointer II.
   (b) She offered a discount.
   (c) She was willing to answer any questions Paul may have.
   (d) She mentioned that there are many orders for Q-pointer II.

2. What type of offer is this?
   (a) general offer (b) free offer
   (c) firm offer (d) conditional offer

3. In general the _______ must accept the offer within the time specified, or no time period is specified, ______________________. If he does not do so, then he will have allowed the offer to terminate.
   (a) offeror – within a reasonable time (b) offeror – after a reasonable time
   (c) offeree – within a reasonable time (d) offeree – after a reasonable time

4. In case of a firm offer, ________________.
   (a) the offeror may revoke it at any time.
   (b) the offeree may accept it within its validity
   (c) it can be amended or revoked without prior notice by the offeror
   (d) it must be accepted with the consent from the offeror.

5. Offer의 문면 상에 "This offer is subject to prior sale"로 명시되어 있다면 다음 중 가장 가까운 내용의 Offer는?
   (a) firm offer (b) counter offer
   (c) conditional offer (d) stock offer

6. 다음 중 매수인이 물품을 판매한 후 판매되지 않은 재고품을 반품할 수 있는 조건부 청약은?
   (a) offer without engagement (b) offer subject to being unsold.
   (c) offer subject to prior sale (d) offer on sale or return

7. In view of ruling price in this market, your price is rather stiff.
(a) 이 시장에서의 가격을 볼 때 귀사의 가격은 아주 높습니다.
(b) 이 시장에서 가격을 비교할 때 귀사의 가격은 다소 낮은 편입니다.
(c) 이 시장에서 현재의 가격에 비추어 귀사의 가격은 다소 높습니다.
(d) 이 시장에서 현재의 가격은 다른 회사의 가격과 비슷한 수준입니다.

8. Owing to recent ______ in the prices of oil, we must _____ our retail price.
(a) rise – raise (b) raise – rise
(c) rise – rise (d) raise – raise

9. ______ you need any clarification about the machine, please do not ______ to contact me.
(a) Should – hesitate (b) Would – reserve
(c) Might – feel (d) Could – extend

10. Where does the following sentence best fit in the letter? [무역영어 2급]
We'll lock in the prices and begin the paperwork that moves your transaction forward. The terms and pricing on this quotation are guaranteed for only a few remaining days.
(a) If you have made a decision in favor of our system, please let us know right away.
(b) If you think you might want a different system than is described in our quotation, no problem. Just tell us what you have in mind.
(c) We'll give you a revised quote immediately. If you are unsure as to whether you're going to go ahead right now, but think it's a possibility, call me.
(d) I'll extend the terms and prices on the enclosed quotation to you for another 60days.

11. Which of the following is NOT correct according to the letter? [무역영어 2급]
Thank you for your letter dated March 15, 2013 for the 5,000 pieces of Plastic Cartridge. As you request, we are sending you our offer as attached. Meanwhile, the price is going up slightly since the end of last

month due to the shortage of the raw materials. So, your immediate acceptance would be very much appreciated. We look forward to an early reply.

(a) This is a letter to offer.
(b) The price may go up if this offer is not accepted this time.
(c) Because of rise in overhead cost, the price has been increased.
(d) This is a reply to the letter of March 15, 2013.

[12~13] Answer the following questions. [무역영어 2급]

Dear Ms. Park
Due to the increase in raw material costs, we must unfortunately raise the cost of our merchandise to you. We have tried to avoid raising our prices, but we can no longer put up with. We have enclosed our new price list for your review which goes into effect on November 24. Any orders placed between now and October 30 will be honored at the lower prices. We wish that you will understand the necessity for this price increase.

12. Which of the followings is NOT TRUE according to the letter?
(a) There will be a price increase.
(b) Customers can buy the products at the lower price on September 30.
(c) It is impossible to keep supplying the merchandise at the present price.
(d) The seller is not in a position to accept the vendors' request for the price hike.

13. Which of the following would be a replacement for underlined 'honored'?
(a) met (b) made
(c) paid (d) offered

Situation 8

Q-pointer II에 대하여 반대오퍼(Counter offer)를 보내다.

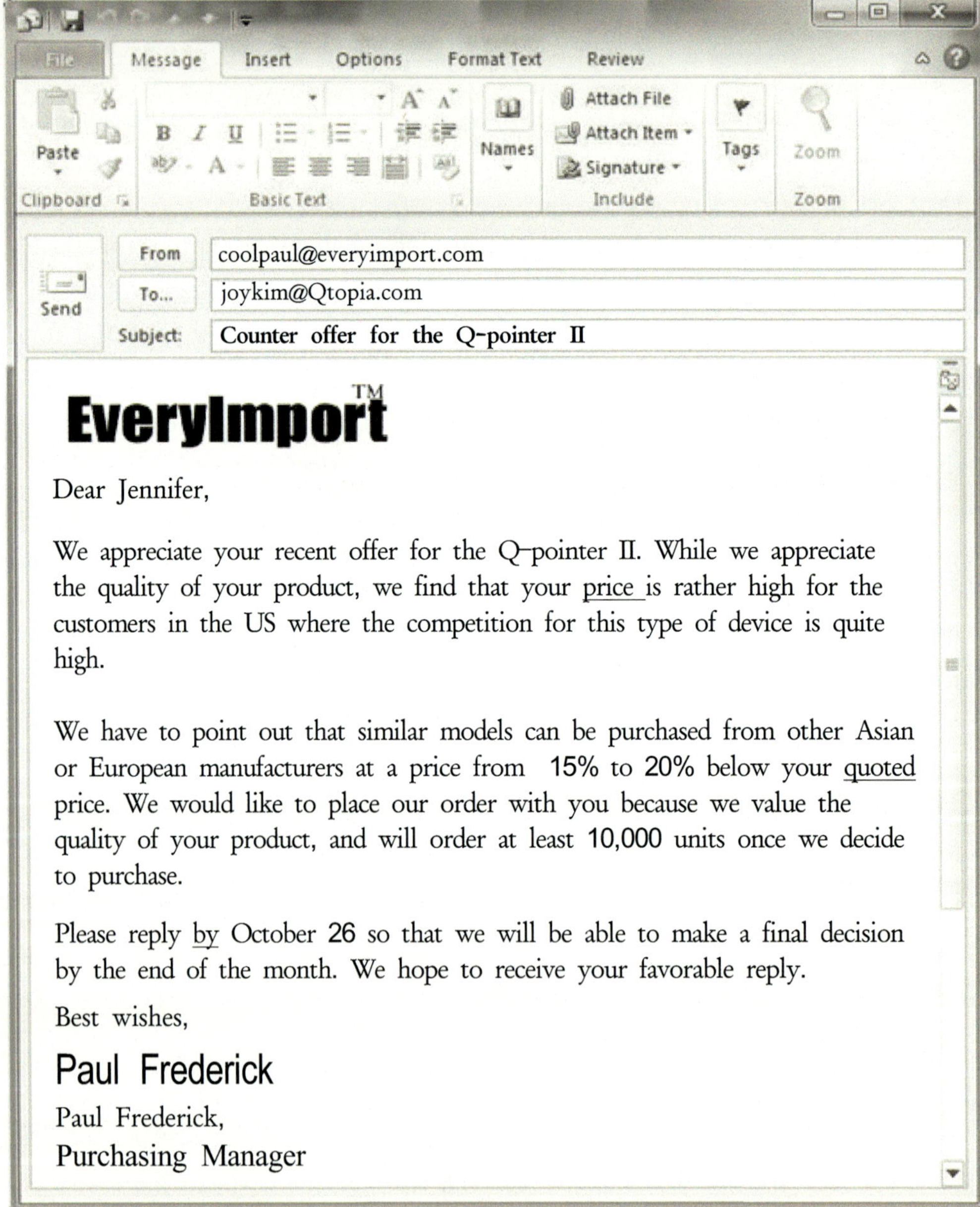

From: coolpaul@everyimport.com
To...: joykim@Qtopia.com
Subject: Counter offer for the Q-pointer II

EveryImport™

Dear Jennifer,

We appreciate your recent offer for the Q-pointer II. While we appreciate the quality of your product, we find that your price is rather high for the customers in the US where the competition for this type of device is quite high.

We have to point out that similar models can be purchased from other Asian or European manufacturers at a price from 15% to 20% below your quoted price. We would like to place our order with you because we value the quality of your product, and will order at least 10,000 units once we decide to purchase.

Please reply by October 26 so that we will be able to make a final decision by the end of the month. We hope to receive your favorable reply.

Best wishes,

Paul Frederick

Paul Frederick,
Purchasing Manager

Synopsis

Qtopia에서 개당 $30의 firm offer를 받은 EveryImport에서는 이 가격이 경쟁이 심한 미국시장에서 너무 높다는 판단 아래 counter offer를 보냈다. 아시아나 유럽의 다른 제조사로부터 비슷한 제품이 15~20% 정도 낮은 가격에 들어오고 있음을 강조하면서 가격인하를 유도하고 있다. 특히 구매를 결정하게 되면 한 번에 최소한 10,000대의 대량주문을 할 것임도 상기시키고 있다. 그리고 이 달 말까지 최종 결정을 할 수 있게 늦어도 26일까지는 이 counter offer에 대한 회신을 달라고 밝히고 있다.

counter offer

오퍼에 대하여 offeree가 가격 등 거래조건에 만족하지 못하면 offerer에게 새로운 조건으로 다시 offer를 보내게 되는데 이를 반대오퍼(counter offer)라고 부른다. 이는 원래의 오퍼(original offer)에 대한 거절이고 동시에 새로운 오퍼가 된다. 따라서 original offer는 counter offer에 의하여 소멸된다. 국제거래에 있어서 한 번의 오퍼로 거래가 성립되기는 어렵고 original offer에 대하여 수차례의 counter offer가 되풀이 된 후에 매도인과 매수인 사이에 합의가 이루어져 거래가 이루어지는 것이 일반적이다.

price(II)

'가격이 높다(비싸다)'라는 표현은 high, unreasonable, unworkable 등을 써서,

- Your price is rather high.
- This item is unreasonably high-priced.
- It is high in price.

또, price가 필요하지 않은 단어들로는 expensive와 costly가 있다.

expensive: 같은 종류의 물건으로서 싼 것도 있으나 그 중에서 비싼, 고급의,
an expensive car 고급차.
costly: 원래 비싼 것으로 같은 종류의 것에 싼 것은 별로 없는,
costly jewels: 고가의 보석

'가격이 낮다(싸다)'의 표현은 low, competitive, reasonable, best possible, lowest possible, moderate, modest, workable 등을 쓸 수 있고, 아주 최저가격이라는 의미로 rock-bottom을 쓸 수 있다.

- The price of this item is low.
- This item is low in price.
- This item is low-priced.
- This is our lowest possible price.
- If your price is competitive, we will place a large order with you.

price라는 단어가 필요하지 않은 표현으로는 cheap과 inexpensive가 있다.

- This car is cheap. (*cheap에는 '싸구려'라는 의미를 내포할 때도 있다.)

quote/quotation

일반적인 뜻은 '인용하다' '인용'이지만 commercial한 의미로는 '가격을 견적하다', '견적가격' 혹은 '가격을 매기다' '매긴 가격'을 말한다.

- The price they quoted to us is too high.
- Can you quote us FOB prices on the following items?
- You need to get a number of quotations from different builders.

시간을 나타내는 전치사

의미상 미묘한 차이가 있으므로 특히 명확한 표현을 해야 하는 Business에서는 주의할 필요가 있다. 먼저, by는 어떤 행동(action)이나 사건(event)이 거기에 표시된 시점을 포함한 일정한 미래의 시점까지를 의미한다. 반면 before는 표시된 시점을 포함하지 않은 미래의 시점까지를 나타낸다.

- We have to make a decision by September 30. (30일 포함)
- We have to make a decision before September 30. (29일까지, 30일 불포함)

특히, Business English에서는 해석의 차이를 미리 피하기 위하여 다음과 같이 명확히 표현하는 경우가 많다.

- We have to make a decision on or before September 30. (30일 포함)

until/ till/ through/ to/ up to는 어떤 동작이나 상태가 표시한 시점을 포함하여 미래의 시점까지 계속된다는 의미를 내포하고 있다.

- Can I stay until the weekend?
- Yes, but you have to leave by(until) Monday midday at the latest.

역시 명확한 표현을 위하여 including이나 inclusive를 써서,

- Qualcom holds a right to buy the machine until and including September 30.
- This L/C is valid up to August 21 inclusive.

from ~ to의 경우 역시 표시 시점을 포함하는 것으로 해석된다. 그러나 after는 표시시 점을 포함하지 않는다.

Shipment will be made on any date from May 20 to May 25.
(선적은 5월 20일에서 25일 사이 어떤 날인가에 될 것입니다.)
Shipment will be made after May 20.
(선적은 5월 20일 이후(21일부터 어느 날)에 될 것입니다.)

명확한 표현을 위하여 inclusive(포함)와 exclusive(제외)를 써서 from May 20 inclusive to May 25 exclusive와 같이 쓰기도 한다. 이에 대해 UCP 600 Article 3에서는 다음과 같이 정의하고 있다. (UCP: Uniform Customs and Practice for Commercial Documentary Credit의 약자로 신용장통일규칙을 말한다. 이에 대한 설명은 Situation 16 참조)

- The words "to", "until", "till", "from" and "between" when used to determine a period of shipment include the date or dates mentioned, and the words "before" and "after" exclude the date mentioned. (선적기간을 정할 때 "to", "until", "till", "from" and "between"은 언급된 날짜를 포함하며 "before" and "after"는 언급된 날짜를 포함하지 않는다.)

Practice Tests - Situation 8

1. What does Paul mention to make Jennifer accept his request?
   (a) He likes the quality of Jennifer's product.
   (b) He will place a large order once he decides to order.
   (c) He says he needs Jennifer's reply by October 26.
   (d) He hopes to receive a favorable reply.

2. What type of letter is it?
   (a) order sheet (b) firm offer
   (c) counter offer (d) conditional offer

3. Why does Paul think the price is too high for customers in the US?
   (a) because customers in the US know the quality of Q-pointer II
   (b) because there are many similar products with lower price in the US.
   (c) because he has to make a decision by October 26.
   (d) because he appreciates the quality of Q-pointer II.

4. As a step for trade contract, the offeree can issue a(an) after amending the terms and conditions of an offer received from the offeror.
   (a) business proposal (b) firm offer
   (c) counter offer (d) inquiry

5. 다음 중 밑줄 친 부분의 해석이 잘못된 것을 고르시오.
   In view of the quotations ruling in this market, your price is slightly stiff. Digital cameras are now in fierce competition here in our market and your competitors are making endeavors to get our business by offering lower prices than yours.
   (a) ~을 고려할 때 (b) 극심하게 비싼
   (c) 열띤 경쟁에 (d) 노력하고 있습니다.

6. The Commerce Department reports that orders to US factories for manufactured goods last month had the largest-ever decline, caused mostly by a sharp drop in orders for airplanes and electronic equipment.

(a) costly (b) cost
(c) costs (d) much cost

7. To improve our chances of getting his order, I told him I would give him the extra-firm mattresses at the price for the firm ones.

(a) quotation (b) quote
(c) quoted (d) quoting

8. Job application forms will be available in November and must be submitted the end of December.

(a) on (b) to
(c) from (d) by

9. Which one does NOT include August 10?

(a) Registration by August 10 is $220.
(b) Registration from August 10 till August 15 is $220.
(c) Registration after August 10 is $220.
(d) Registration through August 10 is $220.

10. Which one does NOT include August 10?

(a) We should arrive there on or before August 10.
(b) We should stay there until August 10.
(c) You should report to us before August 10 inclusive.
(d) You should report to us after August 10.

11. Your offer ( ) our requirement both in price and quality. However, we need the shipped goods ( ) the latest by the end of September. Please let us know your acceptance ( ) the morning of July 20.

(a) meets – for – by (b) suits – at – till
(c) meets – at – by (d) suits – for – till

12. 다음 문장의 괄호 안에 들어갈 가장 적절한 단어를 고르시오. [무역영어 2급]

A reply to an offer which purports to be an acceptance but contains additions, limitations or other modifications constitutes a (   ).

(a) offer
(b) firm offer
(c) free offer
(d) counter offer

13. What is the stage of the contract in terms of legal respect? [무역영어 2급]

Thank you for your offer No. T-301, which we received yesterday. We agree that your offer draws our attention but the price seems too high. May we ask you what your discount for large order is?

(a) Rejection of offer
(b) Acceptance of offer
(c) Conclusion of contract
(d) Order against approval

14. What is the MOST appropriate title of the letter? [무역영어 2급]

Your offer meets our requirement both in price and quality. But we need the goods shipped at the latest by the end of November.

(a) Counter offer requesting early shipment
(b) Counter offer accepted
(c) Asking for shipping schedule
(d) Offer asking early shipment

15. Which of the following has a similar meaning to the sentence below? [무역영어 2급]

Imports decreased slightly over last year.

(a) We saw a slight decrease of imports last year
(b) Decrease of imports was remarkable last year
(c) Last year recorded slight increase compared to this year
(d) There has been a slight increase in imports since last year

16. What is the main purpose of this letter? [무역영어 2급]

Although you have emphasized popularity of your product, we have now a very powerful competitor in the market here, which is commanding an excellent reputation. Their commodity is lower in price by 15% and the

design and style are much superior. Our retail stores report that yours will be competing with it if the price is reduced by USD45.

(a) To request price reduction
(b) To give an advice about the products
(c) To inform the reputation of competitors
(d) To report the opinion of retail stores

17. Which of the following has a DIFFERENT meaning from others?

[무역영어 2급]

(a) The order is accepted subject to an L/C being received by us not later than September 15.
(b) We will accept this order if we receive an L/C before September 15.
(c) The order will be effected as long as an L/C arrives by September 15.
(d) In case where an L/C reaches us till September 15, the payment will be made.

Situation 9

Q-pointer II의 counter offer에 대하여 대체품을 제시하다.

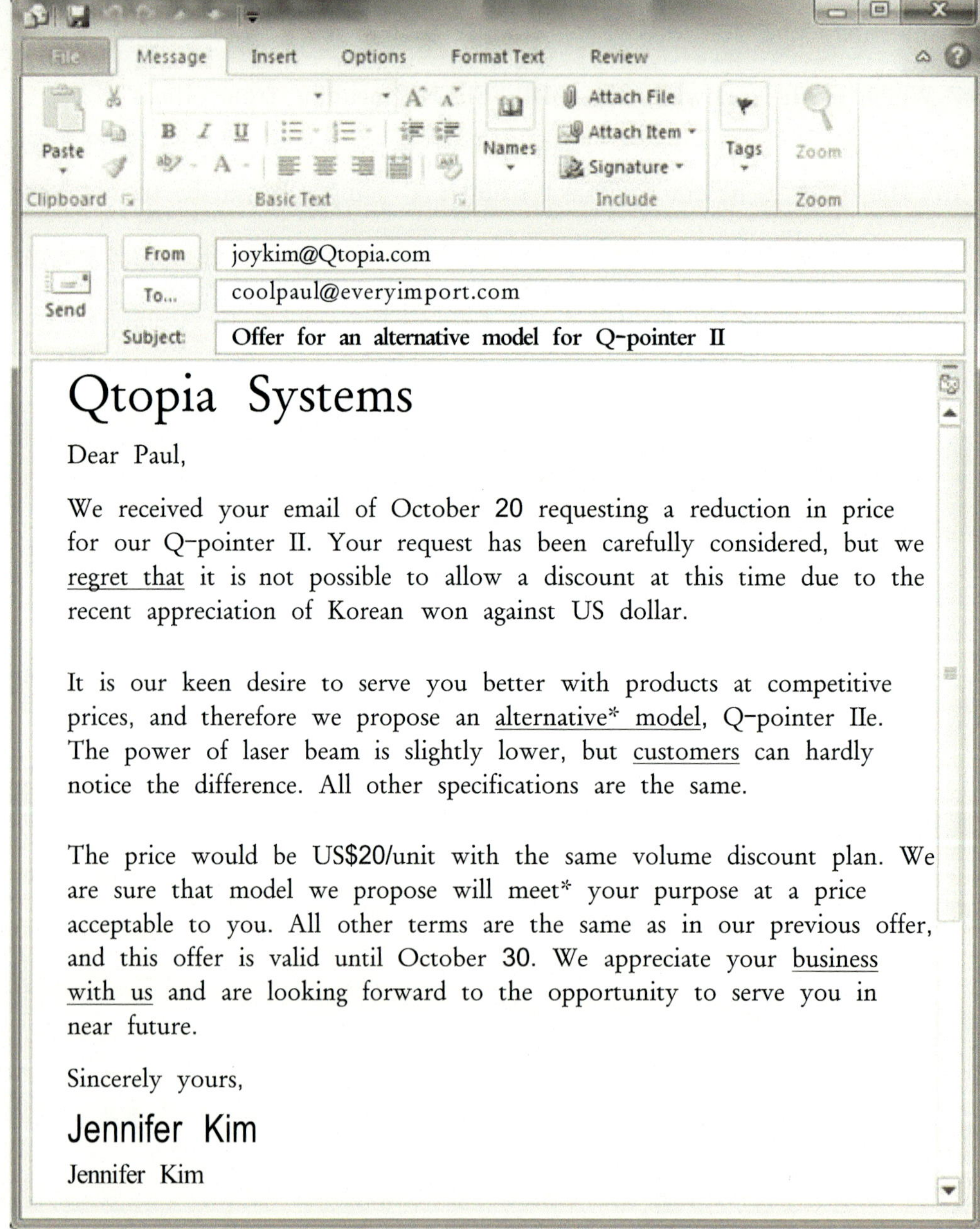

From: joykim@Qtopia.com
To: coolpaul@everyimport.com
Subject: Offer for an alternative model for Q-pointer II

Qtopia Systems

Dear Paul,

We received your email of October 20 requesting a reduction in price for our Q-pointer II. Your request has been carefully considered, but we regret that it is not possible to allow a discount at this time due to the recent appreciation of Korean won against US dollar.

It is our keen desire to serve you better with products at competitive prices, and therefore we propose an alternative* model, Q-pointer IIe. The power of laser beam is slightly lower, but customers can hardly notice the difference. All other specifications are the same.

The price would be US$20/unit with the same volume discount plan. We are sure that model we propose will meet* your purpose at a price acceptable to you. All other terms are the same as in our previous offer, and this offer is valid until October 30. We appreciate your business with us and are looking forward to the opportunity to serve you in near future.

Sincerely yours,

Jennifer Kim

Jennifer Kim

Synopsis

가격인하(a reduction in price)를 요구 받은 Qtopia 측에서 이를 신중히 생각해 본 결과(carefully considered) 최근 원화의 대미 달러 절상(appreciation of Korean Won against US dollar)때문에 이를 수용하기 어렵다고 말하고, 다른 모델 (alternative model)을 다시 offer 하고 있다. 약간 출력이 약하긴 하지만 소비자들은 거의 차이점을 느끼지 못할 것이고 가격은 낮다는 점을 강조하여 이번 offer를 수용하도록 유도하고 있다.

* alternative [ɔ:ltə́:rnətiv, æl–] n. a. (하나를) 선택해야 할 양자(의), 양자택일(의)
  · alternative medicine: 대체의학 · alternative plan: 대안

*meet v. (주문, 요구 등에) 응하다. (의무, 조건 등을) 만족시키다. satisfy, honor, fulfill
  · Our online catalog has been tailored to meet your special needs.

◈ regret

'~를 유감스럽게 생각합니다'. 국제무역거래에서 상대방의 제의나 요청, 주문품의 미도착, 손상, 수량부족, 물품착오 등 상대방에게 사과나 유감의 표명을 해야 할 경우가 자주 발생하게 된다. 이럴 경우 유감의 내용 앞에

We regret that~
I regret to say that ~
Regrettably~
It is with regret that~
I regret to inform you that~ To our regret~
It is regretted that~ Unfortunately~

등을 쓰면 표현을 부드럽게 해 준다. 비슷한 표현으로 We are sorry that ~이 있지만, 이 표현은 책임이 일방적으로 자신 쪽에 있다는 것을 인정해버리는 어감이 있으므로 사용을 주의해서 써야 한다. 대화체에서 이런 상황을 표현해야 할 경우에는 I am afraid ~를 쓰면 상대방에게 불필요한 불쾌감을 주지 않고 원만하게 대화를 진행할 수 있다.

- You have entered wrong id number.라고 단정적으로 표현하기보다는,
- I am afraid you have entered wrong id number.은 완곡한 표현이 된다.
- I'll be late. 는 늦겠다고 단정적으로 말하는 것이지만
- I am afraid I'll be late. 라고 하면 '죄송하지만 늦을 것 같다'는 표현이 된다.

No.라고 딱 끊어서 말하기 어려울 때에도 I am afraid not. 정도로 표현하면 '유감이지만 어쩔 수 없다' 정도의 표현이 된다.

◈ alternative model

business에서 협상을 하다보면 대안이나 대체품을 제시하여야 할 경우가 많이 생긴다. 여기서 alternative는 이런 의미로 쓰였다. 대안이나 대체품을 제시할 때는 이외에도 substitute, replacement, similar, another, nearest 등의 단어가 사용된다.

- I can offer you a substitute of slightly lower quality with much lower price.
- We recommend Model No. 986, which is an up-dated replacement of No. 886.
- We'd like to suggest a very similar item at USD200.00 instead.
- The goods you ordered are out of stock temporarily, and therefore we ask you to choose another model from the enclosed catalog.
- We regret to inform you that we are not able to supply you with the exact article you ordered, but can suggest you the nearest one in our catalog.

substitute는 때때로 원(original) 상품의 대용품이라는 느낌을 주어 business에서 사용할 때 주의할 필요가 있다. 반면 alternative는 '같은 둘 중의 하나'라는 느낌을 준다.

- He substituted for the teacher who was out of town.
- He is a substitute teacher. (줄여서 sub teacher 혹은 그냥 sub라고도 함)
- Herb teas can be a pleasant substitute for coffee.
- substitute goods: 대체재, 예) 커피와 홍차
  [cf] complementary goods: 보완재 예) 커피와 설탕
- You have the alternative of bread or rice. (양쪽 다는 안 됨)
- The alternative possibilities are neutrality or war. (중립 혹은 전쟁)

customer

Business English에서 고객의 표현은 여러 가지가 있고 내용에 따라 용도가 달리 쓰이므로 주의해서 사용해야 한다. 가장 일반적으로 회사나 상점의 고객은 customer라고 한다. 또 회계사, 변호사, 상담회사 등 전문직의 고객은 client라고 하고, 비행기, 기차 등의 손님은 passenger라고 한다. 한편 일반적인 방문객은 visitor나 guest를 쓸 수 있지만, 사교상의 손님, 파티에 초대된 사람은 guest를 쓰고 전람회나 박람회를 찾은 손님은 visitor를 쓴다.

- Recently we have many online customers in our cyber shopping mall.
- The accountant granted 10% friendly discounts for her clients.
- No passengers are allowed to smoke during the flight.
- Jennifer invited many guests in the opening ceremony of the store.
- We have huge visitors in our annual international trade fair.

business with~

'~와 거래를 하다'는 의미로 다음과 같이 표현할 수도 있다.

- enter into business connections with ~
- do business with ~
- make a deal with ~
- have(establish) business transactions with ~
- have(open) an account with ~

"거래 맺기를 간절히 원하다."는 표현은

- It is our keen desire to establish a business relation with you.
- We are writing to you with a keen desire to open an account with you.
- We are anxious to have business transactions with you.
- We are deeply interested in making a deal with you.

반대로 '거래를 끊다'는 stop [break off] business relations [connections] with ~

- We have broken off business connections with the Smith & Co., Inc.

Practice Tests - Situation 9

1. What is Jennifer offering for the request of price reduction?
   (a) suggesting to look for other supplier (b) accepting the request as it is
   (c) cutting the deal (d) recommending another model

2. Why does Jennifer NOT accept Paul's request?
   (a) because customers can hardly notice the difference
   (b) due to recent appreciation of Korean Won against US dollar
   (c) because Jennifer wants to take Paul as her customer.
   (d) due to the fact that all other specifications are the same.

3. What is NOT true about the e-mail in Situation 9?
   (a) Q-pointer IIe is different from Q-pointer II only in terms of price.
   (b) EveryImport should respond by October 30 to make a deal.
   (c) Qtopia is eager to make business relationship with EveryImport.
   (d) Recently, Korean Won has been appreciated.

4. I________ I have another appointment at that time and will not be able to attend.
   (a) regrettable (b) am happy
   (c) regret (d) unfortunately

5. Margarine and butter are ________ goods.
   (a) complementary (b) independent
   (c) substitute (d) supplementary

6. A ________ will not terminate the offer when it is consistent with the idea that ________ is still keeping the original under consideration.
   (a) counter offer – offeror (b) conditional offer – offeror
   (c) counter offer – offeree (d) conditional offer – offeree

7. Fill the _____ with an appropriate word.

Paul invited many _______ in the opening ceremony of the museum. We have huge in our annual international trade fair.

The online shopping mall has many loyal.

All _______ should refrain from smoking during the flight.

The lawyer granted 10% friendly discounts for her ________.

(a) visitors – customers – passengers – clients – guests
(b) customers – passengers – clients– guests – visitors
(c) guests – visitors – customers – passengers – clients
(d) passengers – clients– guests – visitors – customers

8. 다음 중 밑줄친 부분과 바꾸어 쓰기에 적합하지 않은 것을 고르시오.

[무역영어 2급]

We have been very pleased to serve you and hope to establish a pleasant business connection with your company.

(a) to open a pleasant business with
(b) to commence a pleasant business with
(c) to terminate a pleasant business with
(d) to enter into a pleasant business relations with

9. 다음 중 ⓐ~ⓓ가 가리키는 것이 나머지와 다른 하나를 고르시오. [무역영어 2급]

We were glad to learn that you had decided to place a large order. All the items ordered are in stock except the two dozen cushion covers in strawberry pink. Stocks of ⓐthese have been sold out since we quoted for ⓑthem and the makers inform us that it takes another four weeks before they can send ⓒthem.

Instead, we have substituted covers in deep orange, identical in design and quality with those ordered. ⓓThey are rich–looking and most attractive and very popular with our other customers. We hope you will like them.

(a) ⓐ these (b) ⓑ them (c) ⓒ them (d) ⓓ They

10. Which of the following does NOT fit in the blanks? [무역영어 2급]

> This letter is in response to your inquiry regarding our flexibility in the discount rate we offer for (1)______. Our established discount is 2% of the total invoiced amount (2)__________. This figure is not one that has been arbitrarily chosen, but is based on cost, overhead and profit. To increase this discount rate for all of our accounts would seriously jeopardize our firm and (3)_______ would be both unfair and unethical. I believe that you will find that the (4)_________ our customers is standard in the industry. We consider you a most valued customer and hope that you can appreciate our position in this matter.

(a) (1) early settlement of accounts
(b) (2) when payment is received within 10 days of delivery
(c) (3) to increase the rate for an individual account
(d) (4) 10% discount rate we are offered

11. Which of the following is NOT properly corrected? [무역영어 2급]

I am very pleased with the invitation to the Expert Seminar (1) <u>at</u> May 8. Unfortunately, I cannot go to the events as I (2) <u>had had</u> important meeting with (3) <u>clients</u> to attend to. I will be happy to participate in any of your special events on another occasion. I wish you the best of luck on the (4) <u>that is coming</u> Seminar.

(a) (1) at → on (b) (2) had had → had been
(c) (3) clients → customers (d) (4) that is coming → upcoming

12. Which one is NOT APPROPRIATE as part of the reply to the letter below? [무역영어 1급]

> Thank you for your fax of July 5, requesting an offer on our mattress. We offer you firm, subject to your acceptance reaching us by July 20. Our terms and conditions are as follows:
>
> Items: mattress(queen size) Quantity: 300 units
> Price: USD1,100.00 per unit, CIF New York
> Shipment: During May
> Payment: Draft at sight under an Irrevocable L/C

(a) We need the goods in early June, so we would like to make a counter offer changing only shipment term.
(b) Thank you for your firm offer, and we are pleased to accept your offer as specified in our Purchase Note enclosed.
(c) Thank you for your letter requesting us to make an offer, and we would like to make an offer.
(d) We regret to say that we are not able to accept your offer because of high price comparing those of your competitors.

13. Which one would most likely appear before the passages? [무역영어 1급]

However, as you agreed, the recent political change discussed in our previous correspondence has totally changed the prospects on which our original plans had been based. Consequently, although our initial desires remain unchanged, it is impossible for us to set up even a tentative timetable for the purchase. We sincerely hope further political progress will provide us with another opportunity to move toward realization of this project.

(a) Your email of May 8 requesting clarification of our intention in the proposed purchase of your facilities has been thoroughly studied.
(b) We would like to inform you of our prerequisites for meeting your request to market our X3P4 model in South Africa at the earliest possible date.
(c) Attached are the advertising brochures requested in your email of May 8. Additionally, you will routinely receive new material as it becomes available.
(d) Your repeated request to postpone submission of your 2012–2013 P/L statement and your 2013–2014 comprehensive business plans have been acknowledged.

14. Which of the following best fits the blank in the letter? [무역영어 1급]

Your urgent request for delaying the three percent F.O.B. price increase effective from October shipment has been given every consideration. Admittedly, being able to maintain the current F.O.B. price to insure maximum market penetration would be to our mutual benefit. ____.

One of the main reasons for this is the fact that our new line of products has been substantially upgraded. You are encouraged to recognize the qualitative advantage has given you over competitors and the additional cost has meant to us. Your full understanding and quick approval of our offering price would be most appreciated.

(a) In consideration of the above, it is our deep regret that we are not able to accommodate your request for further reduction in our prices.
(b) The final review of our cost structure fortunately enables us to find room for an extra 3 percent discount in your favor without compromising the quality of service.
(c) However, maintaining the current price structure would leave us in the red.
(d) Nevertheless, if price is your prime concern due to the limited budget for this purchase, we can offer an alternative model.

Situation 10

Q-pointer IIe에 대한 오퍼를 받아들이고 정식 매매계약을 하자고 제의하다.

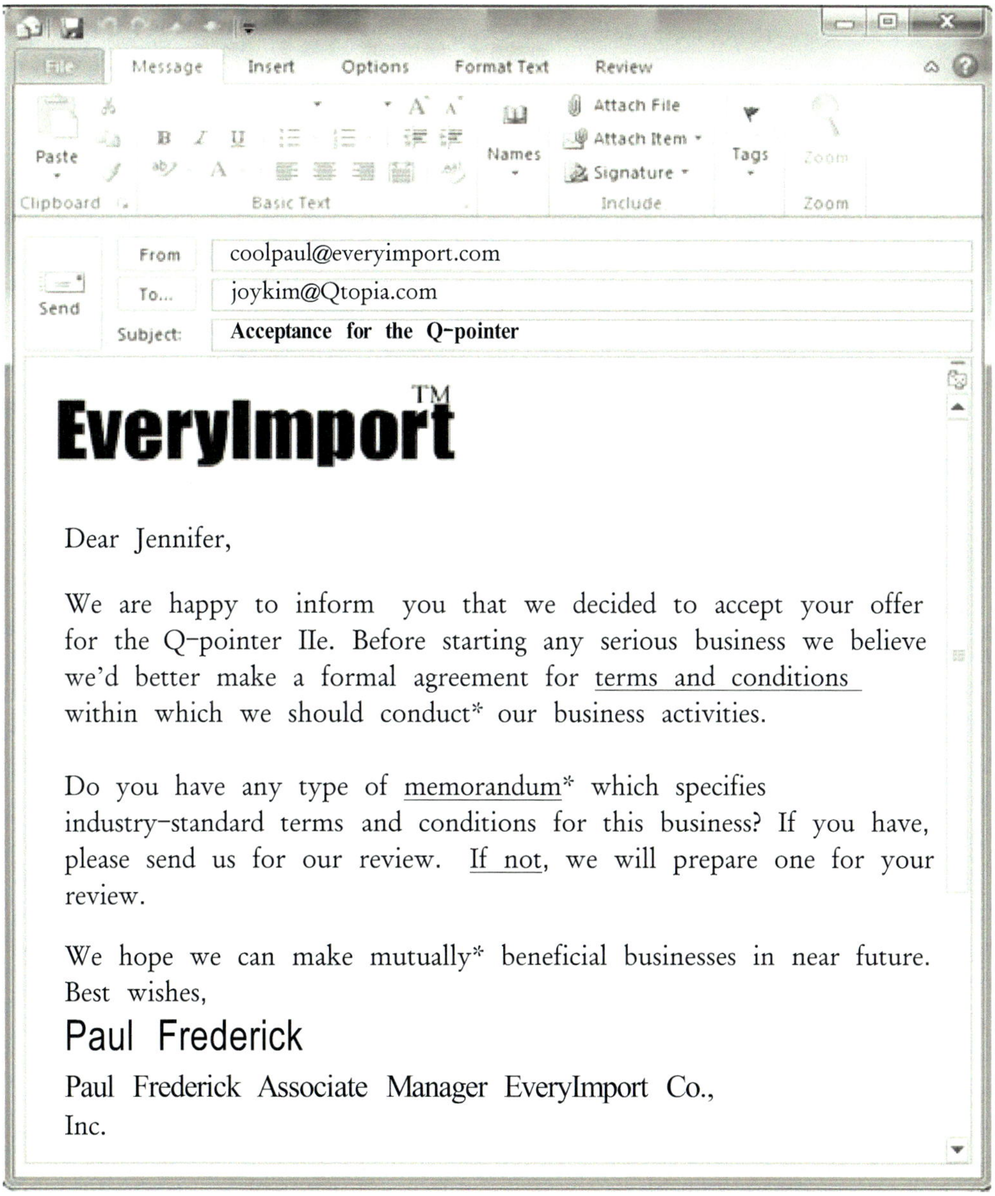

File | Message | Insert | Options | Format Text | Review

Paste | Clipboard | Basic Text | Names | Attach File | Attach Item | Signature | Include | Tags | Zoom

Send

From: coolpaul@everyimport.com

To...: joykim@Qtopia.com

Subject: **Acceptance for the Q-pointer**

EveryImport™

Dear Jennifer,

We are happy to inform you that we decided to accept your offer for the Q-pointer IIe. Before starting any serious business we believe we'd better make a formal agreement for terms and conditions within which we should conduct* our business activities.

Do you have any type of memorandum* which specifies industry-standard terms and conditions for this business? If you have, please send us for our review. If not, we will prepare one for your review.

We hope we can make mutually* beneficial businesses in near future.
Best wishes,

Paul Frederick

Paul Frederick Associate Manager EveryImport Co., Inc.

Synopsis

Q-pointer IIe에 대한 offer를 EveryImport가 받아들이고(accept) 본격적인 거래를 시작하기 전에 앞으로 거래를 할 조건들에 대하여 공식적인 계약서 작성을 제의하고 있다. Paul은 Jennifer에게 Qtopia측에서 업계표준으로(industry-standard) 쓰는 조건들에 관한 양해각서(memorandum)가 있는지 묻고 있다. 있다면 자신들이 검토할 수 있도록 보내주고, 없다면 자신들이 작성해서 보내겠다는 뜻을 전달하고 있다.

*conduct v. n. (특정한) 활동을 하다. 행동

- When you conduct an activity or task, you organize it and carry it out.
- The game has a strict code of conduct.

*memorandum n. (아직 정식으로 서명되지 않은) 각서, memo, minute, note

*mutually adv. 서로, 상호간에

- mutually beneficial(supportive) relation: 상방 간에 이익(도움)이 되는 관계
- mutually satisfactory(agreeable) terms and conditions: 상호 만족할 만한 조건
- mutually convenient time: 서로 편리한 시간
- mutually exclusive ideas: 상호 배타적인 생각

◈ acceptance & contract

승낙(acceptance)이란 offeree가 offerer에 대하여 그 오퍼에 대하여 거래를 성립시킬 목적으로 행하는 의사표시를 말한다. 이는 오퍼의 모든 조건에 대하여 동의하는 무조건적인 것이며, 유효기간 내에 오퍼에 명시된 방법에 따라 이루어져야 한다. 조건부 승낙을 하는 경우 이는 counter offer가 되며 본래의 오퍼를 거절한 것으로 본다. 오퍼의 승낙은 매매계약을 성립시키는 효력을 가지고 있다. 즉, 오퍼에는 주로 거래조건들이 기재되어 있기 때문에 특별히 별도의 계약서를 작성하지 않고 offer sheet을 그대로 계약서로 이용할 수 있다. 일반적인 무역계약은 다음과 같은 방법으로 이루어진다.

첫째, 오퍼에 대한 승낙으로 계약이 성립된다. offer sheet에는 주요 거래조건들이 기재되어 있다. 따라서 별도의 계약서를 작성하지 않고 offer sheet을 그대로 계약서로 사용할 수 있다. 즉, 수출(입)상이 발행한 offer를 수입(출)상이 최종 승낙(acceptance)의 표시로 offer sheet에 서명하면 그것이 곧 계약서가 된다.

둘째, 판매확인서(sales note)에 의하여 계약이 성립된다. 수출상의 offer에 대한 수입상의 acceptance가 바로 이루어지지 않고 counter offer가 수차례 오고간 경우, 최종 승낙을 받은 수출상은 offer의 내용을 최종 확인하여 후일 분쟁의 소지를 줄일 필요가

있다. 이렇게 수출상이 작성하여 수입상에게 보내는 특정 물품의 판매확인서를 sales note라고 한다. 이 경우 수출상은 sales note를 2통 작성하여 서명한 후 수입상에게 보낸다. 수입상은 이에 이의가 없으면 서명을 하여 1통은 자신이 보관하고 다른 1통은 수출상에게 보냄으로써 계약이 성립된다.

셋째, 구매주문서(purchase order)에 의하여 계약이 성립된다. 수입상이 특정 물품을 일정한 조건으로 구매하겠다는 의사표시가 purchase order이다. 이는 sales note와는 반대로 수입자가 주도적으로 계약의 내용을 작성하고 수출상의 최종 acceptance를 받는 형식 의 계약을 말한다.

넷째, 일반거래계약(general sales contract)에 의하여 계약이 성립된다. 동일한 거래상 대방과 지속적으로 거래가 이루어지는 경우, 수출입 관련 당사자들이 계약내용에 대하여 구체적으로 협의를 하여 계약을 체결하는 방식이다. 계약서에는 품질, 가격, 수량, 포장, 보험, 선적, 지불, 분쟁해결 조건 등이 기재된다. 수출입 본 계약의 체결에는 건별로 별도의 계약을 체결하는 개별계약(case by case contract)과 처음 계약을 맺을 때 품종이나 총액만을 정하고 그 밖의 내용은 후일에 협정하도록 하는 포괄계약(master contract)의 두 가지 방법이 있다.

◈ terms and conditions

term은 '경계, 한계, 기한, 기간'을 의미하지만 Business English에서는 이자 등의 '지불기한'을 나타내거나 그와 같은 기한을 결정하는 여러 조항, 즉 '지불조건'을 의미한다. 또 '계약, 협정, 매매, 지불 등을 포괄하는 의미의 조건'을 뜻하기도 한다. 단, 이러한 의미로 쓰일 경우는 반드시 복수형 terms를 사용한다.

- They will assist you to interpret the terms of the new contract.
- We would like to know what the terms of payment will be.

terms와 같이 쓰이는 용어로 conditions이 있는데, terms가 거래에 관련된 조건을 나타낼 경우에만 사용되는 데에 비하여 conditions은 보다 일반적인 '조건, 제약' 등의 뜻으로 쓰인다. 보통은 구별하지 않고 terms and conditions로 사용된다.

- We came to an agreement with Crown under the terms and conditions outlined in our Memorandum No. 125.

여기에서 condition 역시 복수형 conditions로 쓰인다. 다음은 단수와 복수의 의미가 다르게 쓰이는 것들의 예이다.

term 기한　terms 조건　condition 상태　conditions 조건　advice 충고
advices 통지　notice 통보　notices 공지　work 일　works 작품

◈ Memorandum of Understanding: MOU(양해각서)

원래는 본 조약이나 정식 계약의 체결에 앞서 국가 사이에 이루어지는 문서로 된 합의를 가리키지만, 지금은 좀 더 포괄적 의미로 쓰인다. MOU는 당사국 사이의 외교교섭 결과에 따라 서로 양해된 사항을 확인·기록하거나, 본 조약·협정의 후속 조치를 목적으로 작성한다. 공식적으로는 법적 구속력을 갖지는 않지만, 조약과 같은 효력을 갖는다.

기업 사이에 합의해 작성하는 양해각서는 주로 정식계약을 체결하기에 앞서, 쌍방의 의견을 미리 조율하고 확인하는 상징적 차원에서 이루어지는 것이 보통이다. 일반적으로 법적 구속력은 없지만 내용에 따라 구속력을 가질 수 있기 때문에 작성할 때나 서명할 때 각각의 조항에 충실해야 한다.

• MOU is a document that describes the general principles of an agreement between parties, but does not amount to a substantive contract. (MOU는 실질적 계약은 아니지만 계약의 일반 원칙을 명시한 문서이다.)

MOU와 비슷한 성격의 LOI(Letter Of Intent: 의향서)는 국제거래에 관한 협상단계(정식 계약체결의 이전단계)에서 당사자의 의도나 목적, 합의사항 등을 확인하기 위해 문서로 작성하는 예비적 합의의 일종으로, 일방의 의사표시에 의해 작성되기도 하고 합의에 의해 작성되기도 한다. 주로 계약서와 비슷한 형태를 취하지만 당사자를 구속하지는 않는 것이 일반적이다. MOU와 LOI의 성격을 비교하자면 LOI는 어떤 사업에 대한 당사자의 의지의 표현을 기록한 것이고 MOU는 한 단계 더 진전된 서류라고 할 수 있다.

• LOI is a document outlining an agreement between two or more parties before the agreement is finalized. (LOI는 둘 혹은 그 이상 당사자 간 계약이 확정되기 전에 계약의 개요를 명시한 문서이다.)

◈ if not ~

if 다음에 앞에서 언급한 내용을 부정하거나 반복해야 하는 경우 'not' 이나 'so'를 각각 써서 다음과 같이 표현한다.

- I might see you tomorrow. If not, then it'll be Saturday.
  (= If I don't see you tomorrow ~)
- Are you free tomorrow? If so, let's go out for lunch.
  (= If you are free tomorrow ~)

if는 이외에도 다음과 같이 줄여서 쓰인다.

- If in doubt, ask for help. (= If you are in doubt ~)
- If about to go on a long journey, try to save money. (= If you are about ~)
- I am not angry. If anything, I feel a little surprise. (= If there is anything ~)
- There is little, if any, good evidence for UFO. (= if there is any)
- Usually, if not always, we resort to internet for international trade.
  (= if it is not always, 항상은 아니더라도 보통은 우리는 국제거래에서 인터넷에 의존한다.)

Practice Tests - Situation 10

1. Which of the following is not what Paul did?
   (a) accepting the offer
   (b) asking to make a formal contract
   (c) sending an industry-standard memorandum
   (d) hoping to make mutually beneficial businesses

2. What does Jennifer mostly likely do after reading this email?
   (a) confirming the order
   (b) asking to make a formal contract
   (c) processing the order as soon as possible
   (d) sending an industry-standard memorandum

3. Which of the following best fits the blank in the dialog below? [무역영어 1급]
   A: Let me clarify my basic position. I would like to make a contract with you.
   B: ____
   A: I understand it, but please take a look at the current market situation. It's getting tougher because there are many start-up companies.
   B: How about if we lower the price?
   A: How much would you be willing to lower it? B: I'd be willing to reduce it by 10 percent.
   A: In that case, I could guarantee 25,000 units on a yearly basis. B: That sounds good.
   (a) If you guarantee that your products have a warranty period of 210 days, I don't see why we shouldn't.
   (b) I would like you to lower the prices. What would be the minimum order to receive a 4.5% discount?
   (c) I'm afraid we can't accept that because of the financial problems we are facing.
   (d) If you guarantee an order of 25,000 units per year, I don't see why we shouldn't.

Situation 11

Qtopia에서 계약서 초안을 보내다.

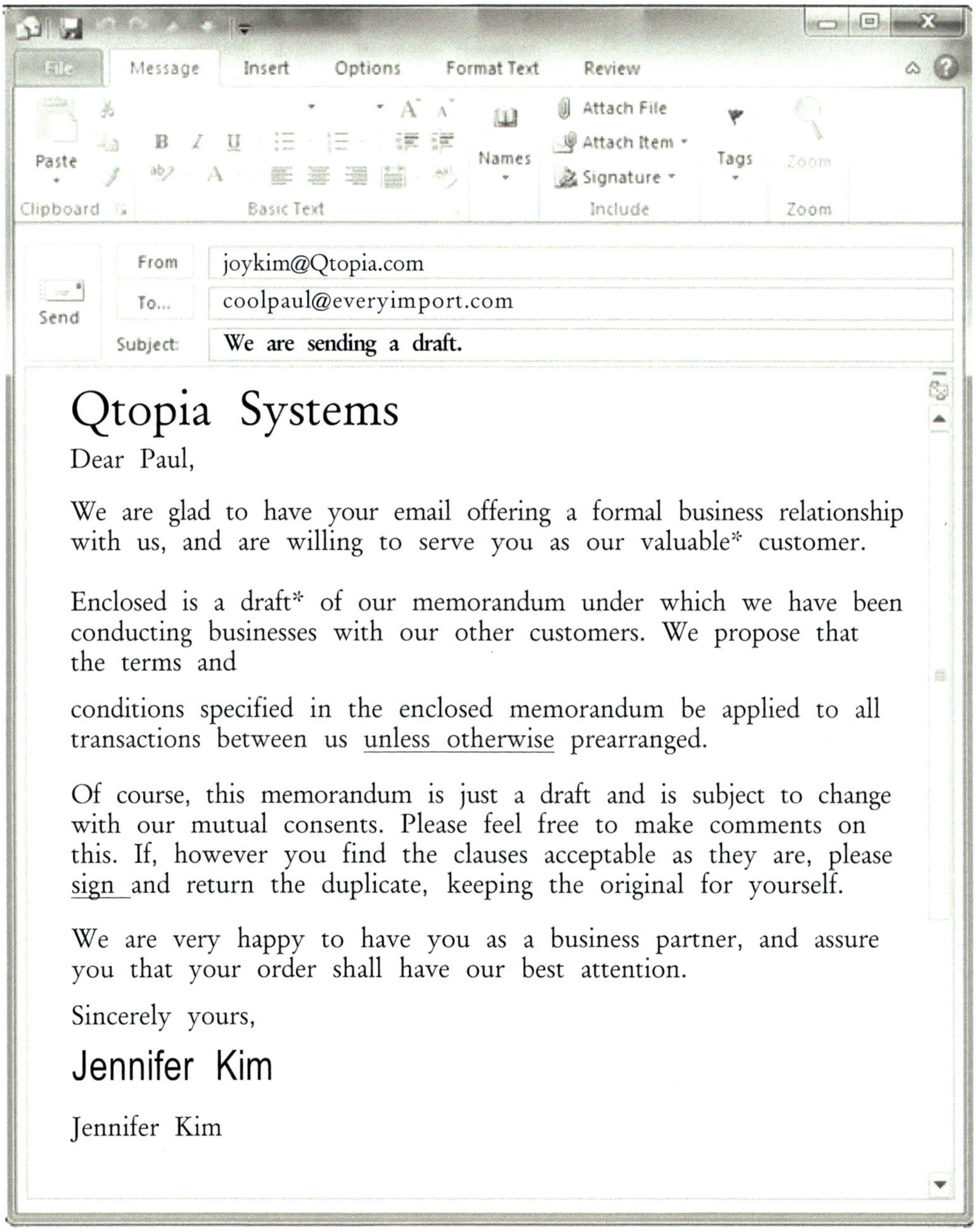

From: joykim@Qtopia.com
To...: coolpaul@everyimport.com
Subject: We are sending a draft.

Qtopia Systems

Dear Paul,

We are glad to have your email offering a formal business relationship with us, and are willing to serve you as our valuable* customer.

Enclosed is a draft* of our memorandum under which we have been conducting businesses with our other customers. We propose that the terms and

conditions specified in the enclosed memorandum be applied to all transactions between us unless otherwise prearranged.

Of course, this memorandum is just a draft and is subject to change with our mutual consents. Please feel free to make comments on this. If, however you find the clauses acceptable as they are, please sign and return the duplicate, keeping the original for yourself.

We are very happy to have you as a business partner, and assure you that your order shall have our best attention.

Sincerely yours,

Jennifer Kim

Jennifer Kim

Synopsis

오퍼를 수락해줘서 고맙다는 메일을 계약서 초안(draft)과 함께 Qtopia의 Jennifer가 EveryImport의 Paul에게 보냈다. 초안에 명시한 조건들은 별도로 달리 정하지 않는 한 모든 거래에 적용키로 하는 것이다. 물론 지금 보낸 memorandum은 가본으로 상호 동의에 의하여 수정될 수 있는 것이므로 의견이 있으면 알려달라고 하였다. 그러나 모든 조건을 현재 그대로 받아들일 수 있다면 2부를 만들어서 서명한 후 원본은 보관 하고 사본은 자신들에게 보내달라고 요청하고 있다.

* valuable [vǽljuəbl] a. valued, useful, important, profitable, beneficial, 소중한(cf.)
invaluable: valuable, priceless, 가치를 평가할 수 없을 정도로 귀중한(opp.)
valueless: of no value, worthless, 쓸모없는

* draft, draught[영국식] [dræft, drɑːft] n.
① 도안, 밑그림, 설계도.
② (계약서나 원고의) 초안, 초고
③ [상업] 환어음(bill of exchange), 지급 명령서
④ [미국] 징병, 징모(conscription); [스포츠] 신인 선수 선발 제, 드래프트제(制).

◈ unless otherwise ~

except if의 의미로 '~별도로 ~가 없다면'의 의미로 계약서나 법조문 등에 자주 쓰인다.

unless otherwise	contracted	별도로 계약하지 않는 한
	indicated	별도로 지정되어 있지 않는 한
	stated	별도로 언급되어 있지 않는 한
	noted	별도로 공지되지 않는 한
	instructed [directed]	별도로 지시되어 있지 않는 한
	specified	별도로 규정하지 않는 한
	agreed(in writing)	(문서로) 별도로 합의 하지 않은 한
	required(by law)	(법에서) 별도로 요구하지 않는 한
	excluded(via mutual agreement)	(상호합의로) 별도로 제외하지 않는 한
	provided(by the Congress)	(국회에서) 별도로 정하지 않는 한

다음과 같이 otherwise와 뒤에 오는 동사의 위치를 바꾸어서도 쓰인다.

- Unless otherwise stated, discounts, gift items do not apply on sales items.
  = Unless stated otherwise, discounts, gift items do not apply on sales items.
  = Unless you state otherwise, discounts, gift items do not apply on sales items.

- Please note that all shipment will be made by air unless otherwise indicated.
  = Please note that all shipment will be made by air unless indicated otherwise.
  = Please note that all shipment will be made by air unless you indicate otherwise.

sign

sign은 동사로 '서명하다'의 의미이지만 명사로는 '기호', '표시'의 의미로 쓰이고 '서명'의 의미는 없다. 서명을 말할 때는 signature를 사용한다.

- They finally reached a conclusion and signed a contract.
- Would you please sign your name here?
- May I have your signature, please?

sign

signature는 서류 등에 기입하는 서명 외에 연예인 등 유명인에게 받는 사인의 의미로도 쓰이지만, autograph는 유명인에게 받는 사인의 의미로만 쓰인다.

- A group of girls asked the actor for his autograph.

sign

Practice Tests - Situation 11

1. If you say something is _____, you mean that is not useful, or worth nothing.
   (a) valueless (b) valuable
   (c) invaluable (d) valued

2. You'll have to be on your toe if you want to get the actor's _________.
   (a) sign (b) autobiography
   (c) autograph (d) signal

3. Which of the following is true according to the letter below? [무역영어 1급]

> We are glad to have your email offering a formal business relationship with us, and are willing to serve you as our valued customer. Enclosed is a draft of our memorandum with which we have been conducting business with our other customers.
>
> Of course, this memorandum is just a draft and is subject to change with our mutual consents. Please feel free to make comments on this. If, however, you find the clauses acceptable as they are, please sign and return the duplicate, keeping the original for yourself.

(a) The exporter is sending the letter to the importer in order to offer a formal business partnership.
(b) The proposed terms and conditions in the memorandum can be applied to transactions only if one party agrees in advance.
(c) The enclosed draft of a memorandum is the final version and therefore is subject to change.
(d) The other party will send a copy of the signed memorandum to the exporter unless they disagree with the proposed terms and conditions.

Situation 12

Qtopia와 EveryImport이 서명한 매매계약서

SALES AGREEMENT

This Agreement is made on October 23, 2014 by and between Every Import Co., Inc., at 3434 Sunset Blvd. Los Angeles, CA, USA ("Buyer") and Qtopia Systems Co., Inc. at 134 Seocho-dong Seocho-ku, Seoul, Korea ("Seller").

Sale of Goods The buyer shall purchase from the seller and the seller shall sell to the buyer newly manufactured laser pointer for smartphone ("Goods") subject to the terms and conditions herein provided.

Quality The specification of the Goods shall be prescribed and specified on specification attached hereto as Exhibit 1.

Quantity For 2 years commencing October 25, 2014, the buyer shall purchase from the seller and the seller shall sell to the buyer [one hundred thousands (100,000) sets] of the Goods per year to make the total quantities of the sale of the Goods [two hundred thousands (200,000) sets] during October 25, 2014 to September 30, 2016.

Price The agreed unit price of each Goods is twenty U.S. Dollars (US$20.00) on CIF Los Angeles basis. The price is fixed and effective up to shipments performed on or before November, 2015, and thereafter the price shall be readjusted every six(6) months according to Seller's request.

Packing The Goods shall be packed and marked in the customary manner for exporting. In case special instructions are necessary, buyer shall furnish seller with such instructions in time for preparation or shipment of the Goods.

Insurance The Seller shall effect marine insurance on all shipments on ICC(B) for 110% of the invoice amount.

Shipment Date of Bill of Lading constitutes time of shipment. In case of force majeure one month's delay is allowed. After the delay allowed the seller must get the buyer's consent before shipping Goods that are late, and it is at the buyer's option either to accept the delayed shipment or to cancel the order, in which case notice of cancellation should be delivered immediately.

Warranty Each Goods supplied by the Seller is hereby expressly warranted to be free from defect in material and workmanship under normal use and service. The warranty shall be limited to a period of 12 months after delivery thereof to the Buyer under storage in a roofed warehouse.

Payment Except otherwise agreed by the parties, all payments for the Goods shall be made in United States Dollars by an irrevocable letter of credit in favor of the Seller. The letter of credit shall be established by the Buyer at least one month prior to each scheduled shipment date, and to be negotiable at sight against draft and to be valid no less than thirty(30) days after the latest date allowed for the shipment.

Aftersales Service The Seller may, upon request of the Buyer and consent of the Seller, dispatch some experient technicians to some places in U.S.A. for the purpose of rendering effective after sales service in connection with the Goods.

Claim & Arbitration All disputes, controversies, or differences which may arise between the parties, out of, or in relation to, or in connection with this contract, or for the breach there of, shall be finally settled by arbitration in Seoul, Korea in accordance with the Commercial Arbitration Rules of the Korean Commercial Arbitration Board. The award rendered by the arbitrator(s) shall be final and binding upon both parties concerned.

Buyer,
EveryImport Co., Inc.
3434 Sunset Blvd.
Los Angeles, CA 93456
Nike Jordan
Nike
Jordan
President

Seller,
Qtopia Systems Co., Inc.
134 Seo Cho-dong Seo Cho-ku,
Seoul 137-071, Korea
James A. Sung
James A. Sung
President

Synopsis

이 계약서는 2014년 10월 23일 EveryImport, 3434 Sunset Blvd. Los Angeles, CA, USA('매수인')과 Qtopia Systems Co., Inc. at 134 Seocho-dong Seocho-ku, Seoul, Korea('매도인') 사이에 체결한다.

- 상품: 매수인은 매도인으로부터 구입하고 매도인은 스마트폰용 레이저 포인터(상품)를 여기에 명시한 조건에 따라 판매한다.
- 품질: 제품의 규격은 첨부 1에 명시한 바에 따른다.
- 수량: 2014년 10월 25일부터 시작하여 2년 동안 매년 100,000개를 매수인은 매도인으로부터 구매를 하여야 하며, 매도인은 매수인에게 판매를 하여, 2014년 10월 25일부터 2016년 9월 30일까지 총 200,000개 거래가 이루어지도록 한다.
- 가격: 상품의 단가는 CIF 기준 20 미국 달러이다. 이는 2015년 10월까지는 고정되어 있고 그 후로는 매도인의 요청으로 매 6개월마다 조정될 수 있다.
- 포장: 상품의 포장과 표기방법은 통상적인 수출방식에 따른다. 특별한 방식이 요구될 경우, 매수인은 매도인이 상품의 선적 또는 사전준비에 필요한 시간을 제공하여야 한다.
- 보험: 매도인은 ICC(B)조건으로 송장의 110% 금액에 대하여 해상운송보험에 가입하여야 한다.
- 선적: B/L의 일자는 선적일자를 말한다. 불가항력의 경우 1개월의 지연이 가능 하지만 그 기간이 지나면 매도인은 매수인으로부터 상품의 선적 전에 동의를 구해야 한다. 이 경우 지연된 선적물을 인수 혹은 취소의 여부는 매수인에게 선택권이 있다. 취소의 경우에는 이를 즉시 통지하여야 한다.
- 보증: 매도인이 인도한 모든 상품에 대하여 정상적인 사용을 조건으로 재료와 기술상의 하자가 없음을 명시적으로 보증한다. 보증은 매수인의 창고에 입하된 후 12개월까지 유효하다.
- 지불: 당사자간 달리 합의하지 않는 한 상품대금은 매도인을 수익자로 하는 취소불능 신용장으로 결제하여야 한다. 신용장은 예정 선적일자보다 최소한 한 달 전에 개설되어야 하며, 일람출급화환어음으로 결제되고, 허용된 최후 선적일로부터 최소한 30일 동안 유효한 조건이여야 한다.
- 분쟁 및 조정: 이 계약과 관련하여, 계약에 벗어난 또는 연계되어 당사자간에 일어나는 모든 분쟁, 논쟁, 의견차이 또는 불이행은 서울에서 상사중재원(Commercial Arbitration Board)의 상사중재규칙(Commercial Arbitration Rules)에 따라 최종적으로 해결한다. 상사원의 결정은 최종적이고 양측 모두에게 구속력이 있다.

Practice Tests - Situation 12

1. A Sales Contract includes a clause stated as "Draft(s) shall be drawn at sight, documents attached, for the full invoice value under an irrevocable Credit which shall be issued within 10 days after the conclusion of the contract". What is the terms this clause is related to?

(a) Arbitration Terms (b) Trade Terms
(c) Quality Terms (d) Payment Terms

2. 다음 ( )에 들어갈 가장 적당한 단어를 고르시오.

『Seller shall not be responsible for non-shipment or late shipment in whole or in part by reason of ( ), such as fires, floods, earthquakes, tempests, strikes, lockouts, and other industrial disputes, mobilization, war, threat of war, riots, civil commotions, hostilities, blockade, and any other contingencies beyond Seller' control.』

(a) Claims (b) Breach of contract
(c) Infringement (d) Force Majeure

3. 각 조항에 대한 설명으로 올바르지 않은 것은? [무역영어 2급]

1. Quantity: Quantities quoted are subject to a variation of plus or minus ten(10) percent.
2. Insurance: Insurance shall be effected by Seller.
3. Claims: No claim shall be entertained before the payment is made or the draft is duly honored.
4. Arbitration: The arbitral award shall be final and binding both parties.

(a) Quantity: it shows 'More or Less clause'
(b) Insurance: the Seller should make a contract for insurance.
(c) Claims: the Buyer should make claims before he pays.
(d) Arbitration: the arbitral award can't be appealed.

[4~5] The followings are parts of a contract for international sale of goods. Answer the questions. [무역영어 1급]

Description: Blue jeans(Item no: Chalie-0924)

Quantity: 2,000 PCs

Unit Price: USD22.50/pc CFR Sydney

port Total amount: USD45,000 only

Payment: Under documents against payment at sight in U.S. dollar

Shipment: Not later than January 15, 2012

POL/PLD: Korean port / Sydney port

Insurance: To be covered by buyer

Inspection: No need

Packing: 20 pieces to be packed in a carton and each piece has to be packed with poly bag

....

Article 11. If the seller fails to deliver any or all of the products within the time period specified in the Agreement, the Buyer shall deduct from the Contract Price, as liquidated damages, a sum equivalent to 2% of the price of the delayed products for each week of delay until to a maximum deduction of 10% of the price of the delayed products. Once the maximum is reached, the Buyer may terminate this Agreement.

....

Article 18. The Trade Terms under this agreement shall be governed and interpreted under the provisions of Incoterms 2010. This Agreement shall be governed and

construed in all respects under and by United Nations Convention on Contract for International Sale of Goods(1980). In the event of conflict between United Nations Convention on Contract for International Sale of Goods(1980) and Incoterms 2010, Incoterms 2010 shall prevail and govern.

4. Which of the following is CORRECT according to the contract above?
   (a) If the Seller delays the shipment more than 5 weeks, the Buyer may declare termination of the contract.
   (b) Since United Nations Convention on Contract for International Sale of Goods(1980) is a governing law, it has a priority over Incoterms 2010 if there is any conflict.
   (c) The Buyer can get deduction of USD90 if the Seller makes shipment on January 20, 2012 as liquidated damages.
   (d) The Seller and the Buyer agree to settle any dispute by arbitration under United Nations Convention on Contract for International Sale of Goods (1980).

5. Which of the following is INCORRECT according to the contract above?
[무역영어 1급]
   (a) The Seller is not obliged to insure goods.
   (b) The risk is transferred from the Seller to the Buyer at the Sydney port.
   (c) The Seller should deliver the goods up to the Sydney port at his own cost.
   (d) 100 cartons should be delivered to the Buyer.

6. Which of the followings is NOT CORRECT according to the contract below?
[무역영어 1급]

CONTRACT
Product: 100% Cotton Yarn
Type: 80's/3, 70's/2, 60's/3
Quantity: One hundred(100) bales each
Packing: 400 Lbs for each bale
Shipment: During January by State Marine Line
Prices: 0.50, 0.40, 0.30 respectively(USD) per lb., F.O.B. Sydney
Insurance: As usual
Payment: By 90 d/s draft against confirmed letter of credit
Remark: If you cannot secure space on s/s "Big Bear", voy. No. 145, please cable immediately

(a) The total quantity of order is 300 bales.
(b) The weight of one bale is 400 Lbs.
(c) The price per lb for 70's/2 is USD 0.40 excluding the cost for carriage.
(d) The goods should be shipped on s/s "Big Bear" which is appointed by the seller.

7. What can be inferred from the passage below? [무역영어 1급]

Countries have different endowments of factors of production. They differ in population density, labor skills, climate, raw materials, capital equipment, etc.. These differences tend to persist because factors are relatively immobile between countries. Obviously land and climate are totally immobile, but even with labor and capital there tend to be more restrictions(physical, social, cultural or legal) on their international movement than on their movement within countries. Thus, the ability to supply goods differs between countries.

(a) The relative costs of producing goods will vary from country to country.
(b) Only one country can have a comparative advantage over another in the production of a commodity.
(c) Trade can benefit all countries if they produce the goods in the same category.
(d) If countries are to gain from trade, they should place a ban on imports.

Situation 13

Q-pointer IIe에 대한 첫 주문을 하다.

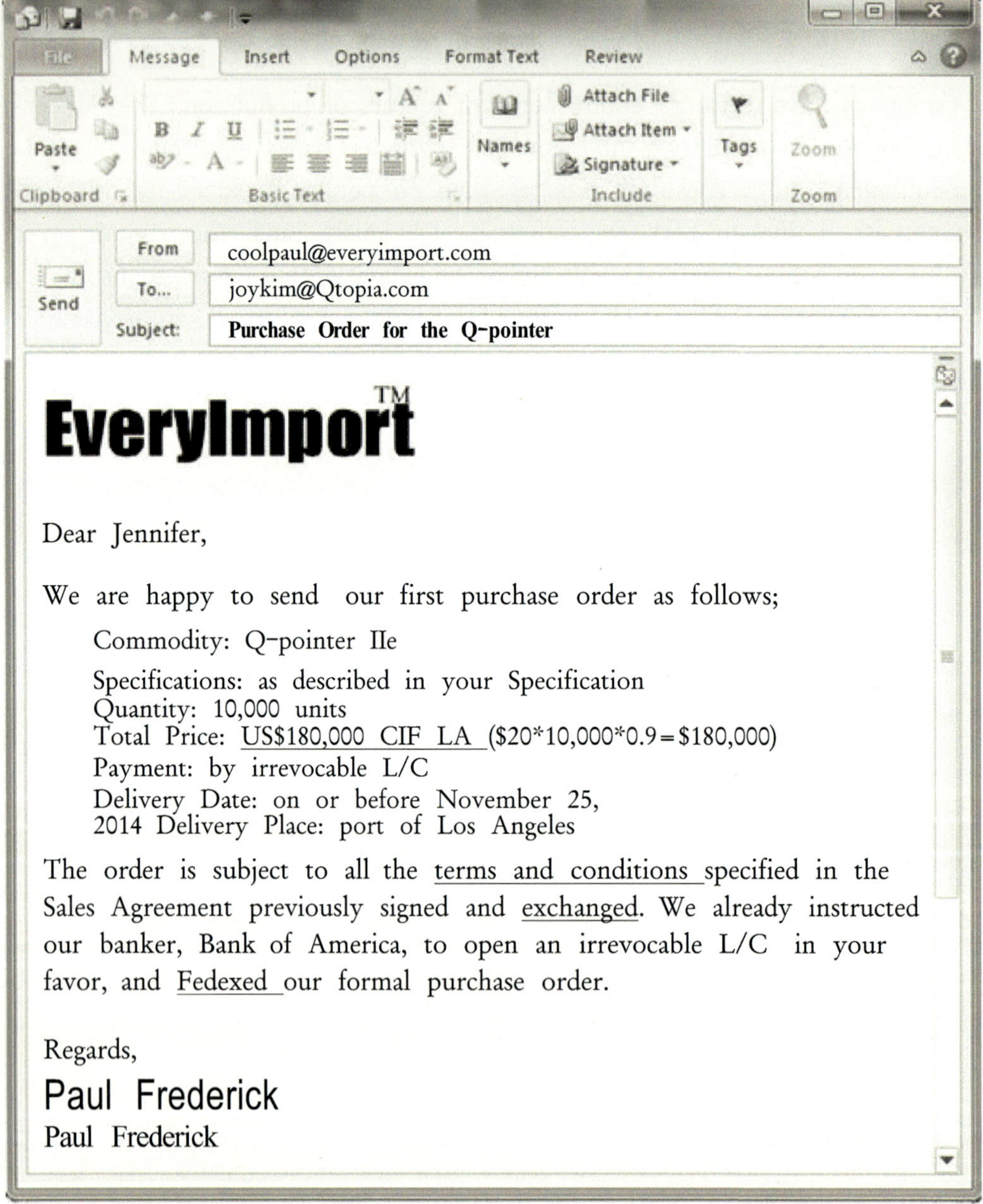

From: coolpaul@everyimport.com
To...: joykim@Qtopia.com
Subject: **Purchase Order for the Q-pointer**

EveryImport™

Dear Jennifer,

We are happy to send our first purchase order as follows;

Commodity: Q-pointer IIe
Specifications: as described in your Specification
Quantity: 10,000 units
Total Price: US$180,000 CIF LA ($20*10,000*0.9=$180,000)
Payment: by irrevocable L/C
Delivery Date: on or before November 25,
2014 Delivery Place: port of Los Angeles

The order is subject to all the terms and conditions specified in the Sales Agreement previously signed and exchanged. We already instructed our banker, Bank of America, to open an irrevocable L/C in your favor, and Fedexed our formal purchase order.

Regards,

Paul Frederick
Paul Frederick

Synopsis

Q-pointer IIe에 대한 첫 주문을 e-mail로 Qtopia 측에 보내고 있다. 거래조건 중, 특히 논란이 되었던 가격은 10,000 units에 대하여 10%의 할인율을 적용하여 총 US$180,000이 되었음을 밝히고 있다. 이 모든 조건들은 앞서 체결한 매매계약서에 근거한 것이라는 것을 밝히고 있다. 또한 거래 은행에 Qtopia를 beneficiary로 하는 irrevocable L/C을 개설하도록 요청하였고 정식 주문서를 Fedex로(Federal Express, 특급우편) 보냈다는 것도 통보하고 있다.

◈ Terms of Price(가격조건)

국제무역에서 가격을 나타내는 방법 중의 하나이다. 국제무역은 서로 멀리 떨어져있는 당사자간의 거래이기 때문에 특히 운송비(freight)와 보험(insurance)의 부담을 누가 하느냐에 따라 여러 가지 가격조건이 생긴다. 이러한 혼란을 방지하기 위하여 ICC (International Chamber of Commerce; 국제상업회의소)가 제정한 INCOTERMS (International Rules for the Interpretation of Trade Terms: 무역거래조건의 해석에 관한 국제 규칙)를 따르는 것이 일반적이다. INCOTERMS는 1936년 처음 제정된 이래 2000년까지 여러 차례 개정되었고 최근 들어서는 세계경제의 블록화로 국경의 의미가 퇴색되고, 순수 국내 상거래에도 Incoterms 조건들이 이용되는 실정 등을 고려하여 INCOTERMS 2010이 제정되었다. INCOTERMS 2010은 복합운송조건 7가지와 해상운송조건 4가지의 총 11가지 조건으로 구성되어 있다. 다음은 이에 대한 설명이다.

RULES FOR ANY MODE OR MODES OF TRANSPORT(**복합운송조건**)

[EXW] EX Works [작업장인도]

"EX" works means that the seller delivers when it places the goods at the disposal of the buyer at the seller's premises or at another named place(i.e. works, factory, warehouse, etc.). The seller does not need to load the goods on any collecting vehicle, nor does it need to clear the goods for export, where such clearance is applicable.

"공장인도"란 매도인이 매도인의 구내 또는 기타 지정된 장소(예를 들면, 작업장, 공장, 창고 등)에 화물을 매수인의 임의처분상태에 있을 수 있도록 전달하는 것을 말한다. 매도인은 화물을 운송차량에 적재할 필요도 없고 수출통관이 필요한 경우에 그와 같은 수출절차를 수행해야 할 필요가 없다.

[FCA] Free CArrier [운송인인도]

"Free Carrier" means that the seller delivers the goods to the carrier or another person nominated by the buyer at the seller's premises or another named place. The parties are well advised to specify as clearly as possible the point within the named place of delivery, as the risk passes to the buyer at that point.

"운송인인도"란 매도인이 매도인의 구내 혹은 다른 지정된 장소에서 운송인 혹은 매수인이 지정한 제3자에게 화물은 인도하는 것을 의미한다. 당사자들은 화물에 대한 위험이 지정된 장소에서 이전됨으로 화물인도장소를 가능한 한 명확히 명시하는 것이 필요하다.

[CPT] Carriage Paid To [운송비지급]

"Carriage Paid To" means that the seller delivers the goods to the carrier or another person nominated by the seller at an agreed place(if any such place is agreed between parties) and that the seller must contract for and pay the costs of carriage necessary to bring the goods to the named place of destination.

"운송비지급"이란 (쌍방간의 합의에 의해 정한 장소가 있는 경우) 그 지정장소에서 매도인 자신이 지명한 운송인 혹은 제3자에게 화물을 인도하는 것을 말하며, 매도인은 그 지정된 목적지까지 화물을 운송하고 운송하는데 필요한 비용을 지불하도록 계약하여야 한다.

[CIP] Carriage and Insurance Paid to [운송비보험료지급]

"Carriage and Insurance Paid to" means that the seller delivers the goods to the carrier or another person nominated by the seller at an agreed place(if any such place is agreed between the parties) and that the seller must contract for an pay the costs of carriage necessary to bring the goods to the named place of destination.

'The seller also contracts for insurance cover against the buyer's risk of loss of or damage to the goods during the carriage. The buyer should note that under CIP the seller is required to obtain insurance only on minimum cover. Should the buyer wish to have more insurance protection, it will need either to agree as much expressly with the seller or to make its own extra insurance arrangements."

"운송비보험료지급"이란 (쌍방간의 합의에 의해 정한 장소가 있는 경우) 그 지정 장소에서 매도인 자신이 지명한 운송인 혹은 제3자에게 화물을 인도하는 것을 말하며,

매도인은 그 지정된 목적지까지 화물을 운송하고 운송하는데 필요한 비용을 지불하도록 계약하여야 한다.

매도인은 또한 운송도중 발생할 수 있는 화물의 멸실이나 손상에 대한 매수인의 위험에 대한 보험료를 지불하도록 계약하여야 한다. CIP 조건하에서는 매도인이 화물에 대하여 최소한의 보장만을 하는 보험을 가입하도록 되어 있음을 매수인은 주의하여야 한다. 매수인이 보다 확장된 범위의 보험을 원할 경우 매도인에게 이와 같은 의사를 명시적으로 나타내거나 혹은 추가보험을 매수인의 비용으로 가입하여야 한다.

[DAT] Delivered At Terminal [터미널인도]

"Delivered at Terminal" means that the seller delivers when the goods, once unloaded from the arriving means of transport, are placed at the disposal of the buyer at a named terminal at the named port or place of destination. "Terminal" includes any place, whether covered or not, such as a quay, warehouse, container yard or road, rail or air cargo terminal. The seller bears all risks involved in bringing the goods to and unloading them at the terminal at the named port or place of destination.

"터미널인도"란 매도인이 지정된 항구 혹은 목적지의 터미널까지 화물을 운송하고 사용한 운송수단으로부터 화물을 하역한 상태로 매수인에게 인도하는 조건을 의미한다. 터미널은 지붕이 있건 없건 상관없이 예를 들면 부두, 창고, 컨테이너 야적장, 도로, 철도 혹은 항공화물 터미널을 의미한다. 매도인은 화물을 지정된 항구 혹은 지정된 목적지의 터미널까지 운송하고 그곳에서 화물을 하역하는데 따른 모든 위험을 부담한다.

[DAP] Delivered At Place [지정장소인도]

"Delivered at Place" means that the seller delivers when the goods are placed at the disposal of the buyer on the arriving means of transport ready for unloading at the named place of destination. The seller bears all risks involved in bringing the goods to the named place.

"지정장소인도"란 매도인이 목적지의 지정된 장소에 화물은 하역하지 않은 상태로 매수인에게 인도하는 조건을 의미한다. 매도인은 지정된 장소까지 화물을 운반하는데 따른 모든 위험을 부담한다.

[DDP] Delivered Duty Paid [관세지급인도]

"Delivered Duty Paid" means that the seller delivers the goods when the goods are placed at the disposal of the buyer, cleared for import on the arriving means of transport ready for unloading at the named place of destination. The seller bears all the costs and risks involved in bringing the goods to the place of destination and has an obligation to clear the goods not only for export but also for import, to pay any duty for both export and import and to carry out all customs formalities.

"관세지급인도"란 매도인이 수입통관을 마치고 사용된 운송수단에서 화물을 하역하지 않은 상태로 지정된 목적지에서 매수자의 임의처분 상태로 화물을 매수인에게 인도하는 것을 의미한다. 매도인은 목적지까지 화물을 운반하는데 따른 모든 비용과 위험을 부담하고 또한 수출입 관세 및 기타 세관 수수료 지급을 포함한 통관 절차를 수행하여야 할 의무가 있다.

RULES FOR SEA AND INLAND WATERWAY TRANSPORT(해상운송조건)

[FAS] Free Alongside Ship [선측인도]

"Free Alongside Ship" means that the seller delivers when the goods are placed alongside the vessel(e.g., on a quay or a barge) nominated by the buyer at the named port of shipment. The risk of loss of or damage to the goods passes when the goods are alongside the ship, and the buyer bears all costs from that moment onwards.

"선측인도"란 매수자가 지정한 선박의 선측(예를 들면 부도 혹은 바지선)에서 화물을 인도하는 것을 의미한다. 화물의 멸실과 손상에 대한 모든 책임은 화물이 선측에 위치하는 순간 전이되고 그 이후의 모든 비용에 책임은 매수인에게 있다.

[FOB] Free On Board [본선인도]

"Free On Board" means that the seller delivers the goods on board the vessel nominated by the buyer at the named port of shipment or procures the goods already so delivered. The risk of loss of or damage to the goods passes when the goods are on board the vessel, and the buyer bears all costs from that moment onwards.

"본선인도"는 매도인이 지정한 선적항에서 매수인이 지목한 선박의 갑판에 화물을 적재하거나 혹은 그렇게 인도될 수 있도록 화물을 확보하는 것을 의미한다. 화물이 적재된

시점에 화물의 멸실이나 손상에 대한 위험이 전이되며, 매수인은 그 이후의 모든 비용을 부담한다.

[CFR] Cost and Freight [운임 포함]

"Cost and Freight" means that the seller delivers the goods on board the vessel or procures the goods already so delivered. The risk of loss of or damage to the goods passes when the goods are on board the vessel. The seller must contract for and pay the costs and freight necessary to bring the goods to the named port of destination.

"운임포함"은 매도인이 선박의 갑판에 화물을 적재하거나 혹은 그렇게 인도될 수 있도록 화물을 확보하는 것을 의미한다. 화물이 적재된 시점에 화물의 멸실이나 손상에 대한 위험이 전이되며, 매수인은 그 이후의 모든 비용을 부담한다. 화물을 지정된 목적항까지 운반하는데 필요한 비용과 운임을 매도인이 부담하도록 계약하여야 한다.

[CIF] Cost, Insurance and Freight [운송보험료 포함]

"Cost, Insurance and Freight" means that the seller delivers the goods on board the vessel or procures the goods already so delivered. The risk of loss of or damage to the goods passes when the goods are on board the vessel. The seller must contract for and pay the costs and freight necessary to bring the goods to the named port of destination.

'The seller also contracts for insurance cover against the buyer's risk of loss of or damage to the goods during the carriage. The buyer should note that under CIF the seller is required to obtain insurance only on minimum cover. Should the buyer wish to have more insurance protection, it will need either to agree as much expressly with the seller or to make its own extra insurance arrangements."

"운임보험료포함"은 매도인이 선박의 갑판에 화물을 적재거나 혹은 그렇게 인도될 수 있도록 화물을 확보하는 것을 의미한다. 화물이 적재된 시점에 화물의 멸실이나 손상에 대한 위험이 전이되며, 매수인은 그 이후의 모든 비용을 부담한다. 화물을 지정된 목적항까지 운반하는데 필요한 비용과 운임을 매도인이 부담하도록 계약하여야 한다.

매도인은 또한 운송도중 발생할 수 있는 화물의 멸실이나 손상에 대한 매수인의 위험에 대한 보험료를 지불하도록 계약하여야 한다. CIF 조건하에서는 매도인이 화물에 대하여 최소한의 보장만을 하는 보험을 가입하도록 되어 있음을 매수인은 주의하여야 한다.

매수인이 보다 확장된 범위의 보험을 원할 경우 매도인에게 이와 같은 의사를 명시적으로 나타내거나 혹은 추가 보험을 매수인의 비용으로 가입하여야 한다.

(Source: International Chamber of Commerce, Incoterms, 2010)

아래 표는 위의 11가지 조건들의 수출상(seller)와 수입상(buyer)의 비용분기점을 요약한 것이다. 이들 조건 중 해상운송에서 가장 널리 쓰이는 것이 CIF와 FOB 조건이다. 가격을 견적(quote)할 때에는 예를 들어 USD250.00 CIF LA라고 되어 있다면 도착항이 LA이고 LA도착 때까지의 운임과 보험비용을 포함한 가격이 미화 250.00불이라는 것을 말한다. USD200.00 FOB Incheon라고 표시하였다면 출발항이 Incheon으로 인천항에 정박한 배의 갑판 위에까지 수출물건을 선적하는데 필요한 비용을 포함한 가격이 미화 200불이라는 표시이다. 영문으로 쓸 때 CIF, FOB 혹은 cif, fob와 같이 대·소문자 모두 가능하다.

	Any Transport		Sea/Inland Waterway Transport				Any Transport				
	EXW	FCA	FAS	FOB	CFR	CIF	CPT	CIP	DAT	DAP	DDP
Export Packing	S	S	S	S	S	S	S	S	S	S	S
Container/Vehicle Loading	B	S	S	S	S	S	S	S	S	S	S
Export Clearance	B	S	S	S	S	S	S	S	S	S	S
Delivery to Port of Export	B	S	S	S	S	S	S	S	S	S	S
Origin Terminal Charges	B	B	S	S	S	S	S	S	S	S	S
Main Carrier Loading	B	B	B	S	S	S	S	S	S	S	S
Freight/Carriage	B	B	B	B	S	S	S	S	S	S	S
Insurance	B	B	B	B	B	S	B	S	S	S	S
Destination Arrival Charges	B	B	B	B	B	B	S	S	S	S	S
Main Carrier Unloading	B	B	B	B	B	B	B	B	S	S	S
Import Customs Clearance	B	B	B	B	B	B	B	B	B	B	S
Delivery to Destination	B	B	B	B	B	B	B	B	B	S	S
Unloading at Destination	B	B	B	B	B	B	B	B	B	B	B

S=Seller, B=Buyer

여기에서 한 가지 주의할 점은 C 조건들의 경우 비용의 분기점과 위험의 분기점이 서로 다르다는 것이다. 예를 들어 CIF조건은 FOB조건에 해상운임과 보험료 의무를 수출상이 부담하도록 추가한 조건이다. 즉, CIF조건에서는 수출상이 비록 목적항까지의 해상운임과 보험료를 지불하지만 수출상의 책임은 화물이 본선의 갑판에 적재될 때 종료된다. 따라서 운송도중의 사고에 대한 책임은 수입상에게 있고, 사고발생시 수입상이 보험회사에 손해배상을 청구하여야 한다. 아래 표는 각 조건들의 인도시점(point of delivery), 위험의 분기점(risk transfer), 그리고 비용의 분기점(charges transfer)을 정리한 것이다.

	Point of Delivery	Risk Transfer	Charges Transfer
EXW	At warehouse Named Place	= point of delivery	=point of delivery
FCA	On truck at Named Place	= point of delivery	=point of delivery
FAS	At Named Port Alongside Ship	= point of delivery	=point of delivery
FOB	At Named Port On Board Ship	= point of delivery	=point of delivery
CFR	On Board Vessel at Point of Shipment	= point of delivery	FOB + Freight
CIF	On Board Vessel at Point of Shipment	= point of delivery	FOB + Insurance + Freight
CPT	On Board Vessel at Point of Shipment	= point of delivery	FCA + Carriage
CIP	On Board Vessel at Point of Shipment	= point of delivery	FCA + Insurance + Carriage
DAT	Unload at the Port or Cargo Terminal Named Place	= point of delivery	=point of delivery
DAP	On delivering Carrier at Named Place	= point of delivery	=point of delivery
DDP	On Delivering Carrier at Named Place & Tax Paid	= point of delivery	=point of delivery

◈ exchange/change

exchange와 change는 구입한 물건을 '교환하다'의 의미로 쓰일 때만 같은 의미로 쓰인다.

- Can I exchange(=change) theses shirts? They don't fit.
- A long time ago Indians used to exchange(~~change~~) furs for guns.
- At Christmas, may family always exchanges(~~changes~~) gifts.
- I had to change(~~exchange~~) my plan because of the weather.
- Would my mind changing(~~exchanging~~) seats?
- We have to change(~~exchanging~~) buses two times to reach there.

Fedex

일반적인 express delivery를 courier[kə́:riər](특급우편)라고 한다.

- It will be shipped to you by courier at our expense.

그런데 고유명사인 미국의 대표적인 특급 택배회사인 Federal Express가 일반 동사화 되어서 '특급택배로 부치다'의 의미로 특히 business에서 구어체로 사용되기도 한다. 구어체적인 표현이긴 하지만 간단하게 표현하기 위하여 이메일 등에서 자주 쓰인다. 본문의 내 용을 좀더 formal 하게 표현하면, We sent our formal purchase order via(by) Fedex.이 된다. 이와 함께 또 다른 택배회사인 DHL(Dalsey, Hillblom, Lynn 세 사람의 창업자 이니셜)이나 UPS(United Parcel Service)도 비슷하게 쓰인다.

- If you found the document, please DHL(UPS) it back to me.
  (서류를 찾으면 DHL(UPS)로 보내주세요.)

이처럼 고유명사를 동사로 쓰이는 또 다른 예는 복사기 제조업체인 Xerox이다. Please Xerox this. 하면 Please make a photocopy of this. (복사해 주세요)의 의미이다. 또 복사물의 뜻으로는 photocopy가 일반적이지만, Xeroxcopy도 쓰이며 copy machine의 의미로 Xerox machine이 많이 쓰인다. Xerox는 [zíəraks]로 읽는다. 이것이 업계를 대표하는 회사나 제품이 갖는 premium이다. 또한 최근에는 "인터넷에서 검색한다"는 의미로 대표적 검색엔진인 Google이나 Yahoo를 동사화해서 I Google it. 혹은 Do you Yahoo?와 같이 쓰기도 한다.

- Everytime I want to know something, I Google it. (뭔가를 알고 싶으면 인터넷에서 검색한다.)

이런 표현들은 일상생활이나 business에서는 편리하게 쓸 수 있지만 구어체적인 표현이므로 공식적인 문서에서는 피하는 것이 좋다.

Practice Tests - Situation 13

1. What type of letter is it?

(a) acceptance
(b) counter-offer
(c) purchase order
(d) confirmation letter

2. What did Paul do before he sent this e-mail?

(a) He instructed Jennifer's bank to open an L/C for him.
(b) He signed on the Sales Contract.
(c) He was processing the order.
(d) He sent the formal order sheet to Jennifer by Fedex.

3. What will Jennifer do after receiving this e-mail?

(a) She will sign the Sales Contract.
(b) She will ask Fedex to send an irrevocable L/C to Paul.
(c) She will instruct her bank to open an L/C.
(d) She will acknowledge and execute the order.

4. If you receive an L/C stating "USD200,000.00 FOB Incheon", what is the port of destination?

(a) Incheon
(b) do not know exactly
(c) anywhere
(d) Incheon or any port in Korea

5. The seller pays all delivery costs to when the goods are on board ship at a named port. The buyer pays all other costs. What term is it?

(a) FOB
(b) CIF
(c) DAT
(d) DDP

6. Under "CIF New York" what's the meaning of 'New York'?

(a) port of loading
(b) port of unloading
(c) port of loading and unloading
(d) can not determine

[7~10] Followings are the parts of INCOTERMS 2010. Choose the one that best fills the blanks.

7. "Delivered Duty Paid" means that the (   ) delivers the goods when the goods are placed at the disposal of the (   ), cleared for import on the arriving means of transport ready for unloading at the named place of destination. The (   ) bears all the costs and risks involved in bringing the goods to the place of destination and has an obligation to clear the goods not only for export but also for import, to pay any duty for both export and import and to carry out all customs formalities.

(a) seller – buyer – seller
(b) seller – seller – seller
(c) buyer – seller – seller
(d) buyer – buyer – buyer

8. (   ) means that the seller delivers when it places the goods at the disposal of the buyer at the seller's premises or another named place(i.e. works, factory, warehouse, etc.). The seller does not need to load the goods on any collecting vehicle, nor does it need to clear the goods for export, where such clearance is applicable.

(a) FOB
(b) EXW
(c) DAT
(d) DDP

9. "Free Alongside Ship" means that the seller delivers when the goods are placed alongside the vessel(e.g., on a quay or a barge) nominated by the buyer at the named port of shipment. The risk of loss of or damage to the goods passes when the goods are alongside the ship, and the( ) bears all costs from that moment onwards.

(a) buyer
(b) seller
(c) carrier
(d) customer

10. (   ) means that the seller delivers the goods on board the vessel or procures the goods already so delivered. The risk of loss of or damage to the goods passes when the goods are on board the vessel. The seller must contract for and pay the costs and freight necessary to bring the goods to the named port of destination. The seller also contracts for insurance cover against the buyer's risk of loss of or damage to the goods during the carriage.

(a) CIF (b) FOB (c) DAT (d) DDP

11. With the following cost information, choose the one that correctly calculate the export price for FAS, FOB, CIF, and DDP terms based on INCORTERMS 2010.

Production Cost:	US$200,000
Delivery Cost(From Factory to Port):	2,000
Export Clearance Fee:	1,000
Loading Fee:	2,000
Freight:	10,000
Insurance Premium:	5,000
Main Carrier Unloading Fee:	2,000
Import Clearance Fee:	1,000
Delivery Cost(From port to the buyer's premise):	2,000
Unlooding at destination	1,000

(a) US$202,000-204,000-220,000-224,000
(b) US$202,0 0-204,0 0-210,0 0-2 5,0 0
(c) US$203,000-205,000-210,000-224,000
(d) US$203,0 0-205,0 0-2 0,0 0-2 5,0 0

12. Read the following and answer. [무역영어 2급]

OFFER SHEET

Messrs. Walt Mart
Date: 15 April, 2011
Goods: 200 PCS of Ladies Jacket, USD250 per piece
Shipment: within 30days after receipt of Letter of
Credit Port of Loading: Busan
Destination: New York Packing: 20 feet
container
Validity: one month from issuance of this
offer Payment: at sight by negotiation
Insurance: to be covered by seller Advising bank: Citi, Sanggong Branch

13. What is most possible price terms for the goods?

(a) CIF Busan USD25,000
(b) FOB Busan USD50,000
(c) FOB New York USD25,000
(d) CIF New York USD50,000

14. 다음 매매계약서에서 빈칸에 들어갈 단어가 순서대로 짝지어진 것을 고르시오.

[무역영어 2급]

FOB basis: [ ] shall nominate its preferred shipping company and shall book shipping space. Meanwhile, [ ] shall inform pre-shipping information to [ ] such as name of the commodity, quantity, package, total weight and expected cargo ready date at the port of shipment.

(a) buyer - seller - buyer
(b) seller - seller - buyer
(c) buyer - buyer - seller
(d) seller - buyer - seller

15. The contract terms are 'FCA Busan Container Depot'. Which of the following transport documents would be acceptable to the importer?

[무역영어 2급]

(a) Air waybill, marked 'freight payable at destination'
(b) Bill of Lading, marked 'freight paid'.
(c) Combined Bill of lading marked 'freight payable at destination'.
(d) Multimodal Bill of lading marked 'freight paid'.

16. Which of the following is most likely to come BEFORE the passage below?

[무역영어 1급]

For the past 5 years ABC has provided 25% of our business, and the loss of this contract will reduce operating revenues. This means that we'll have to lay off three technicians and two consultants.

(a) ABC has just informed us that we must be strict about our records for trip reimbursement. According to ABC, we are required to have bills for any expense over USD25.
(b) I regret to announce that ABC has opted not to renew its contact with us because its business is in financial trouble and its changing its business model.
(c) We have recently been acquired by ABC and find it necessary to streamline our operations dramatically.

(d) We have worked out an arrangement with ABC to keep our costs down. As our firm has grown, so has ABC.

17. Which of the following fits LEAST in the letter? [무역영어 1급]

Dear Mr. Woods,

Good morning. In your last email you made mention of an interest in "home alarm systems." (a) However, could you please provide a bit more details? (b) Although Ms. Jane Smith is working at the Public Relations Divisions, she knows the most about the case.

I am writing to inquire as to the model of home alarm systems you are most interested in: (c) for example, an alarm system for an apartment is different from one for a house, and we have home systems designed simply for a door, and systems designed for an entire home.

(d) I am attaching an e-catalogue of some of our products; perhaps you could select from it the items which best suit your needs. In any event, please email me again at your first convenience.

Situation 14

Q-pointer IIe 주문에 대한 확인을 하다.

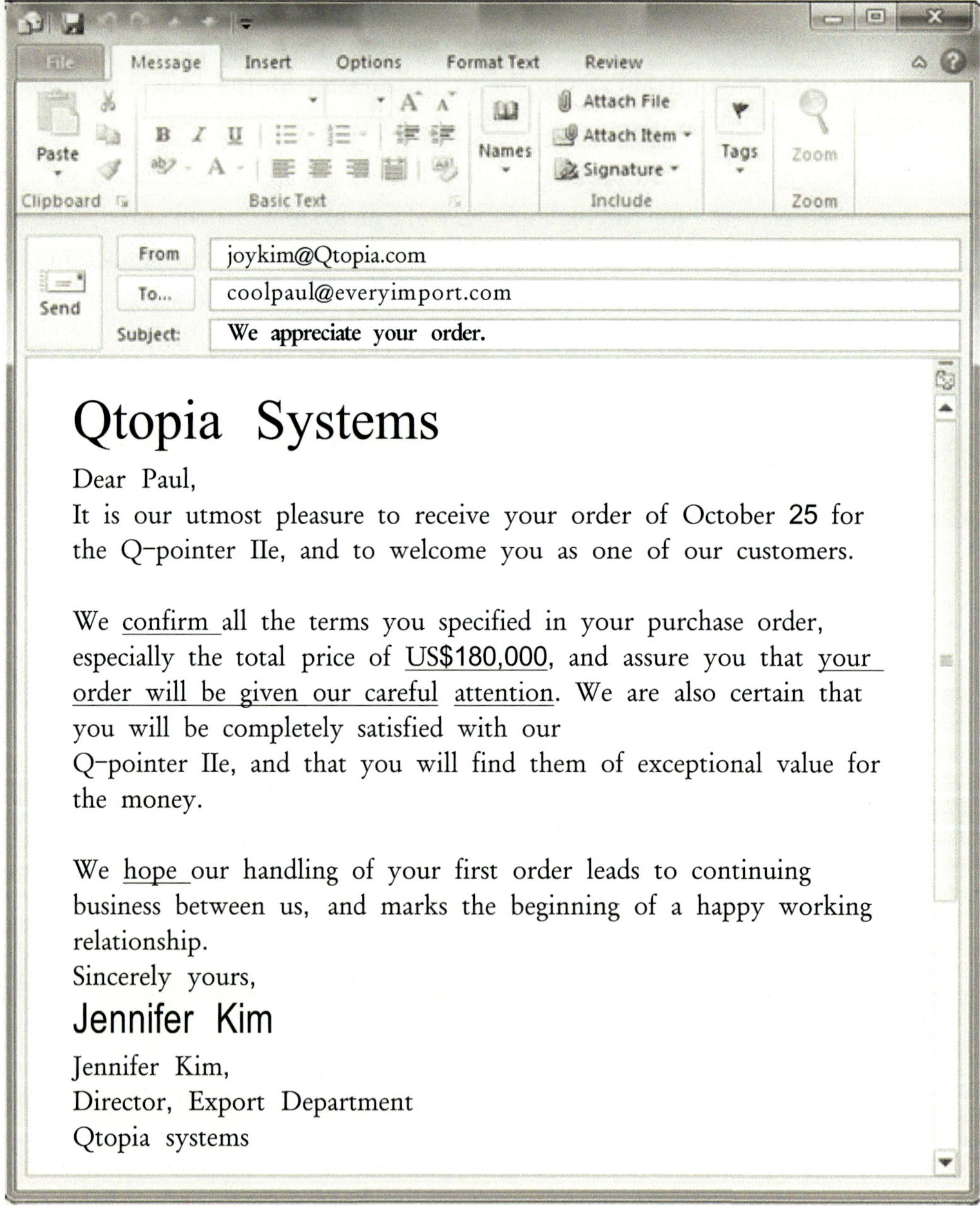

From: joykim@Qtopia.com
To: coolpaul@everyimport.com
Subject: We appreciate your order.

Qtopia Systems

Dear Paul,
It is our utmost pleasure to receive your order of October 25 for the Q-pointer IIe, and to welcome you as one of our customers.

We confirm all the terms you specified in your purchase order, especially the total price of US$180,000, and assure you that your order will be given our careful attention. We are also certain that you will be completely satisfied with our
Q-pointer IIe, and that you will find them of exceptional value for the money.

We hope our handling of your first order leads to continuing business between us, and marks the beginning of a happy working relationship.
Sincerely yours,

Jennifer Kim

Jennifer Kim,
Director, Export Department
Qtopia systems

Synopsis

Qtopia 측에서 EveryImport 측에게 주문에 대하여 지극히(utmost) 감사하며, 새로운 고객으로 환영한다는 것을 밝히고 있다. 구매서에 있는 모든 조건들, 특히 가격이 180,000불임을 확인하면서, 주문을 아주 주의 깊게 처리할 것임을 밝히고 있다. Q-pointer IIe에 대하여 만족할 것임을 확신하며 가격에 비하여 우수한 가치(exceptional value for the money)를 지녔음을 알게 될 것이라는 점도 언급하고 있다. Qtopia는 이번 주문을 통하여 EveryImport과 계속적인 관계가 지속되고, 새로운 관계의 시작점이 되기를 희망하고 있다.

◈ confirm

주문을 받게 되면 그 주문에 대한 확인서를 보내는 것이 필요하다. 확인서에는 주요 매매조건에 대한 언급이 필요하며 필요한 사항이 누락되어 있으면 상대방에게 다시 조회하여 분명히 해둘 필요가 있다. 이때 쓸 수 있는 표현으로 confirm과 acknowledge가 있다. acknowledge는 confirm과 같은 의미로 쓰이기도 하지만, '(~의 승인을) 확인하다, 인증, 인정하다'의 의미를 내포하고 있다.

We are pleased to confirm our telephone conversion this morning as follows:
Please acknowledge our order No. 1234.

USD180,000의 읽기
USD180,000: one hundred eighty thousand US dollars
$18.25: eighteen dollars and twenty-five cents 혹은 eighteen twenty-five
₩30,000,000: Thirty million won(won은 복수로 쓰지 않음)
€20.56(Euro20.56) Twenty euros and fifty-six cents
£81.25: eighty-one pounds and twenty-five pence(1 penny)
¥35.40: thirty-five yen and forty sen(yen, sen은 복수로 쓰지 않음)

신용장, 어음, 영수증 등 금액을 정확히 써야 하는 경우에는 숫자와 함께 문자표기를 하는 경우가 많다. 이때 문자표기 금액 앞에 'Say'를 뒤에는 'Only'를 쓰는 경우도 있다.

USD180,000: SAY US DOLLARS ONE HUNDRED EIGHTY THOUSAND ONLY

US Dollar

penny
($0.01)
1 cent

nickel
($0.05)
5 cents

dime
($0.1)
10 cents

quarter
($0.25)
25 cents

half
dollar($0.50)
잘 통용 안됨

dollar
($1)

$1.00

$5.00

$10.00

$20.00

$50.00

$100.00

Euro

◈ Your order will be given our careful attention.

= We will pay [give/draw] careful attention to your order.

= Your order will receive [attract] our careful attention.

"귀사의 주문은 우리의 세심한 주의를 받을 것입니다"의 의미이다. 이외에도 attention에 붙을 수 있는 형용사들은,

the best attention(최대한의 주의)
close attention(세심한 주의)
full attention(충분한 주의)
special attention(특별한 주의)
every attention(모든 주의)
particular attention(특별한 주의)

◈ hope

'~을 바라다'의 의미로 쓰이는 hope와 유사한 단어들 몇 가지를 소개한다.

hope와 expect

hope는 '뭔가 좋은 것(혹은 자기가 원하는 것)이 일어나길 기대하는 것'이라면 expect는 (좋은 일이건 나쁜 일이건, 자기가 원하는 것이든 원하지 않는 것이든 상관없이) '뭔가가 일어날 것이라는 것을 알고 기대하는 것'이다. 다음 예를 보면 좀 더 명확해진다.

- She is expecting a baby. (=She is pregnant.)
- She is hoping it will be a girl.

- I am expecting Paul to phone at two o'clock.
- I hope he gets some good news.

hope와 wish

hope은 실현가능한 희망을 나타내고, wish는 실현 불가능한 현재의 희망 혹은 얻고 싶은 것을 희망할 때 쓰인다. 이런 의미로 쓰일 때는 hope that ~, wish that ~의 형태로 쓰인다.

- I hope that you can come to the party.
  ~~wish~~ ~~would~~
- I hope you feel better tomorrow.
  ~~wish~~

- We hope you will be satisfied with the consignment.
  (= We wish you would be satisfied with the consignment.)

hope를 사용한 문장이 일반적으로 '선적품에 만족하시길 희망합니다.'이고 wish를 사용하면, "선적품이 맘에 안들더라도 받아주시길 희망합니다."의 느낌을 준다. 이와 같이 wish는 가정법과 같은 성격을 가져서, that ~ 이하의 절에 과거의 시제를 사용한다.

- I wish(that) I were better looking. (더 잘생겼더라면 좋았을걸.)
- I wish(that) I were taller. (키가 더 컸더라면 좋았을걸.)
- We all wish(that) the snow would stay forever. (눈이 계속 남아있길 바람.)
- Don't you wish(that) you could fly? (날아보기를 원하지 않니?)

하지만 wish는 that ~의 절 형태가 아닌 I wish you ~와 같이 쓰이면 좋은 희망을 나타낼 때 쓰인다.

- I wish you a merry Christmas. (즐거운 크리스마스가 되길 바랍니다.)
- We all wish you a quick recovery. (우리 모두 쾌유를 빕니다.)

또한 hope와 wish는 to 부정사를 동반하여 want의 의미로 많이 쓰인다.

- I hope to go to China. (= I want to go to China.)
- She hopes to get a decent job.
- I wish to express my sincere thanks.
- If you wish to reserve a table, please contact me.

본문에 쓰인, "We hope our handling of your first order leads to continuing business between us, and marks the beginning of a happy working relationship."에서 hope는 앞으로 실현가능한 희망적인 바람을 나타낸다. 즉, "이번 첫 주문을 처리를 잘해서 앞으로 지속적인 거래관계가 계속되길 바라며, 이것이 서로 원만한 관계의 시작이 되기를 희망합니다."의 의미이다.

Practice Tests - Situation 14

1. What is not true about the e-mail in Situation 14?
   (a) Jennifer is acknowledging Paul's order.
   (b) Jennifer will give her careful attention to Paul's order.
   (c) Paul finds that the products have exceptional value for the money.
   (d) The total price is USD180,000.

2. What is Jennifer supposed to do after sending this e-mail?
   (a) placing the order (b) processing the order
   (c) taking the order (d) cancelling the order

3. Sara Oliver, a company spokeswoman, ________________ the movie is controversial and may be unpopular with some customers.
   (a) acknowledges (b) knowledges
   (c) acknowledgements (d) knowledging

4. 괄호 안에 들어갈 수 있는 가장 적절한 단어는?
   We ( ) our handling of your first order leads to continuing business between us, and marks the beginning of a happy working relationship.
   (a) expect (b) wish
   (c) hope (d) think

5. 다음 중 어색한 문장을 고르시오.
   (a) I hope that we can receive your order.
   (b) I wish that we could receive your order.
   (c) We hope you will be satisfied with the consignment.
   (d) We wish you would be satisfied with the consignment.

6. If you want to be a successful negotiator and sales person you should:
   - know your ( ) and its main features.
   - know the strengths and ( ) of competing product.

- find out a person who makes the (　　　) decisions in your client's firm.
- listen to what your (　　　) tells you.

(a) product – weakness – final – client
(b) customer – weakness – buying – client
(c) product – specification – final – manager
(d) customer – specification – buying – manager

7. 아래는 어떤 서신의 일부인가? [무역영어 2급]

We are pleased to confirm your order for 1,000 units of electronic calculators amounting to $100,000. As requested, we are preparing to make shipment by the end of September and would request you to issue an irrevocable L/C in our favor as soon as possible, valid until October 20. Immediately upon receipt of your L/C, we will ship your order.

(a) Order acknowledgement　　(b) Firm offer
(c) Import inquiry　　(d) Advise of shipment

8. The following are some standard elements of a business plan. In what order do you think they should come in the actual plan? [무역영어 1급]

(A) Financial analysis. gives details of the business's performance, and existing finance and assets, sales forecasts, and projected financial statements.
(B) Executive summary. a one-page summary or overview of what the business plan is about and what it will contain.
(C) Implementation plan. describes sales and marketing and operational strategies.
(D) Market opportunity. briefly describes what the company or business plans to do, the target market, its needs, current products and services.

(a) C–A–B–D　　(b) B–A–C–D
(c) A–D–B–C　　(d) B–D–A–C

9. Which of the following fits the blanks? [무역영어 1급]

You are probably aware that Justin's has opened a new store in the Bethabara Shopping Center. To celebrate the occasion, we are having a Grand Opening Sale, and every Justin store will be in on it. EVERYTHING in ALL our stores will be marked down 10~30%. Designer jeans that were \$60~\$90 are now \$40~\$60. An assortment of 100% silk blouses, originally \$60~\$95, are on sale for \$40~\$65. The savings are incredible. The sale is for one day only, January 31.

________ letters like the above are commonly used by business to announce sales or stimulate patronage. They have an advantage over other forms of advertising(such as television, radio, or newspaper ads) because letters can be aimed selectively at the ___________ audience most likely to buy. By doing this, they would reach customers with the clearest need for the product.

(a) Retail sales – specific
(b) Inquiry – general
(c) Confirmation – specific
(d) Commitment – general

10. Which of the following is LEAST likely to be part of the document? [무역영어 1급]

I'd like your approval for an Intranet seminar we are planning in October. (a) This will be a kickoff seminar for the introduction of the Korean version of Intra 2013. An outline of the seminar is attached. (b) Our target attendance is 200, including both existing and prospective customers. We are expecting 80 million won in sales for the 2Q of this years. (c) The estimated cost is 3 million won. A spreadsheet showing the cost breakdown and cost/benefit analysis is also attached. (d) As we need to secure retail shelf space, please allow us to suggest a new deadline. This is a great opportunity to gain wide exposure of Intra 2013 in the Korean business community. I look forward to receiving your approval.

The story here tells you that History Repeat Itself.

Lincoln was elected in 1860.
Kennedy was elected in 1960.
There are seven letters in each name. Both Presidents were slain on Friday.
Both were slain in presence of their wives.
Both were shot in the head.
Both were directly concerned with Civil Rights.
Kennedy's secretary Lincoln warned him not to go to Dallas.
Lincoln's secretary Kennedy warned him not to go to the theater.
Both Presidents lost their sons while they were in White House.
Lincoln was slain in a theater names Ford, and Kennedy was slain in a car named Lincoln made by Ford.

Both of their successors were named Johnson; Andrew Johnson, Lyndon Johnson.
Each name contains 13 letters. Andrew Johnson was born in 1808. Lyndon Johnson was born in 1908.
Lincoln's assassin, John Wilkes Booth was born in 1839
Kennedy's assassin, Lee Harvey Oswald was born in 1939.
Each name contains 15 letters.
Booth shot Lincoln in a theater and hid in a warehouse. Oswald shot Kennedy from a warehouse and hid in a theater.
Booth and Oswald were murdered before trial could be arranged.
Both Wives had been previously engaged to someone else.
Both married a dark-haired twenty-four year old woman at time of marriage.
Both Lost a sister before becoming president.
Both Lost a son while serving as president.

For more shocking facts visit
www.near-death.com/experiences/reincarnation08.html

Situation 15

Q-pointer IIe에 대한 신용장 개설을 통보하다.

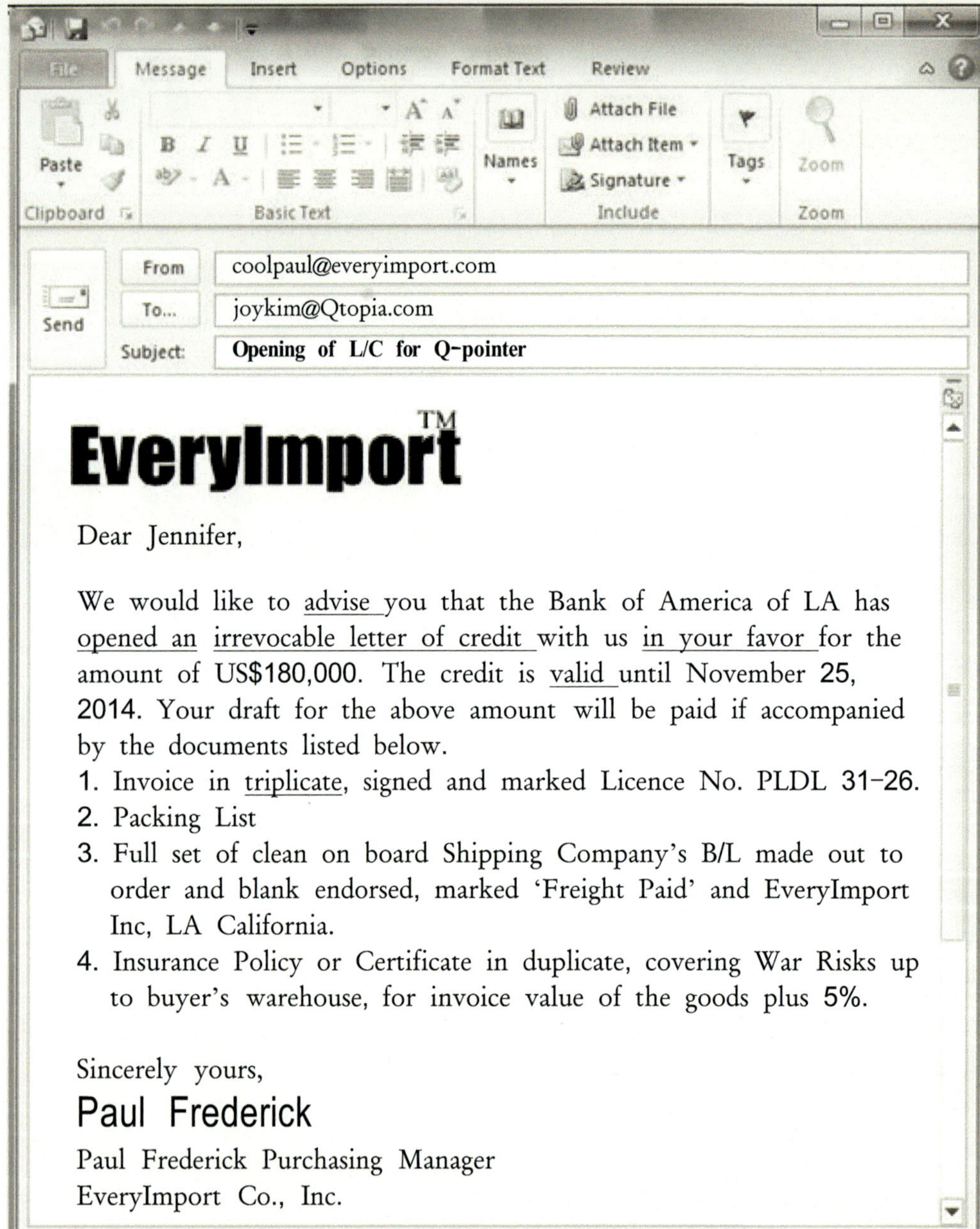

Dear Jennifer,

We would like to advise you that the Bank of America of LA has opened an irrevocable letter of credit with us in your favor for the amount of US$180,000. The credit is valid until November 25, 2014. Your draft for the above amount will be paid if accompanied by the documents listed below.

1. Invoice in triplicate, signed and marked Licence No. PLDL 31-26.
2. Packing List
3. Full set of clean on board Shipping Company's B/L made out to order and blank endorsed, marked 'Freight Paid' and EveryImport Inc, LA California.
4. Insurance Policy or Certificate in duplicate, covering War Risks up to buyer's warehouse, for invoice value of the goods plus 5%.

Sincerely yours,

Paul Frederick

Paul Frederick Purchasing Manager
EveryImport Co., Inc.

Synopsis

EveryImport측에서 수출입대금 180,000불에 대한 irrevocable L/C를 Qtopia를 수익자로 해서(in your favor) Bank of America가 개설하였음을 통지(advise)하고 있다. 신용장의 유효기간은 11월 25일(valid until)이며, invoice 3부(in triplicate), packing list, 지시식(to order)이여서 백지배서(blank endorsed)가 가능하고 운임지급과 EveryImport LA표시가 되어있는 무사고 선적선하증권, 수입자의 창고까지 전쟁위험을 담보를 포함하고 invoice상의 가액에 5%를 더한 금액까지 담보를 증명하는 보험증권 2부(in duplicate)의 4가지 서류와 함께 환어음(draft)을 발행하면 대금이 지급될 것(the above amount will be paid)임을 밝히고 있다.

◈ L/C의 개념

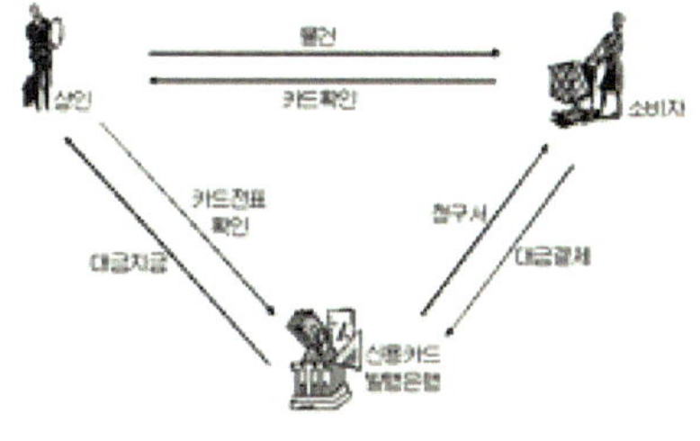

신용장(L/C: letter of credit)이란 무역 거래의 대금결제 및 상품수입을 원활하게하기 위하여 수출상의 요청에 따라 수입상의 거래 은행이 발행하는 것으로 L/C상에 명시된 조건과 수출상 이 제시하는 서류가 일치하면 수출대금 지급을 확약하는 증서(instrument)이다. 이 L/C는 수출상에게는 대금이 결제되지 않을 위험을 제거해 주고 수입상에게는 물품을 확실하게 인수할 수 있게 해주는 제도로써 오늘날 국제무역거래에서 널리 이용되고 있다.

L/C는 우리가 일상생활에서 많이 쓰는 신용카드(credit card)와 유사한 성격을 가지고 있다. credit card로 거래를 할 때 물건을 파는 상인은 카드를 가진 사람을 믿는 것이 아니라 카드를 발행한 은행을 믿고 물건을 파는 것이다. 즉, 물건의 대금을 은행으로부터 받을 수 있기 때문에 현금을 받는 대신 카드만을 확인하고 물건을 팔 수 있는 것이다. 최종 소비자가 은행에 물건대금을 지급하고 안하고는 물건을 판 상인하고 상관없는 것이고, 은행과 소비자 간에 해결할 문제인 것이다. 은행이 credit card를 발행할 때 소비자의 신용상태를 먼저 파악하는 것은 이 때문이다.

L/C에 의한 국제거래에 있어서도 수출상(상인)은 수입상(소비자)을 믿는 것이 아니라 은 행이 대금지급을 확약한 L/C를 믿고 계약물품을 안심하고 수출할 수 있는 것이다. 여기에서도 역시 수출상은 L/C에서 요구하는 서류만 준비하여 은행에 제시하여 수출대금을 받을 수 있고 수입상이 대금을 결제하고 안하고는 수입상과 은행과의 문제이다.

따라서 L/C를 발행하는 은행 역시 수입상의 신용상태를 파악한 후 수입상으로부터 충분한 담보금이나 채권보전조치를 취한 후에 L/C를 발행해 준다.

◈ L/C의 거래과정

신용장은 기본적으로 4개의 당사자가 있다. a) 수출상(exporter), b) 수입상(importer), c) 개설은행(issuing bank), d) 통지은행(advising bank) 혹은 매입은행(negotiating bank) 구체적인 거래과정은 아래 그림을 보면서 설명한다.

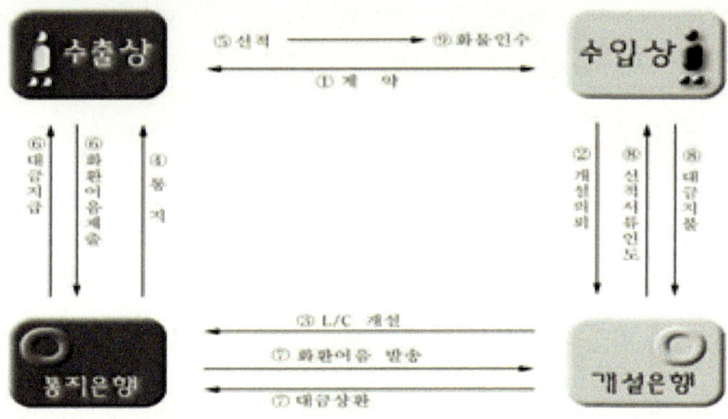

① 거래당사자인 exporter와 importer간에 Sales Contract이 이루어진다.

② importer는 자기 거래은행에 L/C의 개설을 의뢰한다.

③ importer의 거래은행은 수입상의 신용평가에 근거하여 또는 importer로부터 담보를 요구하여 이에 만족하면 L/C에 포함된 지시와 조건에 따라서 상품에 대해 지불을 보증하는 신용장을 개설한다. 이 은행은 L/C를 발급한 은행, 즉 개설은행(issuing bank)이 된다. issuing bank는 수출국에 소재한 자행의 지점 혹은 업무제휴를 맺은 수출국의 은행으로 신용장을 개설한다.

④ L/C를 받은 수출국에 소재한 은행은 exporter에게 L/C의 도착을 확인하여 통지(advise)해 준다. 이 은행을 통지은행(advising bank)이라고 부른다.

⑤ 신용장을 받은 수출상은 계약대로 상품을 수입업자에게 선적한다.

⑥ 수출상은 선하증권(Bill of Lading, Situation18 참조)을 선박회사에서 발급 받고 보험증권, 상업송장 등 신용장에서 요구하는 서류를 구비한 다음 환어음(Bill of Exchange, Situation 20 참조)을 은행에 제시하고 상품대금을 지급 받는다. 이 은행을 매입은행(negotiating bank)이라고 부른다. 보통은 advising bank가

negotiating bank가 된다.

⑦ draft를 매입한 negotiating bank는 exporter에게 지급한 어음대금을 결제 받기 위해 L/C issuing bank에 draft와 exporter가 제출한 shipping documents를 보낸다.

⑧ issuing bank는 shipping documents를 importer에게 인도해 주면서 상품대금을 받아 negotiating bank에 대금상환을 한다.

⑨ importer는 선적서류를 선박회사에 제출하고 화물을 인도 받는다.

advise

일반적인 의미의 '충고하다' 이외에 business에서는 '통보, 통지하다'의 의미로 많이 쓰인다. 신용장에서 advising bank는 신용장을 수익자에게 통지해 주는 통지은행이다. 명사형인 advice는 충고의 의미일 경우 셀 수 없는 명사이기 때문에 an advice, good advices와 같이 쓰지 않고, "a word [bit, piece]of advice"와 같이 쓴다. 그러나 통지의 의미일 경우에는 a remittance advice(송금통지), shipping advices(선적통지), an advice slip(통지전표)와 같이 셀 수 있는 명사로 사용된다.

open an L/C

~ open(issue, establish) an L/C: "수입업자가 자사의 거래은행을 통하여 신용장을 개설하였다"의 의미이다. 또 We instructed our banker to open an L/C ~: "수입업자가 자사 의 거래은행에 신용장 개설을 지시하다" 의미이다. (letter of credit의 약어 L/C는 an L/C로 쓰임) 이외에도 신용장에 관련된 표현으로는,

apply for an L/C	신용장 개설을 의뢰하다.
cable(wire) an L/C	신용장을 전신으로 열다
cancel an L/C	신용장을 취소하다
amend an L/C	신용장을 수정하다
extend an L/C	신용장 기한을 연장하다
increase an L/C	신용장 금액을 늘리다
advise(notify) an L/C	신용장을 통지하다.
transfer an L/C	신용장을 양도하다.
withdraw an L/C	신용장을 철회하다.

in your favor

"귀사를 수익자(beneficiary)로"의 의미이다. 무역거래에서 L/C로 가장 많은 혜택(benefit)을 받는 측이 대금 지급을 공신력 있는 은행으로부터 확약을 받는 수출자이기 때문에 L/C거래에서 수출상을 수익자(beneficiary)라고 부른다. 구체적인 회사를 명시하려면 in favor of ~를 사용하여,

- We opened an L/C in favor of Qtopia.

신용장 금액을 명시할 때에는 for나 for the amount of를 사용하여,

- We opened an L/C in your favor for the amount of USD180,000.00.
  (귀사를 수익자로 하여 미화 180,000불에 대한 신용장을 개설하였습니다.)

valid

오퍼나 신용장에서 '~까지 유효하다'를 표현할 때 많이 쓰는 단어이다. firm offer는 유효기간(validity)이 정해져 있는 offer를 말하고, 신용장도 유효기간이 정해져 있어서 그 기간 안에 관련 서류와 함께 환어음을 매입시켜야 대금을 회수할 수 있다. valid와 같은 의미로 expire(만기가 되다)를 쓸 수도 있다.

- This L/C is valid until October 25. (= This L/C expires on October 25.)

valid의 반대말은 invalid 혹은 void를 쓴다. The expired L/C is invalid [void]. 만기가 끝난 신용장은 무효이다.

triplicate

Business에서는 계약서를 비롯한 많은 서류들을 여러 부 작성할 경우가 많다. 이때 원본(1부)을 orignal이라고 부르고 2부 이상은

duplicate(2부) triplicate(3부) quadruplicate(4부)
quintuplicate(5부) sextuplicate(6부) septuplicate(7부)
octuplicate(8부) nonuplicate(9부) decuplicate(10부)

Practice Tests - Situation 15

1. What can you learn about the shipping of the contracted goods?
   (a) They will be shipped before November 25, 2014.
   (b) They will be shipped after November 25, 2014.
   (c) They will be shipped on November 25, 2014.
   (d) We can not determine with this e-mail.

2. Who will pay the freight for the goods?
   (a) Qtopia systems
   (b) EveryImport
   (c) Bank of America
   (d) can not determine

3. How many invoice(s) does the L/C require?
   (a) one copy
   (b) two copies
   (c) three copies
   (d) four copies

4. Upon receiving your confirmation we will _____ our bank to _________ an L/C in your ____.
   (a) open – instruct – favor
   (b) favor – open – instruct
   (c) open – favor – instruct
   (d) instruct – open – favor

5. 취소불능 신용장을 개설한 은행이 수익자에게 대금을 지급하기 위한 두 가지 전제조건을 올바르게 기술한 것을 고르시오.
   (A) provided all documents as stipulated in the Credit have been presented
   (B) when the goods as stipulated in the Credit have been delivered to the Applicant.
   (C) where all terms and conditions of the Credit are complied with
   (D) when the agreed settlement has been made by the Applicant against the presentation of the documents in order.
   (a) (A) and (B) only
   (b) (D) and (B) only
   (c) (C) and (D) only
   (d) (A) and (C) only

6. Banker's Irrevocable Letter of Credit shall be opened (   ) the Seller immediately upon contract and be maintained at least fifteen days after expiry date of shipment for negotiating of relative draft.

(a) on favor of
(b) on account of
(c) in favor of
(d) in account of

7. Choose most suitable one for bracket. [무역영어 2급]

Commercial risk arises from factors like the non-acceptance of goods by buyer. In order to prevent such a commercial risk, a bank is involved (   ) seller by way of issuing letter of credit.

(a) in favour of
(b) on behalf of
(c) for account of
(d) on account of

8. 다음 문장을 가장 적절하게 바꾼 것을 고르시오. [무역영어 2급]

We are very sorry. We didn't send you an email upon issuing the LC.

→ We are very sorry for (   ).

(a) not sending you an email upon issuing the LC.
(b) sending not you an email upon issuing the LC.
(c) didn't send you an email upon issuing the LC.
(d) didn't send an email to you upon issuing the LC.

9. Which of the following is NOT true according to the letter below?

[무역영어 2급]

I have completed and enclose your form for an irrevocable credit of $12,000USD to be opened with the Shinhan Bank, Seoul, in favor of Eletron Co., Seoul, for a consignment of home theater systems, the credit to be valid until September 30.

When the consignment is shipped the company will draw on the Shinhan Bank at 30 days after sight; the draft will be accompanied by bills of lading(3/3), invoice and certificate or policy of insurance.

(a) The importer wrote the letter instructing their Bank to open a letter of credit together with the Shinhan Bank in Seoul.

(b) An application form for documentary credit completed by the importer was included in the letter.

(c) After receiving this letter, the issuing bank will contact the advising bank in Seoul to notify the opening of credit.

(d) The exporter wrote the letter to instruct the bank in Seoul to open an irrevocable credit.

10. The followings are some standard elements of a trade process. Please put the sentences in the appropriate order. [무역영어 2급]

(A) All models can be supplied by the middle of January 2012, subject to our receiving your firm order by 15th November. Our C.I.F prices are understood to be for transport to Busan. If you would prefer the goods to be sent by air, there will be extra charges

(B) Please send us your latest catalogue, and quote your lowest prices for auto mobile tires. If your price meets our condition, we will consider commencing business with you. Please quote CIF Busan prices. Payment is normally made by letter of credit.

(C) We are glad to confirm our shipment yesterday. We have a pleasure in enclosing an invoice and non-negotiable copy of Bill of Landing covering our shipment.

(D) According to our contract, your orders are immediately ready for shipment. Thus we request you to open L/C covering your order.

(a) (A)-(B)-(D)-(C) (b) (B)-(A)-(D)-(C)

(c) (A)-(B)-(C)-(D) (d) (D)-(A)-(C)-(B)

11. Which of the following is NOT appropriate to fit in the blanks? [무역영어 2급]

We have a pleasure to ((a)) our order. We have ((b)) First Bank of America of New York, to ((c)) a Confirmed and Irrevocable Letter of Credit ((d)) for USD35,000.

(a) enclose (b) instructed (c) issue (d) in our favor

12. 신용장 개설을 통보하는 서신에서 영작이 잘못된 것을 고르시오.

[무역영어 2급]

(a) The L/C will be issued and (b) will cable to the Woori Bank, Korea, which is correspondent of our bank, and (c) you will be notified. We hope (d) you will execute the present order with your usual attention and promptness.

13. Which of the following is grammatically INCORRECT? [무역영어 2급]

<u>Regarding</u> your order No. XYZ-090721, we regret <u>informing</u> you that we have not been <u>informed</u> of any Letter of Credit <u>opening</u> from you.

(a) Regarding (b) informing (c) informed (d) opening

Situation 16

Q-pointer IIe 수출을 위한 신용장의 견본

Letter of Credit ①

Bank of America Higher Standards
1243 Sunrise Ave. LA, CA 93422
Tel. 923-234-3928 Fax. 923-234-3929

Gentlemen,
Without adding your confirmation, please advise the below referenced beneficiary of the following letter of credit details:

② Form of Documentary Credit	Irrevocable x123456
③ BOA reference	October 26, 2014
④ Issue date Date of expiry Place of expiry	November 25, 2014
⑤ Advised thru	Seoul
	Bank of America
	143 Changkyo-dong, Choong-ku Seoul
⑥ Beneficiary	100-220 Republic of Korea
	Qtopia systems Co., Inc.
	134 Seocho-dong, Seocho-ku, Seoul 130-070
⑦ For Account of	Republic of Korea
	EveryImport Co., Inc
	3434 Sunset Blvd
⑧ Currency / Amount	Los Angeles, CA 93456
⑨ Purchase terms	US$180,000 Not to Exceed CIF Los
⑩ Drafts Drawn on for At By	Angeles
	Bank of America, LA
⑪ Partial Shipments Transhipments	1.1 Percent of Invoice Value
	Sight Payment
	Prohibited Prohibited
⑫ Latest Shipment Date	November 20, 2014
⑬ Port of Loading Port of Destination	Incheon
	Los Angeles
⑭ Merchandise Description	10,000 units Q-pointer IIe

⑮ Drafts must be accompanied by the following documents:

1. Invoice in triplicate, signed and marked Licence No. PLDL 31-26.
2. Packing List
3. Full set of clean on board Shipping Company's B/L made out to our order and blank endorsed, marked 'Freight Paid' and EveryImport Inc, LA California.
4. Insurance Policy or Certificate in duplicate, covering War Risks up to buyer's warehouse, for invoice value of the goods plus 5%.

Relating to:

Drafts must be drawn and negotiated no later than November 25, 2014. Drafts drawn hereunder must be marked: "Drawn under the Bank of America Los Angeles Letter of Credit number x123456" and indicate the date hereof.

This Letter of Credit is subject to the uniform customs and practice for Documentary Credit (1993 Revision) International Chamber of Commerce Publication No. 500

Synopsis

Letter of Credit은 기능에 따라 다양한 종류와 형태가 있지만 일반적으로 Situation 13과 같은 내용으로 구성되어 있다. 이 신용장은 Q-pointer IIe 수입을 위하여 LA의 EveryImport의 거래은행인 Bank of America가 Qtopia systems를 수익자로 하여 발행한 신용장이다. 다음은 각 항목에 대한 설명이다.

① 개설은행(issuing bank): 수입상의 거래은행으로서 수입상의 요청으로 신용장을 개설한 은행이다. 수출상 또는 수출상으로부터 선적서류를 양도받은 매입은행 등에게 신용장대금을 지급해야 할 의무를 부담하는 은행이다.

② 신용장의 종류: irrevocable L/C, 즉 취소불능신용장임을 나타내고 있다.

③ 신용장번호: 이 번호는 B/E, B/L, invoice 등 shipping document에 명시된다.

④ 신용장 개설일자 및 유효기일(date of issue and expiry): 개설은행은 개설일자로부터 신용장의 유효기일까지만 수출상에게 지급확약을 하고 있다. 따라서 수출상은 신용자의 유효기일 전에 선적을 마치고 유효기일까지는 관련 선적서류를 첨부한 환어음을 제출하여야만 수출대금을 받을 수 있다. 이 신용장의 아래 부분에 'Drafts must be drawn and negotiated no later than November 25, 2014'이라고 다시 한번 신용장의 유효기일을 밝히고 있다.

⑤ 통지은행(advising bank): 개설은행의 지시 및 전달사항을 수출상에게 전달할 의무를 진 수출국의 은행이다. 보통 수출국에 있는 개설은행의 본·지점이나 환거래은행 이 통지은행이 된다.

⑥ 수익자(beneficiary): 신용장 상에 표기된 선적서류를 제시하고 대금을 수령하는 수출상으로서 신용장에 표기된 물품을 공급할 의무를 부담하는 자를 말한다. 신용장이 개설되면 가장 큰 혜택(benefit)을 받는 당사자가 수출상이기 때문에 수익자라고 부른다.

⑦ 개설의뢰인(applicant): 신용장의 개설을 신청하는 수입상으로 개설은행에게 신용장대금을 결제해야 하는 의무를 부담한다. 보통 'for account of'의 다음에 상호와 주소가 기재된다.

⑧ 신용장금액: 신용장에 의하여 발행되는 환어음의 발행 한도액이다. 즉, 수출상이 수출대금으로 청구할 수 있는 최대의 금액이다. 금액표시 앞에는 통화표시를 해야 한다. 특히 $를 표시통화로 하는 국가가 많으므로 US$, CD$ HK$ 등으로 분명하게 표시되어야 한다.

⑨ 가격조건: CIF LA 등으로 표시한다. 여기에서 LA는 도착항을 의미한다. FOB 조건의 경우는 선적항을 표시하여 FOB Incheon과 같이 기재한다.

⑩ 환어음(draft) 관련 사항: 수출상이 수출대금의 청구를 위하여 발행한 환어음을 매입하여 대금을 지급하는 은행을 지급은행(paying bank)이라고 한다. 여기에서는 통지은행인 Bank of America의 서울 지점이 지급은행의 역할을 하고 있다. 'at sight'로 표시되어 있어서 일람출급어음(sight bill)이 발행된다. 이 경우 수출상은 어음의 매입과 동시에 수출대금을 지급 받을 수 있다. 이와는 달리 'at 30 days after sight' 등으로 표시되어 있다면 이는 기한부어음(usance bill)을 의미하고 수출상은 어음매입 후 30일이 지나서야 수출

Letters of Credit are an important financial vehicle in today's global economy.

대금을 회수할 수 있다. 이러한 기한부어음을 인수하는 은행을 인수은행(accepting bank)이라고 한다. 환어음에 표시되는 금액은 보통 송장금액과 일치하기 때문에 'for 100% of invoice value 또는 for full invoice value' 등으로 표시한다.

⑪ 분할선적(partial shipment) 및 환적(transshipment): 이 L/C의 경우 'prohibited'라고 명시되어 분할선적 및 환적을 허용하지 않고 있다. 이러한 표시가 없거나 'allowed'나 'permitted' 등의 표시가 있으면 분할선적 및 환적이 허용된다.

⑫ 선적기일(latest shipment date): 선적일의 기준은 선적서류의 발행일자 또는 선적이나 발송을 증명하는 접수인의 일자이다. 선적기일이 표시되어 있지 않으면 신용장의 유효기일까지 선적해야 한다.

⑬ 선적항 및 도착항(port of loading and destination): 복합운송의 경우는 선적지나 목적지가 기재되고 해상운송의 경우는 선적항이나 도착항이 표시된다.

⑭ 물품의 명세(merchandise description): 선적한 물품의 명세로 매매계약과 일치하여야 하고 이것은 다시 송장의 내용과도 일치하여야 한다.

⑮ 선적서류: 환어음을 매입시킬 때 선적의 증거나 수입상의 요청으로 매매계약서상에 명시되어 있는 서류들이다. 이 신용장의 경우, 상업송장, 포장명세서, 보험증서, 무사고선하증권을 요구하고 있다.

◈ L/C의 종류

Irrevocable L/C

Under Irrevocable L/C terms, L/C cannot be cancelled or withdrawn after is has been opened and notified to the exporter(who is the beneficiary of L/C) as long as there is no agreement on cancellation or withdrawal among the applicant of L/C, opening bank and the beneficiary.

취소불능신용장(irrevocable L/C)은 issuing bank가 L/C에 따라 발행한 어음을 인수할 의무를 지며 일방적으로 취소(revoke)할 수 없고 특히 수출상을 포함한 모든 당사자들의 동의 없이 수정할 수 없다.

Confirmed L/C

The confirmed L/C is the one which is confirmed and guaranteed by a third party bank for the payment in the event that the opening bank becomes bankrupt. The exporter can be assured of a safe transaction if the L/C is confirmed by a leading bank.

확인신용장(confirmed L/C)이란 개설은행 이외의 제3의 은행(confirming bank)이 issuing bank의 요청에 의하여 수익자, 즉 수출상이 발행한 어음의 지급, 인수 또는 매입을 약정한 L/C를 말하며, 그런 경우 두 은행 모두 L/C에 따라 발행한 어음을 인수할 의무가 있다.

Sight L/C and Usance or Acceptance L/C

If the L/C terms demand that the Bill of Exchange drawn by the exporter is the type which requires the importer to pay at sight, i.e. when the bill is presented to him by the paying bank, L/C with such terms is called Sight L/C. On the other hand, the L/C which has terms allowing the importer a deferred payment is called Usance or Acceptance L/C.

일람출급신용장(sight L/C)은 신용장에 의해서 발행되는 어음이 일람출급어음(sight draft)인 경우를 말하며 환어음상 지급인을 개설은행으로 한다. 취소불능신용장인 경우에는 개설은행이 지급을 확약한 것이므로 신용장조건에 일치하는 서류를 제시하기만 하면 개설은행은 즉시 대금을 지급을 해야 한다. 기한부신용장(Usance or Acceptance L/C)은 기한부어음의 발행을 요구하는 신용장이며 기한부신용장의 수익자는 일정기간 후에 어음금액의 전액을 지급 받든지 또는 그 기간 동안의 이자를 사전에 할인하여 지급 받을 수 있다. 수입상은 화물을 인수한 후 어음의 유예기간 동안에 수입물품을 매각하여 어음의 만기가 도래하면 상환할 수 있다.

Restricted L/C and General or Open L/C

Under the terms of a Restricted L/C(sometimes called special L/C), only a specific bank which is usually the notifying bank can purchase a bill of exchange from the exporter. However, under the terms of a General or Open L/C, the purchasing bank is not specified, hence the exporter can present the bill of exchange to any bank and receive payment.

특정신용장(restricted or special L/C)은 신용장상의 수익자가 선적을 완료한 후 발행하는 환어음의 매입은행을 특정은행으로 한정하고 있는 신용장이며, 매입제한신용장이라고도 한다. 보통신용장(general or open L/C)은 어음매입을 특정 은행으로 제한하지 않고 아무 은행에서나 자유롭게 할 수 있도록 되어 있는 신용장이다.

Non-transferable L/C and Transferable L/C

The beneficiary(exporter) can transfer the Transferable L/C to a third party, but he is unable to do this with the Non-transferable L/C.

양도가능신용장(transferable L/C)은 수익자가 신용장 금액의 전부 또는 일부를 제3자에게 양도할 수 있는 권한을 부여받은 신용장을 말하고, 수익자가 신용장을 제3자에게 양도할 수 없는 신용장을 양도불능신용장(non-transferable L/C)이라 한다.

신용장은 본래 양도가 불가능한 증서이므로 'transferable'이란 문구가 신용장 상에 명기되지 않으면 양도불능신용장이다. 양도는 지급, 인수 또는 매입을 행하도록 수권받은 은행만이 할 수 있고 양도은행이 합의한 범위와 방법에 의해서만 양도될 수 있다.

Negotiation L/C and Straight L/C

Negotiation L/C refers to a credit where the issuer expressly indicates the credit is available by negotiation, or where its issuer's obligation extends to its drawers, endorsers, and bona fide holder for value for drafts drawn under it. Straight L/C refers to a credit that requires drafts to be presented to a specific party such at the issuing bank or more often at the advising bank.

매입신용장(negotiation L/C)이란 발행자가 신용장에 의하여 발행되는 어음에 대하여 명시적으로 지급하겠다는 신용장을 말한다. 발행자의 지급의무는 어음의 발행인(drawer), 배서인(endorser) 및 선의의 소지인(bona fide holder) 모두에게 있다. 지급신용장(straight L/C)은 신용장 개설은행 혹은 주로 통지은행 앞으로 어음이 발행되어 제시되면 지급하겠다는 약정을 하는 신용장이다.

◈ L/C와 UCP

신용장거래에서는 수출상과 수입상 사이에 은행이 개입되기 때문에 상호간의 권리와 의무를 규정하여 둘 필요가 있다. 더욱이 법률체계가 다른 국가 간의 거래에 쓰이는 신용장의 경우 준거법의 필요성이 제기되어 왔다. 이에 따라 1933년 국제상업회의소에서 처음으로 신용장 통일규칙(UCP 600: Uniform Customs and Practice for Documentary Credit)을 제정한 이래 현재는 2007년에 개정된 제6차 통일규칙을 사용하고 있다. 이 규칙은 신용장의 기본원리와 각 당사자 간의 권리와 의무를 규정하고 있다.

L/C의 독립성

신용장은 매매계약에 근거하여 개설되는 것이지만, 일단 신용장이 개설되면 신용장은 매매계약으로부터 독립되어(UCP 600, 제4조) 그 자체로서 별도의 법률관계를 형성한다. 이를 신용장 통일규칙 제4조에서는 다음과 같이 규정하고 있다.

"Credits, by their nature, are separate transactions from the sales or other contract(s) on which they may be based and banks are in no way concerned with or bound by such contract(s), …."

따라서 수입상은 신용장조건과 매매계약조건이 서로 다르다는 점을 이유로 대금지급을 지연 또는 취소할 수 없으며, 매매계약이 취소되었다 할지라도 신용장 조건대로 이행한 수출상은 신용장의 독립성에 의해 보호를 받을 수 있다.

L/C의 추상성

신용장거래에 있어서 모든 관계 당사자는 서류상의 거래를 하는 것이지 그러한 서류들이 관련되어 있는 상품, 용역 또는 계약이행상의 거래를 하는 것이 아니다. 따라서 신용장 거래에서 수출상이 물품을 선적하고 신용장에서 요구하는 서류를 제시하면 은행은 그 서류만을 가지고 수리 여부를 판단한다. 그 이유는 신용장거래에 개입한 은행은 물품거래의 당사자가 아니므로 은행은 매매당사자 간의 매매목적물인 물품에 대하여 알 수가 없기 때문이다.

따라서 신용장을 받은 수출상은 개설된 신용장이 매매계약서에 있는 내용과 일치하는지를 확인하여 불일치(discrepancy)가 발견되면 즉시 은행을 통하여 신용장의 정정을 요구하여야 한다. 또한 신용장에서 요구한 선적서류상의 조건과 신용장의 조건에 불일치가 있으면 은행에서 환어음의 매입을 거절하게 되므로 반드시 일치된 서류를 제출하여야 한다.

L/C의 한계

신용장은 국제거래를 촉진시켜 주는 수단이지만, 신용장이 개설되었다고 모든 것이 다 원만하게 해결되는 것은 아니다. 다시 말해서 신용장도 이행할 수 없는 몇 가지 제한과 제약점들이 있다.

첫째, 신용장은 하나의 독립된 지급수단이 될 수 없다는 점이다. 신용장은 계약의 성질을 지니고 있는 것이기 때문에 특정 조건에 부합하는 제반 서류를 지정된 기일 내에 제시하면 지불하겠다는 은행의 약속증서이지 그 자체가 유통될 수 있는 어음과 같은 수단은

아니다.

둘째, 신용장거래가 반드시 계약상품이 인수된다고 보장하지 않는다는 점이다. 신용장의 거래는 어디까지나 서류상의 거래이기 때문에 서류상으로만 신용장의 조건을 충족시키면 은행은 대금지불을 하게 되나, 서류의 작성자가 성실하지 못한 경우에 나쁜 물품을 선적하고 서류만 신용장 내용대로 작성하여 제시하여도 대금을 지급해야 한다.

Practice Tests - Situation 16

1. Based on the L/C in Situation 16 who is the beneficiary?
   (a) Bank of America
   (b) Qtopia systems
   (c) EveryImport Co.
   (d) can not determine

2. According to the L/C when the shipment should be made?
   (a) by October 26, 2014
   (b) by November 20, 2014
   (c) within 15 days from October 26, 2014
   (d) within 15 days from November 20, 2014

3. Is the L/C confirmed L/C?
   (a) Yes
   (b) No
   (c) it depends on advising bank
   (d) can not determine

4. Under this L/C what type of draft(bill of exchange) will be issued?
   (a) at sight draft
   (b) term draft
   (c) plain draft
   (d) 60 days after sight draft

5. Choose the document not required under this L/C.
   (a) packing list
   (b) B/L
   (c) insurance certificate
   (d) certificate of origin

6. Based on the information in this L/C who will pay the insurance premium?
   (a) Bank of America, Incheon
   (b) Bank of America, LA
   (c) Qtopia systems
   (d) EveryImport Co.

7. Based on the information in this L/C who will pay the ocean freight?
   (a) Bank of America, Incheon
   (b) Bank of America, LA
   (c) Qtopia systems
   (d) EveryImport Co.

8. What are the ports of loading and unloading, respectively?

(a) Incheon – L/A (b) L/A – Incheon

(c) Incheon – New York (d) L/A – New York

9. 다음 빈 칸에 들어갈 적절한 말끼리 연결된 것을 고르시오. [무역영어 2급]

( ) shipments are permitted. ( ) is not permitted.

All drafts, drawn hereunder must state the number, date, and name of establishing bank of this ( ).

The amount and date of payment/acceptance/negotiation of each draft must be ( ) on the reverse there of.

(a) Multimodal – Throughtransportation – L/C – specified

(b) Partial – Transshipment – credit – endorsed

(c) Multimodal – Transshipment – L/C – specified

(d) Partial – Transshipment – invoice – written

10. 다음 빈 칸에 들어갈 적절한 말을 고르시오. [무역영어 2급]

Documentary Credits are a preferred method of payment in comparison to Advance Payment/Open Account /Documentary Collections due to: ( )

(a) comfort provided by the independent undertakings of banks.

(b) opportunity for the buyers to examine the goods before payment.

(c) no credit risk to the buyer with full cash cover.

(d) presentation of documents through the channel of banks.

11. 다음 중 다른 문장과 성격이 다른 것을 고르시오. [무역영어 2급]

(a) We are informed that the original of this credit had been forwarded directly to you.

(b) We would ask you to establish an irrevocable letter of credit in our favor.

(c) They have informed of advising L/C to you.

(d) We are notified by Korea Bank that they have issued a credit.

[12~13] 다음 신용장 개설은행 변경요청 서신을 보고 물음에 답하시오. [무역영어 2급]

ⓐ We thankfully received your fax of today regarding the shipment of the Water Valve.

ⓑ We would like to advise that the banks in Korea hardly purchase L/C opened by Indonesian banks due to the present financial situation of Indonesia.

ⓒ We have contacted many times and have made every effort to persuade them. But, it was out of our control.

ⓓ So, we kindly ask you to change L/C opening bank which should be an international first class bank or change payment terms to T/T remittance basis.

12. Please put the sentences in the correct order.

(a) ⓑ-ⓐ-ⓒ-ⓓ (b) ⓐ-ⓑ-ⓒ-ⓓ
(c) ⓑ-ⓐ-ⓓ-ⓒ (d) ⓑ-ⓒ-ⓓ-ⓐ

13. 밑줄 친 purchase 부분을 고려하였을 때 위 서신에서 언급되고 있는 신용장의 종류를 고르시오.

(a) negotiation L/C (b) payment L/C
(c) acceptance L/C (d) confirm L/C

[14~16] Read the following and answer the questions. [무역영어 2급]

ⓐ We are happy to inform you of our shipment covering your order No. ACE-2301 for US$50,000. After shipment, the documents have been submitted to Woori Bank, Seoul branch ⓑ where the L/C is limited for negotiation. Your kind cooperation for timely payment would be appreciated.

14. What is the main purpose of the letter?

(a) To request shipment (b) To request issuance of L/C
(c) To draw attention on payment (d) To request negotiation

15. 밑줄 친 ⓐ We와 같은 이를 나타내는 단어가 아닌 것을 고르시오.

(a) Drawer (b) Seller

(c) Beneficiary (d) Debtor

16. 밑줄 친 ⓑ를 참고로 하여 두 당사자 간의 거래에 사용되는 신용장의 종류를 고르시오.

(a) Open L/C (b) Restricted L/C

(c) General L/C (d) Freely negotiable L/C

Situation 17

Q-pointer IIe의 선적을 EveryImport에 통보하다.

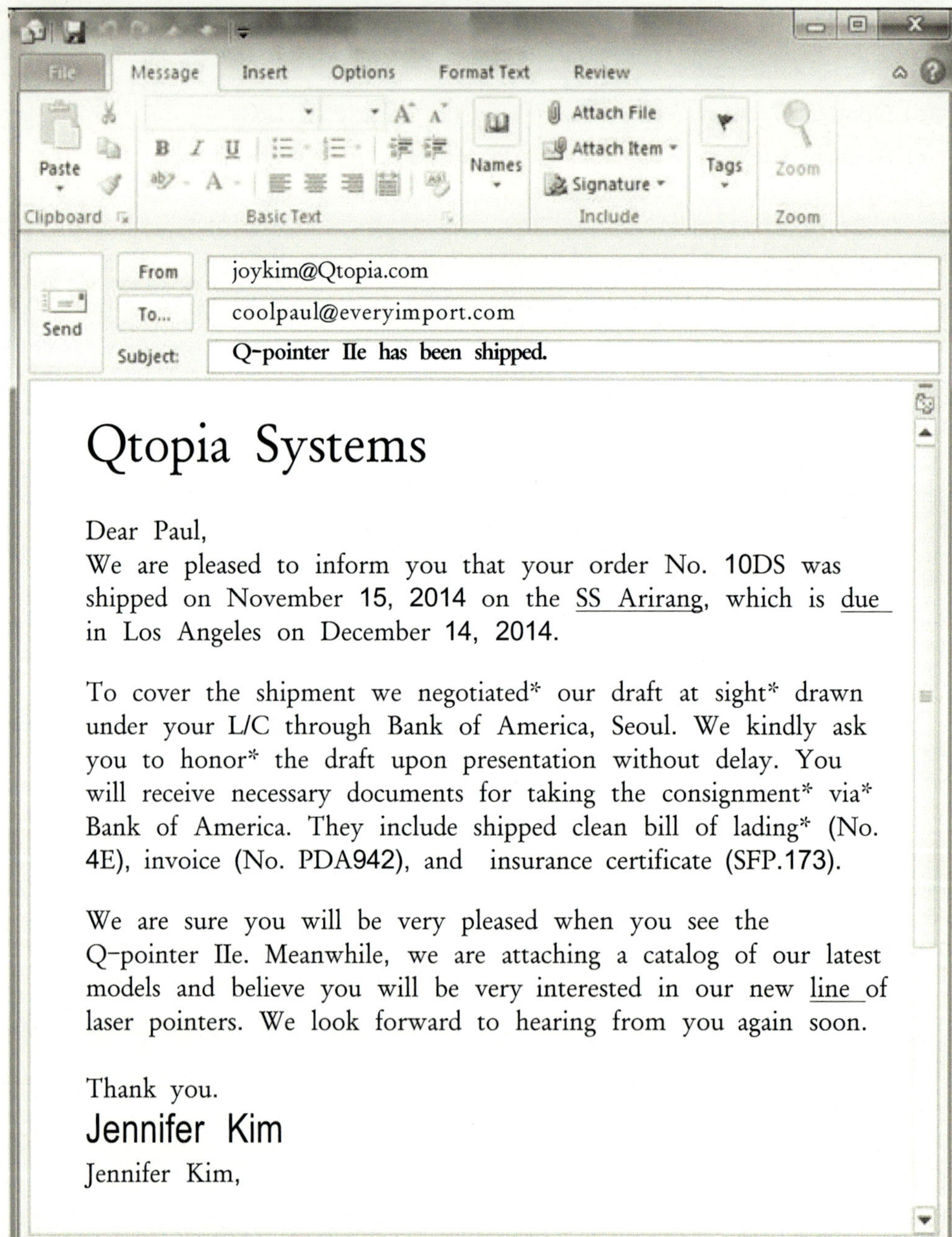

Qtopia Systems

Dear Paul,
We are pleased to inform you that your order No. 10DS was shipped on November 15, 2014 on the SS Arirang, which is due in Los Angeles on December 14, 2014.

To cover the shipment we negotiated* our draft at sight* drawn under your L/C through Bank of America, Seoul. We kindly ask you to honor* the draft upon presentation without delay. You will receive necessary documents for taking the consignment* via* Bank of America. They include shipped clean bill of lading* (No. 4E), invoice (No. PDA942), and insurance certificate (SFP.173).

We are sure you will be very pleased when you see the Q-pointer IIe. Meanwhile, we are attaching a catalog of our latest models and believe you will be very interested in our new line of laser pointers. We look forward to hearing from you again soon.

Thank you.
Jennifer Kim
Jennifer Kim,

Synopsis

Qtopia는 EveryImport에서 보내준 주문서에 따라 Q-pointer IIe 10,000대를 12월 14일에 LA에 도착예정(due in LA)인 Arirang호에 선적을 완료했음을 통보하고 있다. 그리고 서울에 있는 Bank of America에 신용장에 따라 발행된 어음(drawn under your L/C)을 매입(negotiate)하여 대금을 회수하였으니까 어음이 제시되면 수리(honor)해달라고 요구하고 있다. 또한 L/C issuing bank인 Bank of America를 통하여 consignment를 찾는데 필요한 선적 서류들(선적선하증권, 인보이스, 그리고 보험서류)을 입수할 수 있을 것이라고 밝히고 있다. Q-pointer IIe를 받아보면 만족할 것임을 확신한다는 말과 새로운 제품에 대한 catalog를 첨부하여 지속적인 거래관계 유지를 위한 필요한 조치를 취하고 있다.

*negotiate v.
① 협상하다.
② [상업] (어음 등을) 매입하다. 현금으로 바꾸다.

*at sight: 보자마자, [상업] 제시하자 마자, 일람불(一覽拂)의
수출대금의 지급이 어음의 제시 즉시 이루어지는 경우의 어음을 draft at sight 혹은 sight bill이라 부른다. 이와는 반대로 어음 제시 후 일정기간이 지난 후에 대금의 지급이 이루어지는 방식을 usance bill(기한부어음)이라고 한다.

*honor n. v.
① 예우하다. 존중하다.
② [상업] (어음 등을) 인수하여(기일에) 지불하다.

*consignment [kənsainmənt] n.
① 선박, 항공기, 트럭 등의 운송수단에 적재된 화물이라는 의미의 적재화물, 위탁판매물.
② 위탁판매물. consignment sale: 위탁판매, consignment trade: 위탁판매무역 v. consign: 위탁하다. 위임하다. (위탁판매를 위하여) 발송하다. 탁송하다.

*via [vaiə, vi:ə]
(어떤 장소를) 경유하여, ~을 통하여, via Dubai: 두바이를 경유하여, via email: 이메일로

*lading [leidiŋ] n.
화물, 적재, 선적 v. lade: 싣다(load). (배, 열차 등에) 싣다. bill of lading: 선하증권

SS Arirang

선박을 표시할 때 선박 이름 앞에 보통,

SS: Steam Ship(스팀을 동력으로 사용하는 선박, 증기터빈과 같이)
MV, MS: Motor Vessel, Motor Ship(엔진으로 추진하는 선박)
MT: Motor Tanker(엔진으로 추진하는 탱커선)
TS: Turbo Ship(turbo 엔진이 장착된 선박)
CS: Container ship(컨테이너 선박)

RV: Research Vessel(조사선)
IB: Ice-Breaker(극지방에서 얼음을 깨는데 쓰는 쇄빙선)
USS: United States Ship(미국해군 함정)
HMS: His Majesty's Ship(영국해군 함정)

등을 붙인다. 이것은 동력원을 나타내면서 선박의 종류를 표현하기도 하지만 꼭 정해진 것은 아니다. 예를 들면, 엔진으로 추진하는 선박에 SS를 쓰기도 하고 탱커선에 MV를 붙이는 경우도 있다. 붙이는 형식은 SS, ss, M/S, m/s, c.s. R.V. 모두 가능하다. Steam Ship은 현재는 운항되지 않지만 옛날의 흔적으로 사용된다.

due

due는 다음과 같은 여러 가지 의미로 사용된다.

① 지급 기일이 된, 만기(滿期)가 된. [cf.] overdue 지급기일이 지난
② (선박·열차·비행기 따위가) 도착 예정인, 출산 예정인
③ '~ to do의 형태로' ~할 예정인, ~하기로 되어 있는.
④ (돈·보수·고려 따위가) 응당 치러져야 할.
⑤ 마땅한, 적당한, 당연한, 합당한. [opp] undue: 불필요한, 부당한
⑥ '~ to의 형식으로' ~에 기인하는, ~의 탓으로 돌려야 할.

- The bill is due today. [cf] The bill is already overdue. ①
- The ship is due on May 10. • When is your baby due? ②
- The time capsule is due to open today. ③
- The money is due to Thomas. ④

- We have a due margin for delay. [opp] Do not put undue pressure on her. ⑤
- The failure is due to his ignorance. ⑥

due는 또 명사로 쓰여서 복수형 dues의 형태로 duties(지급금, 부과금, 회비, 요금, 수수료, 임금)의 의미로 쓰인다.

- Subject to the following conditions, a non-Federal interest may levy harbor dues.
  (다음과 같은 조항에 근거하여 비연방 주체가 항구세를 부과할 수 있다.)

line

Business English에서 line은 업종, 품목을 말할 때 쓰인다. 본문에서처럼 new line of laser pointers 하면, '새로운 레이저 포인터 취급품목'을 의미한다. line of business는 사업 분야, line of products(or goods)는 취급품목을 의미한다.

- Are you interested in this line of business?(이 사업에 관심 있나요?)
- I will send further particulars of our special line.

line은 또 line of credit(= credit limit)의 의미로도 쓰인다.

- To extend the line of credit you may need future orders.

선박회사 혹은 항공회사를 말할 때에도 line을 써서 a shipping line(선박회사), a bus line(버스회사)으로 표현하고, 구어체에서 '직업, 하는 일'의 의미로도 쓰인다.

- What line of business are you in? (무슨 일에 종사하시나요?)
- What your line?
- I am in the vacuum cleaner line. (진공청소기 사업을 하고 있습니다.)

Practice Tests - Situation 17

1. What will mostly NOT happen after Paul receives this letter?
   (a) Paul will obtain necessary documents to take the consignment.
   (b) Paul will honor the draft.
   (c) Paul will examine the catalog of the latest models.
   (d) Paul will visit Bank of America to negotiate the draft.

2. Where is the Bank of America in paragraph 3 located?
   (a) Seoul (b) Incheon
   (c) Los Angeles (d) New York

3. Our site has information about ________ charged by harbor operator.
   (a) due (b) dues
   (c) charge (d) charges

4. Novelty Products Inc. plans to release a new ______ of flavored toothpicks, including mint, coffee, and lemon.
   (a) business (b) producer
   (c) line (d) commerce
   of flavored toothpicks,

5. Put the sentences above in good order. [무역영어 2급]
   Dear Import Manager,
   (A) We have shipped 10,000 sets of mobile phone by KE612, which is scheduled to depart at Incheon International Airport on 2 PM, 15 April.
   (B) With regard to your e-mail of 15 Mar, we are pleased to inform that:
   (C) We hope that the goods will reach you on time and please make it sure that the goods are acceptable to you within 10 days of arrival.
   (D) As requested, copy of Airway Bill, commercial invoice and packing list will be sent to you upon the shipment.

Sincerely yours,

Sangong Corporation

(a) (A)–(B)–(D)–(C) (b) (A)–(B)–(C)–(D)

(c) (B)–(C)–(A)–(D) (d) (B)–(A)–(D)–(C)

6. What is the main purpose of this letter? [무역영어 2급]

The terms of the credit authorize you to draw at 30 days after sight on the bank in London for the amount of your invoice after each shipment of one container. Before accepting the draft, the bank will require you to produce the following documents: one copy of bills of lading, one copy of the invoice of covering CIF London, a certificate or policy of insurance and certificate of origin. We will expect your first consignment around the middle of next month.

(a) Suspension of payment
(b) Refusal of documentary bill
(c) Notification of documentary credit
(d) Request to a bank to forward a bill

7. What is the purpose of the following letter? [무역영어 2급]

As you know, PENTAX is required to submit all documents and drawings per clause 8.2 Form A of the contract. However, many documents are past due and have not been submitted and approved yet. In addition, the 'For Construction' issue of the Datasheet, Calculation Sheet and Outline Dimension & Service Detail Drawings have not been submitted. PENTAX's submittal delays are impacting our engineering schedule and may be adversely affecting construction. Please advise by return fax when these documents will be submitted.

(a) to instruct PENTAX to send overdue documents
(b) to request PENTAX to give the details of many documents
(c) to order PENTAX to change the engineering schedule
(d) to require PENTAX to fax all the documents

8. Which is most correct according to the following? [무역영어 2급]

We are pleased to inform you that your order No.1555, has been shipped on 05

March on the SS EverMore Asia which is due in Jakarta in 20 days.

(a) The carrier will accept the cargo in 20 days.
(b) The buyer have arranged the shipment.
(c) The seller informs the shipment to a carrier.
(d) The ship may arrive at Jakarta on 25 March.

9. Which of the following is most suitable for the blanks (A) and (B)?

[무역영어 2급]

Against this shipment, we have drawn a draft (A) BMB Bank, London at sight for USD90,000 under the terms of letter of credit (B) the ANA Bank, Seoul.

(a) at – to
(b) to – through
(c) on – through
(d) for – to

10. Which of the following is grammatically INCORRECT? [무역영어 2급, 2012]

We (a) are pleased to advise that your order (b) has been shipped by the S.S. Venus (c) which is (d) due on sail from Busan to Hongkong.

11. 다음 글을 읽고 내용의 흐름상 어색한 것을 고르시오. [무역영어 2급]

Dear Mr. Keton:

Subject: Copies of Instructional software

Thank you for order No.PB0211 included with your letter of October 14.

(a) Enclosed is Pro Forma Invoice F91-131 for $2,000,000.
(b) Payment by bank draft will insure quick delivery.
(c) We sometimes have problems owing to the delay of shipment.
(d) The software will be dispatched immediately on receipt of your payment.

Thank you for giving us this opportunity to be of service.

[12~13] Answer the following questions [무역영어 2급]

a) We have enclosed a simplified financial statement form for your convenience.

b) Thank you again for your order, and we are looking forward to a long and mutually rewarding business relationship.

c) To enable us to extend the line of credit you may need for future orders, will you send us the usual credit information?

d) It was with great pleasure that we received your recent order which was entered for immediate shipment at our regular 30 day terms.

12. Please put the following sentences in order.

(a) c–a–b–d (b) d–c–a–b

(c) a–c–d–b (d) c–d–b–a

13. What is a similar expression for 'line of credit'?

(a) credit limit (b) letter of credit

(c) credit package (d) credit note

14. Which of the following is MOST likely to appear right AFTER the passage? [무역영어 1급]

The next project group meeting will be held at our office on May 11. The proposed agenda is as follows:

Agenda:

a) Manning requirements to September 2013

b) Expenditures to September

c) A farewell party for Mr. Keller

(a) I greatly appreciate your concern for my attendance at this honorable meeting.

(b) It would be appreciated if you would confirm at your earliest convenience whether you will be able to attend this meeting.

(c) I am sorry to report that completing the minutes of the project meeting last week will take a little longer than I thought.

(d) In closing, I would again like to thank you for your understanding and for the great efforts you made to accommodate my schedule.

Situation 18

Q-pointer IIe의 선적을 마치고 선박회사가 발행한 Bill of Lading

① **Shipper** *Qtopia systems Co. Inc.* *134 Seocho-dong Seocho-ku* *Seoul, 130-070 Korea*	**K.S. LINE** **Korea Shipping Corporation**
② **Consignee** *to order of Bank of America*	**COMBINED TRANSPORT BILL OF LADING** RECEIVED in good apparent good order and condition except as otherwise noted the number of Containers or other packages or units enumerated below for transportation from the place of delivery subject to the terms hereof. One of the original Bills of Lading must be surrendered duly endorsed in exchange for the Goods of delivery Order. On Presentation of this document (duly endorsed) to the Carrier by or on behalf of the Holder, the rights and liabilities arising in accordance with the terms hereof shall (without prejudice to any rule of common law or statute rendering them binding on the Merchant) become binding in all respects between the Carrier and the Holder as though the contract evidenced hereby had been made between them.
③ **Notify Party** *EveryImport Co. Inc.* *3434 Sunset Boulevard* *LA, California 93456*	

④ **Pre-Carriage by**	⑤ **Place of Receipt**
pre-carriage trucker	*Incheon, CY*

⑥ **Ocean Vessel**	⑦ **Voyage No.**	⑧ **Port of Loading**	⑨ **B/L No.**
Arirang	*02W*	[illegible]	[illegible]

⑩ **Port of Discharge**	⑪ **Place of Delivery**	⑫ **Final destination**
Los Angeles, USA	*Los Angeles, CY*	*Los Angeles, USA*

⑬ **Container No.**	⑭ **Seal No. Mark**	⑮ **No. of Pkgs Container**	⑯ **Description of Goods**	⑰ **Gross Weigh**	⑱ **Measurement**
[illegible]	*EImport* *Los Angeles* *C/S No.1-200* *Made in Korea*	*(RF)40'×2* *200CTNs*	*10,000 Q-pointer le Laser Pointer*	*1,750KGs*	*91,500CBM*

⑲ **Total No. of Containers or Packages(in word)** *two hundred cartons only*

⑳ **Freight Prepaid at**	**Freight Payable at**	**Place Issue**
Incheon, Korea		*Incheon, Korea*
Total Prepaid	**No. of Original B/L**	**Date of Issue**
USD17,000.00		*November 15, 2014*

IN WITNESS whereof the number of original Bills of Lading stated below have been signed, one of which being accomplished, the other(s) to be void.

Shipped on Board

Date *November 15, 2014*

By Smith Captain

Korea Shipping Corporation

◈ Bill of Lading(B/L)의 개념

선적을 마치게 되면 선박회사는 하주에게 선하증권(bill of lading: B/L)을 발행한다. 이 선하증권은 선박회사가 하주로부터 위탁받은 화물을 선적하였거나 또는 선적을 하기 위하여 화물을 받은 사실을 증명해주는 수령증(a receipt)이며, 증권의 소지자에게 해당 물품의 소유권이 있음을 나타내는 권리증서(a document of title)이다. 또한 하주와 선박회사간의 해상운송계약이 체결되었음을 증명하는 서류(an evidence of contract of carriage)이다.

이러한 선하증권은 선적화물을 대표하는 증서이고 인도나 배서(endorsement)에 의해 전매될 수 있는 유통성(negotiable) 유가증권이므로 이 증권을 소지하고 있다는 것은 선적화물 그 자체를 소유하고 있는 것과 동일하다. 해상운송에서는 일반적으로 선하증권이 화물보다 먼저 수입상에게 전달되기 때문에 선하증권의 전매를 통하여 상품의 매매가 가능하도록 유통성 유가증권으로 발행하는 것이다. 선하증권은 발행하는 선박회사에 따라 여러 가지가 있으며 최근에는 기존의 종이서류를 대신하여 EDI를 이용한 전자식 선하증권(electronic B/L)의 이용도 늘어나고 있다.

Situation 18의 선하증권은 Qtopia systems가 Q-pointer IIe의 선적을 마치고 선박회사로부터 발급 받은 B/L이다. 다음은 이에 대한 설명이다.

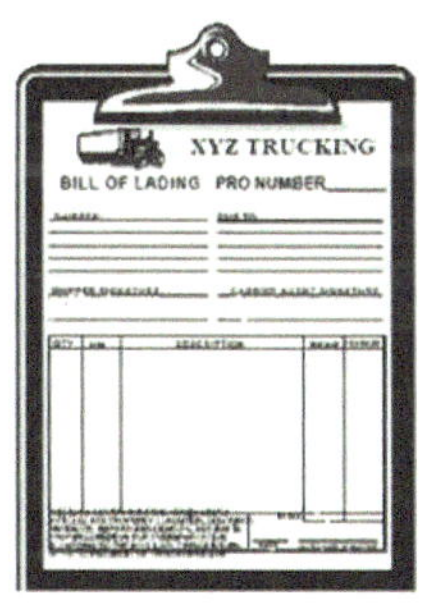

① Shipper: 화물을 보내는 회사명, 주소를 적는다.

② Consignee: 화물 수취인. 신용장을 사용할 경우 보통 수취인은 지정되지 않고 그냥 to order 혹은 to the order of (name of bank)만 쓴다. 신용장의 대금을 개설의뢰인, 즉 수입업자가 지불할 때까지는 선하증권과 화물의 소유주는 은행으로 되어있고, 그 은행은 수입업자가 대금의 미지급 시 화물을 임의로 처리할 수 있는 권리를 가지고 있다. 그런데 수취인이 지정되어 있다면 은행으로서는 임의로 처분할 수 있는 권리가 없어지므로 이와 같이 표시하게 한다. 그러나 신용장 거래가 아닌 추심이나 전신환(T/T) 방식에 의한 거래의 경우에는 consignee란에 수입업자가 기재된다.

③ Notify Party: 통지선, 수입업자 또는 수입업자가 지정하는 대리인(화물도착시 연락처)이 기재된다.

④ Pre-Carriage By: 복합운송의 경우 육상, 해상, 항공 중 적어도 두 가지 이상의 다른 운송방법에 의해 일관 수송되게 된다. 이때 주운송의 전 단계에서 물품을

운송한 운송수단을 Pre-Carriage By란에 기재한다. 주로 컨테이너 화물에 사용되며 pre carry by truck 혹은 pre-carriage train과 같이 기재한다.

⑤ Place of Receipt: 화물을 보내는 측으로부터 운송회사가 화물을 인도 받은 장소를 말한다. Incheon CY[1] 혹은 Busan CFS[2] 등으로 기재된다.

⑥ Ocean Vessel: 화물을 수송하는 선박명

⑦ Voyage No.: 운송회사나 선박회사가 임의로 정한 일련번호

⑧ Port of Loading: 화물이 선적된 항구명 및 국명

⑨ B/L No.: 선박회사가 임의로 정한 B/L의 일련번호

⑩ Port of Discharge: 화물이 하역되는 항구명 및 국명

⑪ Place of Delivery: 운송인이 책임지고 운송하여 수하인에게 인도하여 주는 장소

⑫ Final destination: 화물의 최종 목적지. 복합운송이 아닌 경우 기재되지 않는 경우가 많다.

⑬ Container No.: 화물이 적재되는 container 번호를 기재한다.

⑭ Seal No. & Marks: container에 적재된 화물에 봉인을 한 seal 번호와 화인(mark)을 기재한다.

⑮ No. of Pkgs. Container: container 숫자나 기타 포장 갯수를 기재한다.

⑯ Description of Goods: invoice나 packing list에 기재된 상품내용을 기재한다.

⑰ Gross Weight: 화물의 중량이 기재된다. 복수의 물품이 선적되는 경우는 각 물품의 중량이 따로 기재되어야 한다.

⑱ Measurement: 화물의 용적

⑲ Total No. of Containers or Packages(in word): container나 포장물의 총 갯수

⑳ Freight Prepaid at: 수출자 운임지불조건(예: CIF)의 경우 운임이 지불되는 장소를 나타낸다. 운임이 지불되지 않으면 운송회사는 B/L을 발행하지 않는다.

Freight Payable at: 수입자 운임지불조건(예: FOB)의 경우 운임이 지불되는 장소가 기재된다. 운임이 지불되지 않으면 운송회사는 화물지시인도서(D/O: Delivery Order)를 발행하지 않는다.

Place Issue: B/L의 발행장소를 기재한다.

Total Prepaid: 총 지불된 운임을 기재한다.

---

1) CY(Container Yard): 선박회사가 화물이 적입되어 있는 컨테이너를 본선에 선적하기 위하여 화주로부터 인수하거나 본선에서 양륙된 컨테이너를 화주에게 인도하기 위하여 지정된 장소.

2) CFS(Container Freight Station): 컨테이너를 채울 수 없는 화물 LCL(Less than Container Load)을 컨테이너에 적입(Vanning)하거나 수입화물을 혼재 컨테이너에서 끄집어내서(Devanning) 하주에게 인도하는 업무를 행하는 장소.

No. of Original B/L: 선하증권은 일반적으로 3통이 발행되고 선박회사는 이 중 어느 하나만 제시해도 화물을 내주게 되어있다. 따라서 은행은 3통을 모두 수령해야 화물에 대한 실질적 권리를 행사할 수 있기 때문에 신용장에는 항상 FULL SET의 선하증권을 제시할 것을 요구한다.

Date of Issue: 선하증권이 발행된 날짜.

Shipped on Board: 화물의 선적이 완료된 날자. 보통은 B/L 발행날자와 일치한다. 발행일자가 선적일자보다 늦을 수는 있지만, 반대의 경우는 은행은 매입을 거절할 수 있다. On Board Date 하단에 B/L 발행자의 서명이 들어간다.

◈ B/L의 종류

Shipped B/L and Received B/L

선적선하증권(shipped or on board B/L)은 화물이 실제로 선적된 후에 발행되는 증권으로 증권면에 "shipped", "shipped on board"와 같이 실질적으로 화물의 선적 완료를 표시한 문구가 있다. 모든 선하증권은 선적선하증권으로 발행되어야 하는 것이 원칙이다. 수취선하증권(received for shipment B/L)은 운송인이 선적을 약속한 화물을 하주가 지정된 창고에 입고시킨 후 하주가 요구할 경우 선적 전에 발행되는 증권이다. 이는 예정된 선박에 선적되지 않는 경우가 있기 때문에 신용장에 "received B/L acceptable"에 상응하는 문구가 없으면 은행에서 매입을 거절한다.

A 'shipped' or 'shipped on board' B/L, which indicates that the goods have been received on board ship. A 'received for shipment' B/L which means that the shipping company has taken delivery of the goods but has not placed them on board the vessel. It may be marked 'shipped on board'(or similar expression) once the goods have been received on the vessel. This is known as the 'on board' notation and must be dated by the shipping company.

Clean B/L and Foul B/L

무사고선하증권(clean B/L)은 본선상에 계약화물을 선적할 때 그 화물의 상태가 양호하고 수량이 맞아 비고란(remarks)에 아무 것도 기재되지 않은 증권을 말한다. 증권면에는 "shipped on board in apparent good order and condition"이라는 표시가 된다. 사고부 선하증권(foul, dirty, or claused B/L)은 비고란에 "6 bags torn", "5 packages short in dispute", "3 cases loose strap" 등 선박회사가 인수할 당시 포장

상태가 불완전하거나 수량이 모자라면 이 사실을 증권 상에 기재하는 선하증권이다. 사고부선하증권은 선하증권으 로서의 가치가 없기 때문에 하주는 수량을 채워 넣거나 재포장하여 무사고 선하증권을 발급받아야 한다. 그러나 시간적 여유가 없을 때에는 화주가 파손이나 부족한 화물에 대해서 책임을 지겠다는 파손화물보상장(letter of indemnity: L/I)을 제출하고 무사고 선하증권을 발급받을 수 있다.

Clean B/L is a B/L for goods issued by a shipping line that indicates that the goods were received in "apparent good order and condition", without damage or other irregularities. Foul B/L is a B/L for goods issued by a carrier with an indication that the goods were damaged when received. When a bank refuses to accept a foul B/L, the shipper may obtain a clean B/L. To acquire this, the shipper signs a letter of indemnity, which is an inducement to obtain the clean B/L through the dock or mate's receipt, given on delivery of the goods to dock or ship, showing that the shipment was damaged or in bad condition. This acts as a form of guarantee whereby the shipper accords a claim settlement against a steamship by a B/L holder resulting from a clean bill being issued.

Straight B/L and Order B/L

기명식선하증권(straight B/L)은 B/L의 수하인(consignee)란에 수하인인 수입상의 이름이 기재된 선하증권으로 무역화물에는 이용되지 않고 이삿짐 또는 개인의 물품을 발송하는 경우에 많이 이용된다. 유통이 되지 않으므로 송하인의 배서는 필요가 없다. 지시식 선하증권(order B/L)은 B/L의 수하인 란에 특정의 수하인명이 기재되지 않고 단순히 "to order", "to order of shipper", "to order of bank"와 같이 지시인(order)만 기재하여 유통을 목적으로 한 선하증권을 말한다. 무역거래에서는 원칙적으로 지시식 선하증권을 사용한다.

Straight B/L is a non-negotiable B/L in which the goods are consigned directly to a named consignee. Order B/L is a negotiable B/L made out to the order of a named party.

Combined Transport B/L

수출국의 화물인수장소로부터 수입국의 인도 장소까지 육상, 해상, 항공 중 적어도 두 가지 이상의 다른 운송방법에 의해 일관 수송되는 경우에 발행되는 운송증권을 복합운송

선하증권(combined transport B/L)이라고 한다. 주로 container 화물에 사용된다.

If ocean transport forms only part of the complete journey and overland transport has to be used as well, a 'Combined Transport Bill of Lading' can be issued to cover all stages of the journey. Containers play an important role in international business and 'container' Bills of Lading may be issued to cover goods from port to port or from inland point of departure to inland point of destination.

Through B/L

해상과 육상을 교대로 이용하여 운송하거나, 둘 이상의 해상운송인과 육상운송인이 결합하여 운송할 경우 최초의 운송인이 전구간의 운송에 대하여 책임을 지고 발행하는 증권을 통과선하증권(through B/L)이라고 한다. 운송구간 중 해상운송이 반드시 있어야 한다.

A through bill of lading involves the use of at least two different modes of transport from road, rail, air, and sea.

Short Form B/L

약식선하증권(short form B/L)은 선하증권으로서의 필요기재사항을 갖추고 있지만 보통 선하증권의 배서약관이 생략된 것으로서 최근 미국을 비롯한 여러 나라에서 널리 사용되고 있다. 이 약식선하증권에 관하여 어떤 분쟁이 생기면 long form B/L의 약관에 따른 다는 문언이 기재되어 있다.

A short form bill of lading on which the detailed conditions of transportation are not listed in full, but instead there is a statement which declares them to be incorporated by reference, and states the place where they are available.

Stale B/L

기간경과선하증권(stale B/L)이란 선적이 완료되면 선적일자에 발행되어 수출상은 상품대금을 회수하기 위해 발급일자 후 21일 이내(UCP 600 14조)에 매입은행에 선하증권을 제시하여야 하는데 이 기간 내에 제시하지 않은 선하증권이다. 신용장 상에 "stale B/L acceptable"에 상당하는 문구가 없으면 은행에서 매입을 거절한다.

Stale B/L is the one that has not been presented to the issuing bank within a reasonable time after its date precluding its arrival at the port of discharge by the time the related goods arrive.

UCP 600 Article 14

A presentation including one or more original transport documents subject to articles 19, 20, 21, 22, 23, 24 or 25 must be made by or on behalf of the beneficiary not later than 21 calendar days after the date of shipment as described in these rules, but in any event not later than the expiry date of the credit.

Red B/L

적색선하증권(red B/L)은 선하증권과 보험증권을 결합시킨 것으로서 이 증권에 기재된 화물이 항해 중에 사고가 발생하면 이 사고에 대하여 선박회사가 보상해 주는 선하증권이다. 이 경우 선박회사는 모든 적색선하증권의 발행권을 일괄부보하게 되므로 손해부담을 보험회사가 진다. 그러나 운임에 보험료가 추가되므로 결과적으로 보험료는 송화인이 부담하는 것이 된다.

A red B/L is the one that combines a B/L and an insurance certificate, and the shipping company which issues this type of B/L takes the responsibility for the consignment while it is in transit.

Third Part B/L

선하증권에 표시되는 송화인(shipper)은 일반적으로 신용장의 수익자이지만, 중계무역의 경우 수출입 당사자가 아닌 제3자가 송화인이 되는 경우가 있다. 이때 사용하는 것을 제3자 선하증권(third party B/L, neutral party B/L)이라고 부른다. 신용장에 별도의 명시가 없는 한 은행은 이를 수리하도록 신용장 통일규칙에서 정하고 있다.

Where the goods are shipped by someone else than the exporter(Seller), a 'third party' B/L is issued. It is acceptable if the third party shipper endorses it in favor of the beneficiary(sellers) who, in turn, either endorses it in blank or as stipulated in L/C.

Practice Tests - Situation 18

1. Situation 18의 선하증권의 성격에 대하여 맞게 설명한 것은?
   (a) shipped B/L – clean B/L – straight B/L – short form B/L
   (b) received B/L – foul B/L – straight B/L – red B/L
   (c) on board B/L – foul B/L – order B/L – stale B/L
   (d) shipped B/L – clean B/L – order B/L – combined transport B/L

2. Based on the B/L in Situation 18 who paid the ocean freight?
   (a) Qtopia systems Co., Inc. (b) EveryImport Co., Inc.
   (c) Bank of America (d) freight is not paid yet.

3. Where was the B/L in Situation 18 issued?
   (a) Incheon (b) LA
   (c) Pusan (d) New York

4. A document that establishes the terms of a contract between a shipper and a transportation company under which freight is to be moved between specified points for a specified charge. It serves as a document of title, a contract of carriage, and a receipt for goods.
   (a) bill of exchange (b) bill of sale
   bill of lading (d) bill of unloading

5. 다음 중 밑줄 친 부분의 해석이 잘못된 것은?
   Documents were refused due to (a) <u>the following discrepancies</u>:
   (1) B/L does not show (b) <u>"freight collect"</u>.
   (2) Commodity description in B/L was (c) <u>altered without authority</u>.
   (E) B/L was (d) <u>not endorsed as instructed</u>.
   (a) 다음과 같은 하자 (b) 운임후불
   (c) 허가 없이 변경 (d) 지시대로 발행되지 않음

6. A bill of lading issued by a shipping line for a voyage requiring on carriage, thus involving at least one transshipment.

(a) Stale B/L (b) Through B/L
(c) Order B/L (d) Short Form B/L

7. When there is no intention of the shipper to transfer the title of the lot to anyone except the consignee, is issued in the name of particular consignee.

(a) clean B/L (b) red B/L
(c) order B/L (d) straight B/L

8. If you find your cargo defective on the verge of shipment, you will have to tender ( ) to the shipping company to get a clean bill of lading.

(a) shipping request (b) letter of indemnity
(c) letter of guarantee (d) letter of compensation

9. A "shipped" B/L bill of lading is also called ( ) particularly in the United States.

(a) received B/L (b) order B/L
(c) through B/L (d) on board B/L

10. Bank of America가 발행한 신용장에 "Full set of clean on board Shipping Company's B/L made out to our order and blank endorsed, marked 'Freight Paid' and EveryImport Inc, LA California."라고 언급되어 있다면 이를 근거로 작성된 B/L의 consignee 란에는 어떻게 표시되어야 하는가?

(a) to order of Bank of America (b) to order
(c) to order of Shipper (d) to order of Consignee

12. Which of the following is most suitable for the blank in an insurance assessor's report below? [무역영어 1급]

Our finding is that the claim is not acceptable as goods were shipped ( ) in packing according to the Bill of Lading

(a) corrected (b) cleaned
(c) claused (d) cleared

[12~13] Read the following and answer the questions. [무역영어 1급]

(a) When you are introduced to a woman, offer her the same handshake that you would offer a man. However, be aware that some physical contact that might be acceptable with a male colleague would be considered inappropriate with a woman. For example, you should not clasp a female colleague on the shoulder as you might do with a man. In fact, it is a good idea never to touch a colleague of either sex beyond giving him or her a handshake. This is because you never know when a touch might be misconstrued.

(b) You can think of shaking hands as the American equivalent of bowing. Americans generally shake hands not only when they are introduced to someone for the first time, but at subsequent meetings as well. Businesspeople usually shake hands both before and after a business meeting.

(c) Knowing how and when to shake hands is an important skill when you are doing business in the United States.

(d) When you are greeting a colleague, extend your hand and offer a firm shake. Do not shake your colleague's hand too enthusiastically, but also avoid giving a limp handshake because this may convey an impression of weakness. In the United States, you should generally not bow when being introduced, although it is sometimes difficult for Koreans to break this habit!

(e) Although it is customary in some countries for a man to kiss a woman's hand when they are introduced, this is not common or appropriate in the United States.

12. According to the passage, which of the following statements about shaking hands is true?

(a) The handshake that you offer a man should be much firmer than the one you offer a woman.
(b) You should never shake hands with the same person more than once.
(c) A very weak handshake may give colleagues the wrong impression of you.
(d) You should always shake hands as vigorously and enthusiastically as possible.

13. Please put the paragraphs in the box in the most appropriate order.

(a) c–b–d–a–e　　(b) d–b–c–a–e

(c) a–d–b–e–c　　(d) c–d–e–a–b

Situation 19

Q-pointer IIe의 Commercial Invoice

<table>
<tr><td colspan="5">Commercial Invoice
Qtopia Systems
134 Seocho-dong, Seocho-ku, Seoul 130-070, Republic of Korea</td></tr>
<tr><td colspan="2">Seller
Qtopia systems Co. Inc.
134 Seocho-dong, Seocho-ku,
Seoul 130-070 Republicof Korea</td><td colspan="3">Invoice No. and date
C-0001 December 15, 2014
L/C No. and date
x123456 October 26, 2014</td></tr>
<tr><td colspan="2">Consignee
totheorder of Bank of America</td><td colspan="3">Buyer(if other than consignee)
EveryImport Co. Inc.
3434 Sunset Boulevard
LA, California 93456</td></tr>
<tr><td colspan="2">Departure date
December 15, 2014</td><td colspan="3">Other references</td></tr>
<tr><td>Vessel
Arirang</td><td>From
Incheon, Korea</td><td colspan="3" rowspan="2">Terms of delivery and payment
CIF Incheon, Korea At Sight</td></tr>
<tr><td colspan="2">To
Los Angeles, U.S.A.</td></tr>
<tr><td>Shipping marks</td><td>Goods description</td><td>Quantity</td><td>Unit price</td><td>Amount</td></tr>
<tr><td>EImport
Los Angeles
C/S No.1-200
Made in Korea</td><td>Q-pointer IIe
Laser
Pointer</td><td>10,000PCS</td><td>@USD180.00</td><td>USD180,000.00</td></tr>
<tr><td colspan="2">Phone: 82-2-2374-4785
Fax: 82-2-2374-4788
E-mail: systems@Qtopia.com</td><td colspan="3">Signature of Exporter
Wangsoo Kim</td></tr>
</table>

◈ Commercial Invoice

상업송장(commercial invoice)이란 수출상이 수입상 앞으로 발행하는 것으로, 물품의 명세서와 물품에 대한 대금청구서 역할을 한다. 또한 수출상이 매매계약에 따라 물품을 제공하였다는 계약이행의 입증서류이기도 하다. 상업송장은 수출상의 입장에서는 무역대금을 결제받기 위한 주요 서류일 뿐만이 아니라 출하안내, 과세자료, 수출수속절차상 세관 등에 제공하게 되는 서류이다. 수입상측에서는 수입통관수속에 필수적인 서류가 된다. 따라서 상업송장에 나타난 내용, 즉 품명, 수량, 단가 및 금액은 계약서와 일치하여야 한다. 또한 신용장거래의 경우에는 신용장의 조건과 상업송장의 조건이 일치하여야 한다. 상업송장은 무역계약을 이행하고 거래조건에 따라 작성되는 선적송장(shipping invoice), 가격계산의 기초로 사용되는 견적송장(pro-forma invoice), 견본을 송부할 때 작성되는 견본송장(sample invoice), 위탁매매시에 사용되는 위탁매매송장(consignment invoice)이 있다. 이 가운데 국제무역에서 흔히 말하는 송장이란 선적송장을 의미한다. 상업송장은 원칙적으로 신용장의 수익자(수출상)가 발행하여야 하며, 신용장 개설의뢰인(수입상) 앞으로 발행되어야 한다.

상업송장 이외에 영사송장과 세관송장이 있다. 영사송장(consular invoice)은 수입국에서의 수입관세 탈세나, 외화도피, 덤핑 등을 방지하거나 수출국소재 공관의 사증료 수입을 증대시키기 위하여 수출국주재 수입국 영사가 작성해 주는 서류이다. 세관송장(customs invoice)은 영사송장과 같이 과세가격기준 결정, 덤핑유무판정, 수입통계 등을 목적으로 수출상이 직접 작성한다. 세관송장은 수입국에 따라 양식이 정해져 있으며 수출가격분석(cost breakdown)을 정확히 하여야 한다.

Commercial Invoice: A commercial document that itemizes a transaction between a buyer and a seller. An invoice will usually include the quantity of purchase, price of goods and/or services, date, parties involved, unique invoice number, and tax information. If goods or services were purchased on credit, the invoice will usually specify the terms of the deal, and provide information on the available methods of payment.

Pro Forma Invoice: A preliminary bill of sale sent to buyers in advance of a shipment or delivery of goods. Typically, it gives a description of the purchased items, notes the cost, as well as other important information like shipping weight and transport charges.

Consular Invoice: A document certifying a shipment of goods and shows information such as the consignor, consignee and value of the shipment. A consular invoice can be obtained through a consular representative of the country you're shipping to. The consular invoice is required by some countries to facilitate customs and collection of taxes.

Customs Invoice: Extended form of commercial invoice required by customs (often in a specified format) in which the exporter states the description, quantity and selling price, freight, insurance, and packing costs, terms of delivery and payment, weight and/or volume of the goods for the purpose of determining customs import value at the port of destination.

◈ Other Shipping Documents

Packing List

포장명세서(packing list)란 적재화물의 포장 및 포장단위별 명세, 순중량(net weight), 총중량(gross weight), 용적(measurement), 화인(shipping marks), 포장개수(number of packages) 등을 기재한 상업송장의 보조서류로 수출상이 수입상 앞으로 작성하는 서류이다.

Certificate of Origin

원산지증명서(C/O: certificate of origin)란 수출물품의 원산지를 증명하는 서류이다. 원산지증명서는 수입상이 물품을 수입할 때 관세협약 등에 의해 협정관세율을 적용 받거나 덤핑방지 등 무역정책상 또는 무역통계를 목적으로 요청하게 된다. 현재 국제적으로 통용되고 있는 원산지 인정기준은 다음과 같다.

① 자국의 영토에서 채굴한 광물, 수확된 농·임산물, 사육된 축산물, 수렵물
② 자국의 영해에서 포획 또는 채취한 수산물
③ 자국 영해 밖의 해상이나 지층에서 채취한 광물 및 수산물
④ 공해상에서 자국의 국기를 게양한 선박이 포획한 수산물 또는 그 가공물
⑤ 자국에서 생산된 자재를 사용하여 제조 가공한 물품
⑥ 외국산 원자재를 사용하여 생산된 물품으로서 가공과정에서 새로운 상품적 특성이 발생된 물품

이상의 여섯 가지 조건 중 어느 한 조건을 충족하면 원산지로 인정하는 것이 국제적인 관례이다.

Certificate of Weight and Measurement

중량 및 용적증명서(certificate of weight and measurement)란 수출화물을 선적하기에 앞서 공인검량인(public weighter)에 의해 화물의 순중량, 총중량, 용적을 계량하여 발급해 주는 서류이며 운송화물에 대한 해상운임을 산출하는 기초가 된다. 선박회사측은 총중량과 용적을 자료로 하여 선하증권을 발급하게 된다.

Inspection Certificate

검사증명서(inspection certificate)란 물품의 품질에 대하여 매매계약시 품질의 결정방법과 시기 등을 고려하여 수입상의 요청에 의하여 수출상이 제공하는 검사결과에 대한 증명서이다.

Health Certificate

위생증명서(health certificate; sanitary certificate; veterinary certificate)란 식료품, 약품, 동물의 가죽류 등을 수출하는 경우에 수입국 보건기준에 합치된 것을 수입할 수 있도록 관리하기 위하여 수입상의 요구에 의해 수출국의 위생검사 당국에서 발행하는 서류이다.

Quarantine Certificate

검역증명서(quarantine certificate)는 위생증명서의 일종으로 특히 식물이나 동물 또는 동물의 부산물 등을 수출하는 경우 전염병 등 세균의 침입을 예방하기 위하여 수출국에서 소독, 방역 또는 검역을 실시하고 발급하여 주는 서류를 말한다.

Practice Tests - Situation 19

1. 다음 문장의 괄호 안에 들어갈 적합한 단어나 구로 구성된 것을 고르시오.

To ( ) difficulties with the Customs ( ) here, please ( ) sure that our Shipping Instructions be carefully ( ).

(a) make – Authorities – observed – avoid
(b) avoid – make – Authorities – observed
(c) avoid – observed – Authorities – make
(d) avoid – Authorities – make – observed

2. ( ) is addendum to the commercial invoice and identifies contents of individual package.

(a) Bill of Exchange
(b) Letter of Credit
(c) Letter of Guarantee
(d) Packing List

3. 다음은 무역거래에서 사용되는 서류에 대한 설명이다. 연결이 잘된 것은?

(1) This is a document which is tendered by shipper to shipping company in order to get clean bill of lading.

(2) This is a itemized list issued by exporter showing quantity, description of goods, unit price, total amount, full name/address of importer, and dates.

(3) This is a document certified by an official of importing country in the exporting country showing information such as the consignor, consignee and value of the shipment.

(4) This document is an invitation to the buyer to place an order and often required by him so that authorities of the importer's country grant him an import licence and/or foreign exchange permit.

	(1)	(2)	(3)	(4)
(a)	commercial invoice	letter of indemnity	pro-forma invoice	consular invoice
(b)	commercial invoice	letter of indemnity	consular invoice	pro-forma invoice
(c)	letter of indemnity	commercial invoice	consular invoice	pro-forma invoice
(d)	letter of indemnity	consular invoice	commercial invoice	pro-forma invoice

4. Which statement is NOT correct according to the dialogue? [무역영어 1급]

Greene: I have good news for you. The budget for the research study that you want to do for the new concept you're planning to launch has been approved.

Chris: That's really great!

Greene: I know. Well, you'd better request information from market research agencies to get this project started.

Chris: Yes, I will definitely do that.

Greene: By the way, there's an advertising congress next month. Have you seen the invitation?

Chris: Yes, I have. But I'm afraid I can't make it to the ad congress. It's on the same day as my sister's wedding.

(a) The invitation to the Advertising Congress has been sent to Chris.
(b) Chris wants to launch the new concept.
(c) Chris is unable to take part in the Advertising Congress because of her personal matter.
(d) The new research study of Chris does not require a financial support.

Situation 20

Q-pointer IIe의 수출대금 회수를 위해 발행한 Bill of Exchange

Bill of Exchange

No: ABC-9330

Exchange For USD180,000.00 November 14, 2014

At xxx sight① of this First Bill of Exchange(second of the same tenor and date being unpaid)② pay to Bank of America, Seoul or order③ the sum of US Dollars One Hundred Eighty Thousand only.

Value received and charge the same to account of EveryImport Co., Inc.④

DRAWN UNDER THE BANK OF AMERICA LETTER OF CREDIT No. x123456 DATED October 26, 2014.

To: Bank of America,
Los Angeles⑤

Qtopia systems Co., Inc

Jennifer Kim⑥
Director, Export Department

Bill of Exchange

No: ABC-9330

Exchange For USD180,000.00 November 14, 2014

At xxx sight① of this Second Bill of Exchange(first of the same tenor and date being unpaid)② pay to Bank of America, Seoul or order③ the sum of US Dollars One Hundred Eighty Thousand only.

Value received and charge the same to account of EveryImport Co., Inc.④

DRAWN UNDER THE BANK OF AMERICA LETTER OF CREDIT No. x123456 DATED October 26, 2014.

To: Bank of America,
Los Angeles⑤

Qtopia systems Co., Inc

Jennifer Kim⑥
Director, Export Department

◈ Bill of Exchange

Draft라고도 하며, 우리말로 환(換)어음이라고 부른다. 국내거래에서 어음은 물품의 납품을 받은 매수인이 1개월, 3개월 등 일정기간이 지나면 매도인에게 물품의 대금 지급을 확약하겠다는 증서이다. 그러나 국제간 거래에서의 어음은 물품의 수출상(매도인)이 수출대금을 은행을 통해서 수입상(매수인)에게 청구하는 청구서의 성격을 가진다. 따라서 환어음의 흐름은 국내거래와는 반대이고, 이 때문에 환어음을 역환(逆換: adverse exchange)이라고도 부른다. Situation 20은 Qtopia의 Jennifer가 대금의 회수를 위하여 선적서류와 함께 은행에 매입시킨 환어음이다.

① At Sight: 일람출금환어음을 나타낸다. Situation 16의 신용장에 따라 대금의 지급이 어음을 제시하면 즉시 이루어지는 일람출급방식으로 발행되었다.

② First Bill of Exchange(second of the same tenor and date being unpaid): 환어음 은 통상 안전상 2부가 발행되는데 먼저 도착하는 것이 효력을 갖는다. 이 어음의 경우 첫 장이고, 두 번째 장이 먼저 도착하여 대금이 지급되지 않았으면 이 어음에 따라 지급하라는 내용이다. 둘째 장은 Second Bill of Exchange(first of the same tenor and date being unpaid)와 같이 기재된다.

③ pay to Bank of America, Seoul or order: 수취인(payee)의 표시. payee는 어음에 정해진 금액을 지급받을 자(또는 지급받을 자를 지시하는 자)를 말한다. 여기에서는 "pay to Bank of America, Seoul or order"라고 되어 있어서 Bank of America나 Bank of America가 지명하는 사람에게 지급하라는 의미이다. 이것은 배서(endorsement)를 통하여 어음을 유통시키기 위한 것이다. 이것을 지시식이라고 한다. 여기에 기재되는 은행은 대개는 수출국의 negotiating bank가 된다. 환어음은 이외에도 다음과 같은 방식으로 발행된다:
기명식: pay to Bank of America
소지인식: pay to bearer(어음의 소지인(bearer)에게 지급)
선택소지인식: pay to Bank of America or bearer

④ Value received and charge the same to account of Every Import: 어음 발행인이 어음의 금액(value)은 이미 매입은행을 통하여 받았다(received)는 뜻이고 수입자인 EveryImport의 계정(account)에서 같은(the same) 금액을 청구(charge)하라는 뜻이다.

⑤ 지급인(payer/drawee) 및 지급지: 환어음의 밑 부분 발행인의 서명 옆 To 이하에 기재된다. 대개는 신용장의 issuing bank가 된다. 환어음은 반드시 개설은행(기타

환어음의 지급인) 앞으로 발행해야 하며, 개설의뢰인(여기서는 EveryImport) 앞으로 발행된 환어음은 인정되지 않는다. 물론 궁극적인 대금의 payer는 수입상이지만 L/C 거래의 경우 은행이 지급을 보증하는 것이므로 개설은행이 대금의 지급인(payer)이 되고 개설은행은 수입상의 계정에서 해당되는 금액만큼을 인출하게 된다.

⑥ 발행자(drawer)의 서명날인: 발행자는 beneficiary인 수출자가 된다. 여기에서는 Qtopia systems이다.

환어음과 관련된 당사자의 명칭을 정리하면 아래 표와 같다.

exporter		drawer: 환어음 발행인
bank in exporting country	negotiating bank (advising bank)	payee: 수취인
bank in importing country	paying bank (issuing bank)	payer/drawee 지급인 [신용장 거래]
importer		payer/drawee: 지급인 [추심거래]

◈ draft에 관련된 표현들

draw a draft + [on(지급인)/at(지급방법)/for(금액)/under(조건)] 어음을 발행하다.
present a draft: 어음을 제시하다.
accept a draft: 어음을 인수하다.
negotiate a draft: 어음을 할인하여 매입하다.
honor(protect, pay, settle) a draft: 어음 대금을 지급하다.
dishonor a draft: 어음 대금 지급을 거절하다.
protest a draft: 부도 어음에 대하여 법률적 대응을 하다.

· To cover the shipment we have drawn on you at sight through the Bank of America under the L/C No. 100, and ask you to honor the draft upon presentation. (선적대금 회수를 위하여 당사는 Bank of America를 통해 L/C No. 100에 의거하여 귀사 앞으로 일람출급 환어음을 발행하였으므로 어음이 제시되면 대금을 지급해 주실 것을 부탁드립니다.)

◈ negotiation vs. honor

negotiation과 honor는 둘 다 수출대금에 대하여 지급한다는 의미를 갖지만 그 기능에 차이가 있다. negotiation은 수출상인 beneficiary가 신용장에서 요구한 관련 선적서류와 대금의 지급청구서인 draft를 수출지의 negotiating(or advising) bank에 제시하고 negotiation을 통하여 수출지에서 대금을 지급받는 것이다. honor는 negotiation의 과정을 통해 제시된 draft에 대하여 수입지에서 issuing bank가 대금을 negotiating bank에 지급하는 것을 말한다. 이에 대하여 UCP 600에서는 다음과 같이 정의하고 있다.

Negotiation means the purchase by the nominated bank of drafts(drawn on a bank other than the nominated bank) and/or documents under a complying presentation, by advancing or agreeing to advance funds to the beneficiary on or before the banking day on which reimbursement is due to the nominated bank.

매입(negotiation)이라 함은 상환이 지정은행에게 행해져야 하는 은행영업일 또는 그 이전 수익자에게 대금을 선지급 또는 선지급 하기로 약정함으로써 일치하는 제시에 대한 환어음(지정은행이 아닌 은행을 지급인으로 하여 발행된) 및/또는 서류를 지정은행이 매입하는 것을 말한다.

Honor means:

a. to pay at sight if the credit is available by sight payment.
b. to incur a deferred payment undertaking and pay at maturity if the credit is available by deferred payment.
c. to accept a bill of exchange("draft") drawn by the beneficiary and pay at maturity if the credit is available by acceptance.

지급(honor)이라 함은 다음을 말한다.

a. 신용장이 일람지급에 의하여 사용가능한 경우 일람지급 하는 것.
b. 신용장이 연지급에 의하여 사용가능한 경우 연지급을 확약하고 만기일에 지급하는 것.
c. 신용장이 인수에 의하여 사용가능한 경우 수익자가 발행한 환어음("어음")을 인수하고 만기일에 지급하는 것.

Practice Tests - Situation 20

1. A ________ is an unconditional order issued by a person or business which directs the recipient to pay a fixed sum of money to a third party at a future date. The future date may be either fixed or negotiable.

(a) bill of lading (b) bill of rights
(c) bill of exchange (d) bill of unconditional order

2. To ______ shipment we have ________ our draft on Bank of America at 60 days after _______ for the invoice amount of USD180,000 under your L/C.

(a) make – issued – draft (b) cover – drawn – draft
(c) cover – drawn – sight (d) make – issued – sight

3. Choose the one that incorrectly describe the following bill of exchange.

BILL OF EXCHANGE

No. JR-2354 TOKYO, JAPAN APRIL 27, 2015
FOR CAN$10,275.00

At 60 days after sight on the FIRST bill of exchange(Second of the same tenor and date being unpaid) pay to Japan International Bank or order the sum of CANADA DOLLAR TEN THOUSAND TWO HUNDRED AND SEVENTY-FIVE ONLY.

Value received and charge the same to account of VP INTERCANADA, LTD. Drawn under Bank of Canada, L/C No. 345 dated March 18, 2015

TO: Bank of Canada
Toronto Canada

HPK Trading Co. Ltd.
Hiroshima Honda
Hiroshima Honda, President

(a) The drawer of this B/E is HPK Trading Co. Ltd.
(b) The drawee of this B/E is VP INTERCANADA, LTD.
(c) Japan International Bank is supposed to pay to the HPK Trading Co. Ltd.
(d) This B/E is negotiable by endorsement.

4. In international transactions, who will initially draw a bill of exchange?
(a) importer (b) exporter
(c) importer's bank (d) exporter's bank

5. In international transactions, who will eventually honor a bill of exchange?
(a) importer (b) exporter
(c) importer's bank (d) exporter's bank

6. 다음 괄호 안에 있는 단어들을 순서에 맞게 배열한 것을 고르시오. [무역영어 2급]
We thank you for your email informing us that [negotiated / sight / 90 days / draft / your / after / at / have / you] under the credit No. 86523.
(a) you negotiated your draft at 90 days after sight have
(b) you negotiated your draft after 90 days at sight have
(c) you have negotiated your draft at 90 days after sight
(d) you have negotiated your draft after sight at 90 days

7. Which of the following is NOT correct according to the letter below?
[무역영어 2급]

Dear Mr. Parker,

Your order No. 9021 was shipped on October 10, 2011 -on the Red Dragon due in Liverpool on November 21. We have informed your agents, Eddis Jones, who will make arrangements for the consignment to be sent on to you as soon as they receive the shipping documents for clearance.

Our bank's agents, WestEnd Bank Ltd., London, will hand over the documents: shipped clean bill of lading(No. 347865), invoice(No. DF 3314), and insurance certificate(AR 435 098), once you have accepted our bill.

We are sure you will be impressed by the machines, and that they will find a ready market in your country. Meanwhile, we enclose a catalogue of our new models. We look forward to hearing from you again in due course.

Hue Colbert, Export Manager

(a) West End Bank Ltd. will hand the documents to Mr. Parker's forwarding agent in Liverpool, who will then be able to collect the consignment.

(b) Mr. Parker must accept the bill of exchange before he receives the shipping documents.
(c) Mr. Colbert will now accept the bill that the Mr. Parker's company has drawn on them and send the documents to Mr. Colbert's bank's agent.
(d) It can be inferred that the consignment is in good condition since the B/L is clear.

8. 다음 중 밑줄 친 단어 대신 사용할 수 있는 것을 고르시오. [무역영어 2급]

We have forwarded all the documents required in L/C and attached the copies of them. We would like you to <u>honor</u> the draft on presentation.

(a) dishonor (b) settle
(c) honoring (d) pride

9. Which of the following is NOT correct? [무역영어 1급]

BILL OF EXCHANGE

FOR USD 15,230.00

At 60 days after sight on the FIRST bill of exchange(Second of the same tenor and date being unpaid) pay to Indonesian National Bank or order the sum of US DOLLAR FIFTEEN THOUSAND TWO HUNDRED AND THIRTY ONLY.

Value received and charge the same amount of Top Export, LTD. Drawn under Bank of Seoul, L/C No. 213 dated May 25, 2013

TO: Bank of Seoul

HPK Trading Co.
Jusuf Kalla

(a) This BoE is negotiable by endorsement.
(b) The drawee of this BoE is Top Export.
(c) The drawer of this BoE is HPK Trading Co.
(d) Indonesian National Bank is supposed to buy BoE from HPK Trading Co.

10. 다음 국제물품매매계약서에 관한 설명 중 잘못된 것은? [무역영어 2급]

Payment: Draft shall be drawn at 30 days under Irrevocable Letter of Credit which should be opened in favor of Seller immediately upon the contract, for the invoice value with full set of shipping documents, namely, Bill of Lading, Insurance Policy, Commercial Invoice and other documents.

(a) The Seller should draw a sight draft for payment.
(b) The Seller will be a beneficiary according to this contract.
(c) The amount of L/C should be the same as the invoice value.
(d) The Seller should present a B/L in order to get payment.

11. Which of the followings is NOT a correct meaning for the underlined in the draft below? [무역영어 1급]

BILL OF EXCHANGE

FOR US$50,000

At ..... Sight of this FIRST of Exchange(SECOND of the same tenor and date being unpaid) pay to (a) The Korea Exchange Bank, or order the sum of Dollars Fifty Thousand Only Value received and (b) charge the same to account of Chicago Trading Co., Inc., Chicago, Drawn under(c) Busey Bank of Champaign L/C No.1000 dated November 30, 2012

TO(d) Busey Bank Of Champaign　　　　Tae Jon Trading Co., Ltd.

(a) – the negotiating bank of this draft
(b) – credit fifty thousand dollars to the account of Chicago Trading Co., Inc.,
(c) – the issuing bank of L/C No.1000
(d) – the drawee of this draft

12. 다음 UCP 600에서의 결제(Honour)의 정의 중 그 표현이 맞지 않는 것을 고르시오. [기출, 국제무역사]

(a) It means to pay at sight if the credit is available by sight payment.
(b) It means to advance or agree to advance funds to the beneficiary on or before the banking day on which reimbursement is due to the nominated bank.
(c) It means to accept a bill of exchange(draft) drawn by the beneficiary and pay at maturity if the credit is available by acceptance.
(d) It means to incur a deferred payment undertaking and pay at maturity if the credit is available by deferred payment.

13. 다음 문장의 의미에 맞도록 괄호 안에 들어갈 적당한 것을 고르시오.

[기출, 국제무역사]

Your draft was not honored, please negotiate for the matter with the (A) and let him/her (B) it at once.

(a) drawer – protest
(b) drawee – protect
(c) payee – protect
(d) payer – protest

Situation 21

Q-pointer IIe의 도착과 일부 결함품의 발생을 통보하다.

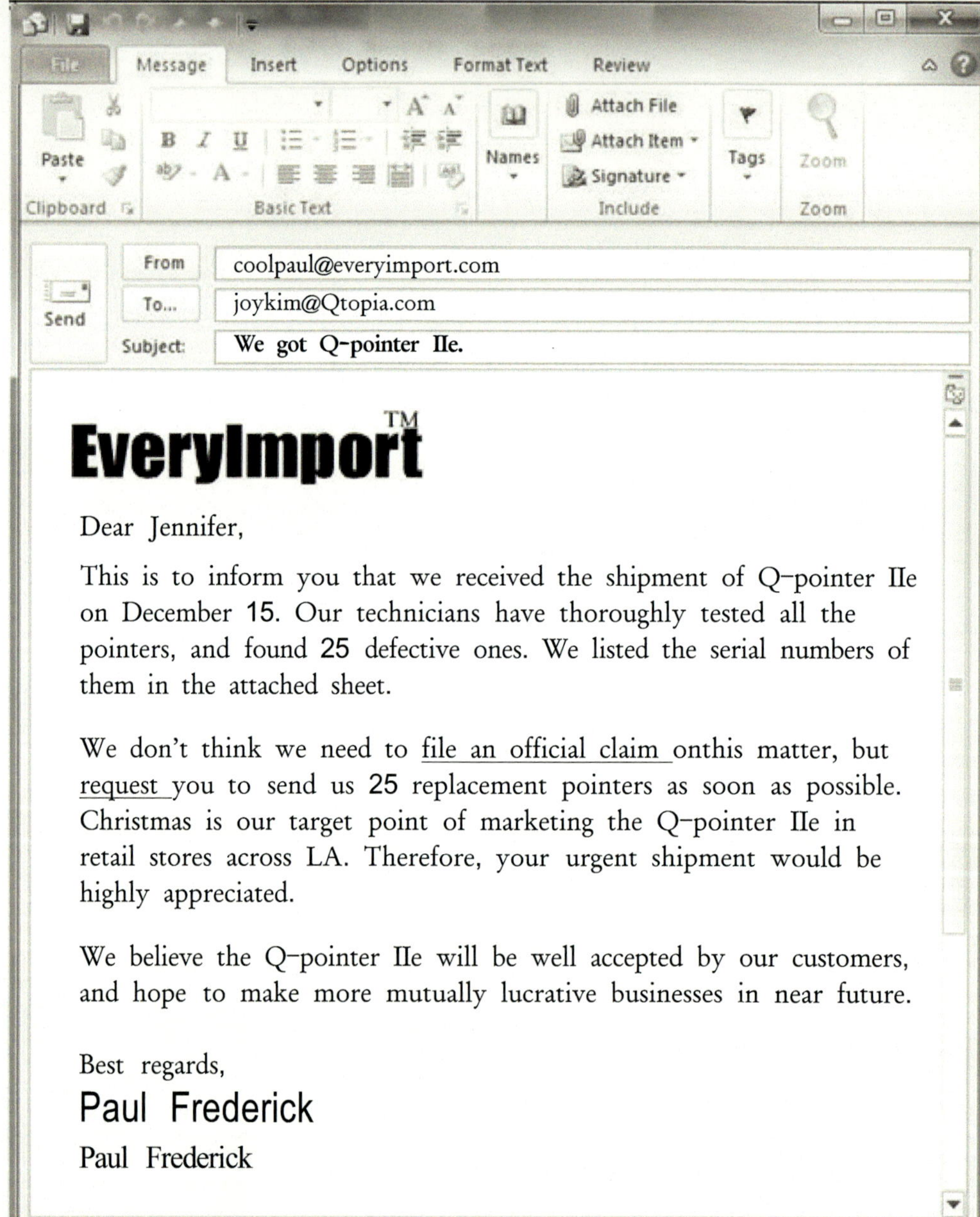

From: coolpaul@everyimport.com
To: joykim@Qtopia.com
Subject: We got Q-pointer IIe.

EveryImport™

Dear Jennifer,

This is to inform you that we received the shipment of Q-pointer IIe on December 15. Our technicians have thoroughly tested all the pointers, and found 25 defective ones. We listed the serial numbers of them in the attached sheet.

We don't think we need to file an official claim onthis matter, but request you to send us 25 replacement pointers as soon as possible. Christmas is our target point of marketing the Q-pointer IIe in retail stores across LA. Therefore, your urgent shipment would be highly appreciated.

We believe the Q-pointer IIe will be well accepted by our customers, and hope to make more mutually lucrative businesses in near future.

Best regards,

Paul Frederick

Paul Frederick

Synopsis

Q-pointer IIe를 인수해서 technician들이 모든 기계를 철저히(thoroughly) 점검한 결과 25개의 결함품(defective ones)이 있음을 통보하고 있다. 이 문제로 공식적인 클레임을 제기할 필요는 없다고 생각하지만 크리스마스를 겨냥해서 물건을 출시할 예정(our target point of marketing)이기 때문에 결함품에 대하여 조속히 교환해줄 것을 요구하고 있다. Q-pointer IIe가 소비자들에게 인기가 있을 것이라고 믿으며 (well accepted) 가까운 장래에 서로 이익이 되는(mutually lucrative) 거래관계를 맺을 수 있게 되기를 바란다는 말로 메일을 마무리하고 있다.

◈ claim

국제무역거래에서 claim이란 매매계약당사자의 일방이 계약이행을 위반함으로써 다른 일방이 이로 인하여 입은 손해의 배상을 청구하는 것을 말한다. 이는 단순히 불만(complaint)과는 구분이 되며, 구체적인 청구가 수반되는 것만 claim에 해당된다.

무역클레임의 해결방법은 당사자간의 해결과 제3자를 통한 해결이 있다. 당사자 간의 해결방법은 당사자간에 직접 교섭하여 우의적으로 해결하는 방법을 말한다. 청구권을 포기(waiver of claim)하고 상대방에 대하여는 다른 조건으로 만족시켜 주거나 클레임의 청구액이 근소하여 클레임을 제기하지 않고 거래를 계속하여 자사에 이익을 가져오는 해결방법이다. 당사자간 자주적인 교섭과 양보로 분쟁을 해결하는 방법으로 화해(amicable settlement)하는 방법도 있다. 당사자 간에 원만하게 해결할 수 없어 쌍방의 주장이 대립하는 경우 제3자가 개입하여 분쟁을 해결하게 되는데, 이러한 방법으로는 알선, 조정, 중재, 소송 등이 있다.

① 알선(intercession, recommendation)

알선이란 공정한 제3자가 당사자의 일방 또는 쌍방의 요청에 의하여 사건에 개입, 해결이 될 수 있도록 조언하는 것을 말한다. 이는 쌍방의 협력이 없으면 실패로 돌아가며, 강제력은 없으나 제3자가 당사자에게 강한 영향력을 미침으로써 분쟁을 해결할 수 있다.

② 조정(conciliation, mediation)

조정은 양 당사자가 공정한 제3자를 조정인으로 선임하고, 조정인이 제시하는 해결안(조정안)에 양 당사자가 합의함으로써 분쟁을 해결하는 방법이다. 조정은 쌍방의 합의에 의해서 행해지고 당사자의 제시된 조정안을 수락할 의무가 없으므로 만약 어느 일방이 조정안에 불복하면 결국 조정은 실패로 돌아간다.

③ 중재(arbitration)

중재란 당사자간의 합의로 사법상의 법률관계를 법원의 소송절차에 의하지 않고 제3자인 중재인(arbitrator)을 선임하여 그 분쟁을 중재인에게 맡겨 중재인의 판단에 양 당사자가 절대 복종함으로써 최종적으로 해결하는 방법이다.

④ 소송(litigation)

소송은 국가공권력(사법재판)에 의한 분쟁해결 방법이며, 외국과의 사법협정이 체결되어 있지 않기 때문에 그 판결은 외국에서 승인 및 집행이 보장되지 않는다. 따라서 소송에 의하여 클레임을 해결하려는 경우에는 피제기자가 거주하는 국가에서 현지 변호사를 법정 대리인으로 선임하여 소송절차를 진행하여야 한다.

◈ claim letter

Situation 21은 일종의 claim을 제기하는 메일이다. business에서는 거래된 제품이나 서비스에 대하여 문제제기를 할 경우가 빈번히 있기 때문에 claim을 제기할 때는 자기의 입장과 상대방을 모두 고려하여 서신을 작성할 필요가 있다.

문제를 제기하라.

claim을 제기할 때에는 지체 없이 해야 한다. 지체가 되면 상대방에 대하여 설득력도 떨어질 뿐만 아니라 시간이 지남에 따라 누락되게 되는 사안도 생길 수 있기 때문이다. claim letter의 도입부분에 문제를 제기해서 미안하다는(we are sorry to have to write to you about...), 유감이라는(we regret to inform you that....) 등의 표현을 쓸 필요는 없다. 단순히 다음과 같이 시작하는 것이 좋다.

- This is to inform you that.....
- We would like to let you know that....
- I am writing to complain about....
- I am writing regarding your order No. AG33, which we received today.

감정적으로 쓰지 마라.

다분히 감정적이고 무례한 표현을 피해야 한다. claim의 원인이 거래상대방의 잘못이

아닐 수도 있고, 실수라 하더라도 거래를 하다보면 어쩔 수 없이 일어나는 일일 수 있기 때문에 감정적이고 무례한 표현은 사태의 해결에 전혀 도움이 되지 않는다. 예를 들면 다음과 같은 무례하고 직설적인 표현들은

- You neglected to specify the color of the item you ordered.
- You made an error on the invoice.
- You fail to enclose the check you mentioned in your letter of May 9.

다음과 같이 정중한 표현으로 바꿔 쓰는 것이 좋다.

- Let me know the color of the item you ordered.
- There appears to be an error on the invoice.
- You will probably have discovered that the check you meant to enclose in your letter of May 9 was missing.

특히, fault(your fault, our fault)나 blame(you are to blame)과 같은 단어는 피하는 것이 좋다.

- Your dispatch division is to blame for the wrong shipment of the goods.
  → The mistake must be connected with the dispatch of the goods.

문제를 설명하라.

문제의 원인이 어디에 있는지 알고 있다면 상대방에 정중히 설명하는 것이 좋다.

- This is obviously due to your poor packing of the goods because they have been placed without any padding.
- Could you ask your shipping department to check my code carefully in future? My number is 5678, but they have sent me a statement coded 5578.
- Please ask your accounts department to correct our address. Our correct address is 1814 Stratford Drive instead of 1814 Stateford Drive.

해결책을 제시하라.

문제의 해결방안이 있다면 상대방에게 제시하는 것도 필요하다.

- We have to request that you send us 25 replacement batteries.
- The best solution would be for me to send the wrong ones to you.
- The pocket calculators have been damaged so badly and are not in salable condition. The best solution would be for us to return them and to request a full refund plus shipping expense.

◈ file a claim [complaint, petition, lawsuit, bankruptcy, legal action]

'클레임 혹은 소송을 제기하다'라고 표현할 때에는 주로 file을 사용한다. file 이외에도 lodge, enter, submit, place 등을 쓴다.

A에게 B에 대한 클레임을 제기하다. file a claim with A for B

= file a claim for + 손해배상금액 with A
= file a claim for the amount of 손해배상금액
= lodge(enter/bring forward) a claim with A
= submit a claim to A
= place a claim before A

- We file a claim with EveryImport for the damage.
- He has filed a claim for $5,000 with the insurance company.
- Bankruptcy should only be filed when all other options have been eliminated.
- Jewish groups said they would file a lawsuit against the company.
- The company filed a legal action on July 24 requesting the information.

claim을 동사형으로 써서 표현하기도 한다.

- He claimed one thousand dollars for the damaged articles.
- He claimed a lot of money for the amount of harm he experienced.

◈ request

business에서는 '~요구하다, ~희망하다 ~제안하다, ~추천하다' 등의 동사(request, advise, agree, ask, command, decide, demand, insist, order, propose, recommend, request, suggest)가 많이 쓰인다. 이 동사들의 다양한 표현 pattern을 request를 사용한 예시로 정확히 알아보자.

1) 3형식 request+목적어 [명사]

- Please feel free to request any further information about our products.

2) 3형식 request+목적어 [명사절: that ~~ 주어+(should)+동사]

- We request you that you(should) contact Qtopia.

이와 같은 형태에서 should는 생략하고 쓰는 경우가 많다. 따라서 that 이하의 절에 3인칭이 오더라도 동사의 원형이 쓰이는 점에 주의해야 한다.

- We request him that he contact Cellopia for the product.
- I propose that the loan be reduced.
- I recommend that the work be done at once.

그러나 항상 동사의 원형이 기계적으로 오는 것은 아니므로 문장의 내용을 먼저 파악해야 한다.

- He insisted that he had attended the meeting. (사실에 대한 주장)
- Dr. Tran's work suggests that the earth became a true planet about 30 million years earlier than previous estimates. (암시)

3) 5형식 request+목적어+ 목적격보어 [to 부정사]

- We request him to remit the past dues immediately.

4) request는 전치사가 필요 없는 타동사이므로 request for ~로 쓰지 않는다. 그러나 request가 명사로 쓰이면 for가 필요함에 주의할 것!!

- We request(~~for~~) the honor of your company. (참석해 주시면 영광이겠습니다.)
- How do I make a request <u>for</u> the information about the computer?.

Practice Tests - Situation 21

1. What is EveryImport trying to say in this e-mail?
   (a) They received the ordered goods on December 15.
   (b) Their technicians have thoroughly tested all the machine they received.
   (c) They are quite satisfied with the overall test results.
   (d) They want replacement laser pointers as soon as possible.

2. What does EveryImport think about the marketability of Q-pointer IIe?
   (a) They believe it will sell briskly in LA.
   (b) They found the Q-pointer IIe defective.
   (c) They are trying to sell the Q-pointer IIe during Christmas holidays.
   (d) They want to make mutually beneficial business.

3. Which expression is NOT appropriate when you write a claim letter?
   (a) The goods we ordered on May 10 have arrived in damaged condition.
   (b) Please look into the matter and let us know your instruction by today.
   (c) You fail to send the goods of the same standard as the sample.
   (d) Your early settlement would be highly appreciated.

4. Automobile manufacturers insist that the relationship between fuel economy and safety ________ yet fully understood.
   (a) should not be　　　　(b) is not
   (c) not be　　　　(d) were not

5. 다음 빈 칸에 들어갈 적절한 말끼리 연결된 것을 고르시오. [무역영어 2급]
   This is a reminder that your payment of $100.000 for 5 sets of drilling machine(delivered on Oct 10) is now (　　　). You may have (　　　) the matter (　　　), so please check and (　　　) the payment by the end of this month.
   (a) overdue - overlooked - by mistake - remit
   (b) underpaid - deficit - unexpectedly - confirm

(c) on time - done – clearly – send
(d) payable - transferred – latter – arrange

[6~7] Answer the following questions [무역영어 2급]

Dear Mr. Jason,
In my letter of 12 December, I explained that the merchandise I ordered from you hadn't arrived. I am attaching a copy of correspondence for your convenience.
Having received neither the merchandise nor a response to my previous letter, I am requesting that you refund USD 30,000 remitted with my order. Attached is a copy of my cancelled check. I shall be looking forward to receiving my refund promptly.

6. What is the main purpose of the letter?
(a) Request for Refund of Duplicate Payment
(b) Request for Refund on Undelivered Merchandise
(c) Request for Price Quote
(d) Request for Proof of Merchandise Return

7. What does the underlined 'correspondence' mean?

(a) order (b) acceptance
(c) offer (d) draft

8. Which of the following is most likely to come right after the passage? [무역영어 2급]

Dear Mary
We have not received our order #13245 as of today. It was supposed to be here last week. We need to supply our products to our customer by November 11. If the goods do not arrive within a week, we may lose our customer.

(a) Please reship the ordered merchandise and also let us know what you want us to do with the mistaken shipment.
(b) Please let us know immediately the status of the shipment and the date of delivery.

(c) We would appreciate your rushing the missing parts to us.

(d) Please let us know what to do with the rejected goods.

9. Read the following letter and put the sentences(a~d) in the most appropriate order. [무역영어 1급]

a) If this amount has already been paid, please disregard this notice.

b) Our records show that you have an outstanding balance dating back to January, 2013.

c) Your January invoice was for $4405.00 and we have yet to receive this payment. Please find a copy of the invoice enclosed.

d) Otherwise, please forward us the amount owed in full by March 1st, 2013. As our contract indicates, we begin charging 5% interest for any outstanding balances after 30 days.

(a) b–c–a–d (b) b–d–a–c

(c) b–a–d–c (d) c–a–b–d

10. Which of the following is LEAST likely to appear right after the passage? [무역영어 1급]

No news is good news when things are on the right track. However, much to our regret, our repeated requests for payment in full of the outstanding accounts have not been answered nor even acknowledged as of today. Your immediate settlement of the overdue debt is imperative. If we have not received payment by the end of this week, August 20, we will have no choice but to take more serious measures.

(a) We do hope the non–payment is merely an oversight by your staff and not in the least your policy.

(b) Our legal department has been duly notified of this case and is prepared to take action against your company.

(c) Please understand that only your immediate action could rectify this situation.

(d) It is our deep regret that we have to discontinue all our discussions and negotiations to save both of us from further loss of time and money.

11. Which of the following is most appropriate right after the passage?

[무역영어 1급]

With deep concern and regret, we remind you again that our invoice KEAA−1212 has not been paid as of today. Please check with your accounting department if the said remittance has been made or not. Also please advise when your payment will reach us.

(a) If this letter crossed paths with your remittance to us, please disregard this letter. Your earliest confirmation would be much appreciated.

(b) Our letter of September 20 might have reached you at an inopportune time, however, we still wonder why our request for confirmation of the global discount scheme has not been acknowledged by you.

(c) Enclosed is a credit note for $2,345 which reflects the discrepancy we found in our invoice for August 2012. We apologize for the inconvenience caused by a clerical oversight at our end.

(d) Remittance abroad of foreign exchanges from Korea is stringently controlled by the Ministry of Finance and conditioned upon prior approval of related contracts.

Situation 22

결함품 발생에 대하여 사과하고 교환품을 발송하다.

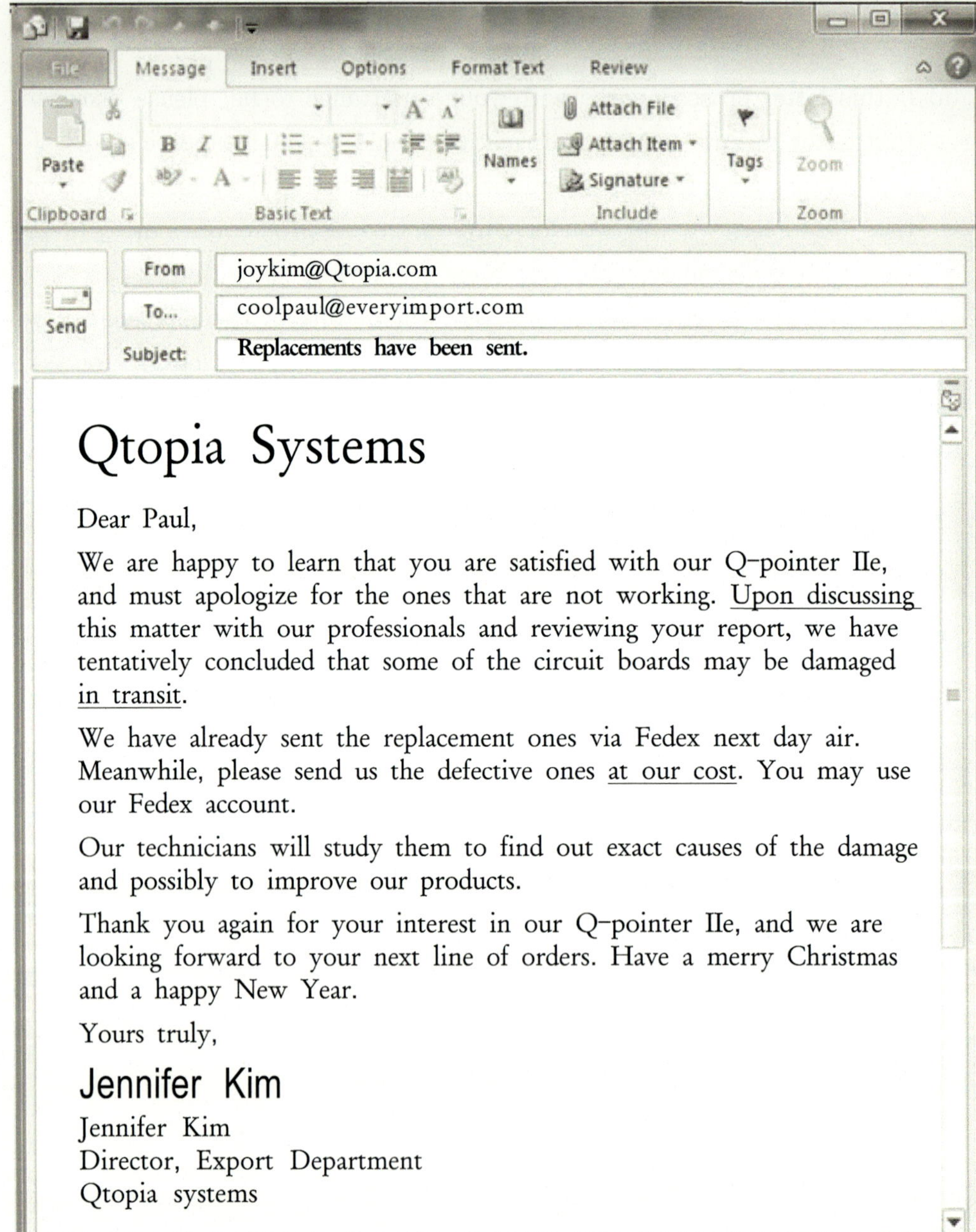

From: joykim@Qtopia.com
To...: coolpaul@everyimport.com
Subject: **Replacements have been sent.**

Qtopia Systems

Dear Paul,

We are happy to learn that you are satisfied with our Q-pointer IIe, and must apologize for the ones that are not working. Upon discussing this matter with our professionals and reviewing your report, we have tentatively concluded that some of the circuit boards may be damaged in transit.

We have already sent the replacement ones via Fedex next day air. Meanwhile, please send us the defective ones at our cost. You may use our Fedex account.

Our technicians will study them to find out exact causes of the damage and possibly to improve our products.

Thank you again for your interest in our Q-pointer IIe, and we are looking forward to your next line of orders. Have a merry Christmas and a happy New Year.

Yours truly,

Jennifer Kim

Jennifer Kim
Director, Export Department
Qtopia systems

Synopsis

일부 제품에서 작동하지 않는다는 통보를 받은 Qtopia의 Jennifer는 이를 기술자들과 상의한 결과 운송과정(in transit)에서 일부 circuit board가 손상되었을 것이라고 잠정적으로 결론(tentatively concluded)짓고, 교환품(replacement)을 Federal Express의 next day air로 보냈음을 통보하고 있다. 결함 제품에 대해서는 Qtopia의 부담으로(at our cost) 돌려줄 것을 요구하고 있다. 기술자들이 결함품을 연구(study)해서 결함원인(exact cause of damage)을 찾는 동시에 가능하면 제품의 개선(possibly to improve our products)에 이용할 것이라는 것을 밝혀 클레임을 신속하게 처리하고 또 완전한 제품을 추구한다는 회사이미지를 부각시키고 있다. 다시 한 번 Q-pointer IIe에 관심을 보여줘서 고맙다는 말과 다음 주문(next line of orders)을 기대한다는 말로 메일을 마무리 지었다.

◈ claim에 대한 대답.

시작

상대방으로 부터 문제제기를 받았고, 문제점에 대하여 알려준 것에 고마움을 표시한다.

- Thank you for your letter of July 7 informing us that...
- We would like to thank you for informing us that....
- In replying to your fax of July 7 in which you told us that....

문제를 조사할 시간을 달라고 요구한다.

제기된 문제에 대하여 즉각적인 조치를 취하기 어려운 경우에는 이메일이나 팩스로 현재 조사가 진행 중임을 알릴 필요가 있다. 침묵으로 일관한다면 상대방은 문제를 해결할 의사가 없는 것으로 생각할 수 있다.

- Upon discussing this matter with our professionals we have tentatively concluded that some of the circuit boards may be damaged in transit. While we cannot give you an explanation at present, we are looking into the problem and will contact you again shortly.
- Please return samples of the items you are dissatisfied with, and I will send them to our factory in Detroit for tests.

문제를 해결하라.

제기된 문제에 대해 책임이 있다면 인정하고, 어떻게 해결할 것인지를 분명히 밝혀야 한다. business란 한번 거래로 끝날 것이 아니므로 지속적인 관계를 위해서는 지금 다소 손해를 보더라도 사태에 대하여 책임감 있는 자세가 필요하다.

- We have already sent the replacement batteries via Fedex next day air. Meanwhile, please send us the defective ones at our cost.
- We apologize sincerely for the trouble caused to you and will take all possible steps to avoid such a mistake again in the future.
- We will, of course, immediately refund the amount you paid for Invoice No. TT-1 and reimburse you for the cost of shipping the defective items back to us.

부당한 문제제기라면 단호히 거부하라.

부당한 문제를 제기해왔다면 단호하지만 정중하게 거절할 필요가 있다. 그러나 책임을 회피한다는 인상을 주지 않도록 충분히 설명을 해 주어야 한다.

- We have thoroughly investigated the matter and concluded that the warranty does not cover the complaint you mentioned in your letter of April 10.
- As the damage occurred after the goods delivered to your warehouse, we are afraid that there is little we can do concerning compensation.
- We have closely compared the articles you returned with our samples and can see no difference between them. Under this circumstances, we must regrettably turn down your request for a full refund.

맺기

제기된 클레임이나 불만에 대하여 이러한 일들이 아주 드물게 일어나는 예외적인 일이라는 것을 밝히고 이런 일이 다시는 일어나지 않을 것임을 주지시키는 것이 바람직하다. 또한 상대방에게 끼친 불편에 대하여 사과하는 것도 잊어서는 안 된다.

- In closing we would like to apologize for the inconvenience, and also point out that this type of error rarely occurs in our company.

• Finally, we must say that this was an exceptional mistake and is unlikely to occur again. Please accept our apologies for the inconvenience.

◈ upon discussing ~

When we discussed the matter ~에서 주어 we가 생략되고 ~ing형태의 문장이 되었다. 다음의 문장들도 비슷한 구조를 가지고 있다.

• While watching the TV program yesterday, I fell asleep.
  = While I was watching ~
• After finishing the high school diploma, what courses can I take?
  = After I finish ~
• (Up)on receiving your confirmation ~ 귀사의 확인을 받는 즉시
  = Upon receipt of your confirmation ~
  = As soon as we receive your confirmation ~
  = When we receive your confirmation ~
• Since leaving MS a year ago, she has stayed close to the IT industry.
  = Since she left ~

그러나 각 절의 주어가 다르다면 이런 구조의 문장이 불가능하다.

Ex) Since leaving MS a year ago, <u>the IT industry</u> has experienced a harsh change.
(MS를 일 년 전에 떠난 이래 IT 산업은 심각한 변화를 겪어오고 있다: 앞 문장은 사람이 주어이고 뒤 문장은 IT industry이다.)

동사 discuss는 타동사로 전치사가 필요 없다.

• We discuss ~~about~~ the matter with our professionals and technicians.

◈ in transit

~ while they were transported(운송 도중)의 의미이다. the나 a와 같은 관사가 없이 사용되고 있다. 이처럼 관사 없이 사용되는 관용구는,

in turn 번갈아
in hand 수중에
in public 공적으로
in doubt 의심하여
in private 사적으로
in conclusion 결론적으로
for breakfast 아침으로
at night 밤에
by sea/air/land 해상/항공/육상으로
on sale 판매중인
under control 통제 하에 놓인
under construction 건설 중인
out of danger 위험을 벗어나
without fail 틀림없이
in danger 위험에 처한
in time 늦지 않게
in error 잘못된
in place 적재적소에
in(good) order 질서정연한
for sale 팔려고 내놓은
at risk 위험에 직면하여
by mail/fax 우편/팩스로
by bus/car/train/airplane/boat 교통수단
on time 정시에
under discussion 논의 중인
out of order 고장난
beyond dispute 논란의 여지가 없는
without permission 허가 없이

at our cost

여기에서는 '우리 부담으로'라는 뜻으로 쓰였다. 이와 비슷한 표현은,

- Please return the whole consignment to us, postage and packing forward.
  (운송료와 포장비용을 본사 부담으로 모든 선적품을 되돌려 주시기 바랍니다.)

postage and packing을 P&P로 쓰기도 한다. 한편 '상대방 부담으로' 하려면, charging을 써서,

- The best solution would be to return the wrong articles, charging you P&P.
  (최선의 방법은 운송료와 포장비용을 귀사 부담으로 잘못된 물건을 반품하는 것입니다.)

Practice Tests - Situation 22

1. What is this letter for?
   (a) Jennifer is trying to let Paul know that she is happy.
   (b) Jennifer informs Paul that replacements are ready for shipment.
   (c) Jennifer wishes Paul a happy Christmas.
   (d) Jennifer tries to solve the problem Paul has.

2. Which one is NOT the action Jennifer took after she received claim letter?
   (a) She discussed the matter with the professionals.
   (b) She reviewed the report Paul had filed.
   (c) She sent the replacement laser pointers through express mail.
   (d) She made the technicians study the batteries for improvement.

3. What will Paul do after receiving this email?
   (a) He will place another order.
   (b) He will send the defective batteries to Qtopia systems.
   (c) He will use Qtopia's Fedex account for the next order.
   (d) He will have a happy Christmas.

4. Which is NOT appropriate as a reply to a claim letter?
   (a) I am sorry that the quality of paper in the forms we supplied you was not up to your expectation.
   (b) The terms of sale are described on the invoice we sent you, and perhaps you overlooked them.
   (c) We have been glad to recheck our calculations, but we were unable to find any evidence of error.
   (d) In your May 3 order, you neglected to specify the color of vinyl sheeting you require.

5. Which of the following is the main purpose of the letter? [무역영어 1급]

I deeply regret that at this moment in time I am unable to settle your invoice. The consignment arrived in good condition and as usual. Unfortunately, two days after the arrival of the consignment, disaster struck. After several centimeters of incessant rain, my stockroom was completely flooded and much of the stock damaged or destroyed.

I am able to inform you that the insurers have promised me to settle the damages within the next four weeks. When I receive this, I will take measures to pay as soon as I can.

(a) Refusing an order
(b) Reply to complaint about damage
(c) Request for comprehensive insurance
(d) Request for more time to settle an account

6. Which of the followings is NOT APPROPRIATE as the meaning of ⓐ~ⓓ? [무역영어 1급]

Gentlemen:

We acknowledge the receipt of your letter of October 19 and are extremely sorry that ⓐ causes completely beyond our control have made it impossible for us to keep the delivery date.

ⓑ The recent railway strike held up supplies of coal and raw material and resulted in delays of 5 to 7 weeks. ⓒ We have made every possible effort to speed up delivery but unfortunately have failed without success.

Under the circumstances we have no alternative but to accept your cancellation, but we would ask you to know that ⓓ the delay was in no way caused by any negligence on our part. While offering our sincere apologies we trust that you will continue to place your orders with us.

Faithfully yours,

(a) ⓐ → We cannot make shipment within the delivery date because of causes that we could not control.
(b) ⓑ → Coal and raw material were not supplied in time because of the recent railway strike.
(c) ⓒ → We have done our best to deliver the goods as early as possible.
(d) ⓓ → the delay was resulted from you.

7. Which of the following is LEAST likely to come right before the passage below? [무역영어 1급]

As you will see from the copy enclosed, we warned suppliers that there might be some delay in clearing accounts and replying to correspondence as the move would involve employing new staff who needed time to get used to our accounts and filing systems.

You will be pleased to hear that we have now settled into our new offices and will have a fully trained staff by the end of next month. Meanwhile, I am enclosing a cheque for £20,000 on account, and will send a full settlement of your June statement within the next few days. Could you please note our new address for future reference?

(a) First let me apologize for not having cleared our June statement or replying to your letter of 10 August. However, I am surprised that you did not receive our circular letter informing all our suppliers that we were moving from Milan to Turin.

(b) We are greatly sorry for not making payment for the order of 15 May. However, as you might know we sent our letter on 30 June, explaining about our situation and asking you to excuse our late payment.

(c) Thank you for your enquiry about payment. As we mentioned in our order sheet, our usual terms of payment are D/A with 90 days usance. Therefore, your bill will be cleared out on 30 November, 2012.

(d) We have received your letter of 25 August. However, we regret that you could not get our letter informing our moving. Upon checking our record, the letter was sent on 30 June.

[8~9] Read the following and answer the questions. [무역영어 1급]

An Office Party

An American manager by the name of Bill Morris worked for an American multinational firm. One year later, he was transferred to France. When he began working in the French office, he decided to throw a party for the whole office. (a) <u>He thought it would be a good way to get acquainted with everyone in a less formal environment</u>. He invited everyone in his office, including secretaries and executives, for a big party in his elegant apartment. Everyone accepted the invitation. (b) <u>He was pleased that no one had declined his invitation</u>.

At his apartment Morris served a buffet of snack foods and drinks. The employees could help themselves to whatever they liked. As an informal and relaxed host of the party he could show them that he was an open person and easy to talk to.

(c) He believes that a manager should show a clear sense of authority. The party, however, was not a success. The employees were very uncomfortable as guests. (d) They felt they didn't know Morris well enough to be in his home. They thought he was showing off his money and were not comfortable with one another because they were not used to socializing together.

8. Which of the following is TRUE from the passage?

(a) Since the quality of food was not good, the employees were not satisfactory at the party.

(b) Some workers did not come to Morris' party for they didn't like home parties.

(c) The guests in the party enjoyed the party, and felt at ease.

(d) Morris prepared an informal party to be friendly with the people in the office.

9. Which of the following is AGAINST the logic from the passage?

(a) (b) (c) (d)

Story II

Global gTrade vs. Allgarment Enterprises

등장인물

Eugine Park: Import Manager, Global gTrading Co. Ltd.
Javv Gupta: Director, Export Division Allgarment Enterprise
Shoe Shipper: Acting Manager, India Shipping Lines.
Insura Insupers: Manager, Insurance India, Co. Ltd.

줄거리

한국의 전문 무역업체인 Global gTrading의 import manager인 Eugine Park은 인도의 Allgarment Enterprise가 ECplaza 21에 올린 여러 디자인의 의류를 보고 수입하여 판매할 목적으로 director인 Javv Gupta에게 inquiry를 보냈다. 거래조건에 관한 몇 번의 의견 교환 끝에 15%의 할인, CIF가격 조건, 그리고 D/P 방식으로 계약을 맺었다. CIF조건이기 때문에 Javv는 선박화사와 보험회사에 연락을 하여 선복을 확보하고 보험을 들었다. 그러나 선적을 준비하고 있는데 때마침 인도 동부를 강타한 Cyclone 때문에 선박이 파손되고 이에 따라 선적이 지연되었다. 결국 다른 선박을 확보해서 선적을 마무리 하였다. 그 후에도 서로 여러 차례의 거래가 이루어져 신뢰가 확보된 후에는 D/A 방식으로 거래가 이루어졌다. 그런데 어느 날..

Situation 1

Global gTrading이 의류수입을 위한 Inquiry를 보내다.

Global gTrading

124 Dukjin Dong Jeonju, Korea 561-756
Tel: +82-63-270-3049 Fax: +82-63-270-3028
E-mail: gtrading@kornet.net

September 1, 2014

Dear Mr. J. Gupta,

We are a specialist in importing and distributing all kinds of garments across Korea since 1979, and are looking for a manufacturer who can supply us with wide range of hand-crafted knitwear. We were favorably impressed by the designs displayed at your site in ECplaza.

In this type of business we used to make deals by 60-day bill of exchange, D/A. We are also expecting a quantity discount* in addition to a 20% trade discount* off net list prices because we usually place large orders.

If you can agree to the payment terms and concessions* we are asking for, please send us your current catalog and price list. We would also appreciate it if you could send some samples of your knitwears so that we can examine the texture and quality.
We hope to hear from you soon. With best regards,

Eugine Park

Eugine Park Import Manager
Global gTrading Co., Ltd.

Synopsis

Global gTrading의 import manager인 Eugine Park은 인도의 Allgarment Enterprise가 ECplaza에 올린 여러 디자인의 의류를 보고 수입하여 판매할 목적으로 inquiry를 보냈다. 우선 Global gTrading은 한국에서 1979년부터 의류수입 및 유통업에 종사해온 전문회사인데, 수공에 뜨개질 의류를 공급해줄 회사를 찾고 있음을 밝히고 있다. 대금 거래조건은 서류인수 후 60일 결제조건인 D/A(documents against acceptance)로 해왔고, 주로 대량구매를 하기 때문에 표시가격에서 20%의 할인을 기대하고 있다는 것을 밝히고 있다. 이런 대금지급과 할인조건들에 동의한다면 가격표와 함께 최신 catalog를 보내주면 고맙겠다고 말하고 있다. 그리고 섬유(texture)와 품질(quality)을 조사할 수 있도록 샘플을 보내달라고 요구하고 있다.

* quantity discount: =volume discount, 대량주문에 따른 할인
* trade discount: (주로 대량주문을 유도하기 위한) 동업자간 할인
* concession: discount, allowance, reduction, rebate, abatement

◇ we are a specialist~

여기에서 쓰인 We는 하나의 회사를 나타낸다. 따라서 specialists라고 복수로 쓰지 않고 단수로 받아서 a specialist로 쓴다.

- We are a co-operative wholesale society based on New York.
  (co-operative: co-op, 공동출자에 의한 조합)
- We are a large retail store ~
- Our company is a subsidiary of ~

같은 이유로 복수의 회사명이라도 단수로 받는다.

- Hyundai Motors Co. announces that it will donate one trillion won to the social welfare foundation.

그러나 다음과 같이 복수 형태로 쓰이기도 한다.

- We are prime makers and exporters producing office appliances.

garment

옷, 의복을 나타내는 단어에는 여러 가지가 있다. 서로 중복되어서 같이 쓰이는 것도 있지만, 상황에 맞게 용어를 선택할 필요가 있다.

clothes: '의복'을 뜻하는 일반적인 말로, 상의·하의 등을 가리킴.

- She walked upstairs to change her clothes.

clothing: 몸에 걸치는 모든 것을 뜻하는 '의류'로 각종 clothes의 총칭.

- clothing industry: 의류산업

apparel: 공식적인 중요한 행사에 입는 옷

- Women's apparel is offered in petite, regular, and tall models.

garment: 특히 옷을 제조하거나 판매와 관련된 옷을 말할 때 씀

- Our garments have the customers' name tags in the linings.

attire: 입고 있는 옷, 차림새

- Business attire is required for this occasion. (정장이 요구됨)

costume: 영화, 연극, 행사 때의 분장과 관련된 옷

- The actress has eight costume changes during the drama.

wear: 어떤 때나 장소에 맞는 옷을 말할 때

- beach wear(해수욕장 옷), evening wear(저녁 잠옷 류)

outfit: 한 벌의 의상

- She is wearing an outfit she bought yesterday.

dress: 보통 겉에 입는 의복으로 사교 장소 등에 입고 나가는 것. 여성의 드레스.

- She is wearing pink dress.

suit: 정장, 남자의 경우는 jacket, trousers, 여자는 jacket, skirt or trousers

- a dark pin-striped business suit(어두운 줄무늬 정장)

gear: 특정행사나 목적을 위한 옷

- fishing gear(낚시용 옷), riot gear(폭동진압용 옷)

uniform: 군대나 학교 등 특정 단체가 같은 형식으로 입는 옷

- school uniform, military uniform

wardrobe: 소유하고 있는 의상, 연극단체 등의 배우용 costume의 총칭, 옷장.

- the wardrobe department of the theater: 극장의 의상실

manufacturer

제조업자, 생산업자를 나타내는 말에는 maker, manufacturer, producer 등이 있다.

maker는 생산업자에 대한 총칭의 성격이 강하다

- auto maker
- computer maker

manufacturer는 원래 수공업자와 같이 소규모 제조업자에 대하여 사용되었지만, 지금은 대규모의 제조업자를 의미한다.

- car manufacturer
- chemical products manufacturer
- original equipment manufacturer(OEM: 주문자 브랜드로 판매되는 상품을 제조하는 업자)

producer는 경제학적 용어로 consumer(소비자)에 대한 생산자의 개념으로 쓰인다. (producer's price: 생산자 가격) producer(PD)는 영화나 드라마의 제작자라는 의미도 있다.

EC plaza

1995년 이후 세계적으로 인터넷상에 무역전문 사이트가 생겨나기 시작하여 현재 수백개의 사이트들이 운영되고 있다. 이들 사이트는 구매오퍼(offer to buy)와 판매오퍼(offer to sell)를 게시하여 상품을 사고파는 정보를 중계하는 것이 주된 기능이다. 이러한 사이트들을 이용하면 아주 적은 경비와 단순한 작업으로 전 세계 바이어들에게 시간과 공간에 관계없이 상품을 홍보할 수 있으며 바이어를 발굴할 수 있다. 국내·외 대표적인 사이트들은 다음과 같다.

국내	외국
www.ecplaza.net	www.worldbid.com
www.ec21.com	www.alibaba.com
www.kotis.net	www.eceurope.com
www.silkroad21.com	www.ecrobot.com

◈ used to

'언제나 ~했다' '~하는 것이 보통이었다'와 같이 과거의 습관을 나타낸다.

- He used to eat Chinese food. (중국음식을 먹곤 했었다.)
- He used to be one of the professors at the College of Commerce.
  used to의 부정형은 used not to로 쓰지만 구어체에서는 did not use to 혹은 did not used to도 사용된다.
- She used not to answer the phone.
- She did not use(d) to answer the phone.

be used to ~는 '~에 익숙해져 있다'(=be accustomed to)의 의미로 형태는 used to와 비슷하지만 뜻도 다르고 사용법도 다르므로 주의해야 한다. used to의 used는 동사이지만, be used to의 used는 형용사이고 to는 전치사이기 때문에 to 다음에 명사나 동명사가 오고 동사는 올 수 없다.

- He is used to eating Chinese food. (중국음식에 익숙해졌다.)
- I am used/accustomed to making a speech in public.
  ~~to make~~
- I don't frighten her. She is used to it.

be 대신 get이나 become을 써서 쓰기도 한다.

- I am getting used to making a speech in public. (익숙해져 가고 있다.)
- This is how I do things here. You'll soon become used to it. (익숙해질 것이다.)

'사용하다'의 의미로 쓰이는 동사 use가 수동태 형태로 쓰이면 '~하기 위하여 사용되다'의 의미가 되고 이때는 to 다음에 동사가 올 수 있으므로 문장의 의미로 먼저 파악해야 한다.

- This knife is used to cut the glass. (이 칼은 유리를 자르는 데 사용된다.)
  * '이 칼은 유리를 자르는 데 익숙해져 있다'는 말은 어색함.
- Internet advertisement has been used to promote our products.

◈ Terms of Payment(결제조건)

무역대금의 결제방법은 크게 송금결제(remittance), 추심결제(documentary collection), 신용장(letter of credit)결제가 있다.

송금결제는 계약 물품의 인도 전, 인도와 동시, 또는 인도 후에 전신환(T/T: telegraphic transfer) 또는 우편환(M/T: mail transfer)을 이용하여 대금을 결제하는 단순 송금방식이다. 송금결제방식에는 CWO, CAD, COD가 있다.

추심결제는 수출상이 수입상 앞으로 발행한 환어음(bill of exchange)에 선적서류를 첨부하여 수출상 거래은행에 추심(collection)을 의뢰하면 은행은 은행 간 추심을 통하여 수입상 거래은행에서 선적서류와 상환으로 대금을 결제하는 방식이다. 추심결제에는 어음지급 서류인도조건(D/P: documents against payment)과 어음인수 서류인도조건(D/A: documents against acceptance)방식이 있다.

위의 두 가지 결제방법은 수출상과 수입상 중 어느 일방에게만 유리하고 상대방에게는 대금회수나 물품 인수의 보장이 없는 것이 특징이다. 따라서 이러한 방식은 매매상대방을 신뢰할 수 없을 때에는 사용하기 어렵다. 이러한 이유 때문에 특히 국제무역에서는 매매당사자 이외에 제3자인 은행이 개입하여 대금의 지급을 보장하는 신용장(letter of credit) 결제방식이 많이 쓰인다. L/C에 대하여서는 Story I에서 알아보았음으로 여기에서는 송금 결제와 추심결제에 대하여 알아본다.

송금결제

CWO(Cash With Order)

수입상이 물품구입 주문과 동시에 대금을 전부 지불하고 수출상은 일정한 기일 내 이에 상응하는 물품을 선적하는 것을 말한다. 즉, cash in advance(선불) 거래 방식이다.

CAD(Cash Against Documents)

수출상이 상품을 선적하고 이를 증명할 수 있는 선하증권, 보험증권, 상업송장 등 주요 선적서류를 수출지의 수입상의 대리점이나 거래은행에 제시하고 수출대금을 받는 방식이다.

COD(Cash On Delivery)

계약물품이 수입지에 도착하면 수입상이 물품의 품질이나 수량 등을 검사한 후 그 물품과 상환으로 수출대금을 현금으로 결제해 주는 방식이다. 수입국의 수출상의 해외 지점 등이 수출상이 보낸 서류를 받아서 수입상에게 전달한 후 물품의 검사가 끝나면 수출대금을 받는 방식을 취한다.

추심결제

D/P(Documents against Payment: 어음지급 서류인도조건)

어음지급 서류인도조건은 수출상이 수입상과의 매매계약에 따라 물품을 선적하고 구비된 서류에 일람출급환어음(sight bill or demand draft)을 발행 첨부하여 자기거래 은행(추 심의뢰은행)을 통하여 수입상 거래은행인 수입국의 은행 앞으로 그 어음대금을 추심 의뢰하면 수입국측 은행(추심은행)은 수입상에게 어음을 제시하여 그 어음금액의 일람지급을 받고 서류를 인도하는 거래방식을 말한다. 수입상이 대금지급을 하지 않고는 선적서류를 인수하지 못하기 때문에 수출상의 입장에서는 D/A조건보다 유리하다.

D/A(Documents against Acceptance: 어음인수 서류인도조건)

어음인수서류인도조건은 거래와 대금을 추심하는 경로는 같으나 D/P와 다른 점은 수출상이 일람 후 정기 또는 확정일 출급 환어음(usance bill or time draft)을 발행하고 수입 상 거래은행인 추심은행은 환어음을 수입상에게 제시하여 그 제시된 어음을 일람지급 받지 않고 인수만 받음으로써 서류를 인도한 후 만기일에 대금을 지급 받는 거래방식이다. 즉, 수입상은 인도받은 서류로 물품을 찾은 다음 판매하여 그 대금으로 어음의 기일 내에 결제하게 된다.

◈ agree to

'~에 찬성하다'의 의미로 agree to 다음에는 사물, agree with 다음에는 사람이 오는 것이 일반적이다.

- She agreed to both requests.
- I see your point but I am not sure I agree with you.

그러나 사람이건 사물이건 with를 쓰는 경향이 많다.

- I agree with every word you have just said.
- She said she totally agreed with my opinion.

이외에 agree는 to + do, on + ~ing, ~that의 형태로 쓰인다.

She agreed to stay here.

We agree on going there together.

He agreed that we won the game.

◈ sample

국제간의 거래에서는 제품의 품질이나 성격을 파악하기 위하여 sample을 주고받는 경우가 많이 생긴다. 이럴 때는,

- We shall be glad if you will send us samples of flour of medium quality.
- Would you please send the samples to us for testing the quality?
- When replying, could you please enclose sample patterns of fabrics.

sample은 거래를 활성화하기 위하여 필요하지만 소량 샘플을 요구한 후 더 많은 샘플을 요구하거나 샘플을 자주 요구하는 buyer는 일단 거래의사는 별로 없고 sample만을 사취하 기 위한 무역 사기범일 가능성이 많으므로 의심해 봐야 한다. 샘플은 무상으로 줄 수 있는 한도가 넘어가는 경우 대금을 요청하거나 송금을 받은 후 샘플을 발송하여야 한다. 이럴 때는 다음과 같은 표현을 쓸 수 있다.

- For our regular customer, the sample can be sent free of charge. Please, however, understand that we shall be forced to charge sample cost and freight to all of the new buyers until the first transaction is made.

sample: 실제 거래되는 상품의 일부, 현물 견본

pattern: 의상, 도안이 상품의 품질을 결정하는 직물류 등의 견본

specimen: 동일 종류에 속하는 것, 전체를 대표하는 견본

swatch: 직물의 일부 견본

standard: 현물 견본으로 매매하기 어려운 상품의 견본

Practice Tests - Situation 1

1. What type of letter is it?
   (a) An inquiry from an exporter to an importer.
   (b) An offer from an exporter to an importer.
   (c) An inquiry from an importer to an exporter.
   (d) An offer from an exporter to an importer.

2. What is NOT true about this letter?
   (a) Mr. Park wants to make a deal by usance bill.
   (b) Mr. Park searched the websites to find suppliers.
   (c) Mr. Gupta sent Mr. Park some samples of the garments.
   (d) Mr. Gupta's company put an advertisement on EC plaza 21.

3. In this type of business we ______ make deals by 60-day bill of exchange.
   (a) are used to (b) are accustomed to
   (c) used to (d) get used to

4. I am getting used to ________ a speech in public.
   (a) make (b) making
   (c) made (d) have made

5. If you can ____________ the payment terms and concessions we are asking ____, please send us your current catalog and price list.
   (a) agree with - to (b) agree to - for
   (c) agree for - to (d) agree on - for

6. We are also expecting a quantity discount in addition to a 20% trade discount net list prices because we usually place large orders.
   (a) from (b) in
   (c) out of (d) off

7. For our regular customer, the ______ can be sent free of charge. Please, however, understand that we shall be forced to charge _______ cost and freight to all of the new buyers until the first transaction is made.

(a) merchandise (b) cargo
(c) particle (d) sample

8. If a draft is payable upon presentation to the drawee, it is classified as ____________.

(a) demand draft (b) time draft
(c) usance bill (d) D/A

9. 괄호 안에 가장 적합한 문장은?

A: Would you tell me your terms of payment?

B: We require full payment within 30 d/s. But a 8% discount will be allowed for cash payment.

A: We prefer the former terms of payment. Then when shall we pay for it?

B: Shipping documents will be dispatched to you through the bank, ( ).

(a) and you must remit the invoice amount within 30 days after receipt of them.
(b) and you must remit the invoice amount as soon as you receive them.
(c) and we will remit the invoice amount within 30 days after receipt of them.
(d) and we will remit the invoice amount as soon as we receive them.

10. Under the D/A bill the documents are handed over to consignee from the bank upon his acceptance of the bill, whereas under ( ) the documents are not handed over to the consignee until he pays his bill.

(a) clean B/L (b) documentary bill
(c) D/P bill (d) sight bill

11. Choose the correct one.

(a) They usually do business on a draft at sight under documents against payment, and think that these terms will suit you.

(b) They usually do business on a draft at sight under documents against acceptance, and think that these terms will suit to you.

(c) They usually do business on a draft as sights under documents against payment, and think that these terms will suit to you.

(d) They usually do business on a draft as sight under documents against acceptance, and think that these terms will suit you.

12. 다음은 어떤 지급조건의 거래에서 사용된 문장인가? [무역영어 2급]

We have accepted you bill of exchange for USD35,800 drawn at 120 days after sight and duly received the relevant documents. the bill will be paid by us on a fixed date.

(a) D/P (b) D/A
(c) COD (d) CAD

13. 다음을 가장 올바르게 영작한 것을 고르시오. [무역영어 2급]

귀사가 통상 사용하는 지불 조건을 일람 30일 후 지불조건방식으로 바꾸시겠습니까?

(a) Would you depart from your usual terms of payment to 30 days after sight under D/P?

(b) Would you mind if we change your usual terms of 30 days to our new terms of payment after at sight?

(c) Would you mind if we change your usual terms of 30 days to our new terms of payment after at sight?

(d) Would you depart from your usual terms of payment to 30 days after sight under D/A?

14. Which of the followings is NOT TRUE according to the letter?

[무역영어 2급]

Regarding payments terms, we are regretful to say that it would not be possible for us to accept your proposal of D/A 180 days basis transaction due to conservative sales policy of our company after financial crisis.

Hence, we would like to ask you to consider Usance Letter of Credit on 180 days basis.

(a) This is a reply to a letter requesting collection terms.
(b) This letter gives a negative response to the request.
(c) This letter suggests a different payment terms.
(d) This letter rejects the request because of short credit period.

15. Below is the opening part of a letter. What is the purpose of this letter? [무역영어 2급]

Thank you for your recent application for 60-day terms of credit. However, we are not in a position to grant you credit at this time.

(a) to answer a extension request.
(b) to propose the new payment terms.
(c) to refuse payment terms requested.
(d) to grant the credit requested.

[16~17] Read the following, and answer the questions. [무역영어 1급]

I called on World Colorants on Monday.

They currently import raw materials from Europe, but are interested in finding lower-cost sources of materials of the same quality. In the report I've included a list of materials they are looking for along with their target prices.

The 8% commission will barely cover our expenses, and we'll need at least 10%.

If we can meet those prices, I'm pretty sure we can get this account.

I'd like to discuss pricing with you.

16. Which of the following is AGAINST the logic from the letter?

(a) (A) (b) (B) (c) (C) (d) (D)

17. What type of the document is it?

(a) Call Report (b) Request for Special Billing
(c) Notice of Rate Change (d) Payment Authorized

Situation 2

Allgarment Enterprises가 Inquiry에 reply하다.

37-2 Bridgeway Colony, 2nd Street, Tirupur, Tamilnadu India 641607
Telephone: +91-421-2232-880
Facsimile: +91-42-2232-888

September 2, 2014

Dear Mr. Eugine Park,

This morning I am very pleased to find your fax saying that you are positively considering our knitwears. We would have no problem in supplying you from our wide selection of garments.

By DHL we will send our winter catalog and price list quoting prices CIF Busan along with 3 pieces of our sample garments for you to review. We are sure that you will find a ready sale for our goods in Korea.

For orders of USD20,000 or more we will make a 5% discount off the list prices, but the usual allowance for a trade discount in India is 15%. We always deal on payment by sight draft, documents against payment (D/P). However, we will be willing to reconsider this term once we establish a firm trading association with you.

We hope very much that we can reach an agreement on the terms quoted. Yours sincerely,

Javv Gupta

Javv Gupta, Director Export Division Allgarment Enterprises

Synopsis

Global gTrading의 inquiry를 받은 Allgarment의 Javv Gupta는 감사의 표시와 함께 여러 종류의 의류가 있으니 공급하는데 문제가 없을 것임을 밝히고 있다. 대량 주문 할인은 미화 20,000 이상이면 순 가격에서 5%이고, 인도에서 동업자간 할인은 15%이므로 이런 조건을 제시하고 있다. 결제는 일람출급어음 방식으로 해오고 있지만, 일단 거래가 성사되고 확실한 관계가 유지되면 상대방(수입자, 여기서는 Global gTrading)에게 더 유리한 조건을 고려하겠다고 말하고 있다. CIF Busan으로 견적한 price list, winter catalog, 그리고 3종류의 sample을 DHL로 보내겠다고 밝히고, 한국에서 잘 팔릴 것이며 계약이 성사되길 바란다고 편지를 마감하고 있다.

◈ find a ready sale

'~이 잘 팔리다'의 뜻이다. sell을 사용하면 본문의 내용을 이렇게 고칠 수 있다.

- We are sure that our products will sell well in Korea.

on sale은 '판매'라는 뜻과 함께 '평소보다 싸게 판매'한다는 뜻도 가지고 있다.

- English textbook and dictionaries are on sale everywhere. (판매 중이다.)
- She bought a dress on sale at Macy's. (싸게 샀다.)

for sale은 '(원래 팔지 않는 것을) 팔려고 내놓았다'는 의미이다.

- His house is for sale at $160,000.
- These fine jewelries are not for sale. (비매품이다.)

clearance sale: 재고정리 염가판매
bargain sale: 할인판매
closing down sale: 점포정리 판매
cash sale, sale for cash(money): 현금판매
credit sale, sale on credit(account): 외상판매
back-to-school sale: 개학 맞이 할인판매
Thanksgiving sale: 추수감사절 할인판매
after Christmas sale: 크리스마스 지난 후 할인판매

anniversary sale: 점포개점 기념 할인판매
garage/yard sale: 개인 중고품 판매(주로 주말에 개인집 차고나 마당에서 함)
fundraising sale: 특정 기금 모금을 위한 자선판매

◈ goods

'상품, 제품, 화물' 등의 의미로 쓰이는 말은 여러 가지가 있다 그 중에서 가장 일반적으로 쓰이는 단어는 goods이다.

goods는 항상 복수로 쓰이기 때문에 this good은 틀린 표현이고 these goods이나 the goods로 표현한다. 또한 goods 다음에 오는 동사도 복수형으로 쓴다.

- Goods are things that are made to be sold. (goods는 팔기 위해 만든 물건이다.)

seasonal goods: 계절품
(high) quality goods: 고급품
defective goods: 불량품
goods in stock: 재고품
sundry goods: 잡화
durable goods: 내구재
goods and services: 재화와 용역
public goods: 공공재화
household goods: 가정용품
finished goods: 완제품
semi-manufactured goods: 반제품
goods made to order: 주문품
goods in process: 제작중인 물건
non-durable goods: 소비재
substitute goods: 대체재
private goods: 사유재물

merchandise는 특히 시장에 나와서 거래되는 goods를 말한다. uncountable noun 이므로 복수형으로 쓰이지 않고 동사도 단수가 온다. 집합적 의미의 상품을 말한다.

- Merchandise is goods that are bought, sold, or traded.
  (merchandise는 사고, 팔리고, 거래되는 goods를 말한다.)
- When goods are put on the market they are called merchandise.
  (goods이 시장에 나오면 merchandise가 된다.)

gift merchandise: 선물용품
musical merchandise: 음악용품
general merchandise: 잡화
unsold merchandise: 판매 되지 않은 상품

Harry Potter merchandise: Harry Potter 관련 상품(책, 인형, 게임 등)

article은 물건, 물품으로 countable noun이다. 따라서 articles로 쓸 수 있다.

article(s) of furniture: 가구
necessary article: 필수품
luxury article: 고급품
coarse article: 조잡품
articles of food: 식료품
articles of export: 수출품
domestic article: 국산품
imported article: 수입품

commodity는 상품, 물품, 물산(특히 곡물, 식료품 등 일차 상품)을 말한다. 복수형으로 쓰여서 일용품, 필수품의 의미로도 쓰인다.

marketable commodity: 시장성이 좋은 상품
perishable commodity: 부패하기 쉬운 상품
commodity exchange: 상품거래시장(곡물, 원유, 원당 등을 거래하는 시장)
financial commodity market: 금융상품시장(주식, 채권, 외환 등을 거래하는 시장)
household commodities: 가정용품

product는 천연물과 공산품 양쪽의 생산물, 제품을 말하는 countable noun이다.

industrial products: 공산품
agricultural products: 농산물
natural products: 천연산물
fishery products: 해산물
forestry products: 임산물
foreign products: 외제

produce는 명사형으로 특히 농산물, 수확물 등을 말한다. uncountable noun이므로 항상 단수이고 한 개의 생산물은 a piece of produce, 한 종류의 생산품은 an item of produce로 쓴다. 발음은 동사형과 달리 accent를 앞에 두어서 [prádjuːs, próu-]와 같이 한다.

farm produce: 농산물
produce of factory: 공산품
produce on display: 진열된 농산물

ware는 주로 합성어로 쓰여서 제품, 세공품 등을 말한다.

hardware: 철물, 컴퓨터의 하드웨어
software: 소프트웨어
glassware: 유리제품
tableware: 식탁용 식기류
woodenware: 목기류
luxury wares: 고급품

◈ orders of USD20,000 or more

'미화 20,000 혹은 그 이상의 주문'의 의미이다. 평상문이나 일상대화의 경우 orders more than $20,000 혹은 orders over $20,000면 충분하지만 business에서는 20,000이 포함되느냐 혹은 포함되지 않느냐가 중요한 경우가 많다. For order over $20,000 we will make 5% discount off the list prices.로 표현했다면, 정확히 20,000불의 주문은 어떻게 할 것인지에 대하여 서로 해석의 차이가 있을 수 있다. We have more than 2,000 participants on the meeting.에서와 같이 숫자가 그리 중요하지 않은 경우도 있지만, 대부분의 business에서 특히 금액이나 수량 등의 숫자는 중요한 의미를 가지고 있다. 따라서 처음부터 다음 표를 참조하여 숫자를 명확히 표현하는 습관을 들이는 것이 필요하다.

~ 미만 (해당 수 불포함)	~ 이하 (해당 수 포함)	~ 이상 (해당 수 포함)	~을 초과하다 (해당 수 불포함)
less than~ under ~ [above] ~ below ~	~ or less [below] ~ and under not more than ~	~ or more [above] ~ and over not less than ~	more than ~ over exceeding ~

I have less than $20. ($19.99~$00.01) $20 포함 안 됨
I have $20 or less. ($20.00~$00.01) $20 포함
I have $20 or more. ($20.00~∞) $20 포함
I have more than $20. (20.01~∞) $20 포함 안 됨

◈ make a discount~

'~의 할인을 해 주다(제공하다, 받다)'의 표현은,

make allow give grant offer take receive	a(n)	discount allowance concession reduction rebate abatement	off on	the price the goods the order

'~가격에서 5% 할인'으로 쓰일 때, 전치사는 off가 가장 많이 쓰이고 on도 가능하다. 실무에서 from이나 of를 쓰기도 하지만 정확한 표현은 아니다.

- Now through May 31, all orders receive a 20% discount off the order total.
- You're entitled to take a 2% prompt payment discount off the goods value.
- You can find specials for a discount off the price of the Cook Books.

discount: 일반적인 할인
allowance: 할인, 특히 claim에 대한 조정으로 인한 할인
concession: (양보에 의한) 가격 할인
reduction: (양자 합의에 의한) 할인
rebate: 판매 대금 수령 후 일정금액을 돌려주는 형식의 할인
abatement: 소량의 할인

Practice Tests - Situation 2

1. Which one is NOT what Mr. Gupta said in this letter?
   (a) He was happy to receive an inquiry.
   (b) He is sure their garments will sell well in Korea.
   (c) He is willing to reconsider the payment terms at this time.
   (d) He hopes to reach an agreement on the terms he quoted.

2. What is true about the terms Mr. Gupta is offering?
   (a) The quantity discount is 15%.
   (b) The importer should pay the ocean freight.
   (c) His company wants to make a deal by a time draft.
   (d) His company will insure the goods up to the destination.

3. From the appearances of the buildings and premises of Mr. Petrie, we should think his business was profitable, and that he has ready for all the butter he makes. Butter is used at every meal and on every table, and if the quality is satisfactory will always find a ready .
   (a) sold (b) selling
   (c) sale (d) sell

4. _________ by owner allows you to beat the real estate agents and save thousands on fees! Sell your house today.
   (a) on sale (b) in sale
   (c) for sale (d) off sale

5. When _______ are put on the market they are called _________.
   (a) merchandises – goods (b) goods – merchandises
   (c) goods – merchandise (d) merchandises – good

6. For orders of USD20,000 ___________ we will make a 5% discount off the list prices, but the usual allowance for a trade discount in India is 15%.

(a) or less (b) or more
(c) and under (d) and below

7. 다음을 가장 올바르게 영작한 것을 고르시오. [무역영어 2급]

당사의 제의에 관심이 있다면, 당사는 송장금액에서 10%의 특별할인을 허용해 드리겠습니다.

(a) If you are interested in our proposal, we would like you to allow us a special discount of 10% off the invoice amount.
(b) If you are interested in our proposal, we would like to give you a special allowance of 10% off the invoice amount.
(c) If you are interested in our proposition, we would like you to give us a special discount of 10% off the invoice amount.
(d) If you are interested to our proposal, we would like to allow you a special allowing of 10% off the invoice amount.

[8~9] Read the following letter and answer the questions. [무역영어 1급]

Dear ABC,

I was intrigued by your article in the June issue of American Druggist, and I am interested in learning more about the new networking options you discussed.

I have a client who would benefit greatly from these applications that your company developed specifically for pharmacies. Your system may be the answer to my client's problem, and I would like to learn more. I am particularly

interested in seeing how it tracks and manages data reporting, as now required by the recent FDA mandates.

I will be in Seattle the week of August 18 and would very much like to see this system in operation. Please let me know if this will be convenient.

Sincerely,

BCD

8. Which of the following is NOT inferred according to the letter above?
 (a) BCD is the person who will use the networking if things go well.
 (b) The networking mentioned in the letter is designed specifically for pharmacies.
 (c) Pharmacies are recently mandated to keep the records in operation.
 (d) The client of BCD is concerned about the increasing costs of data handling.

9. What is the most appropriate reason that BCD wrote to ABC?
 (a) To ask an inquiry about the networking ABC has developed
 (b) To introduce his client to ABC
 (c) To ask for an appointment to see the networking operation
 (d) To show his interest about the networking

10. Which of the following is the main purpose of the letter?

[무역영어 1급]

Dear Mr. Torrence,

I have just returned from my trip to Europe today. I would like to thank you, not only for the time and excellent lunch in Brussels last week, but also for the very positive attitude you showed toward the joint project. I am sure you played a very important role in laying the ground work for the decision you indicated.

As I told you, the Executive Committee for the project will be held in Seoul in May 30 especially to review the progress of our project. I would very much like to be able to announce your firm commitment to the Committee at that time.

Thank you again.

Patric Johnson

 (a) To confirm with Mr. Torrence the launch of the new joint project.
 (b) To inform Mr. Torrence of the decision regarding the new joint project.
 (c) To request Mr. Torrence to lay the grounds for the new joint project.
 (d) To ask for Mr. Torrence's active involvement in the new joint project.

11. Which of the following is MOST likely to come before the passage below? [무역영어 1급]

The American manufacturer was pleased with the negotiations, although they had taken much longer than he had planned. They had finally agreed to prices and methods of distribution. The Saudi Arabian distributor asked the American when he could expect his first shipment of clothes. The American answered that they could begin business only when the contracts were written and signed.

(a) An American clothes manufacturer and a Saudi Arabian clothes distributor came to the end of lengthy negotiations in Saudi Arabia.
(a) When the Saudi Arabian heard this, he became extremely insulted. He told the American that he was close to canceling the deal.
(a) The Saudi Arabian businessman said that he thought everything was agreed to and finalized during the negotiations.
(a) The American said that was true, but he still insisted on a written contract. The written contract would say exactly when their business would begin and end and state all the terms they had agreed to.

12. Which of the followings CANNOT replace the ones(A-D) with the same meaning as the ones given in the sentence? [무역영어 1급]

If you can (A) guarantee supply of products strictly (B) in accordance with our specifications, we shall be (C) prepared to (D) place a prompt trial order.

(a) (A) guarantee → secure
(b) (B) in accordance with → conforming to
(c) (C) prepared → appointed
(d) (D) place → give

Situation 3

Global gTrading이 의류수입을 위한 주문을 Allgarment에 보내다.

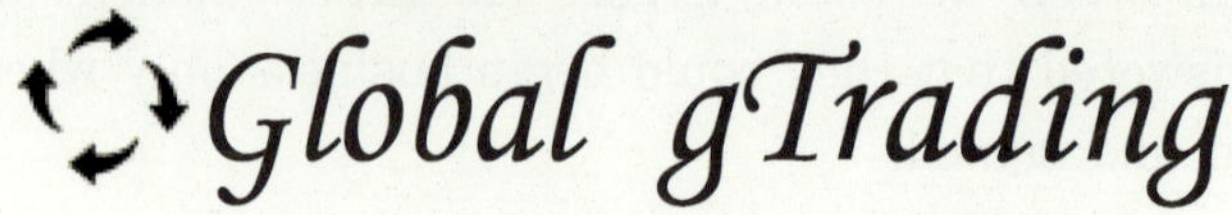

124 Dukjin Dong Jeonju, Korea 561-756
Tel: +82-63-270-3049 Fax: +82-63-270-3028
E-mail: gtrading@kornet.net

Your ref: D/3344
Our ref: Order DR3355

September 14, 2014

Dear Mr. Gupta,

After reviewing your sample and considering your discounts we have decided to place a trial order of 500 garments. Enclosed please find our Order Sheet,
No. DR3355.

For this order, we accept the 15% trade discount you offered, and the terms of payment (sight draft, D/P), but hope you review these terms for future transactions.

Please send the shipping documents and your sight draft to Korea Exchange Bank (Dukjin Branch), 1233 Dukjin-dong Jeonju, Korea 561-733. We would appreciate delivery within the next six weeks, and look forward to your order acknowledgement.
Best wishes,

Eugine Park

Eugine Park,
Import
Manager
Global gTrading Co., Inc.

Synopsis

인도의 Allgarment로부터 받은 샘플과 할인조건을 검토한 후에 Global gTrading의 Eugine Park은 우선 500벌의 시험주문을 하기로 결정했다. Allgarment가 제시한 15%의 trade discount와 일람출급어음에 의한 결제방식을 받아들였다. 결제조건은 추후 거래에서는 다시 결정해 주길 원한다는 점도 밝혀두고 있다. 그리고 선적서류와 일람출급어음을 외환은행을 통해 보내달라고 요구했다. 또 6주 이내에 상품이 인도되게 해달라는 말과 함께 주문 확인(acknowledge)을 부탁했다.

◈ Order Sheet

Order Letter(주문서한)는 order의 내용이 간단한 경우에 사용되며 서한 본문 중에 주문의 내용이 포함된다. 그러나 주문의 내용이 복잡한 경우, 일정한 Order Sheet(주문서)에 주문내용을 기입하고 이것을 매도인에게 보내면 매도인은 acknowledgement of order(주문 승낙서)를 매수인에게 보냄으로써 무역계약은 성립되고 확인된다. Order Letter에는 주문의 의사표시, 주문의 근거(catalog, sample, price list 등), 주문의 내용에 관한 사항이 기재된다. 내용이 복잡한 경우 다음의 Situation 4와 같은 Order Sheet에 항목별로 Order의 내용을 상세히 기재하고 여기에 주문의 의사표시와 주요 거래조건, 기타 희망사항 등을 기재한 Situation 3와 같은 cover letter를 첨부하여 보내게 된다.

◈ delivery

delivery order(D/O): 화물인도지시서
delivery period: 인도기간
date(time) of delivery: 인도기일
delivery terms: 인도조건
installment delivery: 분할인도
full delivery: 전량인도
get(receive, take) delivery: 인도받다
make(give) delivery: 인도하다
ready for delivery: 즉시인도
near delivery: 근일인도
immediate(prompt) delivery: 즉시인도

immediate과 prompt는 '즉시 인도'의 의미로 사용되었지만 즉시의 해석은 각국마다 다를 수 있다. 따라서 신용장통일규칙에서는 이런 용어의 사용을 금하고 있다. near delivery 역시 불명확한 용어이다. 이외에도 as soon as possible, without delay, by an earliest possible date, vessel by first available과 같은 불명확한 표현들은 피해야 한다. business에서는 delivery within six weeks나 September delivery와 같이 명확한 표현을 사용할 필요가 있다.

◈ next

next는 '다음'을 의미한다. 따라서 next Monday, next month라고 하면 다음 월요일, 다음 달을 말한다.

- Shipment will be made next Friday.

위의 문장은 문법적으로는 문제가 없지만 정확성을 요구하는 business에서는 예를 들면 오늘이 월요일이라면 위의 표현은 다가오는 금요일인지 아니면 다음 주 금요일인지 아니면 더 막연히 다음 금요일인지 분명하지 않을 수 있다. 실제로 영어를 모국어로 쓰는 사람들도 예를 들면 오늘이 금요일이라면 3일 후의 "월요일에 보자"라고 말할 때, 아래의 3가지 표현을 모두 섞어서 쓰는 경향이 있다.

- I'll see you on Monday.
- I'll see you this Monday.
- I'll see you next Monday.

일상 대화에서도 말하는 시점이 언제인지에 따라서 혹은 사람에 따라서 다르게 말하고 해석될 가능성이 있다. 일상 대화에서는 다시 물어볼 수도 있고 또 정확히 언제를 말하는지가 중요하지 않을 수도 있지만 business에서는 다른 문제가 야기될 수 있다. 따라서 좀 더 정확한 표현을 다음과 같이 할 필요가 있다.

- Shipment will be made this(coming) Friday. (이번 주 금요일)
- Shipment will be made next coming Friday. (다음 주 금요일)
- Shipment will be made on Friday next week. (다음 주 금요일)

그러나 첫 두 문장 역시 말하는 시점이 주말이고 다음 월요일을 말할 경우 혼란을 줄 여지가 남아있다. 따라서 business writing에서 가장 추천할 수 있는 표현은 정확한 날짜와 함께 쓰는 것이다.

- Shipment will be made next coming Monday, May 27, 2006.

next, this, last는 시간을 나타내는 명사(week, month, year 등)와 함께 쓰이면 부사가 되어서 앞에 전치사 in이나 on이 오지 않는다.

- We will go there in this month.
- We went there in last weekend.
- We will go there in next year.

또 이렇게 쓸 때 next는 the 없이 쓰인다. the next와 next는 문법적으로 엄밀하게 구분하면 차이가 있겠지만 실제 business writing에서는 구별하지 않고 쓰인다.

- Your order will reach you within(the) next few days.
- Shipment will be made sometime in(the) next 7 days.

◈ Company의 종류

회사를 나타내는 말에는 다음과 같이 여러 가지가 있다.

company, firm, concern, enterprise, business organization: 일반적인 회사의 총칭
corporation: 주식회사
　　미국식: Company Incorporated(Co., Inc.)
　　영국식: Company Limited(Co., Ltd.),
PLC(Public Limited Company: 주식이 상장되어 있는 주식회사)

holding company: 지주회사
Chaebol(재벌): Korean conglomerate
Keiretsu(系列): Japanese conglomerate
general trading company: 종합무역상사
individual(sole) proprietorship: 개인회사
partnership: 합명회사
conglomerate: 기업집단
subsidiary company: 자회사
affiliated company: 계열회사
parent company: 모회사
limited partnership: 합자회사
private company: 유한회사
cooperative [co-op] 협동조합
dot-com, dot com company, dot com: 인터넷 관련 사업을 하는 회사
on-going concern: 정상적으로 운영되고 있는 회사
　　[bankrupt company(부도난 회사)에 대비된 개념의 용어]

Practice Tests - Situation 3

1. What kind of letter is it?

(a) A cover letter for an order
(b) An offer sheet
(c) A purchase order
(d) A sales note

2. According to the letter the transaction will be made by

(a) Letter of Credit.
(b) Cash with Order.
(c) Documentary Collection.
(d) Cash on Delivery.

3. Which one is NOT what Mr. Park wants Mr. Gupta to do?

(a) Mr. Park wants Mr. Gupta to review the payment terms.
(b) Mr. Park wants the shipping documents to be sent to KEB.
(c) Mr. Park wants the delivery to be made within the next six weeks.
(d) Mr. Park wants to acknowledge the order.

4. The goods will be delivered week.

(a) in the next
(b) the next
(c) next
(d) next of the

5. Questionably, a larger proportion of bankrupt companies received a audit opinion.

(a) going-concern
(b) limited
(c) private
(d) special

6. 다음 회화의 흐름상 괄호 안에 가장 적합한 표현은?

Insu: In case you open an account with us, we would like to allow you a trade discount.

Jane: What do you mean by the trade discount?

Insu: It is a reduction of the price(   ).

Jane: Thank you for your consideration.

(a) in accordance with the time of payment to induce the client to place a repeat order with us
(b) irrespective of the quantity ordered for the client to offer the highest prices to us
(c) regardless of the time of payment so as to induce the client to place a big order with us
(d) in view of the time of shipment so as to induce the importer to place a big order

7. Further to our telephone conversation on Friday, I am writing to you your order No. TT188, which was _______ with us on March 18. Once again, I must _________ for the delay in processing this order. It will reach you within five working days.

(a) concerning – placed – apologize (b) affecting – made – regret
(c) changing – sold – speak (d) regarding – taken – told

8. Please put the sentences below in the most appropriate order.

[무역영어 1급]

Thank you for your catalogue and price list.

a) They have agreed to pay by letter of credit, which we discussed on the phone last week, and they should deliver before the end of this month.
b) If the colors they have chosen are not in stock, they will accept an alternative provided the designs are those stipulated on the order.
c) They have asked us to instruct you that the 60 sets of crockery ordered should be packed in 6 crates, 10 sets per crates.
d) Please find attached an order(R1423) from our principals, MacKenzie Bros. Ltd., 1–5 Whale Drive, Dawson, Ontario, Canada.
e) Please send any further correspondence relating to shipment or payment direct to MacKenzie Bros.

(a) a – b – c – d – e (b) c – a – e – d – b
(c) d – c – a – b – e (d) e – b – c – a – d

Situation 4

Global gTrading이 보낸 official order sheet

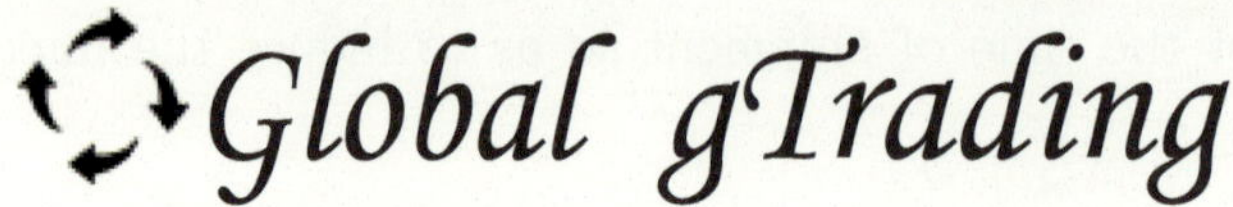

124 Dukjin Dong Jeonju, Korea 561-756
Tel: +82-63-270-3049 Fax: +82-63-270-3028
E-mail: gtrading@kornet.net

Order No. DR3355

Authorized
Eugine Park

Quantity	Item Description	Cat. No.	Price (CIF Busan)
300	Ladies' knitted three-piece sets	D 333	U$30.30 each
100	Ladies' knitted two-piece sets	F 347	U$28.50 each
50	Men's knitted pullover	G 123	U$25.00 each
50	Knitted hats	R 456	U$20.00 each
			Total: U$14,190.00

Comments: 15% Trade Disc. allowed. Pymt. D/P Del. 6 weeks

Date: September 14, 2014

Synopsis

Situation 3에서 언급한 500벌의 시험주문에 대한 정식 주문서이다. Ladies' knitted three-piece sets 300벌, two-piece sets 100벌 Men's pullover 50벌 그리고 Knitted hat 50벌을 우선 주문하기로 했다. 총 대금은 USD14,190이고 여기에서 15%의 trade discount를 받기로 한 점, 결제조건은 D/P: 일람출급서류인도조건, 그리고 delivery는 6주 후에 하기로 한 점 등을 명시하였다.

◈ Terms of Quantity(수량조건)

수출입 물품의 양(quantity)을 규정하는 문제는 분쟁의 소지가 많을 수 있다. 수량단위의 경우 국가간에 도량형 단위가 다른 경우가 있으므로 이의 정확한 표현이 중요하다. 국제무역에 많이 사용되는 수량단위는 다음 표와 같다.

단위	내용	주요용도
중 량	Ton: Long Ton(British Ton = 2,240lbs = 1,016kg) Short Ton(American Ton = 2,000lbs = 907.2kg) Metric Ton(Kilo Ton = 2204lbs = 1,000kg) Pound(lb)	곡물, 원자재
용 적	SF(superfoot): 1 SF = 1 square feet × 1 inch M/T(measurement ton): 1 M/T = 40 cubic feet(cft) CBM: Cubic meter(m^3) Barrel: 원유	액체, 목재
개 수	Dozen: 1 Dozen = 12 pieces Gross: 1 Gross = 12 dozens	잡화류
길 이	Meter, Yard, Feet	직물, 전선
면 적	SF(square foot), SM(square meter)	합판, 타일
포 장	Case, Bag, Bundle, Barrel	원면, 시멘트

수량의 결정시기는 품질조건과 마찬가지로 선적수량조건(shipped quantity terms)과 도착수량조건(landed quantity terms)으로 구별된다. 대부분의 공산품은 선적수량조건으로 계약되나, 비포장상태로 거래되어 운송도중 감량이 예상되는 곡물류, 광산물, 원유 등의 bulk cargo의 경우에는 도착수량조건으로 계약하는 것이 일반적이다.

이러한 bulk cargo의 경우는 계약 시 일정한 과부족을 인정받는 more or less clause (M/L clause: 과부족용인) 조건을 사용할 수 있다. 신용장통일규칙(UCP 600) 30조에 의하면 포장단위 또는 개개 품목에 따라 수량이 명기되어 있을 때에는 이러한 과부족은 적용되지 않지만, 환어음의 발행금액이 신용장금액을 초과하지 않는 범위 내에서 5%까지 과부족이 용인된다.

A tolerance not to exceed 5% more or 5% less than the quantity of the goods is allowed, provided the credit does not state the quantity in terms of a stipulated number of packing units or individual items and the total amount of the drawings does not exceed the amount of the credit.

또한 신용장상에 'about', 'approximately' 같은 표현이 수량이나 금액 앞에 사용되었을 때에는 10%의 범위 내에서 과부족을 허용하는 것으로 해석한다.

The words "about" or "approximately" used in connection with the amount of the credit or the quantity or the unit price stated in the credit are to be construed as allowing a tolerance not to exceed 10% more or 10% less than the amount, the quantity or the unit price to which they refer.

Terms of Quality(품질조건)

무역거래 시 많은 분쟁의 소지가 되는 것이 품질에 관한 조건이다. 따라서 품질 조건에서 규정하여야 할 중요한 내용은 품질의 결정방법, 시기, 증명방법 등이다. 수출입상품의 품질결정은 다음 표와 같은 방법을 이용한다. 국제간의 무역의 경우 장거리 수송이 대부분이기 때문에 같은 상품이라고 하여도 선적 시와 하역 시의 품질이 다를 수 있다. 따라서 계약서상에 품질의 결정시기를 명시하는 것이 바람직하다.

대부분의 공산품의 경우 선적품질조건(shipped quality terms)을 사용하며, 선적 시에 공인검사기관의 품질확인을 받았다면 그 이후의 변질에 대하여 수출상은 면책된다. 반면 농산물이나 어류 등의 경우는 도착지품질조건(landed quality terms)을 사용하는 것이 일반적이다. 이 조건에서는 도착지에서 품질조사를 한 것이 계약조건과 일치하여야 수출상이 면책을 기관에 의뢰하여 감정보고서(survey report)를 발급 받아 이를 근거로 클레임을 제기할 수 있다. 품질결정시기에 관한 별도의 합의가 없으면 FOB나 CIF같은 적재지 매매조건의 경우 선적지의 품질을 기준으로 한다. 반면, DAP나 DDU같은 도착지매매

조건의 경우에 도착지의 품질을 기준으로 한다. 곡물의 경우 TQ(Tale Quale)는 shipped quality term을 RT(Ryle Terms)는 landed quality term을 말한다.

품질의 결정방법	내용	주요용도
견품 매매 (sale by sample)	샘플로 품질을 결정하는 방법으로 가장 널리 쓰인다. 상품의 성질에 따라 품질의 차이가 있을 수 있다는 문구가 필요하다.	대부분의 공산품
상표 매매 (sale by trade mark)	세계적으로 유명한 상품의 경우 상표나 브랜드로 품질을 결정하는 방법이다.	Intel Chips, Coca Cola
명세서 매매 (sale by specification)	해당상품을 자세히 설명하는 명세서, 설계도, 청사진 등을 기준으로 하여 품질을 결정하는 방법	선박, 철도, 의료기기 등의 기계류
표준품 매매 (sale by standard)	FAQ(Fair Average Quality): 동종품질 가운데 중등품을 표준으로 품질을 결정하는 방법	곡물, 과일, 광산품 냉동어류,
	GMQ(Good Merchantable Quality): 물품인도시 매도인이 해당 상품의 판매적격성을 보증하는 조건	목재
	USQ(Usual Standard Quality): 공인검사기관 혹은 공인기준에 의하여 보통품질을 표준품의 품질로 정하는 방법	원면
규격품 매매 (sale by type or grade)	국제적으로 상품의 규격이 정해져 있는 경우에 그 규격을 품질의 기준으로 삼는 방법	ISO9000, KS

Practice Tests - Situation 4

1. When is the delivery scheduled to be made?
   - (a) within 4 weeks
   - (b) within 5 weeks
   - (c) within 6 weeks
   - (d) not specified

2. What sort of discounts have been applied to this order?
   - (a) volume discount
   - (b) special discount
   - (c) trade discount
   - (d) cash discount

3. Why is there only trade discount?
   - (a) because they just ordered 500 pieces.
   - (b) because that's what they agreed.
   - (c) because they placed an order too late.
   - (d) because the total price does not exceed USD20,000.

4. If Global gTrading has further correspondence with Allgarment, what reference would they use?
   - (a) Order no. DR 3354
   - (b) Order no. DR 3355
   - (c) Order no. DR 3355-1
   - (d) Order no. DR. 3356

5. The word "about", "approximately" used in connection with the amount of the Credit or the quantity or the unit price stated in the Credit are to be construed as allowing a difference not to exceed ________________ than the amount or the quantity or the unit price to which they refer.
   - (a) 5% more or 10% less
   - (b) 10% more or 5% less
   - (c) 5% more or 5% less
   - (d) 10% more or 10% less

6. A tolerance not to exceed ____________ than the quantity of the goods is allowed, provided the credit does not state the quantity in terms of a stipulated number of packing units or individual items and the total amount of the drawings does not exceed the amount of the credit.

(a) 5% more or 10% less (b) 10% more or 5% less
(c) 5% more or 5% less (d) 10% more or 10% less

7. 다음 문장의 구성이 논리적으로 잘 배열된 것을 고르시오.

(A) Your prices are not competitive and therefore we are unable to place an order with you at this time, even though we are favorably impressed with your samples.

(B) As we indicated in our last letter, our requirements for this line are large, but the competition in this line is very strong.

(C) We have received your letter of July 20. Thank you for the supply of samples which are in accordance with our expectation.

(D) We trust you will make every effort to revise your prices.

(E) Under such circumstances, we have to ask for your most competitive prices on the particular item, your samples No. 10 which is in high demand.

(a) (C)-(B)-(A)-(D)-(E) (b) (D)-(B)-(A)-(E)-(C)
(c) (C)-(A)-(B)-(E)-(D) (d) (C)-(E)-(B)-(A)-(D)

8. 다음 문장들은 주문서의 내용이다. 순서대로 나열한 것은?

ⓐ We are very interested in the different types of watches on your offer and have decided to place a trial order for the following, if you can guarantee despatch in time to reach us by the end of this month.

ⓑ Thank you for your letter of the 22nd of April forwarding booklet with details of your range of wrist watches.

ⓒ 1 gross "Popular" Watches @ $ 90 per dozen; 1 gross "Aristocrat" Watches @ $ 240 per dozen.

ⓓ We place this order on the clear understanding that the consignment is despatched in time to reach us by the 31st of May and reserve the right to cancel it and to refuse delivery after this date.

ⓔ We suggest payment by bill of exchange drawn on us at 30 days after sight.

Please say whether this is agreeable to you.

(a) ⓐ - ⓑ - ⓒ - ⓓ - ⓔ (b) ⓑ - ⓒ - ⓐ - ⓓ - ⓔ
(c) ⓑ - ⓐ - ⓒ - ⓓ - ⓔ (d) ⓐ - ⓑ - ⓓ - ⓔ - ⓒ

Situation 5

Allgarment가 India Shipping Lines에 선박을 수배하다.

37-2 Bridgeway Colony, 2nd Street, Tirupur, Tamilnadu India 641607
Telephone: +91-421-2232-880
Facsimile: +91-42-2232-888

September 25, 2014

India Shipping Lines
136-2 Bridgeway Colony, 1st Street, Chennia, Tamilnadu India 641607

Dear Sir:

We have 20 boxes of garments for shipment to Busan, South Korea. Each box contains 25 knitwears weighing 5 kilos and measuring 90 X 82 X 120cm.

Please inform us which vessels are available to reach Busan by the end of next month, and let us have your freight rates including lighterage, loading charges, dock dues and all other expenses.
I look forward to your prompt reply. Best regards.

Javv Gupta

Javv Gupta, Director
Export Division
Allgarment
Enterprises

Synopsis

Global gTrading으로부터 order를 받은 Allgarment의 Javv는 CIF조건이기 때문에 선박회사에 연락해서 부산으로 가는 선박의 항해일정을 알아보고 있다. 25개의 knitwear를 20개 box에 나누어서 포장하였고, 각 box의 크기와 무게를 India Shipping Lines에 알려주고, 다음 달 말까지 부산으로 가는 선박의 항해일정과 부선료(浮船料, lighterage), 적재비용(loading charge), 항만세(dock dues), 그 외 모든 비용을 포함한 운임을 알려달라고 요청하고 있다.

◈ each & every

each나 every에는 명사(단수) + 동사(단수)의 형태를 취한다. each나 every 다음에 명사가 둘 이상 연속되어도 단수형 동사가 온다.

- Each business student is required to take the following courses.
  ~~students are~~
- Every business needs to develop its own marketing strategy.
  ~~businesses need~~ ~~their~~
- Each senator and congressman was allocated two seats.
- Every man and woman recognizes their capabilities and their limitations.
  (*대명사 의 경우는 his or her 혹은 their로 받을 수 있음.)
- The soldiers used every means(단수명사) possible to evacuate the civilians.
  군인들은 민간인들을 대피시키기 위해 모든 수단을 동원했다.

each는 부정대명사(주어)로 사용되면 단수로 취급되고(부정) 형용사로 사용될 수 있지만 every는 부정형용사로만 사용된다.

- Each should attend the OJT(on-the-job-training) meeting.
  ~~Every~~ should attend the OJT(on-the-job-training) meeting.
- Each of us needs to attend the meeting.
  ~~Every~~ of us needs to attend the meeting.

[cf] Every one of us ~는 가능.

[cf] This book sells for $40 each(= apiece, individually; 부사로 쓰임).

each and every: each 혹은 every를 강조하기 위하여 쓴다.

- The boss wants each and every employee to be at work on time.
- Each and every man has his day. (모든 사람에게 언젠간 기회가 온다.)

width×length×height

박스나 컨테이너 등의 용적을 가로(width), 세로(length), 높이(height)로 표시할 때는 통상 숫자 중간에 ×를 추가하여 사용하고, 읽을 때는 by를 중간에 넣어서 읽는다. 예를 들어 본문의 90×82×120을 정확히 읽으면 wide, long, high와 by를 사용하여 "ninety centimeters wide by eighty-two centimeters long by hundred twenty centimeters high"가 된다. 그러나 보통은 줄여서 "ninety by eighty-two by hundred twenty centimeters"라고 읽는다. 또 나라나 지역마다 width, length, height의 순서를 다르게 표기할 수도 있으므로 각 단어의 initial을 써서, WLH=90:82:120 혹은 WHL=90:120:82로 표기하기도 한다.

the end of next month

the beginning of March: 3월(1 ~10일)
the middle of March: 3월(11 ~20일)
the end of March: 3월(21~31일)
the first half of March: 3월 전반부(1~15일)
the second half of March: 3월 하반부(16~31일)

UCP 600의 Article 3에 의하면,

The term "first half", "second half" of a month shall be construed respectively as the 1st to the 15th, and 16th to the last day of such month, all dates inclusive.

The term "beginning", "middle", or "end" of a month shall be construed respectively as the 1st to the 10th, the 11th to the 20th, and the 21st to the last of such month, all dates inclusive.

Practice Tests - Situation 5

1. We can assume that the terms of price under the transaction in Situation 5 is _____.

(a) FOB (b) FAS
(c) EXW (d) CIF

2. What is true about the transaction in Situation 5?

(a) The port of loading is located in Korea.
(b) The port of destination is India.
(c) The goods will be delivered by the end of November.
(d) They have 100 kilos of cargo all together.

3. As an option, shipments can be picked up at special events held at the winery around the time of each. These events allow a chance to taste our new releases and meet the wine making team.

(a) shipment (b) shipments
(c) ships (d) ship

4. I have been importing goods from around the world for 7 years now and find that _________ shipment is extremely different. Especially now with homeland security international shipping has become a much bigger headache than ever.

(a) each and every (b) all
(c) most of the (d) almost all

5. The term "first half", "second half" of a month shall be construed respectively as the 1st to the 15th, and 16th to the last day of such month, all dates _________.

(a) exclusive (b) inclusive
(c) excluding (d) including

6. The term "beginning", "middle", or "end" of a month shall be construed respectively as the 1st to the _____, the ____ to the _____, and the _____ to the last of such month, all dates inclusive.

(a) 8th, 9th, 18th, 19th
(b) 10th, 11th, 21st, 22nd
(c) 10th, 11th, 20th, 21st
(d) 11th, 12th, 20th, 21st

7. 다음 중 문법적으로 가장 옳은 문장을 고르시오. [무역영어 2급]

(a) Each of products supplied by the Seller is warranted to be free from defect.
(b) Each products supplied by the Seller are warranted to be free from defect.
(c) Each of the products supplied by the Seller are warranted to be free from defect.
(d) Each product supplied by the Seller is warranted to be free from defect.

8. Below is a reply to a letter. Which of the following is LEAST likely found in the previous letter? [무역영어 1급]

Thank you for your enquiry of 21 April. Enclosed you will find details of our sailing for beginning of next month, from Hong Kong to Busan. You will see that the first available vessel we have will be the Sun Star scheduled to leave on 3 May. Our freight rate for rated goods is USD310 per ton, and I have attached our shipping instruction to the enclosed itinerary.

(a) Inform us first vessel sailing to Busan with freight rates.
(b) Provide us with shipping instruction for the month of April.
(c) Provide us with shipping schedule for the shipment with competitive rates.
(d) Inform us of shipping details with departure to Busan early next month.

9. Which of the following does NOT fit in the letter below? [무역영어 1급]

(a) We will ship 500pcs of cotton goods by the s.s "Arirang V-106" which is due to sail from Busan on May 15 to Hong Kong.
(b) We therefore ask you to quote us your lowest rate for Marine insurance including war risk on the shipment of the goods, valued at USD30,000 by the vessel referred to.

(c) Considering the rates quoted by our competitors, you will find that the rate we are offering is exceptionally low.
(d) Your prompt reply to this letter would be highly appreciated.

10. Which of the following BEST fits the blank in the box below?

[무역영어 1급]

An air transport document, however named, must appear to:
(A) indicate the name of the carrier and be signed by:
- the carrier, or
- a named agent for or on behalf of the carrier.

Any signature by the carrier or agent must be identified as that of the carrier or agent. (　)
(B) indicate that the goods have been accepted for carriage.

(a) The date stated in the notation will be deemed to be the date of shipment.
(b) The person is exempt under the preceding paragraph.
(c) A bank will not examine charter party contracts.
(d) Any signature by an agent must indicate that the agent has signed for or on behalf of the carrier.

11. Which of the following is the main purpose of the letter below?

[무역영어 1급]

We are immediately proud of this union of two important publishing houses. Rothmore-Medico was founded in 1932 by Duglas H. Rothmore, a distinguished medical professional. Rothmore-Medico, long recognized as one of the country's preeminent medical publishers, recently launched Medical Innovations, a sophisticated monthly magazine with a circulation of over 100,000 readers, to health-care professionals, libraries, and hospitals. We welcome Rothmore-Medico into Payne- Wyatt group. Michael Beyer will continue a president of Rothmore, reporting to Payne-Wyatt CEO Clark Trimple.

(a) To announce the anniversary　　(b) To celebrate the launch of the magazine
(c) To introduce new executives　　(d) To announce the acquisition

Situation 6

India Shipping Lines에서 shipping schedule을 보내오다.

India Shipping Lines

136-2 Bridgeway Colony, 1st Street,
Chennia, Tamilnadu India 641607
Telephone: +91-471-2432-680
Facsimile: +91-472-2632-688

September 26, 2014
Dear Mr. Gupta:

Thank you for your fax of yesterday. Enclosed please find details of our sailing schedule from Chennai to Busan, South Korea for the end of this month and the beginning of next month.

As you will see the first available vessel is MV Bombay, which will accept cargo on or about October 1. She is due in Busan on or about October 15. The goods should reach us by 28th of this month for this vessel. The next one will leave for Busan on October 7.

The freight rate from Chennai to Busan is USD35.00(thirty-five US dollars) per cubic meter, which is the lowest possible rate we can quote. A copy of shipping request form is attached in the enclosed itinerary.
Best regards.

Shoe Shipper

Shoe Shipper,
Acting Manager
India Shipping Lines
Enc. Itinerary/Shipping request form

Synopsis

Allgarment Enterprises로부터 부산으로 가는 선박의 schedule을 요청받은 Inida Shipping Lines의 Mr. Shipper는 이달 하순에서 다음 달 초순까지의 부산으로 가는 선박의 항해정보를 Allgarment의 Javv에게 보냈다. 가장 빠른 선박은 Bombay호이고, 이 선박은 10월 1일경에 화물을 선적할 수 있으며 부산도착은 10월 15일이다. 다음 선박은 10월 7일에 있다. 인도의 Chennai에서 부산까지의 운임은 큐빅미터(가로×세로×높이)당 35불로 견적하였고 이 운임은 India Shipping이 견적할 수 있는 가장 낮은 금액임을 강조하고 있다. 동봉한 항해일정(itinerary)에 선적요청서(shipping request: S/R)가 있음을 알려주고 있다.

vessel

배, 선박을 나타내는 말은,

boat: 작은 배

ferry: (양쪽을 오가는) 나룻배, 선박

ship: (boat보다 큰) 일반적인 선박

vessel: 일반적인 선박

liner: 정기선

tramp/tramper: 부정기선

steamer: 증기선

국제거래에 쓰이는 선박의 종류에는 그 용도에 따라 여러 가지가 있다.

- Bulk carrier transports bulk consignments such as grain, wheat, and ores.
- Tanker transports liquid bulk consignments, usually oil.
- Container vessel has special lifting gear and storage space for the containers (large steel boxes) that they transport.
- Passenger cargo vessel concentrates on cargoes, but also carry passenger. They offer more facilities for loading and unloading than passenger liners.
- Passenger liner follows scheduled routes and concentrates on passenger services, but can also carry cargo.

- Roll-on roll-off(Ro-Ro) ferry is a vessel constructed with large doors so that cars and trucks can drive on at one port and off at another without having to unload and reload their cargo.
- Lighter is used for taking goods from a port out to a ship, or vice versa. They can also do the same work as a barge.
- Barge is a large fat-bottom boat which are used to transport goods inland along rivers and canals.

on or about

"on or about"이라는 용어가 선적과 관련하여 사용되었을 때에는 언급된 날을 중심으 로 전후 5일 내에 선적이 이루어지는 것으로 해석한다. [UCP600 Article 3]

- The expression "on or about" or similar will be interpreted as a stipulation that an event is to occur during a period of <u>five calendar days before</u> until <u>five calendar days after</u> the specified date, both start and end dates included.

따라서 본문의 "will accept cargo on or about October 1"는 10월 1일 전 5일부터 후 5일을 포함하여 총 11일 동안 선적을 할 수 있는 것으로 해석한다.

또 Article 3에서는 선적과 관련하여 "prompt", "immediately", "as soon as possible"과 같은 애매한 용어의 사용을 사용하여서는 안 된다고 규정하고 있다. 이런 말이 사용되었을 경우에는 은행은 이를 무시하게 된다.

- Unless required to be used in a document, words such as "prompt", "immediately" or "as soon as possible" will be disregarded.

freight

운임의 지급시기에 따라,

- prepaid freight/freight in advance: 선불운임
- freight collect/freight payable at destination: 후불운임

운임의 부과 단위에 따라,

- measurement cargo(용적화물): 화물의 부피에 따라 부과

- weight cargo(중량화물): 화물의 무게에 따라 부과
- ad valorem rate cargo(종가화물): 화물의 가치에 따라

부과 용선(charter: 선박 전체를 빌리는 것)의 경우는,

- voyage charter(항해용선): 항해구간(A항에서 B항까지)에 따라 부과
- time charter(정기용선): 선박의 크기(tonnage)와 기타 운항비용에 따라 부과
  * 선박의 운항은 선주가 하므로 선원의 임금은 선주가 부담
- bare boat charter(나용선): time charter + 선원의 임금
  * 선박의 운항책임이 선박을 용선한 화주에 있음

운임, 가격, 요금 등으로 쓰이는 용어들은 그 쓰이는 곳이 다음과 같이 조금씩 다르다.

① freight: 주로 해상 운임
② price: 가장 일반적인 가격, 매도자가 붙이는 가격
③ cost: 원가, 제조, 입수, 유지 등을 위하여 지급하는 금액
④ charge: 어떤 일을 행하는데 드는 비용, 동사로 요금을 청구하다.
⑤ rate: 단위당 부과된 금액(전기, 수도, 전화요금 등)
⑥ fee: 의사, 변호사 등의 전문직에 지급하는 수수료, 사례금
⑦ fare: 비행기, 기차, 버스, 택시 등 승객이 지불하는 운임
⑧ rent: 물건을 빌리는데 드는 일당, 주당, 월별 사용료. 사용료를 내고 빌리다.
⑨ bid: 매입자가 제시하는 가격
⑩ quotation: 매입자의 청구에 의해 매도자가 부르는 견적가

- A freight is a price at which a cargo is delivered from one point to another. ①
- What is the price of the machine? ②
- The cost of the camera is top secret. ③
- No charge for the service. They charged 100,000 won for the repair service. ④
- The new water rate will also have an impact on your sewer rate. ⑤
- I didn't know that the lawyers' fees were so high. ⑥

- What is the air fare for the round trip from Seoul to New York? ⑦
- The rent for this apartment is $1,000 per month. ⑧
- The highest bid in for the ancient sword was $1,000,000. ⑨
- Please send your quotation for wheat. ⑩

◈ shipping/shipment

shipping은 원래 선박에 화물을 싣는 것을 말하지만 그 이외에도 항공기, 트럭, 기차 그 밖의 모든 운송수단에 대해서도 사용된다. 따라서 shipping charge도 단순히 발송비용, 운송료 정도로 쓰인다. 운송료와 기타 처리비용을 합해서 shipping & handling charge라고도 한다.

shipping request(S/R): 선적요청서, 수출자가 선복을 요구하는 요청서
shipping order(S/O): 선적지시서; 선박회사가 선장에게 적하를 지시하는 명령서
shipping space: 선복, 선적공간
shipping charges: 선적비용, 운송비용

shipment는 '선박에 짐을 싣는 행위'라는 의미뿐만 아니라 '선적품'이라는 의미도 있다. an order가 '주문'이라는 의미뿐만 아니라 '주문품'의 의미도 있는 것과 마찬가지이다. 또한 shipping과 마찬가지로 shipment도 배에 물건을 싣는 것뿐만 아니라 모든 운송수단에 화물을 싣는 것, 혹은 그 화물을 의미한다.

partial shipment: 분할선적
complete(full) shipment: 완전선적
transshipment: 환적(중간항구에서 화물을 옮겨 싣는 것)
carload(consolidated) shipment: 단일적재
less-than-carload shipment: 혼합적재
deferred(late) shipment: 지연선적
on deck shipment: 갑판선적

◈ Terms of Shipment(선적조건)

선적(shipment)이란 선박, 철도, 화차, 항공기 등에 계약물품을 싣는 것(loading)뿐만 아니라 우편을 이용할 경우의 발송(dispatch), 복합운송의 경우의 수탁(taking in charge)을 포함하는 포괄적 의미이다. 선적계약의 당사자 및 선적방법에 관해서는 INCOTERMS

의 정형거래조건에 규정되어 있으므로 계약을 체결할 때에는 선적시기, 분할선적(partial shipment) 및 환적(transshipment), 지연선적 등에 대하여 명확히 해두어야 한다.

선적시기를 지정하는 방법에는 다음과 같이 특정일을 지정하여 그때가 최종선적일이 되는 특정일 선적조건이 가장 많이 쓰인다.

- Shipment shall be made by May 15, 2015.
- Last shipping date: May 15, 2015.

또 다음과 같이 특정 월을 지정하여 정할 수 있다.

- Shipment shall be made during May. 또는 May shipment(단월조건)
- Shipment shall be made from May to July. 또는 May-July shipment (연월조건)

이 경우 특정 월내의 선적시기와 선적방법(일시 혹은 분할선적)은 특약이 없는 한 seller's option으로 해석한다. 그리고 선적시기가 특정조건이 만족되는 시점을 기준으로 하여 정하는 방법도 있다. 예를 들어,

- Shipment shall be made within 30 days after receipt of L/C.

그러나 Shipment should be made on September 15.와 같이 특정일을 정해버리면 실무 상 이를 맞추기가 매우 어렵기 때문에 피하는 것이 좋다.

주어진 정박기간(laydays, laytime)을 초과하면 화주는 체선료(demurrage)를 부담하게 되는 반면, 정박기간보다 일찍 선적을 완료하면 선박회사로부터 조출료(dispatch money)를 지급받게 된다.

선적물량이 많아서 한 번에 선적하기가 어려운 경우나 수입상의 판매계획, 물류비절감, 시황, 계절적 요인 등으로 인하여 계약물품을 한번에 선적하지 않고 나누어 선적하는 것을 분할선적(partial or installment shipment)이라고 한다. 수입상이 분할선적을 원할 경우 분할횟수, 분할선적수량, 분할선적시기 등을 정할 수 있다('equal shipment during March, April, and May' 또는 'half in April and the balance in May'). 특별히 분할선적을 금지하는 조항이 없는 경우에는 분할선적이 허용되는 것으로 간주된다.

환적(transshipment)은 이미 선적된 계약물품을 최종 목적지까지 운송 도중에 다른 선박이나 그 밖의 다른 운송수단에 옮겨 싣는 것을 말한다. 환적과정에서 생길 수 있는 물품의 손상이나 멸실 등 여러 가지 위험 때문에 이를 피하기 위해서는 계약서에 'transshipment prohibited'라는 문구를 명기해야 한다. 그러나 복합운송이나 목적항까지 직항선이 없는 경우에는 환적을 허용하게 된다. 이 경우 'transshipment permitted' 혹은 환적항을 지정하여 'transshipment at Honolulu permitted'라고 명시할 수 있다. 신용장 거래에서는 환적을 금지한다는 표시가 없으면 환적을 허용하는 것으로 간주한다. 또 환적 금지의 표현이 있더라도 복합운송의 경우 환적의 표시가 있는 선적서류를 인정하고 있다.

계약물품이 선적기일 내에 선적되지 않으면 지연선적(delayed shipment)이 된다. 이 경우 매도인의 고의나 과실에 의한 경우라면 계약위반이 되어 매수인은 계약을 해제하거나 손해배상을 청구할 수 있다. 그러나 선적지연이 천재지변, 파업, 전쟁 등 매도자가 통제할 수 없는 상황, 즉 불가항력(force majeure)에 의한 경우에는 원칙적으로 매도인의 책임은 면제된다. 이 경우 매도인은 불가항력의 존재에 대하여 입증할 책임이 있으므로 상공회의소나 해당국의 대사관 등에서 증명서를 교부받아 매수인에게 보내야 한다.

Practice Tests - Situation 6

1. When is the latest possible date they can ship the goods in case they take the first available vessel?

(a) September 30　　(b) October 1
(c) October 5　　(d) October 6

2. ______________ is a vessel constructed with large doors so that cars and trucks can drive on at one port and off at another without having to unload and reload their cargo.

(a) Roll-on roll-off(Ro-Ro) ferry　　(b) Container vessel
(c) Lighter　　(d) Bulk carrier

3. 다음의 선적기간을 약정하는 문언 중 실무상 바람직하지 않은 것은?

(a) Shipment must be made on September 15.
(b) Shipment must be made on or about September 15.
(c) Shipment must be made not later than September 15.
(d) Shipment must be made within 10 days from the date of contract.

4. 다음 중 UCP 600에 규정되어 있는 바와 다른 것은?

(a) The word "to", "until", "till", "from" and words of similar import applying to any date or period in the Credit referring to shipment will be understood to include the date mentioned.
(a) The word "after" will be understood to exclude the date mentioned.
(a) The term "first half", "second half" of a month shall be construed respectively as the 1st to the 15th, and 16th to the last day of such month, all dates inclusive.
(a) If expression "on or about" or similar expressions are used, banks will interpret them as a stipulation that shipment is to be made during the period from five days before to ten days after the specified date, both end day included.

5. Choose the most appropriate words to complete the sentence.

[무역영어 2급]

Should the number of (   ) be exceeded the charterer must pay (   ); should the work be completed in less than number of days allowed, they receive (   ).

(a) lay days – demurrage – dispatch money
(b) running days – dispatch money – demurrage
(c) lay days – dispatch money – demurrage
(d) shipping days – demurrage – dispatch money

6. Put the following sentences in order. [무역영어 2급]

(A) Please complete it and return it as soon as possible.
(B) MV Pacific Ruby will be loading at number 1 dock from 4 to 8 May inclusive.
(C) We shall be glad to book your 200 boxes for either of these vessels and enclose our shipping form.
(D) Following her is the Golden rose, loading at number 8 dock from 19 to 23 May inclusive.

(a) A. C. B. D
(b) A. D. B. C
(c) C. A. B. D
(d) B. D. C. A

7. Which of the following has a DIFFERENT meaning from others?

[무역영어 2급]

(a) Please do your best to expedite shipment in time.
(b) We ask you to do everything possible to ensure punctual shipment.
(c) It is important that the delivery date should be strictly kept.
(d) We hope that you will deliver the goods at once.

8. Which of the followings is NOT APPROPRIATE as part of the reply to the letter below? [무역영어 1급]

We intend to ship a consignment of dinghies and their equipment to London at the beginning of next month. The consignment consists of ten boats which have been packed into wooden crates marked 1–10, each

measuring 4×2×2.5 meters and weighing 90 kilos.

Could you inform us which vessels are available to reach London before the end of next month, and let us know your freight rates?

(a) You will see that the first available ship we have will be the MV Orient, which will accept cargo from 2 February to 7 February, when she sails.

(b) Our freight rate for crated consignment is USD191.00(one hundred and ninety-one dollars) per ton and I have attached our shipping instructions.

(c) You will see from our list of tariffs where charges are calculated by cubic meter or cubic kilogram and that we offer substantial rebates for regular shipments.

(d) As you can see from our documents, two non-negotiable copies of the B/L and three copies of shipping invoice should be enclosed.

[9~10] Read the following letter and answer the questions. [무역영어 1급]

(A) Your duties will commence at 09:00 on 10 April 2012, but we would appreciate it if you could arrive at 08:30, so that we can introduce you to the staff.

(B) Full details of your terms of employment are on pp. 9-14 of our employees' handbook, HNT 661, but, as we discussed at the interview, your hours will be subject to requirement, and no overtime will be paid.

(C) Your starting salary will be USD16,000, with annual increments of 9 percent in the first three years, and subject to negotiation thereafter.

(D) In addition to the listed fringe benefits, which include a Non-Contributory Pension Scheme at 8% of your gross salary, free medical insurance; staff discounts on our products, etc.

9. Which of the following is correct?

(a) Final interview will be held on 10 April.

(b) Salary will be increased by 8% every year.

(c) The company will pay for extra hours.

(d) The employee does not need to pay medical insurance.

10. Where does the following sentence best fit in the letter above?

I am writing on behalf of Mr. Newman to tell you that you were successful in your interview on 12 March for the post of Credit Analyst.

(a) (A) (b) (B)

(c) (C) (d) (D)

Situation 7

Allgarment가 Insurance India에 보험견적을 의뢰하다.

Allgarment Enterprises

37-2 Bridgeway Colony, 2nd Street, Tirupur, Tamilnadu India 641607
Telephone: +91-421-2232-880
Facsimile: +91-42-2232-888

September 27, 2014

Insurance India
1736-6 Bridgeway Colony, 3rd. Street Chennia, Tamilnadu, 641607
Dear Ms. Insupers,

We will be sending a consignment of 500 garments to Busan, South Korea. The goods will be loaded on the MV Bombay, ex-Chennai October 1 due Busan October 15.

Please quote us your lowest rate of marine cargo insurance, ICC(B), including
S.R.C.C. and T.P.N.D. on the shipment of above articles, valued at CIF Busan US$14,190 by the referred vessel. A copy of commercial invoice and packing details are attached.

Your prompt reply would be greatly appreciated.
Best regards.

Javv Gupta

Javv Gupta, Director
Export Division
Allgarment
Enterprises

Synopsis

부산으로 갈 Bombay호에 shipping space를 확보한 Allgarment의 Javv는 이제 Insurance India에 연락하여서 화물의 종류와 선박에 대하여 알려주고, commercial invoice와 packing list를 보내면서 수출대금 US$14,190에 대한 SRCC와 TPND 특약이 포함된 ICC(B)조건의 보험료에 대한 견적을 의뢰하고 있다.

◈ Terms of Insurance(보험조건)

Situation 7에서처럼 CIF조건의 경우 수출상(Allgarment)이 수입상(Global gTrading)을 위하여 insurance premium(보험료)을 지불하고 보험에 가입하게 된다. [FOB 조건이라면 Global gTrading이 보험에 가입해야 한다.] 여기에서 India Insurance는 insurance policy(보험증서)를 발행하는 insurer 혹은 underwriter(보험자)가 되고, Allgarment는 policy holder(보험계약자)가 된다. [FOB 조건이라면 policy holder는 Global gTrading이 되었을 것이다.]

어느 쪽에서 보험을 계약했건 사고발생시 insurer로부터 보상을 받을 권리가 있는 자인 insured(피보험자)는 수입상인 Global gTrading이 된다. 보험에 드는 대상물, --여기서는 500 piece의 knitwear--을 subject-matter insured(보험목적물)이라고 부른다. 보험에 들기 위해서는 policy holder가 insurable interest(피보험이익)를 가지고 있어야 하며, 보통 대상물의 소유권을 가진 사람이 insurable interest를 가지고 있다.

insurable value(보험가액)는 보험목적물의 market value(시가)를 말하며, insured amount(보험금액)는 insurer가 보험계약에서 insurable value에 의거하여 지급할 수 있는 최고금액이다. full insurance(전부보험)는 insurable value = insured amount인 보험을 말하고 partial insurance 혹은 under insurance란 insurable value > insured amount인 보험이고, over insurance는 반대인 경우로 초과 부분은 무효가 된다. 손해의 종류에는 다음과 같은 것이 있다.

Total Loss(전손)

보험의 목적물이 전부 손실된 경우를 말한다. 여기에는 actual total loss(현실전손)와 constructive total loss(추정전손)가 있는데 현실전손은 보험의 목적물이 전부 없어지

거나 전부 원래의 성질이 바뀌져 본래의 용도를 잃은 경우를 말한다. 추정전손은 전부 없어진 것은 아니지만, 회복불능이나 회복에 비용이 들어 전손으로 간주하는 것을 말한다.

Partial Loss(분손)

분손이란 보험의 목적물이 부분적인 손해를 입은 것을 말하며 보험용어로 해손(average)이라고 부른다. particular average(단독해손)는 피보험자의 피보험이익이 단독으로 겪는 손해를 말하고, general average(공동해손)는 해난을 당하여 공동의 안전을 위하여 행한 행위로 인한 손실이나 비용을 말한다. 이러한 손해는 특정한 당사자만 부담할 것이 아니라 관련된 모든 당사자가 똑같이 부담해야 한다는 의미로 공동해손이라고 한다.

해상보험에서는 런던보험자협회(ILU: Institute of London Underwriters)에서 정한 협회적하약관(ICC: Institute Cargo Clause)이 보험조건 선택의 기준이 되고 있다. ICC는 부보범위에 따라 ICC(A), (B), (C)의 3등급으로 나누고 있다. 이는 1982년 이전의 구약관에서 사용하던 A/R(all risk; 전위험담보), WA(with average; 분손담보), FPA(free from particular average; 단독해손부담보)의 명칭을 변경한 것이다. 현재 신약관과 구약관이 병행하여 사용하고 있다.

위의 세 가지 조건은 보험료에 따른 보험자의 담보범위를 기준으로 구분한 것으로 ICC(A)를 선택하였다면 피보험자는 보험자의 일반면책사항, 운송선박의 불내항성 및 부적합성, 전쟁·파업을 제외한 전손, 공동해손 등의 모든 손해를 보상받게 된다. 그러나 보험료가 높아져서 피보험자의 비용이 증가하게 된다. 따라서 실무적으로는 화물의 종류, 포장방법, 운송방법 등을 고려하여 기본조건인 ICC(B), (C)나 WA, FPA에 열거된 보험조건에 특별약관을 추가하여 부보함으로써 보다 저렴한 보험료로 전위험 담보조건으로 부보하는 것과 동일한 효과를 거둘 수 있다. 특별약관에는 다음과 같은 것들이 있다.

① War Risk(전쟁위험): 해상적하보험에서는 전쟁이나 이에 준하는 위험으로 인한 손해에 대하여 보험자는 면책된다. 따라서 보험계약자가 이를 담보하고자 하면 할증보 험료를 지불하고 협회전쟁약관(Institute War Clause)을 첨부하여야 한다.
② SRCC(Strikes, Riots, and Civil Commotions: 동맹파업위험): 부두노동자들의 파업은 화물에 막대한 피해를 주기 때문에 보험자는 이에 따른 손해에 대해 면책된다. 따라서 이의 담보를 원하는 피보험자는 협회동맹파업·폭동·소요약관을 첨부하여야 한다.

③ TPND(theft, pilferage & non-delivery): 도난(theft)이란 포장된 단위 채로 훔쳐가는 것이고 발하(pilferage)는 포장된 물품 중 일부만 훔쳐가는 좀도둑을 말한다. 불도착(non-delivery)은 화물의 일부가 목적지에 도착하지 않은 경우를 말한다.

④ RFWD(rain and/or fresh water damage): 바닷물 이외에 빗물, 담수로 인한 손해를 담보하는 조건이다.

⑤ COOC(contact with oil and/or other cargo): 선박의 연료나 기계의 기름이 화물과 접촉되어 발생된 손해를 담보하는 조건이다.

⑥ JWOB(jettison & washing over-board): 해난사고 시 갑판상에 적재된 보험가입 화물을 투하하거나 풍랑으로 유실된 손해를 담보하는 조건이다.

consignment

선박, 항공기, 트럭, 기차 등 운송수단에 적재된 화물이라는 의미의 선적품

consignment: 적재화물, 위탁판매화물
shipment: 선적화물
cargo: 적재화물
freight: 운송료라는 뜻 이외에, 적재화물
lading: lade (짐을 싣다)의 명사형, 화물
load: 적재화물, 무거운 짐(burden)

ex-

여기에서 쓰인 ex- 는 from, out of 으로 쓰여서 '~에서', '~을 떠나는'의 의미이다. 따라서 ex-Chennai는 'Chennai를 출발하는'의 뜻이다. 또 ex 다음에 특정 장소를 표시해서 그 장소에서부터(from, out of) seller의 책임이 없음 혹은 그 장소에서부터 buyer의 책임임을 나타내는 용어들이 많다.

ex work(EXW): 작업장 인도(incoterms의 한 조건)
ex bond: 보세구역 인도
ex quay(wharf): 부두인도
ex pier: 부교인도
ex rail: 철도 인도
ex ship: 본선인도
ex warehouse: 창고인도
ex factory price: 공장도 가격

일상용어로는 ex boyfriend, ex wife, ex lover, ex president Clinton과 같이 '이전의' 의미로 쓰인다. 또 명사로 특히 romantic한 관계였던 전 사람을 말하기도 한다.

He is different from my ex. (이 남자는 전 남자와는 다르다)
He is one of my exes. (옛날 남자 중의 하나)

이 외에 자주 쓰이는 단어 중에는,

ex-ante: beforehand(사전)
ex-post: after the fact(사후)
ex-dividend: 배당락, 배당 기준일이 지나 배당받을 권리가 없어진 상태

- Using ex-ante analysis helps to give an idea of future movements in price.
- Companies may try to obtain ex-post data to forecast future earnings.
- If you purchase before the ex-dividend date, you get the dividend.

◈ quote your rate ~

'보험료를 견적해 달라'의 여러 가지 표현

- At what rate can you insure against All Risks on our cargo to Italy?
- Please cover US$150,000 on 5,000 pieces of knitwear against ICC(C).
- Please quote your lowest ICC(A) rate on 1,000 sets of PDA's for US$30,000.
- Please quote us the insurance rate against With Average on our machineries from US$100,000 from Incheon to Singapore.
- Please effect an insurance for US$120,000 on car stereos on ICC(B) from Busan to London, and let us have the insurance policy as soon as possible.
- We want you to open an insurance against All Risks for US$10,000-value of 500 cartons of knitwear per M.S. Bombay from Incheon to New York.

◈ including

including, plus, less는 다음과 같이 달리 쓰인다.

- The price of this merchandise is $300 including 10% sales tax. (세금포함, 300)
- The price of this merchandise is $300, plus 10% sales tax. (300+30=330)
- The price of this merchandise is $300, less 10% discount. (300-30=270)

Practice Tests - Situation 7

1. Mr. Gupta wants ___________.
   (a) to thank Ms. Insupers for her prompt reply.
   (b) to know the price of the goods.
   (c) to inform Ms. Insupers of the arrival of MV Bombay.
   (d) to get a quotation for cargo insurance.

2. Which one is NOT Constructive Total Loss?
   (a) Where the assured is deprived of the possession of his goods by a peril insured against, and it is unlikely that he can recover the goods.
   (b) Where the ship concerned in the adventure is missing, and after the lapse of a reasonable time no news of her has been received.
   (c) Where the assured is deprived of the possession of his ship by a peril insured against, and the cost of recovering the ship would exceed their value when recovered.
   (d) In the case of damage to a ship, where she is so damaged by a peril insured against that the cost of repairing the damage would exceed the value of the ship when repaired.

3. When Matt Saunders meets Jenny Johnson, he thinks he's found the perfect girl. However, he decides to break things off with her when she becomes too needy, controlling, and jealous. Jenny doesn't take it well and decides to get back at him by using her superpowers. Meanwhile, Matt and his co-worker, Hannah start to have a romance with each other which sends Jenny over the edge. Jenny is Matt's ___________.
   (a) wife (b) co-work
   (c) ex-girlfriend (d) mother

4. A statement, "The price of this merchandise is $300, plus 10% sales tax", means you have to pay ___________.
   (a) $270 (b) $300
   (c) $330 (d) not clear

5. What is the purpose of the letter below? [무역영어 1급]

We will be sending a consignment of 500 leisure chairs to Incheon, South Korea. The goods will be loaded on the MV Mumbai, ex-Chennai October 1 due Incheon October 15.

Please quote us your lowest rate of marine cargo insurance, ICC(B), including S.R.C.C. and T.P.N.D. on the shipment of above articles, valued at CIF Incheon US$14,190 by the referred vessel.

A copy of commercial invoice and packing details are attached. Your prompt reply would be greatly appreciated.

(a) To claim under an open cover policy
(b) To request a marine insurance quotation
(c) To provide information about the shipment
(d) To quote a rate for open cover bill

6. Which of the following CANNOT be included in a reply to the letter? [무역영어 1급]

We shall shortly have a consignment of electric shavers, weighing about 20kg, for a customer in Damascus. We wish to send this by air from London. Please let us have details of the cost and any formalities to be observed. The invoice value of the consignment is USD50,000 and we should require insurance cover for this amount plus the costs of sending the consignment.

(a) As you suggest, we will airfreight the goods by own cost.
(b) All our charges including freight, airway bill fee, insurance and our own commission are shown on the attached schedule.
(c) To enable us to prepare your airway bill we shall need the information requested in the enclosed form.
(d) Please telephone me when you are ready to deliver the consignment to our officer at the airport, so that we can prepare to receive it and deal with it promptly.

[7~8] Read the following letter and answer the questions. [무역영어 1급]

We have received the manufacturer's price list and samples you sent us last month. (A)

Now enclose our indent number 342 for goods to be shipped by the TJ Prince due to leave Dover for Alexandria, Egypt on 31 May. (B)

The indent contains full instructions as to packing, insurance and shipping documents. It is important for the goods to be shipped either by the vessel named, or by an earlier vessel. (C)

When we receive the goods we shall pay you the agreed agency commission of 5%. The account for the goods will be settled direct with the manufacturers. (D)

7. What is the purpose of the letter above?

(a) To request a shipment along with insurance
(b) To confirm agent's order
(c) To discuss shipping schedule
(d) To negotiate agency commission

8. Where does the following sentence best fit in the above letter?

If there are any items which cannot be supplied in time for this shipment they should be cancelled.

(a) (A) (b) (B)
(c) (C) (d) (D)

Situation 8

Insurance India에서 Allgarment에 보험 견적을 보내다.

1736-6 Bridgeway Colony, 3rd Street,
Chennia, Tamilnadu India 641607
Telephone: +91-473-2332-780
Facsimile: +91-473-2332-788

September 27, 2014

Dear Mr. Gupta:

Consignment of 500 garments

Thank you for your fax regarding the cover of above consignment.

We are pleased to offer you a port-to-port ICC(B) including S.R.C.C. and T.P.N.D. valued policy at a rate of 2.21% for a total cover of US$15,609 (CIF value+10%). We would stress that this is a very competitive rate.

If the rate is agreeable to you please complete the enclosed proposal form and return it to us. Then, we will effect an insurance on your consignment.

I am looking forward to hearing from you.

Best regards.

Insura Insupers

Insura Insupers
Manager, Quotation
Department Insurance India
Co. Ltd.

Synopsis

Allgarment로부터 보험료 견적을 요청받은 Insurance India의 Insura는 invoice 가격에 10% 희망이익을 더한 금액을 insured amount(보험금액)로 하여 2.21%의 요율로 SRCC와 TPND를 포함한 ICC(B) 조건을 견적하였다. 이 요율은 매우 저렴하다는 것을 밝히고 있다. 동봉한 proposal form을 작성하여 보내주면 보험에 가입해주겠다고 말하고 있다.

◈ valued policy

해상보험의 경우 대부분 valued policy로 가입하게 되는데, 이는 계약 당시에 최고 보상 한도(즉, insured amount)를 commercial invoice 가격에 일정금액[보통 invoice value의 10%: 이를 imaginary profit 혹은 expected profit(희망이익)이라 부른다.]을 가산한 금액으로 미리 정하여 보험에 가입하는 것을 말한다. unvalued policy는 insured amount를 미리 정하지 않고 부보하고, 사고가 발생하면 보험목적물의 market value에 따라 보상하게 된다. 그리고 보험은 보험계약자가 보험청약을 할 때마다 보험자가 개개의 건마다 심사를 하여 인수 여부를 결정하는 개별보험계약(facultative contract or definitive contract)과 반복적 수출입의 경우 매건 별로 보험계약을 체결해야 하는 번거로움과 보험비용 절감을 위하여 일정기간 동안 보험 가입 예상 물동량을 산출하여 보험회사와 포괄적으로 계약을 하는 포괄보험계 약(open cover policy)이 있다.

◈ at a rate of

보험료(premium)의 견적은 %로 한다. 예를 들면 여기에서처럼 at a rate of 2.21%라고 되어 있다면 premium은 CIF가격×1.1(희망이익 10%)×0.0221이 된다.

◈ effect an insurance

'~에 대하여 보험을 가입하다'의 의미로 다음과 같이 표현한다.

We will insure the goods for you subject to ICC(A) with Lloyd's.

We insure the cargo against A/R for US$1,500,000 at a rate of 4.66%.

We have effected(undertake, take) an insurance on the 50 cartons of cloths for you.

◈ 혼동하기 쉬운 단어들

effect: v. ~을 야기시키다, ~실행하다. n. 효과, 결과
affect: v. ~에게 영향을 주다. ~인체하다. n. 정서, 감정(emotion)

- The medicine effected a cure.
- The disease had a devastating effect on the poor.
- Mostly, the disease affected poor people.
- Her affect was very disturbing after she saw the scary movie.

compliment: [kάmpləmənt/k&m-] v. 칭찬하다. n. 칭찬, 경의, 무료
complement: [kάmpləmənt/k&m-] v. 보충하다. n. 보충

- The dean compliments Jennifer on her speech.
- Free tickets are complimentary. (무료로 주는 티켓)
- The menu is complemented by a good wine list.

command: [kəmǽnd] v. 명령하다, 차지하다. n. 명령
commend: [kəménd] v. 칭찬하다, 추천하다(recommend), 맡기다.

- He is a general who commands the army.
- KT&G Corp. commands about 80 of the domestic cigarette market.
- The major commend a fireman for bravery.
- I commend Mr. Black to you.

compare to: 비유되다.
compare with: ~과 ~을 비교하다.

- Earning a doctoral degree has been compared to climbing Everest barefoot.
- The report compares US business etiquette with that of Korea.

decent: [dí:snt] a. nice, modest
descent: [disént] v. n. falling, descending cf. ascent

- My son did a decent job of fixing the broken wall.
- The accident occurred during the plane's descent.

desperate: [déspərət] a. 필사적인, 절망적인, hopeless
disparate: [díspərit, dispǽ–] a. 전혀 다른, different

- This is a desperate solution to the problem.
- The family is in a desperate state. (절망적인 상태)
- They gather news from disparate sources.

disinterested: impartial, unbiased(공정한)
uninterested: not interested(무관심한)

- A disinterested judge gives fair rulings.
- The uninterested judge dozed on the bench. (doze 졸다)

differ from: unlikeness(다른 것)
differ with: divergence of opinion(의견이 다름)

- His paper differs greatly from mine.
- The President differs with Congress regarding welfare.

emigrate: to leave a country(이민을 가다)
immigrate: to enter a new country(이민을 오다)

- Millions emigrated from Europe. (유럽에서 이민을 갔다)
- They immigrated to the USA. (미국으로 이민을 갔다)

illicit: [ilísit] a. 불법적인, unlawful, illegal
elicit: v. 이끌어내다, evoke, draw

- He is suspected of collecting large sum of illicit funds from corporations.
- He elicited a reply from the criminal.

principal: [prínsəpəl] 주요한, central, major
principle: [prínsəpl] 원칙, 규범, standard

- What are the principal products of your hometown?
- He is a man of moral principle. (그는 도덕적 규범을 가지고 있는 사람이다.)

Practice Tests - Situation 8

1. What should Allgarment do to insure the goods?
   (a) They need to send a fax.
   (b) They should make sure that the rate is competitive.
   (c) They should fill out the proposal form.
   (d) They should call to Ms. Insupers first.

2. Seller shall ________ marine insurance on all shipments on ICC(a) including war risk for 110% of invoice value.
   (a) effect (b) affect
   (c) effective (d) affective

3. An insurance policy in which the value of the insured item is defined and agreed at the commencement of the policy is a valued policy. In the event of a total loss the agreed amount is paid by the insurer without the need for further proof of value. There are also unvalued policies, where the value of the goods is not agreed in advance but assessed if loss should occur. This means the client will, if their goods are damaged or destroyed, get the (   ) as compensation.
   (a) fair value (b) predetermined value
   (c) market price (d) resonable price

4. Goods are usually insured for the voyage on an agreed value basis. However, if a client ships regularly with a given company, they might ask for (   ), e.g. for twelve months. The premium would be agreed at the beginning and the client would declare each shipment, without limit on the number of shipments they make. An initial payment would be charged and adjusted according to the number of shipments made over that period.
   (a) regular policy (b) open cover policy
   (c) voyage to voyage policy (d) named policy

5. The hotel offers a complimentary breakfast for the guests.

(a) a breakfast with a reduced charge

(b) a breakfast with a free of charge

(c) a breakfast with a regular charge

(d) a breakfast with a free delivery

6. According to the dialogue, which of the following is true? [무역영어 1급]

Matt: Would you like to go out to dinner tonight? William: Sure. Where do you want to go?

Matt: Well. What do you think of French Food?

William: I love it, but I'm not really in the mood for it today. Matt: Yeah. I'm not either, I guess.

William: Um.... How do you like Mexican food? Matt: Oh, I like it a lot.

William: I do, too. Do you know a nice Mexican restaurant near here? Matt: I know. It's called El Salto. It's near by the station.

William: Terrific! Let's go!

(a) El Salto is a nice French restaurant.

(b) Matt and William want to go different restaurants.

(c) The Mexican restaurant is located near by the station.

(d) Matt has never had Mexican food.

7. Read the following letter for insurance. Which of the following is NOT suitable for the given blank? [무역영어 1급]

Dear Mr. Jones:

At your request, I checked (a) __________ to see why this year's premium had increased. There is indeed (b) ________. You will be pleased to know that you are paying exactly the same rate for insurance this year as last year. The reason your premium is higher is that you increased your coverage.

When you bought your new truck last year, you increased the (c) _______ and added a third driver to your policy. In short, this year's premium simply reflects the fact that your new truck is worth a lot (d) _________. I hope this puts your mind at ease. If you have any other question, please

feel free to stop by my office. It is always a pleasure doing business with you.

(a) on your insurance policy (b) a reasonable explanation
(c) penalty coverage (d) more than your old one

Situation 9

Cyclone 때문에 선적이 지연되다.

Allgarment Enterprises

37-2 Bridgeway Colony, 2nd Street, Tirupur, Tamilnadu India 641607
Telephone: +91-421-2232-880
Facsimile: +91-42-2232-888

October 17, 2014

Dear Mr. Eugine Park,

We regret to inform you that it has become impossible to complete the shipment of your Order No. 3355 as scheduled due to a recent cyclone which has struck the eastern part of India.

Your order was ready for shipment on the MV Bombay, but she suffered serious damage and her October 10th departure was cancelled indefinitely. Moreover, a considerable amount of cargo has been congested and it is quite difficult to secure any other shipping spaces.

Therefore, we are asking to extend the shipping date until the end of this month. Though the delay is beyond our control, we must apologize for any inconvenience you might have. We will try to do our best to ship your order as soon as possible.
Thank you and best regards.

Javv Gupta

Javv Gupta, Director
Export Division
Allgarment
Enterprises

Synopsis

부산으로 갈 Bombay호에 주문품을 선적할 준비를 마쳤으나 때마침 인도의 동부를 강타한 cyclone 때문에 예정대로 선적할 수가 없게 된 Allgarment의 Javv는 Global gTrading의 Eugine에게 연락하여 사정을 설명하고 있다. Bombay호가 심각한 손상을 입어서 출항이 무기한(indefinitely) 연기되었고, 화물이 정체(congested)되어서 다른 선복(shipping space)을 찾는 것도 여의치 않다는 것을 밝히고 선적을 이달 말까지 연장해 달라고 요청하고 있다. 선적지연이 자신들도 어쩔 수 없는 것이긴 하지만(beyond our control), 가능한 한 빨리 선적을 하겠다고 말해 최선을 다하고 있음을 보여주고 있다.

cyclone: 인도양의 태풍
typhoon: 태평양의 태풍
hurricane: 북대서양의 태풍

Seller의 고의, 과실 또는 태만으로 인하여 약정된 기간 내에 선적을 하지 못하게 된 경우(delayed shipment)에는 seller가 책임을 져야한다. 그러나 delayed shipment의 원인이 천재지변(acts of God)이나 전쟁(war) 등의 불가항력(force majeure)일 경우에는 seller는 물품의 선적을 일시 연기시키거나 선적의무를 면제받을 수 있다. 이럴 경우에 대비해서 계약 시에 다음과 같은 force majeure clause를 두는 것이 필요하다.

Force Majeure: Neither party shall be liable in damages or have the right to terminate this Agreement for any delay or default in performing hereunder if such delay or default is caused by conditions beyond its control including, Acts of God,

Government restrictions(including the denial or cancellation of any export or other necessary license), wars, insurrections and/or any other cause beyond the reasonable control of the party whose performance is affected.

불가항력: 다음과 같은 당사자의 통제를 벗어난 사안에 때문에 지연 혹은 계약불이행이 생긴 경우에는 어느 당사자도 그 손해에 대하여 책임이 있거나 계약을 파기할 수 있는 권리를 가지지 않는다. 다음의 사안은 Acts of God, 정부의 규제(수출 혹은 필요한 라이선스의 거부나 취소 포함), 전쟁, 폭동 그리고/혹은 계약의 수행에 영향을 주는 통제 불가능한 어떤 다른 이유를 포함한다.

Force Majeure literally means "greater force". These clauses excuse a party from liability if some unforseen event beyond the control of that party prevents it from performing its obligations under the contract. Typically, force majeure clauses cover natural disasters or other "Acts of God", war, or the failure of third parties—such as suppliers and subcontractors--to perform their obligations to the contracting party. It is important to remember that force majeure clauses are intended to excuse a party only if the failure to perform could not be avoided by the exercise of due care by that party.

Force Majeure는 "greater force"에 의하여 당사자의 통제를 넘어서는 모든 사건을 말한다. 이 조항은 당사자의 통제를 넘어서는 예측 불가능한 사건 때문에 계약상의 의무를 수행하지 못하게 되는 경우에 당사자의 의무를 면제해 주기 위함이다. 이 조항은 당사자가 상당한 주의(due care)를 했음에도 해당의무를 수행하지 못한 경우에만 당사자의 의무를 면제해 주는 점에 유의해야 한다.

◈ impossible

possible과 impossible은 가각 '가능하다', '가능하지 않다'의 의미이고 사람을 주어로 쓰지 않는다.

- It is impossible for us to complete the shipment as scheduled.
  ~~We are impossible to~~
- We can not complete the shipment as scheduled.
- Today, it is possible for us to get overseas news easily with internet.
  ~~we are possible to~~
- Today, we can get overseas news easily with internet.

possible과 probable 동의어지만 의미의 차이가 있다.

probable은 일어날 가능성이 매우 큰 것을 말하고, possible은 이미 일어났거나 조건이 갖추어지면 가능한 것을 말한다.

- She will probably come back. (아마도 꼭 돌아올 것이다.)
- She will possibly come back. (돌아올 수도 있다.)
- It is possible that it will rain, but with such a blue sky it does not seem probable. (비가 올 수도 있지만 이런 푸른 하늘로 봐서는 가능할 것 같지 않다.)
- Snow is possible, though not probable, even at the end of April. (4월 말에 눈이 오는 것은, 가능성이 많지는 않지만, 있을 수 있다.)

schedule

schedule은 명사로 열차, 버스, 항공기의 시간표, 미래에 해야 할 일들의 목록, 그리고 앞으로 할 구체적 단일사항에 대한 언급 등에 쓰인다.

- Do you have the schedule for flight from Incheon to LA?
- I have a busy(full) schedule.
- Do you have a schedule today for the IMF Board meeting for Korea?
- This Sunday I have a schedule to invite foreign diplomats.

또 schedule은 uncountable noun으로 다음과 같이 쓴다.

- He arrived here behind schedule. (계획보다 늦게)
- He arrived here according to schedule. (계획에 따라)
- He arrived here ahead of schedule. (계획보다 먼저)
- He arrived here on schedule. (계획에 맞춰)

동사형으로는, be scheduled to(for)의 형태로 많이 쓰인다.

- He is scheduled to dine with us.
- He is scheduled for a speech.
- He arrived here as(it is) scheduled.

Practice Tests - Situation 9

1. Why did Mr. Gupta write this letter?
   (a) to inform Mr. Park of the recent cyclone in India
   (b) because he cannot secure other shipping spaces
   (c) to show that they are doing their best.
   (d) because his company can not ship the order on time.

2. What did Mr. Gupta want Mr. Park to do?
   (a) He wants Mr. Park to accept his apology.
   (b) He wants to say that they can not process the order.
   (c) He wants Mr. Park to extend the shipping date.
   (d) He wants Mr. Park to know that the delay is beyond their control.

3. Your order was ready for shipment on the MV Bombay, but suffered serious damage and her October 10th departure was cancelled indefinitely.
   (a) he　　(b) she
   (c) they　　(d) we

4. Choose the one that is awkward.
   (a) Shipment will not be completed as scheduled.
   (b) It is impossible to complete the shipment as scheduled.
   (c) We can not complete the shipment as scheduled.
   (d) We are impossible to complete the shipment as scheduled.

5. Though the delay is ___________ we must apologize for any inconvenience you might have. We will try to do our best to ship your order as soon as possible.
   (a) beyond our control　　(b) our fault
   (c) controllable　　(d) evitable

6. On date of shipment send one copy of Notice of Shipment to Buyer's Purchasing Department. Do not deliver _____ unless authorized by Buyer.

(a) behind schedule (b) according to schedule
(c) ahead of schedule (d) on schedule

7. 다음 단어와 관련 있는 것은?

strikes, riots, lockouts, earthquakes, blockades

(a) force majeure clause (b) arbitration clause
(c) escalation clause (d) governing law clause

8. Expression such as "prompt", "immediately", "as soon as possible" and the like should not be used at to dates for shipment in the Letter of Credit. If the term is used banks will ____________.

(a) interpret them as at least 7 business days.
(b) interpret them as 3 business days.
(c) let shipper determine the date.
(d) disregard.

9. These clauses excuse a party from liability if some unforseen event beyond the control of that party prevents it from performing its obligations under the contract. Typically, force majeure clauses cover natural disasters or other "Acts of God", war, or the failure of third parties--such as suppliers and subcontractors—to perform their obligations to the contracting party. It is important to remember that force majeure clauses are intended to excuse a party only if the failure to perform could not be avoided by the exercise of ___________ by that party.

(a) due care (b) full force
(c) carelessness (d) enforcement

10. Fill in the blanks. [무역영어 2급]

Your order No. 5 will be completed( ) March 20 and shipped ( ) the "Easters Quees" scheduled ( ) leave Pusan on March 30. would you please open a letter of credit well in time ( ) the shipment.

(a) around – on – to – for (b) on – in – to – of
(c) by – on – to – on (d) on – on – on – on

Situation 10

Allgarment가 Global gTrading에 주문품이 결국 선적되었음을 통보하다.

37-2 Bridgeway Colony, 2nd Street, Tirupur, Tamilnadu India 641607
Telephone: +91-421-2232-880
Facsimile: +91-42-2232-888

October 28, 2014

Dear Mr. Eugine Park,

Your Order No. 3355

We are pleased to tell you that your above order has finally been shipped on SS Delphia and should reach you within the next 15 days.

Meanwhile, our bank has forwarded the relevant documents and sight draft for USD14,190 to your bank.

We are sure that you will be satisfied with the consignment and apologize again for the delay of the shipment. We are looking forward to your next order.
With best regards.

Javv Gupta

Javv Gupta, Director
Export Division
Allgarment
Enterprises

Synopsis

cyclone 때문에 선적이 지연되었던 Global gTrading의 주문품이 결국 다른 선박 SS Delpia에 선적되었음을 통지하고 있다. Allgarment의 Javv는 수출대금을 받기 위하여 자기 거래은행을 통하여 US$14,190에 대한 일람출급어음을 발행하고 관련 서류와 함께 Global gTrading의 거래은행인 한국의 외환은행에 보냈다. 이 서류를 받으면 선적물을 인수할 수 있을 것이라고 밝히고 있다. 다시 한 번 선적지연에 사과를 하고 선적품에 만족할 것이라는 말로 편지를 마감하고 있다.

◈ say, tell, talk, & speak

우리말로는 전부 '~을(에게) 말하다'의 의미이고 단어에 따라서 서로 교환되어서 쓰이기도 하지만, 각 단어는 의미상으로 쓰이는 용법상으로 차이가 있다.

say는 가장 일반적으로 쓰인다. 대화 중 했던 말을 다시 언급할 때 혹은 말을 직접 인용할 때 사용되며, 말하고 있는 상대를 꼭 나타낼 필요는 없다. say는 항상 타동사로 쓰이고 사람을 목적어로 취하지 않는다. 듣는 상대를 나타낼 경우에는 say to someone으로 사용되지만 이 경우에는 tell을 사용하는 것이 더 일반적이다.

- She said, "He was attractive?" [say + 직접인용문]
- She said that he was attractive. [say + 명사절(that절)]
- She didn't say why he was attractive. (say + 의문사(명사절))
- She said many good words about him. [say + 목적어]
- She said to me that he was attractive. [say + to somebody(전치사구) + 명사절(that절)]
  ~~(said me that)~~

tell은 항상 타동사로 쓰이며, 목적어를 한 개(3형식) 쓸 수도, 두 개(4형식) 쓸 수도 있다. 두 개 쓸 때 간접목적어로는 사람이 와야 한다. 또한, tell은 5형식으로 쓰이고 목적격보어로 to 부정사가 온다. tell은 특히 전달되는 메시지가 정보(information), 사실(truth), 이야기(story, joke) 혹은 지시(instruction)를 나타내는 경우에 쓰인다.

- He told a funny story. [3형식: tell + 목적어)
- He told us about a funny story. [3형식: tell + 목적어 + 전치사 구(about/of ~)]

- He told us a funny story. [4형식: tell + 간접목적어 + 직접목적어]
- He told me that he had a funny story. [4형식: tell + 간접목적어 + 직접목적어 (명사절)]
- He told me how to write funny stories. [4형식: tell + 간접목적어 + 직접목적어 (의문사)]
- He told me why he wrote funny stories. [4형식: tell + 간접목적어 + 직접목적어 (의문사)]
- He told me to listen to his funny story. [5형식: tell + 목적어 + 목적격보어 (to부정사)]

talk는 대화중에 이야기의 내용이 아닌 대화를 한다는 의미를 나타낼 때 쓴다. talk은 "~와 대화하다"의 의미일 경우, to나 with를 동반한다. 대화의 주제를 나타낼 때에는 about을 사용한다. 타동사로서 사용되는 경우 목적어로 사람이나 that절을 쓸 수 없다. 즉, talk는 주로 자동사로 사용되면 3형식 동사로만 사용되고 4형식 동사로 사용될 수 없다.

- She talked to(with) him for about two hours. [talk to/with + somebody]
- We talked about our vacation plans for two hours.
- He is talking nonsense. [talk + 목적어]

speak는 의사전달을 위해 또는 일정한 내용을 전하기 위해 '이야기하다'라는 의미가 있어서 talk보다 형식적인 말에 사용한다. 일정한 내용전달에 사용되다보니 연설하는 경우에 자주 볼 수 있는 단어이며 많은 청중이 있는 공공의 장소에서 말할 때 쓰인다. Speaker라는 단어는 speak에 er을 붙여 연사(연설하는 사람, 웅변가, 스피커, 확성기)라는 의미가 있듯 이 많은 사람에게 전달하는 목적에 사용된다. 쓰이는 용법은 talk과 비슷하고 Say와 만찬가지로 '~에게'라는 대상은 전치사 to를 사용하여 표현해야 한다.

- I was speaking with my boss about possibility of pay raise.

- Paul: Hello, may I speak to Jennifer? (Paul: Jennifer 좀 바꿔주시겠어요?)
  Jennifer: Speaking. (Jennifer: 전데요.)
- The boss spoke to us about the possibility of pay raise.
- Our products speak for themselves. (우리 제품은 써보시면 압니다.)
- Would you please speak up? (크게 좀 말해 주시겠어요?)

Speak는 주로 '(언어)를 말하다'를 의미할 때 타동사로 사용된다.

- She speaks strange things.
- She is good at speaking English.

* Can you speak Korean?로 표현하면 "한국말이나 할 줄 아세요?"의 의미가 되어 약간 무례한 표현이 될 수 있으므로 Do you speak Korean?으로 사용하는 것이 좋다. Could you speak in Korean?은 "한국말로 말해 주세요"를 뜻한다.

◈ reach: 전치사가 필요 없는 타동사

- We must reach (~~at~~) a conclusion before signing a contract.
- The ship will leave (~~from~~) Busan on May 1. (cf. ~depart[sail, clear] from Busan.)
- We regret (~~for~~) the error in our statement.
- She joined (~~into~~) our company five years ago.
- Please visit (~~to~~) our website for more information.
- Please contact (~~to~~) us for more detailed specifications about our products.
- Will you marry (~~with~~) me?
- He requests (~~for~~) permission to enter the conference room.
- Jennifer resembles (~~like~~) her father. (cf. Jennifer looks like her father.)
- You should obey (~~to~~) the rules here.
- He was trying to explain (~~about~~) the problem.
- She attended (~~at~~) the meeting.
- Try to answer (~~to~~) all the questions. (cf. Respond to all the questions.)
- Please try to answer (~~to~~) all the questions. (cf. ... respond to all the questions.)
- The car approaches (~~to~~) the intersection.
- She miraculously survived (~~from~~) the car crash.
- You should remember (~~about~~) the facts before taking any actions.
- The survey team reported (~~about~~) the accident to the board members.
- She managed to describe (~~about~~) the kidnapper.
- The prices will fall (~~down~~) sharply for the next few weeks.
- She accompanied (~~with~~) the guest to the door.
- They didn't mention (~~about~~) it.

Practice Tests - Situation 10

1. The appraiser assessed for the house at 30,000,000 won.

   The information officer at the bank his customers that there were several different kinds of checking accounts available.

   (a) said (b) told (c) talked (d) spoke

2. "Why does everybody like Mrs. Black?"

   "Because she always good after-dinner jokes."

   (a) says (b) speaks (c) tells (d) talks

3. The police _______ the man to get out of the car with his hands in the air.

   (a) said (b) told (c) talked (d) spoke

4. The girls ________ on the phone all the night.

   (a) said (b) told (c) talked (d) spoke

5. Could you _____________________ us more about your trip to South Africa?

   (a) say (b) speak (c) tell (d) talk

6. I _____ that I was going away for two years and couldn't see him anymore.

   (a) said (b) told (c) talked (d) spoke

7. I ______ him that I was going away for two years and couldn't see him anymore.

   (a) said (b) told (c) talked (d) spoke

8. Choose the one that is natural.

   (a) She said me that there will be shipping delays.
   (b) He told about the delayed shipment.
   (c) She talked that the shipment of the goods was delayed.
   (d) The boss spoke to me about the possible pay raise.

9. Choose the one that is awkward.

(a) He said that he was in deep trouble with his boss.
(b) The product speaks for itself.
(c) I speak with my boss about my promotion.
(d) We talked our vacation plan for more than two hours.

10. 다음 괄호에 들어갈 수 있는 말로 적절하지 못한 것은?

We have shipped your goods No. ABC-100 by M/S Arirang due to (   ).

(a) leave from Busan for LA
(b) clear from Busan for LA
(c) depart from Busan for LA
(d) sail from Busan for LA

11. Please be advised that the undermentioned cargo (   ) to you arrived aboard subject vessel on the fourth of April, 2002, at the port of Incheon.

(a) negotiated
(b) mentioned
(c) consigned
(d) paid

12. 다음 중 틀린 문장을 고르시오. [무역영어 2급]

(a) Please contact to us for more details about our terms and conditions.
(b) We regret the error in our invoice.
(c) She talked to him about the pros and cons of the plan.
(d) We must reach a decision before the end of the week.

Situation 11

1년 후, Global gTrading이 Allgarment에 결제조건을 재고해달라고 요청하다.

124 Dukjin Dong Jeonju, Korea 561-756

Tel: +82-63-270-3049 Fax: +82-63-270-3028

E-mail: gtrading@kornet.net

August 27, 2015

Dear Mr. J. Gupta,

We appreciate the documents for our last order No. 4727. We have honored the sight bill, and the bank should send you an advice shortly.

More than a year has passed since we made the first transaction on a D/P basis. We would like you to change it to payment by 60-day bill of exchange, D/A.

When we first contacted you last September you told us that you would be willing to reconsider the terms of payment once we had established a trading association.
We believe that sufficient time has elapsed for us to be allowed the terms we have asked for. If you need references, we will be glad to supply them.
As we are planning to send another order next week, could you please confirm that you agree to these new terms of payment at your earliest convenient date?
With best regards,

Eugine Park

Eugine Park,
Import
Manager
Global gTrading Co., Inc.

Synopsis

한국의 Global gTrading과 인도의 Allgarment Enterprises가 거래를 시작한지도 1년이 지났다. 그동안 약간의 선적지연이 있기는 했지만 서로 별 문제없이 거래를 해왔다. 이에 Global gTrading의 Eugine은 현재 D/P로 되어 있는 결제조건을 자사에게 유리한 외상거래인 60일 D/A조건으로 바꾸었으면 하고 있다. 이것은 처음 거래를 시작할 때 Allgarment측에서 거래관계가 어느 정도 이루어지면 고려해 보기로 한 사항이다. Eugine은 이 점을 Allgarment의 Javv에게 상기시키면서 결제조건을 재고해 달라고 요청하고 있다. 다음 주에 또 주문을 할 예정이니, 이 결제 조건에 동의하는지 알려 달라고 말하고 있다.

once

여기에서 쓰인 once는 조건을 나타내는 부사절로 쓰이면서 '일단 ~하면 ~한다'의 의미로 쓰였다. once는 이런 절을 이끌면서 현재시제로 미래를 나타낸다.

- Once we establish a business relationship, we will be willing to reconsider the terms of payment. (앞으로 좋은 거래관계를 맺으면 미래에 다시 생각해 보겠다.)

주절(main clause)의 시제가 현재(과거)라면, once가 이끄는 절은 그 앞의 시제, 즉 현재 혹은 현재완료(과거완료)가 된다.

- Once you have added $100 in refills in your account, you automatically become a Gold Rewards customer.
  (과거의 어느 시점부터 $100을 충전하면 현재의 시점에 Gold Rewards 고객이 됨)

- Once we had received the merchandise, I was going to write a more objective review of the store.
  (물건을 받아보고 나서 그 가게에 대한 객관적인 평을 쓰려고 하고 있었다.)

이런 의미로 쓰인 once는 as long as, only if와 바꿔 쓸 수 있다.

- As long as we receive payment within this period, no further recovery action will be taken against you and no further costs will be applied.

• Only if we receive your order by 2 pm, the item will reach you on the next business day.

이처럼 시간이나 조건을 나타내는 부사절들은 현재의 시제로 미래를 나타낸다.

• When we receive your order, we will start to make the ordered goods.
• By the time the building is completed, it will be the tallest one.
• Next time I come to New York, I will be a tourist. (다음번에는 관광하러 뉴욕에 올 것이다.)
• The consignment will be put to one side until we receive your instructions.

그러나 문장의 내용에 따라 once가 이끄는 절과 주절이 같은 시제일 수도 있다.

• Once customers come to rely on these systems, they almost never take their business elsewhere.

◈ convenient

• Please visit us at your convenience.
• Please visit us when you find it convenient.
• Please visit us when it is convenient to/for you.
  (~~you are~~) convenient는 사람이 주어로 사용되지 않음.
• When is it convenient for you?
  (~~are you~~)
• What time would be convenient for you?
• Is it convenient for you?
  (~~Are you~~)

convenience는 편리함, 편리한 것.
inconvenience는 불편함, 불편한 것.

• A pickup service will be provided for your convenience.
• We have many modern conveniences. (우리는 많은 문명 이기들을 가지고 있다.)
• We have no inconveniences in living suburb.

Practice Tests - Situation 11

1. The main purpose of this letter is ______________________________.
   (a) to inform the sight bill is honored.
   (b) to tell Mr. Gupta that the bank will soon send an advice.
   (c) to change the payment method.
   (d) to let Mr. Gupta know that order will be made next week.

2. What did Mr. Gupta promise when the first transaction was made?
   (a) He will establish a trading association.
   (b) He will reconsider the terms of payment.
   (c) He will ask reference to change the terms of payment.
   (d) He is planning to make large orders.

3. We will be willing to reconsider the terms of payment once we _______ a trading association.
   (a) had established (b) have established
   (c) established (d) establish

4. We believe that sufficient time has elapsed for us to be allowed the terms we have asked for.
   (a) gone (b) been over
   (c) flown (d) passed

5. Choose the one that is natural.
   (a) Please call me when it is convenient to you.
   (b) Please call me when you are convenient.
   (c) When are you convenient?
   (d) Are you convenient?

6. Which of the following would most likely appear right after the passage?

[무역영어 1급]

We are very sorry to announce that a chip in the Photophone 720, which was shipped to you on December 5, is defective and will be replaced. We ask you that you return all phones to us by January 31. Send them to our main distribution center in your region. Please use overnight express or two-day air. Electronix will pay for all shipping and handling, plus give you a 10% discount on your next order. We will replace the defective chip and ship the Photophone back to you within three business days of receiving it.

(a) We select each item we carry individually, to ensure quality and value for our customers.

(b) Our engineers have discovered defective keypads in some of the Photophone 720 products.

(c) Our goal is to have happy customers who return to us for all of their electronic equipment needs.

(d) We regret any inconvenience this recall may cause and we promise to provide you with quality electronic equipment in the future.

7. 다음을 요약한 것 중 원문과 다른 것을 고르시오. [무역영어 2급]

The demand for your product has more than doubled for the last quarter. So, we would like to place an additional order of three million bars of soap. We need them in one month to meet the increasing demand. Is it possible for you to complete this order in a month?

(a) The demand increased, so we want to place an additional order of three million bars of soap. We want to know whether you can ship them in a month.

(b) The demand has more than doubled. We would like to place an additional order of huge amount and want them to be delivered in a month. We want to know if it is possible.

(c) The demand increased more than we expected. So we want to place an additional order of three million bars of soap. We need them to be here in a month. We want to know whether it is possible.

(d) The demand increased for your product and we want to place an urgent order of three million bars of soap. We know it is possible as you have dealt with similar case before.

8. Which of the following is the LEAST likely reply to the letter below?

[무역영어 1급]

We have received a number of inquires for floor coverings suitable for use on the rough floors which seem to be a feature of much of the new building taking place in this region. It would be helpful if you could send us samples showing your range of suitable coverings. A pattern-card of the designs in which they are supplied would also be very useful

(a) We encourage you to test the samples provided. When you have done this if you feel it would help to discuss the matter we will arrange for our technical representative to arrange to come and see you.
(b) Our price list is enclosed which also shows details of our conditions and terms of trading.
(c) We have today sent to you separately a range of samples specially selected for their hard-wearing qualities.
(d) As part of our efforts to keep down manufacturing costs, I am sure you will understand that we must increase sales by distributing through as many outlets as possible.

9. Who is Ms. Rosen most likely to be? [무역영어 1급]

Dear Ms. Rosen:

We have seen your advertisement on your website and we are interested in the Alpha Rapid Bottler. We are a small company manufacturing soft drinks in the south of Spain. At the moment, we use a Wesco Bottler, but we are interested in hearing more about your equipment. We would be grateful if you could arrange a visit to our factory in the near future.

Yours faithfully

(a) an accountant
(b) a sales consultant
(c) a web designer
(d) an electric contractor

Situation 12

선적품에 문제가 생겼다.

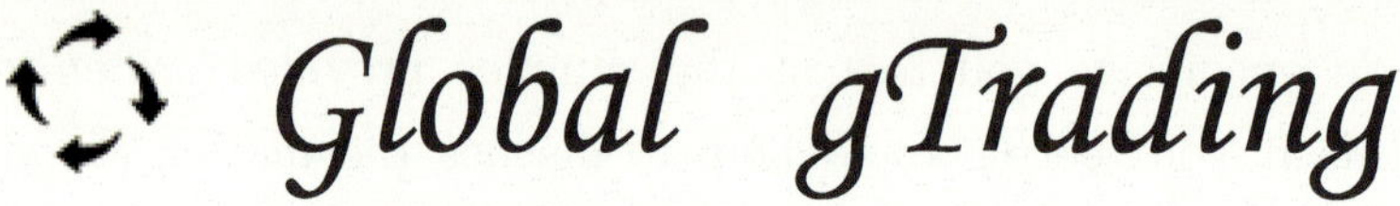

124 Dukjin Dong Jeonju, Korea 561-756
Tel: +82-63-270-3049 Fax: +82-63-270-3028
E-mail: gtrading@kornet.net

September 20, 2015
Dear Mr. Gupta,

Our Order No. 4477

We regret to inform you that 50 out of 400 boxes under the above order were broken open. Some garments were apparently missing and quite a few others are seriously stained and can not be sold as new articles.

From your invoice No.2228 we estimate that total loss amounts to USD15,550.00. As the sale was on a CIF basis and the forwarding company was your agent,
we suggest you contact them with regard to compensation.

You will find a list of the damaged and missing articles enclosed, and the consignment will be put to one side until we receive your instructions.
Regards,

Eugine Park

Eugine Park
Import
Manager
Global gTrading Co., Ltd.

Synopsis

결제조건도 외상거래(D/P에서 D/A로)로 바뀌질 정도로 서로 신뢰를 바탕으로 거래를 해오던 중, Allgarment가 보낸 400box의 의류 중 50box가 뜯겨져서 열린 사고가 발생했다. 의류 중의 일부는 분명히(apparently) 없어졌고, 상당수는(quite a few others) 심하게 더럽혀져서(stained) 상품성이 없어져 버렸다. 이에 Global gTrading의 Eugine 은 이 사실을 Allgarment측에 통보하고 보험회사에 연락해줄 것을 요청했다.

◈ Terms of Packing(포장조건)

장기간 운송을 요하는 수출입화물의 경우 situation 12에서와 같이 포장으로 인한 문제가 발생할 수 있기 때문에 곡물이나 광물과 같은 bulk cargo이거나 자동차나 선박과 같은 비포장화물(unpacked cargo)인 경우를 제외하고는 일정한 수준의 포장(packing)이 필요하다. 포장의 기능은 물품의 보호와 외관상 쉽게 식별하기 위한 것으로 장거리 수송이 필요한 무역거래에 있어서는 계약체결 시 포장재의 선택과 화인(shipping mark) 등에 대하여 약정할 필요가 있다.

포장에는 물품을 낱개로 포장한 최소단위 포장인 개장(unitary packing), 개장한 물품을 보호, 수송 및 보관의 편의성 등을 위하여 재포장한 내장(inner packing), 몇 개의 내장을 목재나 골판지 상자 등으로 선적을 위하여 최종적으로 다시 포장한 외장(outer packing) 등으로 구별할 수 있다. 포장재의 선택은 화물의 성질과 수송지역 및 기간 등을 고려하여 가장 합리적이고 안전한 포장방법을 선택하여야 한다. 일반 공산품의 경우 'Export Standard Packing'으로 표시하여 해당 업계에서 수출품의 포장으로 받아들일 수 있는 정도의 포장을 지칭한다.

shipping mark은 화물의 식별을 용이하게 하기 위하여 주로 importer의 지시에 의해 exporter가 포장화물의 외부포장에 수입업자명, 목적지 상자번호 등의 표식을 하는 것을 말한다. 화인은 invoice나 B/L 등 주요 선적서류에도 표시된다. 화인이 필요한 이유는 운송인이 이들 표시를 보고 취급화물을 invoice나 B/L 등과 대조하여 쉽게 식별하기 위한 것이다. 따라서 화인이 없는 화물은 no mark cargo가 되어 수입상에게 전달되지 않을 수도 있으므로 이를 분명하게 표시하는 것이 중요하다. 화인은 모두 대문자로 표기하는 것이 관습이며 보통 다음 그림과 같이 표시한다.

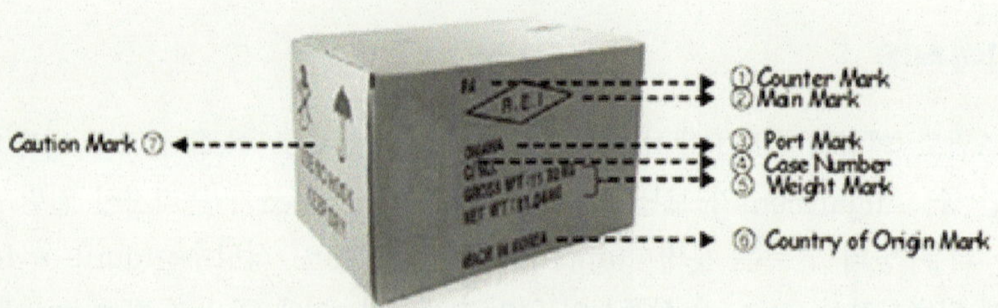

① 주화인(main mark): 주화인은 다른 화물과 식별을 용이하게 하기 위하여 삼각형, 다이아몬드형, 정방형, 마름모형, 타원형 등의 표시를 하고, 그 안에 수입자의 상호 약자를 기재한다.

② 부화인(counter mark): 주화인이 다른 화물과 같을 것에 대비하여 주로 생산자 또는 수출자의 약호를 기재한다.

③ 도착항구표시(port mark): 화물의 선적 또는 양하작업을 용이하게 하고 화물이 잘못 선적 되는 일이 없도록 도착항 등을 표시한다.

④ 화물번호(case number: C/NO.): 포장물이 여러 개인 경우 포장마다 고유번호를 표시하고 또한 총 개수 중에 몇 번째임을 표시한다.

⑤ 중량표시(weight mark): 화물의 gross weight(총중량)과 net weight(순중량)을 표시하며 이는 주로 운임계산과 하역작업에 도움을 주기 위하여 표시한다.

⑥ 원산지표시(country of origin mark): 화물의 생산지표시로 우리나라의 경우 "Made in Korea"로 표시한다.

⑦ 주의표시(caution mark): 화물의 선적 또는 운송 시에 취급상의 주의를 표시한 것으로 보통 포장의 측면에 표시하기 때문에 side mark라고도 한다. 다음과 같이 그림이나 문자 혹은 둘 다 사용해서 보통 붉은색으로 표시한다.

NO HOOKS(갈고리 사용금지)

KEEP DRY(건조한 곳에 둘 것)

FRAGILE(깨지기 쉬움)

THIS SIDE UP(이쪽이 위로)

KEEP AWAY FROM FIRE(화기엄금)

WITH CARE(취급주의)

◈ quite a few(a little)

구어체로 '상당히 많은'의 의미이다. 일반적인 사용법은,

a few people: 긍정적 의미의 몇 명의 사람들(countable noun)
few people: 부정적 의미의 몇 명 안 되는 사람들(countable noun)

- His ideas are difficult, but a few people understand them.
- His ideas are difficult, and few people understand them.

a little water: 긍정적 의미의 약간의 물(uncountable noun)
little water: 부정적 의미의 얼마 안 되는 물(uncountable noun)

- Giver roses a little water every day. (not a lot, but some)
- Cactuses need little water. (not much water)

a little more than: ~보다 약간 많은
little more than: ~에 지나지 않는

- The company get a little more than $5,000,000 of fixed assets.
- The company is little more than a name. (그 회사는 유명무실하다.)

* little은 a little table(작은 테이블), little tables처럼 형용사로 countable noun을 수식할 수 있다.

◈ others

others는 여기서 막연한 사람이나 사물을 나타내는 indefinite pronoun(부정대명사)으로 쓰였다. 쓰이는 법은 수가 한정되어 있을 경우,

- One of two candidates is female while the other is male.
- One of three candidates is female while the others are male.
- Two of three candidates are female while the other is male.
- One of three candidates is from the West, another is from the East, and the other is from the Mid-West.

수가 한정되지 않았을 경우,

- One of the candidates is female while others are male.
- Some of the candidates are female while others are male.

명사를 수식하는 데 쓰이는 another는 an+other로 다음에 항상 단수명사가 온다. 반면 other는 불특정의 다수를 지칭해서 항상 복수명사가 온다. the other는 단수, 복수명사 모두 올 수 있다. (the) others는 대명사로만 쓰이므로 다음에 명사가 올 수 없다.

- He is trying to enter another school. (불특정의 어느 학교)
- He is trying to enter the other school. (특정한 어느 학교)
- He is trying to enter other schools. (불특정의 어느 학교들)
- He is trying to enter the other schools. (특정한 어느 학교들)

- He is trying to enter another ~~schools~~.
- He is trying to enter other ~~school~~.
- He is trying to enter ~~others~~ schools.

◈ amount to

an amount of food: 많은 양의 음식(uncountable noun) = much food
a number of students: 많은 학생들(countable noun) = many students

amount가 '총합이 ~에 이르다', '결과적으로 ~이 되다'라는 동사로 쓰이면 to와 같이 쓰인다.

- This year's net profit amounted to one million dollars.
- The answer amounts to a refusal of proposal. (그 대답은 결국 거절이 된다.)

total도 동사로 쓰여서 amount to와 같은 의미로 쓰인다. 단 to가 없어도 된다.

- The country's export will total(to) $950 million this year.

suggest

여기에서처럼 제의하다, 주장하다의 의미로 쓰일 때, suggest는 다음과 같이 여러 형태로 쓰인다.

- He suggested that they(should)leave all at once. [목적어로 that이 사용될 때 should 생략 가능]
- He suggested going picnic. (목적어로 동명사 사용)
- He suggested which way to take. (목적어로 명사절 사용)
- He suggested her to go to see a doctor. (5형식 목적격 보어로 to 부정사 사용)

Practice Tests - Situation 12

1. Why did Global gTrading write this letter?

(a) to file a lawsuit
(b) to file a claim
(c) to contact the forwarding agent
(d) to sell their product

2. 다음 중 Shipping Mark에 해당하지 않는 것은?

(a) port mark
(b) case number
(c) L/C number
(d) weight mark

3. 다음은 Shipping Mark 중 Cargo Mark이다. 그 의미가 부적절하게 연결된 것을 고르시오.

(a) Stow Away From Heat – 화기엄금
(b) This Side Up – 상하 바로 놓음
(c) Fragile – 부서지기 쉬운 물건(파손주의)
(d) Guard Against Damp – 하적금지

4. Choose the one that is natural.

(a) He is trying to enter another schools.
(b) He is trying to enter other school.
(c) He is trying to enter others schools.
(d) He is trying to enter the other schools.

5. The shipping charges for deliveries to the Netherlands _____ 7.50 per parcel up to 30 kgs.

(a) amount
(b) amount to
(c) amounted
(d) is amount

6. Which would be used to have a similar meaning? [무역영어 2급]

In 2010, we sold 10,083 mobile phones to India, which was about the target.

→ Last year we could (   ) the target by selling (   ) 10,000 mobile phones in India

(a) meet – a little more than (b) achieve – just below
(c) get – little more to (d) obtain – just about

7. 다음 밑줄 친 부분을 가장 바르게 고쳐 쓴 것을 고르시오? [무역영어 2급]

We received the shipment no. 234-kr today. The boxes looked damaged, both stains(apparently from getting wet) and dents. We opened one box and, in fact, most of the books were water-damaged and some were bented and crushed.

We have hundreds of back order that we were hoping to fill with this shipment.

Please let us know how soon you can have this shipment replacement so we can give our customers a date by which they can receive their orders.

(a) stained-dented-bended-back orders-replace
(b) stained-dented-bent-back orders-replaced
(c) stain-dent-bent-back orders-replaced
(d) stain-dent-bended-back order-replaced

8. Which of the following can be inferred from the letter below? [무역영어 1급]

I am writing to inform you that the goods we ordered from your company have not been supplied correctly. On 20 July 2012, we placed an order with your firm for 12,000 light-weight CD cases.

The consignment arrived yesterday, but contained only 1,200 cases. This error put our firm in a difficult position, as we had to make some emergency purchases to fulfill our commitments to all our customers. This caused us considerable inconvenience.

I am writing to ask you to please make up the shortfall immediately and to ensure that such errors do not happen again. Otherwise, we may have to look elsewhere for our supplies.

(a) The importer has decided to change suppliers because of the delay in shipment.
(a) Owing to the error in shipment, customers were not able to make purchases.

(c) The seller has ensured that such error will not happen again.
(d) The importer has requested that the problem be rectified as soon as possible.

9. Which of the following can be included in a reply to the letter below? [무역영어 1급]

We thank you for having shipped our order of handheld vacuum cleaners via the M/V Marina. However, we regret to inform you that 4 cases were found to be crushed and their contents badly damaged. We found that the cases were too fragile and the packing was not sufficient for ocean transaction and so the contents of the crushed cases were broken and are now in an unsaleable condition.

We enclose the authorized surveyor's report showing the damage to be the result of poor packing. We ask you, therefore, either to send us your replacement right away by air freight at your expense or to reimburse us USD980.00 to cover the prices of the damaged goods and our losses accrued for the import duty and charges of the inspector. We will wait for your prompt decision on this matter. Thank you.

(a) We offer our sincere apologies for our mistaken numbering. We found that the packers misread the numbers, and have instructed them to send you our correct goods immediately.
(b) The damage by fungus seems to have been on account of the fact that the goods were exposed in the broken cases to humidity upon landing.
(c) The great pressure of orders for these goods sine you placed an order has made it impossible to produce as we wish, although all of our automated lines have been fully operated.
(d) The packing, however, was in full compliance with the standards for international ocean transportation and the specifications of the packaging were agreed upon by you in the contract. We will need a double checking.

10. Which of the following is the best summary of the letter? [무역영어 1급]

Just as soon as we finished our telephone conversation this morning, I ordered a duplicate shipment of carrel panels sent to you. We are quite

certain that the damages you reported on the first shipment were the result of careless handling by the trucking company—the fixtures were expertly crated and left our plant in perfect condition.

We will, of course, take this matter up with Fastway Transport—but that's our problem, not yours. Just store the damaged materials somewhere out of your way, and we'll have them picked up. We are very sorry about this incident, and we are confident that the delay will be a short one.

(a) The seller assures that the buyer was not aware of the damage and is therefore not to blame.

(b) The buyer insists that any problem with the shipment should be resolved by the seller and the carrier.

(c) The buyer is certain that it returned unsalable merchandise, and thus it doesn't have the right to request for the replacement.

(d) The seller would replace the wrong shipment and assumes that the damage was caused by the carrier.

11. Which of the following can be inferred from the article below?

[무역영어 1급]

Exports from China rose 13.4 percent in December compared with a year ago, while import growth unexpectedly slowed to 11.8 percent because of lower prices and moderating domestic demand. Overall, the Chinese trade surplus shrank to USD155 billion in 2011, from USD183 billion in 2010, as imports picked up and demand for Chinese goods in Europe and elsewhere softened. Despite concerns in China about the slowing pace of economic growth, Capital analysts predicted that China's exports will grow 10 percent this year – less than half of last year's increase. They estimated that imports will increase 13 percent, down from 24.9 percent growth in 2011.

(a) Chinese economic growth is not as impressive as the previous year, however, analysts are optimistic about export growth.

(b) Analysts predict further improvement for the Chinese economic growth.

(c) New trends in Europe have enhanced 10% growth in exports.

(d) Imports influenced by the slowing economy are not expected to increase any further.

Situation 13

문제가 된 선적품에 대하여 Allgarment측에서 답변을 보내다.

Allgarment Enterprises

37-2 Bridgeway Colony, 2nd Street, Tirupur, Tamilnadu India 641607
Telephone: +91-421-2232-880
Facsimile: +91-42-2232-888

September 25, 2015
Dear Mr. Eugine Park,

Thank you for informing us about the damage to our consignment (Invoice. No. 2228). From our previous transactions you will realize that this sort of problem is quite unusual. Nevertheless, we are sorry for the inconvenience it has caused you.
We must, however, point out that this transaction is based on CIF. Therefore, we are free from any liabilities for the shipment from the point the cargos are on board the vessel although we paid the insurance premium for you under CIF terms.
Moreover, the clean on board B/L reveals that everything was in order at the time the goods were loaded onto the ship.

Our best guess is that the accident had happened in transit, and we are willing to cooperate with you to file a claim with Insurance India. It is unlikely that our insurance agent needs to be troubled with this case.

Please contact the Insurance India's claims settling agent in Korea specified in the insurance policy for this matter. If you need further assistance, we will be more than happy to assist you in any way we can.

With best regards.

Javv Gupta

Javv. Gupta, Director
Export Division
Allgarment Enterprises

Synopsis

Global gTrading에 보낸 선적물 중의 일부가 파손되었다는 연락을 받은 Allgarment의 Javv는 이런 일이 아주 드물게 일어나는 일이지만 불편을 끼치게 되어 미안하다는 말로 답장을 시작했다. 그러나 이 거래는 CIF조건이기 때문에 자신들이 보험료를 지불하긴 했지만, 선적물이 본선의 갑판에(on board the vessel) 선적되는 순간 수출상인 자신들의 책임은 없다는 것을 분명히 하고 있다. 더욱이 무사고선적선하증권(clean on board B/L)을 발급받았기 때문에 선적 당시에는 아무 이상이 없었음을 밝히고 있다. Allgarment는 이 사태가 운송도중 일어났을 것이라고 추정하고 있으며, Global gTrading이 보험회사에 보험금을 청구할 수 있도록 기꺼이 협조하겠다고 말하고 있다. 이런 종류의 문제에 대하여 Allgarment측의 보험사인 Insurance India는 별문제 없이 처리해 줄 것이라고 언급하였다. 이 문제에 대하여 한국에 소재하는 Insurance India의 보험금 결제대리인(claims settling agent)에게 연락하는 말과 함께, 더 이상의 도움이 필요하면 기꺼이 돕겠다는 말로 편지를 마무리하고 있다.

◈ CIF조건의 거래에서 보험사고가 발생했을 때

CIF조건에서는 수출자가 보험과 운임을 지급하지만, FOB조건에서와 마찬가지로 수출자의 위험의 부담은 화물이 본선에 선적되는 순간까지이다. 따라서 운송 도중 발생한 보험 사고의 경우, 수입자가 피보험이익을 갖고 있으므로 수입자가 보험을 청구하게 된다. 이 경우 보험청구권자인 수입자는 보험가입지가 아닌 수입국에 소재하므로 사고발생 시 청구의 편의를 위하여 신용장 상에 보험금 지급지를 수입국으로 기재하고, 보험계약서에도 이 업무를 담당할 보험금결제 대리인(Claims Settling Agent)을 지정해 두게 된다. 따라서 Situation 12에서 발생한 보험사고는 수출자인 Allgarment가 아닌 수입자인 Global gTrading이 처리해야 한다.

◈ sort of

sort of, kind of는 원래 '~종류의'라는 의미로 쓰인다. 여기에서도 '이런 종류의 문제는'의 의미로 쓰였다.

- What sort of processor does the computer use?
- We eat the same kind of food everyday.

구어에서는 '어느 정도, 차라리, 어쩐지'의 의미로 쓰인다. 또는 상대가 대답하기 싫거나 곤란한 질문을 했을 때 확실히 말하지 않고 대충 얼버무려는 표현으로도 쓰인다. '그렇다고 할 수 있지', '말하자면 그런 셈이야'라는 의미이다.

- He is sort of angry. (조금 화가 났다.)
- She is, kind of, very pretty. (그녀는 상당히 예쁘다.)
- I sort of expected it. (얼마간은 예상했었다.)
- Do you like her? Sort of. (그렇다고 할 수 있지.)

◈ our best guess ~

We guess that ~의 의미로 영어에서는 이처럼 무생물을 주어로 하는 경우가 많다.

- What has brought you here?
- A few minute's walk brought us to the movie theater.
- Your look suggests that you're having a great time with her.
- The movie reminds me of my old friends.

Practice Tests - Situation 13

1. What is Mr. Gupta's suggestion regarding the damaged and missing goods?
   (a) Allgarment Enterprises is fully responsible for the accident.
   (b) The accident had happened during the transit.
   (c) Global gTrading should file a claim with claims settling agent.
   (d) This sort of accident is quite unusual.

2. Why did Mr. Gupta claim that his company is not responsible for the accident?
   (a) Because the accident had happened in transit.
   (b) Because his company paid the insurance premium.
   (c) Because the clean on board B/L had issued.
   (d) Because it is an unlikely accident.

3. 다음 문장을 영작한 부분 중 틀린 곳을 고르시오.
   가죽제품은 거칠게 제조되었고 볼품없이 질이 떨어지는 경향이 있습니다. 귀사가 원견품과 비교할 수 있도록 견품 2타를 미국 UPS 특사편으로 오늘 발송하였습니다.
   (a) The leather products seem to be too roughly manufactured
   (b) and are inclined to be inferior out of shape.
   (c) Two dozens of samples have today dispatched to you by American UPS courier
   (d) so that you can compare them with your original samples.

4. Which of the following has a different context of writing a letter?
   [무역영어 2급]
   (a) The goods shipped by M/S "Kennedy" leaving Portland on February 14, whose insurance policy is No. M-153, have been damaged during transportation due to bad weather.
   (b) We have received your letter of May 25, and according to your instructions we have effected marine insurance for USD 6,000 on three units of computers from Busan to London per M/S "NamDong" sailing

on August 20 against A/R. We are pleased to send you the insurance policy and our bill of USD 2000 and request you to remit by October 15.

(c) We would like to cover the loss by marine insurance and request you to let us know what particulars you require from us when making our claim. Also please let us have the necessary forms we have to submit to you.

(d) We are very pleased to receive your order, and trust that it will be the first of many orders—the beginning of a long lasting association between our two companies.

5. Put the following sentences in the correct order. [무역영어 2급]

From your email of August 11, it appears that there is misunderstanding of our intention.

(A) We would like you to provide this material as soon as possible, but if your policy does not permit such an accommodation without contract coverage, we will have to reconsider our plans. (B) We are interested in using your new automatic model in our front-wheel-drive vehicles, since we anticipate that demand for manual models will decrease. (C) It was your automatic transaxle, not the manual one, that our CEO, Mr. Danish referred to during his visit on July 25. (D) However, feasibility can only be determined after receiving drawings and specifications from you, due to the regulations in Korea.

Your prompt response would be very much appreciated. Thank you.

(a) C – B – D – A (b) B – C – A – D
(c) A – B – C – D (d) D – A – C – B

6. Which of the following best fits the blank in the letter below?

[무역영어 1급]

Thank you for informing us about the damage to our consignment(Inc. No. 2228).

From our previous transactions you will realize that this sort of problem is quite unusual. Nevertheless, we are sorry for the inconvenience it has caused you.

We must, however, point out that this transaction is based on CIF. Therefore, ________ although we paid the insurance premium for you under CIF terms. Moreover, the clean on board B/L reveals that everything was in order at the time the goods were loaded onto the ship.

Our best guess is that the accident had happened in transit, and we are willing to cooperate with you to file a claim with Insurance Korea. It is unlikely that our insurance agent needs to be troubled with this case.

(a) you have the responsibility to compensate for the expenses incurred due to the damaged shipment

(b) we are free from any liabilities for the shipment from on board of designated vessel

(c) you have no responsibility to hire an independent surveyor who will examine the damaged shipment

(d) we should contact the Insurance Korea's claims settling agent in your city specified in the insurance policy for this matter

거래 단계별 expressions

1. 제품의 소개
2. 회사의 소개
3. 거래처 소개의뢰
4. 상대방을 알게 된 경위 설명
5. 거래를 제의할 때
6. catalog, sample 등을 요청할 때
7. 가격견적을 요청할 때
8. 거래 조건을 제시할 때
9. 신용조회를 할 때
10. 여러 가지의 offer
11. offer를 받아들일 것을 권유하는 표현
12. counteroffer – 가격인하요구
13. counter – offer – 지불조건, 인도시기 등의 협상
14. 가격인하 요구 사절
15. 가격인하 요구를 사절하고 대안을 제시
16. Counter – offer를 받아들일 때
17. 계약에 관한 표현
18. 주문을 할 때
19. 주문을 확인할 때
20. 주문 거절, 변경과 기타 지연상황
21. L/C의 개설
22. L/C조건의 변경
23. 선적완료, 선적지연
24. 해상보험의 가입
25. 선적서류의 송부
26. 수출입 대금의 결제

1. 제품의 소개

With a whopping 1GB of memory, Celltopia II is a powerful tool for the mobile professionals. You can access the Internet while you are on the road with the built-in wireless modem.	1기가 바이트의 대용량 메모리로 무장한 Celltopia II는 이동이 잦은 전문가 여러분께 강력한 도구가 될 것입니다. 내장된 무선 모뎀으로 어디서든 인터넷에 접근할 수 있습니다.
You will find that we are offering a wide selection of quality pre-owned cars, buses and trucks. All are manufactured in Korea and come with our one-year limited warranty for parts and labor.	저희가 다양한 종류의 최고급 중고 자동차, 버스, 트럭을 취급하고 있음을 알게 되실 것입니다. 모두 한국산이며 1년간 무상으로 부품 및 수리비 포함 조건으로 품질을 보증합니다.
We sell four different grades of wheat flour. Our prices are very competitive and extremely attractive. The minimum order is 12,500 metric tons. To get FOB and F&C prices, please contact us.	저희는 4종류의 밀가루를 취급하고 있습니다. 저희 가격은 매우 경쟁력이 있고 매력적입니다. 최소 주문량은 12,500 metric tons입니다. FOB나 F&C 가격 견적을 원하시면 연락주시기 바랍니다.
We can assure you that the Omega II is one of the most outstanding machines on the market, and our confidence in it is supported by our five-year guarantee.	Omega II는 시중에 나와 있는 제품 중 최고급 기계이며 저희는 5년간 보증해 드릴 정도로 품질에 자신 있습니다.
When you have had the opportunity to see the samples for yourself, we feel that you will agree that they are the highest quality.	직접 견본을 보시게 되면 저희 제품이 최고 품질이라는 것에 동의하시리라 생각합니다.
Once you have seen the Gamma 900 in operation we know that you will be impressed by its trouble-free performance.	작동 중인 Gamma 900을 보시면 고장 없는 성능에 감동 받으시리라 생각합니다.

2. 회사의 소개

As a leader in electronic importing firm in Los Angles we would like to know more about your Celltopia II, a mobile internet browser you advertised in the latimes.com.	LA 지역에서 전자제품을 수입하는 일류 회사로서 저희는 귀사가 latimes.com에 광고한 무선 인터넷 검색기인, Celltopia II에 대하여 알고 싶습니다.
We are a specialist in importing and distributing all kinds of garments across Korea since 1979, and are looking for a manufacturer who can supply us with wide range of hand-crafted knit wear.	저희는 1979년부터 각종 의류를 수입하여 보급하는 것을 전문으로 하는 회사이며 수공에 니트웨어를 공급해줄 제조업체를 찾고 있는 중입니다.
I am writing on behalf of our principal in our region, who is interested in importing used vehicles from Korea.	저는 저희 지역에서 한국으로부터 중고 자동차 수입에 관심 있는 저희 고객사를 대신해서 이 글을 쓰고 있습니다.
We have been in the import business of the agricultural products in Korea since 1979, and it is our intention to purchase your wheat flour.	저희는 한국에서 1979년부터 농산물 수입업에 종사해 오고 있는 회사이며 귀사의 밀가루를 구입하고자 합니다.
We have had long experience in supplying top quality medical equipment to every part of the world.	저희는 최고급 의료 장비를 전 세계로 오랫동안 공급한 경험을 가지고 있습니다.
We are one of the main producers of industrial chemicals in Korea, and hope to expand our market into Eastern Europe.	저희는 한국에서 산업용 화학제품을 생산하는 주요 회사 중의 하나이며 동유럽으로 시장을 확대하길 바라고 있습니다.
We have a proud record of more than 20 years in our business as an exporter-importer dealing in general goods, machinery and equipment.	저희는 일반상품, 기계류 및 장비 수출입 상으로 20년이 넘는 역사를 자랑하고 있습니다.

3. 거래처 소개의뢰

We would be grateful if you could provide us with names of US firms having extensive sales networks for our Celltopia II.	당사의 Celltopia II 판매를 위한 광범위한 판매망을 가지고 있는 미국 회사의 이름을 제공해주시면 감사하겠습니다.
Please introduce us to some creditable firms who can supply us with wide range of hand-crafted knit wear.	다양한 수공예 니트웨어를 공급해 줄 수 있는 믿을 만한 회사를 소개해 주시기 바랍니다.
We would appreciate your introducing us one or two reliable distributor who are will to work on an exclusive basis with us in the marketing of our products in China.	독점 방식으로 당사의 제품을 중국에서 판매하고자 하는 믿을 만한 유통회사를 1~2곳 소개해 주시면 감사하겠습니다.
Since we do not yet have any particular business connections in your country, it would be deeply appreciated if you could kindly help us obtain a list to several dependable importer who may be interested in this line of business.	당사는 귀국에 거래 관계가 있는 특정 회사가 없으므로 이 계통에 관심이 있는 믿을 만한 수입회사들의 목록을 구하는데 도움을 주시면 대단히 감사하겠습니다.
We are seeking some reliable firms with whom we can establish business relationship, and would appreciate it if you could introduce us some of them in your region.	당사는 당사와 거래 관계를 수립할 수 있는 믿을 만한 회사를 찾고 있으므로 이런 회사들을 소개해 주시면 감사하겠습니다.
We are looking for an adequate representative to sell our automatic duplicating machines in your country. The representative should have experience with office equipment buyers.	당사는 자동복사기를 귀국에 판매할 적절한 대리점을 찾고 있는 중입니다. 대리점은 사무기기 구매자들과 거래 경험이 있어야 합니다.

4. 상대방을 알게 된 경위 설명

We have seen your advertisement in latimes.com, and are interested in your Celltopia II.	latimes.com에서 귀사의 광고를 보았습니다. 그리고 귀사의 Celltopia II에 관심이 있습니다.
We were favorably impressed by the designs displayed at your site in ECplaza 21.	ECplaza 21의 귀사의 site에 올라와있는 디자인에 좋은 인상을 받았습니다.
Your name has been recommended to us by KOTRA as one of the most reliable exporters of used vehicles.	가장 믿을 만한 중고 자동차 수출상으로 KOTRA가 귀사를 추천하였습니다.
The Korean Consulate in Shanghai has told us that you are looking for an agent in Korea to represent you.	상하이의 한국영사관에서 귀사가 한국 내에서 귀사를 대리할 회사를 찾고 있다고 들었습니다.
Our associates in the garment industry speak highly of your products, and we would like to have more information about them.	의류업에 종사하는 당사의 거래처가 귀사의 제품을 높이 평가하여서 좀 더 많은 정보를 얻고자 합니다.
We have learned from US Chamber of Commerce that you are one of the leading importers of electronic goods.	USCC로부터 귀사가 전자제품의 주요 수입상이라는 것을 알았습니다.
Having found your name in Internet website, we learned that you are manufacturing re-writable and recordable CDs.	귀사를 인터넷 웹사이트에서 발견하고 귀사가 재기록, 재녹음 가능한 CD생산하고 있다는 것을 알았습니다.
Through the courtesy of USDA we have heard your name and address as one of the leading exporters of agricultural products.	USDA의 호의로 주요 농산물 수출상인 귀사의 이름과 주소를 알았습니다.

5. 거래를 제의할 때

We have special interest in opening a business relationship with a top-ranking company.	당사는 최고의 회사와 거래관계를 맺는데 특별한 관심을 가지고 있습니다.
As we have not yet set up any account in Germany we are desirous of entering into business with you.	당사가 아직 독일에는 진출하지 않았기 때문에 귀사와 거래하고 싶습니다.
It is our keen desire to establish a business connection with you soon for our mutual benefit.	상호이익을 창출하기 위하여 귀사와 거래 관계를 맺기를 열망하고 있습니다.
We feel confident that our extensive networks of retailers in Korea will give you a large competitive edge in marketing your products in the Korean market.	당사의 광범위한 소매상 조직은 귀사의 제품을 한국 내에서 판매하는데 커다란 경쟁우위를 가져다 줄 것으로 확신합니다.
We would like to offer our services to promote your products in Korea.	귀사의 제품을 한국에서 알리는데 당사의 서비스를 제공하고자 합니다.
We would like to suggest a business tie-up between our two companies, with your company handling the manufacturing and our company taking care of the marketing and distribution.	귀사가 생산을 담당하고, 당사는 판매와 물류를 담당하는 것을 내용으로 하는 거래 관계를 맺고자 합니다.
We would be very much interested in the possibility of establishing a licensing agreement to manufacture your cosmetics within Korea.	당사는 한국 내에서 귀사의 화장품을 제조하는 라이센스 계약에 관심이 매우 많습니다.
We would like to discuss the possibility of your firm manufacturing the panel for LCD under an OEM agreement.	귀사가 OEM 계약 하에서 LCD 판넬을 제조할 수 있는 가능성에 대하여 논의하고자 합니다.

6. catalog, sample 등을 요청할 때

Please let us know what type of CPU and softwares you installed in the machine. It would be very helpful if you could send us some catalogs with detailed specifications.	CPU의 종류와 어떤 소프트웨어가 제공되어 있는지 알려주시기 바랍니다. 구체적인 스펙이 적힌 카탈로그를 보내주시면 도움이 많이 되겠습니다.
Please send us your current catalog and price list. We would also appreciate it if you could send some samples of your knitwears so that we can examine the texture and quality.	최신 카탈로그와 가격표를 보내주시기 바랍니다. 그리고 저희가 옷감과 품질을 살펴볼 수 있도록 귀사의 니트웨어 견본을 보내주시면 감사하겠습니다.
Although I can check your stocks in your website, I need your most updated list of stocks and export prices.	귀사의 재고를 웹사이트에서 확인할 수는 있지만 최신 재고목록과 수출가격이 필요합니다.
We have heard about your latest equipment in laser surgery and would like to have more details. Please send us any information you can supply.	당사는 귀사의 최신 레이저 수술도구들에 대하여 들었고 좀 더 자세한 내용이 필요합니다. 귀사가 제공할 수 있는 정보를 보내주시기 바랍니다.
Could you please give more information about Celltopia II which you recently advertised in latimes.com?	최근에 귀사가 latimes.com에 광고하신 Celltopia II에 대한 추가 정보를 제공해 주실 수 있겠습니까?
I would appreciate more details about the newly advertised dental cleaning system in your website.	귀사의 웹사이트에 새로 광고하신 구강청정 시스템에 대한 구체적 정보를 보내주 시면 감사하겠습니다.
I would be grateful if you could arrange for one of your sales representatives to call on me with the next two weeks.	2주일 내로 귀사의 판매 대리인이 저에게 전화할 수 있도록 조치해주시면 감사하겠습니다.
When replying, would you please enclose a pattern card?	답장을 보내실 때 패턴카드를 동봉해 주시겠습니까?

7. 가격견적을 요청할 때

We want to know your export price, possible quantity discounts, and payment terms. If the Celltopia II is of the standard we require and the price quoted is competitive, we will place a substantial order.	귀사의 수출가격, 대량구매에 따른 할인, 그리고 결제조건에 대하여 알고 싶습니다. Celltopia II가 당사가 요구하는 수준이고 제시 가격이 경쟁력이 있으면 상당량의 주문을 할 것입니다.
Please quote us your FOB price and let us know other terms and conditions.	FOB가격을 견적해 주시고 다른 거래조건들에 대해서도 알려주십시오.
Please quote all prices CIF Los Angeles.	LA도착 CIF가격으로 견적바랍니다.
We would like to receive your samples of the following goods and their prices quoted in US dollars CIF Incheon.	다음 물품에 대한 견본을 보내주시고, 미국 달러로 견적한 인천 도착 가격을 알려주시기 바랍니다.
We would be grateful if you could send us an itemized estimate giving details of all the costs involved.	각 항목별로 모든 원가를 자세히 밝힌 견적을 보내주시면 감사하겠습니다.
We would appreciate your e-mail by this Friday, giving an estimate for fifty(50) laser cutting machines.	50개의 레이저 커팅 머신에 관한 견적을 이번 금요일까지 e-mail로 보내주시면 감사하겠습니다.
As we are considering ordering more than 1,000 bicycles we would be pleased if you quote us the best discount off your list price for them.	당사는 1,000대 이상의 자전거를 주문할 것을 고려하고 있으므로 최대 할인율은 적용한 가격으로 견적 바랍니다.
Please include all shipping and insurance in your quotation.	견적 시에 선적과 보험비용을 포함해 주시기 바랍니다.

8. 거래 조건을 제시할 때

In this type of business we used to make deals by 60-day bill of exchange, D/A. We are also expecting a quantity discount in addition to a 20% trade discount off net list prices because we usually place large orders.	이런 종류의 거래에서 당사는 60일 후 결제 조건 환어음으로 거래해 왔습니다. 당사는 또한 주로 대량 주문을 하기 때문에 20%의 동업자할인에 추가해서 대량주문에 따른 할인도 기대하고 있습니다.
We usually deal on a 30% trade discount basis with an additional quantity discount for orders over 1,000 units.	당사는 주로 30%의 동업자할인에 추가해서 1,000개 이상의 수량에 대하여 대량주문 할인을 하고 있습니다.
We'd like to point out that we usually settle our accounts on a D/A basis with payment by 30-day bill of exchange.	당사는 주로 30일 후 지불조건의 환어음에 의한 D/A 방식으로 거래해왔음을 언급하고 싶습니다.
We generally do our business on an Irrevocable L/C, under which we draw a draft at 60 d/s. Prices are quoted FOB Busan in US dollars, but we can make up CIF prices, delivery at any port of your country, if you desire.	당사는 일반적으로 60일 기한부 어음을 발행하는 취소불능신용장에 의하여 거래를 합니다. 가격은 부산 출발 FOB 미화로 견적되지만 원하시면 귀국의 어느 항구도착 CIF가격도 제시할 수 있습니다.
We usually do business on an L/C basis, but we are willing to accept D/P if you insist.	당사는 주로 신용장에 의하여 거래하지만 귀사가 원하시면 D/P방식도 가능합니다.
Goods are sold on open account. ~on sight draft. ~on time draft. ~on an L/C.	외상거래입니다. 일람출급어음에 의한 거래입니다. 기한부어음에 의한 거래입니다. 신용장에 의한 거래입니다.
As for payment, we ask you to open an L/C at sight in our favor for the full invoice value immediately upon confirmation of sale.	결제조건으로는 거래 확정 직후 당사를 수익자로 하는 일람출급 신용장을 송장가격 전액에 대하여 개설할 것을 요청합니다.

9. 신용조회를 할 때

Please name your banker and business partner who would tell us your financial and business conditions.	귀사의 재무 상태와 영업 상태를 알 수 있는 거래은행과 거래처를 말씀해주시기 바랍니다.
As for our financial standing you may refer to the Korea Exchange Bank, Head Office, Seoul.	당사의 재무 상태에 관해서 서울 한국 외환은행 본사에 조회해 주십시오.
We may refer you to the Korea Exchange Bank for our financial status.	당사의 재무상태에 관해서는 한국외환 은행에 조회해 주십시오.
EveryImport has referred us to your bank for their financial status.	EveryImport의 재무 상태에 관해 귀 은행에 조회하라고 하였습니다.
Your bank has been referred to us by EveryImport for their financial status.	EveryImport이 그들이 재무 상태를 귀 은행에서 알아보라고 하였습니다.
We would appreciate it if you would kindly let us have your opinion regarding their financial standing. We precisely want to know how long EveryImport has had accounts with you and the promptness in paying bills.	그 회사의 재무 상태에 관한 귀사의 의견을 주시면 대단히 감사하겠습니다. 얼마나 오랫동안 EveryImport와 거래해 왔고 결제는 신속히 처리했는지 정확히 알고 싶습니다.
Would you please inform us confidentially of your opinion about their financial standing?	그 회사의 재무 상태에 대해서 비밀리에 귀사의 의견을 말씀해 주시겠습니까?
We would be very grateful if you could provide us with the information regarding their general reputation.	그 회사의 일반적인 평판에 관한 정보를 당사에 주시면 대단히 감사하겠습니다.
Please give us your candid opinion as to their trustworthiness and way of doing business.	그 회사의 신뢰성과 영업방식에 대한 귀사의 솔직한 의견을 주셨으면 합니다.

We should be grateful if you could supply us with the information you might have regarding their general standing and say whether, in your opinion, they are likely to be reliable for credit up to US$500,000, and whether they settle their account on time.	그 회사의 일반적 상황에 대한 정보가 있으면 알려주시고, 귀사의 의견으로 저희가 그 회사에게 50만 달러까지 신용을 제공해도 괜찮을지, 그리고 대출금 상환을 제 때 하였는지 알려주시기 바랍니다.
We assure you that any information you may supply will be kept in the strictest confidence, and that you will have no responsibility for the information provided.	귀사가 제공한 어떠한 정보라도 철저히 비밀로 할 것이며, 귀사는 정보 제공에 대한 어떠한 책임도 없다는 것을 보증합니다.
Any information you may give us will be held in absolutely confidential.	귀사에서 제공된 정보는 철저히 비밀로 하겠습니다.
Your reply will, of course, be treated as strict confidence.	귀사의 답변은 당연히 철저히 비밀로 하겠습니다.
Please be assured that all correspondence will be held in the strictest confidence.	연락 내용은 모두 철저히 비밀로 하여야 합니다.
Any expenses connected with this credit inquiry will be promptly paid by us upon receipt of your bill.	이 신용조회에 대한 비용은 귀사의 청구서를 받는 즉시 지불할 것입니다.
We shall be glad to reciprocate your courtesy on any similar occasion.	유사한 경우가 발생할 시에 저희도 귀사의 이번 호의에 보답하겠습니다.
We will be pleased to render you similar service when requested.	요청을 하시면 저희도 비슷한 서비스를 제공하겠습니다.

10. 여러 가지의 offer

We are very happy to inform you that we have received favorable responses from the references and offer you firm subject to your reply received here by October 25 as follows:	신용조회처로부터 호의적인 답변이 있어서, 10월 25일까지 유효한 확정청약을 다음과 같이 하게 되어 기쁩니다.
We are making a firm offer, subject to your reply by March 18, on LCD panel at US$40.00 each, CIF Los Angeles.	귀사의 회신을 3월 18일까지 받는 조건으로 LCD패널을 CIF LA 가격으로 개당 40달러에 확정오퍼 합니다.
Concerning your inquiry of September 12, we are glad to make to following offer to you for our new products.	귀사의 9월 12일자 문의에 답하여 당사의 신제품에 대해 아래와 같은 오퍼를 하는 바입니다.
We are pleased to make an offer for this item subject to prior sale since it is our final stock now out of production.	현재 이 제품은 생산이 중단되어서 마지막 재고이기 때문에 선착순 매도 조건으로 오퍼를 냅니다.
Thank you for your inquiry of June 29, against which we are offering you our wheat flour subject to being unsold.	귀사의 6월 29일자 문의에 감사하며 당사의 밀가루에 대하여 재고잔류 조건으로 청약을 합니다.
In order to help our customers we are making an offer on sale or return for our newly designed hats.	당사는 고객을 돕기 위하여 새롭게 디자인된 모자를 반품허용조건으로 청약합니다.
We are pleased to make a special offer of 20% discount on all our products for this month only.	이번 달 동안에만 당사의 모든 물품에 대하여 20% 할인해 주는 특별오퍼를 제공해 드리는 바입니다.
Our following offer is subject to change without notice owing to the frequent fluctuation in the market price.	다음 오퍼는 시장가격의 빈번한 변동으로 인하여 통보 없이 변경될 수 있습니다.

11. offer를 받아들일 것을 권유하는 표현

Now, larger orders are rushing in from many countries and the demand for our Celltopia II in Korea is very strong. Under the circumstances, there is every indication that the price will rise soon.	현재, 많은 주문들이 많은 국가로부터 들어오고 있고, 한국에서 Celltopia Ⅱ의 수요가 매우 좋습니다. 이런 상황으로 가격이 곧 상승될 명백한 조짐을 보이고 있습니다.
Improved production methods have allowed us to offer you our new main boards at prices considerably below those of last year. You will notice that reduction up to 20% has been achieved.	향상된 생산 기술로 지난 해의 가격보다 훨씬 낮은 가격으로 새로운 메인보드를 귀 사에 제공할 수 있게 되었습니다. 최대 20%의 할인이 이루어졌다는 것을 알게 될 것입니다.
You will see from the details of our enclosed offer that all our products are now offered at 2% lower than our usual prices. As our prices are quoted CIF LA, you will agree that they are below those of our competitors.	당사의 정상가격보다 2% 더 낮게 제안한 모든 당사의 제품에 대한 오퍼의 세부사항을 동봉하였습니다. 당사의 가격이 CIF LA 조건으로, 경쟁사들의 것보다 싸다는 것에 동의하실 것입니다.
The current rush of orders from your country will keep all the factories here fully occupied for quite a while. Under these circumstances, we have offered you the very best price with the soonest possible delivery.	현재 귀 국가로부터 주문이 폭주하여 꽤 오랫동안 이곳의 모든 공장들이 가동될 것입니다. 이러한 상황에도 당사는 귀사에(물품이) 가능한 빨리 인도될 수 있도록 하면서 최저의 가격 조건을 제시했습니다.
We can not guarantee that these prices will be available next month because the cost of material is steadily rising.	원자재의 가격이 꾸준히 증가하고 있어서 이 가격이 다음 달에도 가능할 것이라는 확신이 없습니다.
As prices are on the rise, we advise you to accept this offer and order without further delay.	가격이 상승하고 있기 때문에 더 이상의 지연 없이 귀사가 이 오퍼를 수락하여 주문을 하실 것을 권유합니다.

12. counteroffer – 가격인하요구

While we appreciate the quality of your product, we find that your price is rather high for the customers in the US where the competition for this type of device is quite high.	귀사의 상품의 품질을 높게 평가하긴 하지만, 이런 종류의 기계에 대한 경쟁이 심한 미국시장의 소비자들에게는 귀사의 가격은 다소 높습니다.
We have to point out that similar models can be purchased from other Asian or European manufacturers at a price from 15% to 20% below your quoted price.	귀사가 제시한 가격보다 15~20% 저렴한 가격으로 아시아와 유럽 제조업자들로부터 비슷한 모델을 구입할 수 있음을 말씀드리고 싶습니다.
We are not in a position to accept your offer of memory chips. We are obtaining the same quality through another channel at a price far below what you quoted.	귀사의 메모리칩에 대한 오퍼를 받아들일 수 없습니다. 귀사가 언급한 가격보다 훨씬 낮은 가격으로 다른 경로를 통해 같은 품질의 물품을 제공받고 있습니다.
How about reducing your price somewhat, say, to US$20.00 per piece? If you can come down to this price level, we are prepared to place a large order.	개당 가격을 20달러 정도로 낮출 수 있으 신지요? 귀사께서 이 가격대로 내려주시면, 당사는 대량의 주문을 할 계획입니다.
We would like to ask you to reconsider the price.	그 가격을 다시 생각해 주실 것을 요청합니다.
To be perfectly honest, I was somewhat surprised at the price you quoted.	솔직히 말씀드리면, 귀사께서 제시하신 가격에 약간 놀랐습니다.
In view of the current market conditions, we feel the offered price would make it difficult for us to maintain competitiveness.	최근 시장상황을 비추어 보건데, 귀사가 제안한 가격으로는 당사의 경쟁력을 유지하는 데 어려움이 있을 것 같습니다.

13. counter - offer - 지불조건, 인도시기 등의 협상

Your terms of payment by a sight draft are too hard for us. Another firm is granting us the terms of a draft at 60 d/s.	일람출급결제조건은 당사에게는 매우 어렵습니다. 다른 회사는 60일 기한부 어음 조건으로 해주고 있습니다.
If a further discount is not possible, we would like to be able to pay installments. If you could agree to let us pay for the order over a period of two years, we would be ready to place a order.	더 많은 할인이 가능하지 않으면, 분할 지급을 하고 싶습니다. 2년 분할 지급 조건에 동의하시면 당사는 주문을 할 준비가 되어 있습니다.
Your delivery date of December 27 is too late for our winter collection, which should be finished during October.	겨울컬렉션을 위해서 10월 중에는 납품이 끝나야만 하는데 귀사의 12월 27일의 선적은 너무 늦습니다.
We would like to request a revision in the delivery date. We can accept your offer if you can shorten the delivery period.	납품일을 변경을 하고 싶습니다. 귀사께서 납품기간을 단축해 주시면 귀사의 제안을 받아드릴 수 있습니다.
Would it be possible to have the 200kg bags of wheat flour repacked in 100kg bag?	200kg 밀가루 포장을 100kg 포장으로 해 주실 수 있으십니까?
We will surely place another order if you guarantee the quality is equal to the previous shipment.	과거의 선적품과 같은 품질을 귀사께서 보증해 주신다면 다시 주문하겠습니다.

14. 가격인하 요구 사절

Your counter-offer has been carefully considered, but we regret that it is not possible to allow a discount at this time due to the recent appreciation of Korean won against US dollar.	귀사의 반대청약을 신중하게 고려하였습니다만, 최근 달러대비 원화의 평가절상 때문에 이번에 할인해 드릴 수 없음을 유감스럽게 생각합니다.
We regret to say that we are not able to meet all the demands you have made in your counter-offer.	당사는 귀사의 반대청약에 있는 모든 요구에 응할 수 없음을 유감스럽게 생각합니다.
In fact, our revised price barely covers the cost of production, no margin of profit left for us. We will not be able to make any further reductions in price.	사실, 당사의 수정된 가격은 제조원가를 간신히 넘고 있어서 당사에게 남는 이익은 없습니다. 이 가격을 더 이상은 삭감을 할 수 없습니다.
We hope you understand that 20% discount is the maximum we can allow on any order.	어떤 주문에 대해서도 20%의 할인이 당사가 허용할 수 있는 최대라는 것을 이해해 주시기 바랍니다.
We regret that we can't agree to you counteroffer of January 3 because of our policy regarding the minimum order.	최소 주문에 관한 당사의 정책 때문에 1월 3일 귀사의 반대청약에 동의할 수 없음을 유감스럽게 생각합니다.
Although we would very much like to meet as many of your terms as possible, we cannot air freight your order for the same price as by sea.	비록 당사가 가능한 한 귀사의 조건을 맞추려고 하지만 해상운송 가격으로 주문품을 항공편으로 보낼 수 없습니다.
At the moment, the best reduction we could grant you would be 3%.	현재, 당사는 최대 3%의 할인을 귀사에게 제공할 수 있습니다.
We apologize we cannot give you any discount because the price is fixed.	정찰제 가격 때문에 조금의 할인도 해줄 수 없음을 사과드립니다.

15. 가격인하 요구를 사절하고 대안을 제시

It is our keen desire to serve you better with products at competitive prices, and therefore we propose an alternative model, Celltopia IIe. It has a slightly slower processor, but customers can hardly notice the difference. All other specifications are the same.	보다 좋은 제품을 싸게 공급하고 싶은 것이 당사의 희망이므로 다른 제품, Celltopia IIe를 제안합니다. 약간 느린 프로세서가 장착되어 있지만 소비자들은 거의 차이점을 느끼지 못할 것입니다. 다른 모든 사양은 같습니다.
To our regret we are unable to supply you with 12" panel at the price you requested. We have an 8"-panel which sells at a price closer to what you wish to pay.	유감스럽게도 당사는 귀사가 요청한 가격에는 12인치 판넬을 공급할 수 없습니다. 귀사가 지불하기 원하는 가격대에는 8인치 판넬이 있습니다.
The 15% discount you have requested is available for orders of 200 units or more. If you increase your order to this volume, we will be happy to allow you the discount you want.	귀사가 요청한 15%의 할인은 200개 이상의 주문에만 가능합니다. 주문량을 이 수준까지 늘려주시면 귀사가 원하는 할인을 해드리겠습니다.
We are offering you a substitute which is the same price and of similar quality as the goods ordered.	귀사가 원하는 가격에 비슷한 품질의 제품을 대체품으로 제시합니다.
We cannot lower the unit price of our product to the price you requested for the quantity you wish to order. However, if you order a minimum of 500 units, we will grant a 20-percent discount.	현재의 주문 수량으로는 당사 제품의 단가를 귀사가 요청하는 수준까지 내릴 수 없습니다. 그러나 최소주문량을 500개로 하시면 20%의 할인을 해드리겠습니다.
I suggest that you order our 10mm pearl instead of 12mm. 10mm one is priced well within your budgetary requirements.	12mm 진주 대신 10mm 진주를 주문하시길 바랍니다. 10mm 진주는 귀사의 예산범위 내에서 구입하실 수 있습니다.

16. Counter - offer를 받아들일 때

We would like to materialize this business even at some concession, and are therefore prepared to grant you as special discount of 5% for the quantity of 1,000 units, and the terms of a draft at 60 d/s on D/A. We trust that you will obtain a fine sale at these large concession and give us further orders.	저희는 약간의 할인을 감수하고서라도 이 거래를 성사시키고자 1,000개의 주문에 대하여 5%의 특별할인을 제공하고 결제는 60일 후 결제의 D/A방식으로 할 준비가 되어 있습니다. 가격이 대폭 내려감에 따라 잘 팔릴 것으로 기대하며 더 많은 주문을 주실 것으로 믿습니다.
Our price of US$3,125.00 was carefully calculated and it is very difficult for us to allow even the smallest reduction. However, this being the first experience with you, we have decided to accept your offer at U.S.$3,120.00 per unit C.I.F. New York.	당사의 가격 3,125달러는 매우 신중하게 계산된 것으로 조금도 깎아드릴 수 없습니다. 그러나 첫 거래임을 감안하여 CIF New York 조건 개당 미화 3,120의 귀사 오퍼를 받아들이기로 하였습니다.
We have decided to accept your counteroffer of January 28. The modifications you requested will be reflected in the sale contract.	당사는 귀사의 1월 28일자 반대오퍼를 받아들이기로 하였습니다. 수정된 부분은 판매계약서에 반영되어 있을 것입니다.
As we have been doing business with you for many years and you have always been reasonable in you dealings with us, we have decided to agree to your terms.	귀사와 오랫동안 거래를 해왔고 귀사는 항상 거래를 합리적으로 해왔기 때문에 당사는 귀사의 조건에 동의합니다.
The terms stated in your counteroffer of July 1 for our offer No. H-666 are acceptable to us.	당사의 H-666호 오퍼에 관한 귀사의 7월 1일자 반대오퍼는 받아드릴 만합니다.

17. 계약에 관한 표현

Before conducting any serious business we believe we'd better make a formal agreement for terms and conditions under which we should conduct our business activities.	본격적인 거래에 앞서 거래조건에 대한 공식적인 합의서를 작성하는 것이 필요하다고 믿습니다.
Enclosed is a draft of our memorandum with which we have been conducting businesses with our other customers. We propose that the terms and conditions specified in the enclosed memorandum be applied to all transactions between us unless otherwise prearranged.	당사의 다른 고객과 거래할 때 사용한 협정서의 초안을 동봉합니다. 당사는 별도로 정하지 않는 한 이 협정서에 나와 있는 조건으로 모든 거래를 하는 것을 제안합니다.
Of course, this memorandum is just a draft and is subject to change with our mutual consents. Please feel free to make comments on this.	물론 이 협정서는 초안이므로 상호 합의하에 수정이 가능합니다. 의견을 주시기 바랍니다.
We are pleased to enclose our Sales Note covering your order for the Celltopia II.	귀사의 Celltopia II에 관한 주문을 위한 당사의 판매계약서(Sales Note)를 동봉합니다.
We are pleased to issue our Purchase Order for the under mentioned commodities in accordance with the terms and conditions given below.	아래와 같은 조건으로 아래 물품에 대한 구매주문서(Purchase Order)를 보내드립니다.
The buyer shall purchase from the seller and the seller shall sell to the buyer wheat flour for baking purpose (“goods”) subject to the terms and conditions herein provided.	아래의 조건에 따라 구매자는 판매자로부터 구매를 하고 판매자는 구매자에게 제빵용 밀가루(상품)를 판매한다.

18. 주문을 할 때

We are pleased to accept your offer of June 18 and would like to place the following order with you.	당사는 귀사의 6월 18일자 귀사의 오퍼를 받아 들여서 다음과 같이 주문합니다.
For this order, we accept the 15% trade discount you offered, and the terms of payment(sight draft, D/P), but hope you review these terms for future transactions.	이번 주문에 대하여서 당사는 귀사가 제시한 15%의 동업자 할인과 결제조건(일람출급어음, D/P)을 받아들이지만 앞으로 거래에서는 이 조건들을 재고해주셨으면 합니다.
The goods are urgently needed, so make sure that the delivery is made on the specified date.	물건이 긴급히 필요하므로 정해진 날짜에 배달이 될 수 있도록 확인해 주십시오.
Enclosed please find our first order No.123-1 for 20,000MT of the Grade A wheat flour. The order is subject to all the terms and conditions specified in the Sales Agreement previously signed and exchanged.	Grade A의 밀가루 20,000MT에 대한 당사의 첫 주문서 No. 123-1을 동봉합니다. 이 주문은 전에 서명해서 교환한 판매계약서에 명시한 모든 조건에 따라 행해지는 것입니다.
After reviewing your sample and considering your discounts we have decided to place a trial order of 500 garments. Enclosed please find our Order Sheet, No. DR3355.	귀사의 견본을 검토하고 할인조건을 고려한 결과 당사는 500벌을 시험 주문하기로 했습니다. 당사의 주문서 No. DR 3355를 동봉했습니다.
Please accept this letter as our official order for the merchandise mentioned in you offer of May 5. We would appreciate if you would confirm this order by e-mail or fax at your earliest possible date.	이 편지를 귀사의 5월 5일 오퍼에서 언급한 물건의 공식주문으로 받아주시기 바랍니다. 이 주문을 이메일이나 팩스로 가능한 빨리 확인해 주시면 감사하겠습니다.

19. 주문을 확인할 때

It is our utmost pleasure to receive your order of October 25 for the Celltopia IIe, and to welcome you as one of our customers.	10월 25일자 Celltopia lle에 대한 귀사의 주문을 정말 고맙게 생각하며 당사의 고객이 되신 것을 환영합니다.
We confirm all the terms you specified in your purchase order, especially the total price of US$180,000, and assure you that your order will be given our careful attention.	귀사의 구매주문, 특히 총 구매대금이 미화로 18만 달러임을 확인합니다. 그리고 당사는 귀사의 구매주문에 대해 최선을 다하겠습니다.
We are very pleased to accept your order No. 221 of November 22 and confirm that we have all the items in stock.	귀사의 11월 22일자 No.221에 대한 구매주문을 받아 기쁘게 생각하며, 모든 상품의 재고가 있음을 확인합니다.
We trust that the goods you ordered will meet your expectations and hope you will find future opportunity to contact us.	당사는 귀사가 주문하신 상품들이 귀사의 기대에 부응할 것이라고 믿으며, 장래에 당사와 또 연락할 기회가 있게 되길 바랍니다.
Your order No. 124 is now being processed and should be ready for dispatch by the end of this week.	귀사의 주문 No. 124는 지금 처리 중이며, 이번 주말까지는 발송될 것입니다.
Thank you for your order No. T-55 which we received today. We are now dealing with it and you may expect delivery within the next two weeks.	오늘 주문받은 No. T-55에 대해서 감사하게 생각하며 2주 이내에 배달되도록 노력 하고 있습니다.
We are pleased to inform you that we have already made up your order, No. 8828 for 500 sweaters, and now making arrangement for shipment to New York.	당사는 No. 8828의 스웨터 500벌에 대한 생산을 끝냈고, 이젠 뉴욕으로 선적을 준비 중이라는 소식을 말씀드리게 되어 기쁩니다.

20. 주문 거절, 변경과 기타 지연상황

We are sorry to say that we are completely out of stock of the item and it will be five weeks before we get our next delivery.	죄송하지만 그 제품은 당사에 재고가 전혀 없고, 다음 배송까지 5주 정도가 소요될 것 같습니다.
We regret that due to a strike at our factory we are unable to fulfil your order at present.	당사 공장의 파업으로 인하여 현재는 귀사의 주문을 처리하지 못하고 있습니다.
Regretfully, we must turn down your order as it would be difficult for us to manufacture the goods at the price you ask.	유감스럽게도, 귀사가 요구하신 가격으로는 그 제품을 생산할 수 없기 때문에 귀사의 주문을 거절할 수밖에 없습니다.
We apologize for being unable to accept your order. We do hope that we can be of service to you in the future.	귀사의 주문을 처리하지 못하여 죄송스럽게 생각합니다. 당사는 가까운 시일 내에 귀사에게 서비스를 제공할 수 있기를 희망합니다.
The shirt we manufacture are sold by the dozen in one color. I regret that we never sell individual garments.	당사가 생산하는 셔츠는 한 색상 당 12개 묶음으로 판매합니다. 낱개로는 판매할 수 없음을 유감스럽게 생각합니다.
If the alternative model we have suggested is acceptable to you, we would appreciate a fax confirming this.	당사가 제안했던 다른 모델을 귀사가 수용하실 수 있다면, 확인 팩스를 부탁합니다.
Although we can't be of any help on this occasion, I hope there will be other opportunities for us to do business with you.	비록 이번에는 제대로 도움을 못드렸지만, 다음 기회에 당사와 거래할 기회가 있기를 기대합니다.
We are afraid that the digital camera you ordered has been out of production.	귀사가 주문하신 디지털 카메라는 생산 중단된 품목입니다.

21. L/C의 개설

We will soon be ready for shipment of the goods and, therefore, ask you to open a letter of credit as soon as possible to enable us to effect the shipment on time.	조만간 상품들을 선적할 것이므로 신용장을 빠른 시일 내에 개설해 주실 것을 요청합니다.
We would like to advise you that the Bank of America of LA has opened an irrevocable letter of credit in your favor for the amount of US$180,000. The credit is valid until May 25, 2006.	귀사를 수익자로 미화 18만 불 상당의 취소불능신용장을 LA의 Bank of America 측에서 개설하였음을 통보합니다. 신용장의 유효기간은 2006년 5월 25일까지입니다.
We instructed our banker, Bank of America, to open an irrevocable L/C in your favor.	Bank of America에게 귀사를 수익자로 취소불능신용장 개설을 지시해 두었습니다.
We will open an L/C against our order upon receipt of your confirmation of order.	귀사가 당사의 주문을 확인해 주시면 당사는 신용장을 개설할 것입니다.
We would like to call your attention that we have not received the letter of credit covering the order. The L/C should have reached us by yesterday. Your prompt expedition of an irrevocable L/C in our favor is greatly appreciated.	귀사의 주문을 처리할 수 있는 신용장을 아직 받지 못하였음 알려드립니다. 신용장은 어제까지 당사에 도착했어야 했습니다. 당사를 수익자로 한 취소불능신용장을 조속히 개설해 주시면 감사하겠습니다.
Without adding your confirmation, please advise the below referenced beneficiary of the following letter of credit details:	아래의 수익자에게 다음의 신용장의 세부사항을 통지해 주시기 바랍니다. 귀 은행이 이 신용장에 대한 추가적인 확인을 할 필요는 없습니다.
Draft and documents as specified in this L/C must be forwarded to the issuing bank directly by the negotiating bank.	신용장에 명시된 환어음과 제반서류는 반드시 매입은행이 직접 발행은행 앞으로 보내야 합니다.

22. L/C조건의 변경

Upon carefully checking the L/C, however, we found it stipulates 'freight prepaid'. As you might understand we have contracted by FOB basis, and accordingly the term 'freight collect' should be used.	신용장을 자세히 검토한 결과 '운송료 선불'이라는 조항을 발견하게 되었습니다. 귀사가 알다시피 FOB(본선인도조건)로 계약하였으므로 '운송료 착불'로 표시되어야 합니다.
Please have your banker amend the L/C replacing the term 'freight prepaid' with the term 'freight collect'.	'운송료 선불'이라는 문구는 '운송료 착불'로 대체하여 신용장을 수정해 주시기 바랍니다.
Thank you for your email pointing out the discrepancy between our contract and L/C. Upon checking it we found that when our clerk typed the application form for the L/C she made a mistake.	거래조건과 신용장상의 불일치점을 지적한 귀사의 e-mail에 감사합니다. 당사가 조사한 결과 담당자가 신용장 신청서 작성 시에 실수를 하였음을 발견하였습니다.
Given this situation shipment delays are inevitable, and we are not sure when the works can be resumed. We therefore request your L/C No. 7 be amended so the validity is extended to May 15.	이 상황을 감안해볼 때 선적 지연은 불가피하며, 언제 이 일이 재개될지는 확신할 수 없습니다. 따라서 귀사의 신용장 No. 7의 유효기간을 5월 15일까지 연장해 주실 것을 요청합니다.
As requested in your e-mail of April 21 we are pleased to inform you that we had the L/C amended. We have instructed our bankers today to amend the latest shipping date and validity of the Credit to May 10 and May 15, respectively.	4월 21일에 귀사가 e-mail로 요청하신 대로 신용장이 수정되었음을 알려드립니다. 마지막 선적날짜와 신용장 유효기일을 각각 5월 10일과 5월 15일로 수정할 것을 은행에 지시하였습니다.

23. 선적완료, 선적지연

We are pleased to inform you that your order No. 10DS was shipped on November 15, 2006 on the SS Arirang, which is due in Los Angeles on December 14, 2006.	귀사가 주문하신 NO. 10DS는 2006년 11월 15일에 아리랑호에 선적이 완료된 상태이며, 아리랑호는 LA에 2006년 12월 14일에 도착할 예정입니다.
The above order has now been completed and sent to the port of Incheon, where it is awaiting loading on the SS Chinastar, which sails for Shanghai on April 21 arriving April 26.	상기 주문의 처리가 완료되어 물품이 인천 항에서 4월 21일에 출발하여 상하이 26일에 도착 예정인 차이나스타호에 선적될 것을 기다리고 있습니다.
We regret to inform you that it has become impossible to complete the shipment of your Order no.3355 as scheduled due to a recent cyclone which has struck the eastern part of India.	귀사의 주문 No.3355는 유감스럽게도 최근 인도의 동쪽을 강타한 태풍으로 인하여 계획대로 제때에 선적되지 못하고 있습니다.
Your order was ready for shipment on the MV Bombay, but she suffered serious damage and her October 10th departure was cancelled indefinitely. Moreover, a considerable amount of cargo has been congested and it is quite difficult to secure any other shipping spaces.	귀사의 주문이 봄베이호에 선적할 준비는 끝났으나, 태풍으로 인한 선박의 피해로 인해 10월 10일 출항이 무기한 연기되었습니다. 게다가 엄청난 양의 화물들이 선적을 기다리고 있어서 다른 선복을 확보하기가 매우 어렵습니다.
As noted in our e-mail dated April 18, the buses are currently on the port of Incheon for shipment. Unfortunately, however, the port-workers' union began a strike yesterday, and all the loading and unloading works have been canceled.	4월 18일자의 이메일에 언급했듯이, 버스들이 현재 인천항에서 선적을 기다리고 있습니다. 그렇지만 불행하게도 항만 노조가 어제부터 파업에 돌입해 모든 선적과 하역 업무가 이루어지지 않고 있습니다.

24. 해상보험의 가입

Would you please quote us your lowest rate of marine cargo insurance, ICC(B), including S.R.C.C. and T.P.N.D. on the shipment of above articles, valued at CIF Busan US$200,000 by the referred vessel. A copy of commercial invoice and packing details are attached.	CIF 부산 가격으로 미화 20만 불에 해당하는 상기 선적품에 대해 SRCC, TPND 조항을 포함한 ICC(B) 조건으로 귀사의 가장 낮은 보험료를 견적해 주시기 바랍니다. 상업송장 사본 1부와 포장명세서를 첨부합니다.
We are pleased to offer you a port-to-port ICC(B) including S.S.R.C., T.P.N.D. valued policy at a rate of 2.21% for a total cover of US$13,266 CIF value + 10%). We would stress that this is a very competitive rate.	총 13,266달러(CIF가격+10%)에 대해 SSRC, TPND 조항을 포함한 항구에서 항구까지 ICC(B) 조건을 2.21%로 귀사에 견적하게 되어 기쁩니다. 이 보험료율은 매우 경쟁력 있는 것임을 강조하고 싶습니다.
We are pleased to inform you that we have effected insurance against All Risks, including War Risks at a rate of 1.12% to the value of US$300,000.	1.12% 비율로 30만 불에 대하여 전쟁위험을 포함한 전위험담보 조건의 보험이 가입되었음을 통보합니다.
Please cover 110% of the invoice value for 500 sets of GPS on Institute Cargo Clause(B) including W/SRCC.	GPS 500세트에 대하여 W/SRCC를 포함한 ICC(B) 조건으로 송장가격의 110%를 보상하는 보험을 가입해 주십시오.
All shipments are subject to insurance on W.A. for a sum equivalent to the invoice amount plus 10%, unless otherwise specified by agreement.	특별히 달리 정하지 않는 한 모든 선적품은 인보이스 금액에 10% 가산한 금액에 해당하는 금액을 보상하는 분손담보 조건의 보험에 가입되어 있어야 합니다.
We will continue to be making regular shipments, and wondered if you could arrange open cover for US$100,000 against all risks to insure consignments.	당사는 정기적으로 선적을 할 예정이므로 귀사가 미화 10만 불에 대하여 전손담보조건의 포괄예정보험(open cover)을 가입해 주실 수 있는지 알고 싶습니다.

25. 선적서류의 송부

You will receive necessary documents for taking the consignment via Bank of America. They include shipped clean bill of lading(No. 4E), invoice NO. PDA942), and insurance certificate NO. SFP.173).	선적품을 찾기 위한 필요서류들을 Bank of America를 통해 받게 될 것입니다. 그 서류들은 선하증권(NO. 4E), 송장(NO. PDA942), 그리고 보험증권(NO. SFP.173)입니다.
Attached please find copies of all shipping documents: commercial invoice, clean on board B/L, and certificate of origin. The originals with our bill of exchange at 60 days after sight were forwarded to the L/C issuing bank, China Trust Bank through our negotiating bank, Hana Bank in Seoul.	모든 선적서류, 즉 상업송장, 선하증권, 원산지증명서 사본을 첨부하였으니 확인하십시오. 60일 상환 환어음을 포함한 원본서류는 당사의 지급은행인 서울의 하나은행을 통해 LC 개설은행인 China Trust Bank에 전달되었습니다.
When we have the necessary documents we will transfer them to Hana Bank, your bank's agent here, and they will forward them to the China Trust Bank.	관련 서류들이 준비되면 이곳의 귀사의 은행대리점인 하나은행에게 전달할 것이고 그들은(하나은행) 그 서류들을 China Trust Bank에 전달할 것입니다.
We cannot take possession of the goods as we have not yet received the shipping documents. We would appreciate if you would send us one set of copies of documents so that our bank can issue a Letter of Guarantee.	당사는 선적서류를 받지 않는 한 물품에 대한 소유권을 취할 수 없습니다. 당사의 거래은행에서 LG(수입화물선취보증서)를 발행할 수 있도록 모든 서류 사본 1세트를 당사에게 보내주셨으면 고맙겠습니다.
As requested, two copies of the non-negotiable B/L and three copies of commercial invoice are enclosed.	귀사의 요구에 따라 유통불능선하증권 사본 2부와 상업송장사본 3부가 동봉되었습니다.
We are waiting for an on board ocean B/L from India Lines and it will be airmailed to you with the commercial invoice and insurance policy.	당사는 India Lines로부터 선적선하증권을 기다리고 있고, 상업송장과 보험증권과 함께 귀사에게 항공우편으로 보내겠습니다.

26. 수출입 대금의 결제

To cover the shipment we negotiated our draft at sight drawn under your L/C through Bank of America, Seoul. We kindly ask you to honor the draft on presentation without delay.	상기 선적품에 대한 귀사의 LC 조건대로 당사는 일람출급환어음을 서울의 Bank of America에 매입시켰습니다. 환어음이 제시되면 바로 결제해 주시면 감사하겠습니다.
We have received the shipping documents today and your draft was duly honored by the L/C issuing bank.	당사는 선적서류를 오늘 받았고 귀사의 환어음은 LC개설은행을 통해 정히 처리되었습니다.
Our bank also has advised us that the proceeds of our L/C against your invoice, No. UU-2, have now been credited to your account.	당사의 은행이 귀사의 송장 UU-2에 대한 LC의 결제금액이 귀사의 구좌에 입금되었음을 통보해 왔습니다.
As we are expanding our business here, we are planning to place a series of orders with you in near future. Although we have paid by the L/C this time, we would like, if possible, to settle future account based on document against acceptance (D/A) to facilitate the transaction as well as to avoid bank charges.	지금 당사의 사업을 확대하고자, 근시일내에 귀사에 연속적인 주문을 내려고 합니다. 당사가 현재는 LC조건으로 대금을 지불하였지만 가능하시다면 앞으로는 업무를 용이하게 할 뿐 아니라 은행 수수료를 피할 수 있는 DA(어음인수 서류인도 조건) 조건으로 거래를 하였으면 합니다.
We appreciate the documents for our last order No. 4727. We have honored the sight bill, and the bank should send you an advice shortly.	당사의 지난번 4727호 오더에 대한 서류 감사합니다. 당사는 일람출급환어음을 인수하였고 은행에서 귀사에게 곧 통지할 것입니다.
More than a year has passed since we made the first transaction on a D/P basis. We would like you to change it to payment by 60-day bill of exchange, D/A.	첫 거래를 DP(어음지급 서류인도 조건) 조건으로 한 이후 일 년 이상이 지났습니다. 당사는 60일 기한부 어음, D/A조건으로 변경했으면 합니다.

claim의 제기

Our technicians have thoroughly tested all the machines, and found 25 defective batteries. Although we are quite satisfied with the overall test results, we have to request that you send us 25 replacement batteries as soon as possible.	당사의 기술자들이 철저하게 모든 기계들은 시험했고, 25개의 결함있는 배터리를 발견했습니다. 당사는 전체적으로 테스트 결과에 만족합니다만, 25개 대체 배터리를 가능한 빨리 보내주시기를 바랍니다.
We regret to inform you that 50 out of 400 boxes under the above order were broken open. Some garments were apparently missing and quite a few others are seriously stained and can not be sold as new articles.	상기 오더에서 400개 박스 중 50개가 열린 채 파손되었음을 알리게 되어 유감스럽습니다. 일부 의류는 확실히 없어졌고 다른 의류에는 심각하게 오염되어 있어서 신상품으로 도저히 팔릴 수 없는 상태입니다.
Because of the large number of complaints filed by their customers, our client has returned nearly entire order.	그들의 손님들에 의해 접수된 수많은 불만 사항들 때문에, 당사의 고객은 주문품 거의 모두를 반송했습니다.
Upon unpacking the goods, we found that the colors of the goods are not the same as those of the sample.	포장을 뜯자마자 당사는 물품의 색상이 샘플의 색상과 같지 않았음을 발견했습니다.
To our regret there's only 12 articles in each box instead of 20 as shown in your Invoice NO. 1244.	실망스럽게도 송장번호 1244에서 명시된 대로 각 박스 당 20개가 아닌 12개의 제품만 있었습니다.
Please let us know if you want to take the goods back or let us sell them at a discount of 20 percent.	이 물품을 반송할 것인지 당사가 20퍼센트 할인해서 판매할 수 있도록 할 것인지 알려주십시오.
We hope you will take care of this matter carefully and suggest your solution as soon as possible.	귀사가 이 문제를 심사숙고하여 해결책을 가능한 빨리 제시하여 주시기를 바랍니다.

claim의 해결

We must apologize for the batteries that are not working. Upon discussing this matter with our professionals and reviewing your report we have tentatively concluded that some of the circuit boards may be damaged in transit. We have already sent the replacement batteries via Fedex next day air.	당사는 배터리가 잘 작동하지 않은 점에 대해 죄송하게 생각합니다. 이 문제를 당사의 전문가와 함께 토론하고 귀사의 보고서를 검토한 결과 회로기판의 일부가 운송 중에 손상을 입은 것으로 잠정적으로 결정지었습니다. 당사는 이미 대체 배터리를 다음날 도착 Fedex 항공편으로 발송하였습니다.
The defect may be due to a fault in a machine, and we are now checking all the machines. Meanwhile, we will offer 10% allowance for the defective goods.	그 결함는 기계의 결함 때문인 것 같고 당사는 모든 기계를 지금 확인하고 있습니다. 동시에 당사는 이 불량품에 대해 10% 할인해 드리겠습니다.
We must point out that this transaction is based on CIF. Therefore, we are free from any liabilities for the shipment from the point the cargos pass the rail of designated vessel although we paid the insurance premium for you under CIF terms.	당사는 이 운송조건이 CIF에 근거한 것임을 강조하고자 합니다. 그러므로 당사가 CIF 조건하에 보험료를 지급하였더라도 당사는 물품이 지정된 선박의 난간을 통과하는 시점부터 선적품에 대한 어떤 의무도 없습니다.
Under this circumstance, we hope you will understand why we are not in position to accept your claim.	이런 상황에서 당사가 귀사의 요구를 받아 드릴 수 있는 입장이 아님을 양해해 주시기를 바랍니다.
Please let us know what settlement you consider fair under these circumstances.	귀사가 이 상황에서 공정하다고 생각되는 해결책이 무엇인지 알려주십시오.
We suggest that this claim be settled in accordance with the arbitration rule of the Korean Commercial Arbitration Board.	당사는 이 요구사항이 한국 상사중재원의 중재규정에 의해 해결되기를 바랍니다.

How to write your resume

영문이력서는 resumé[rèzuméi] 혹은 CV(Curriculum vitae[−váiti:, vi:tai])라고 한다. 국문 이력서와 달리 일정한 형식이 있지는 않지만 통상적으로 쓰이는 내용과 스타일은 정해져 있다. 따라서 다른 지원자들과 구별되게끔 창조적이고 깔끔하면서 자신만의 강점을 부각시킬 수 있게 작성하는 것이 중요하다.

영문이력서의 내용

1. Contact Information

보통 이력서의 맨 위에 작성자의 이름과 주소 및 전화, 이메일, 홈페이지 주소 등의 연락처를 기재한다.

2. Objective

이력서를 작성하는 목적을 기재한다. 지원하고자 하는 기관의 희망직종을 1~2줄로 적는 것이 적당하다. 꼭 필요한 항목은 아니지만 이력서를 보는 상대방에게 한눈에 어떤 직종을 원하는지를 알리기 위함이다.

Sample Objectives

- An entry level position as a marketing assistant.
- Electrical engineering internship.
- To obtain a position in finance.
- A program coordinator position in a community organization working with youth.

- To apply decision and systems analysis to strategic planning in the telecommunications industry.

3. Summary of Qualifications or Profile.

이 항목에는 특정 포지션에 지원하는 이력서 작성자의 경력이나 자격 등을 요약해서 서술한다. 문장형식 혹은 단문형식으로 2~3줄 정도 기재하는 것이 일반적이다. Objective와 마찬가지로 꼭 필요한 항목은 아니지만 이력서 작성자의 자질을 요약해서 보여줄 수 있는 항목이다.

Sample Qualifications

Over five years of broad-based management experience, including operations, analysis, budgeting, and process improvement; demonstrated track record of managing multiple projects and providing quality, on time deliveries. Experienced in managing and motivating staff; excellent communication skills.

- More than three years experience in retail and food management.
- Retail internship with Walmart.
- Proficient in MS Office, Power Point, Windows XP and the Internet.

4. Education

지원자가 졸업한 학교, 학위, 성적, 졸업년도 등의 학력을 기재한다. 학교를 막 졸업해서 경력이 많지 않은 경우에는 지원하는 직종과 관련된 수강과목을 적는 것도 바람직하다. 대학원을 졸업했을 경우, 학위논문이 지원하는 직종과 관련 있는 경우에는 학위의 제목과 간단한 요약을 첨가하는 것도 좋다. 학교 졸업 후 경력이 많이 있는 경우에는 Education 부분은 다음의 Work Experience 부분 뒤에 간략히 졸업한 학교 및 학위 정도를 기재해서 상대적으로 Experience 부분을 강조할 필요가 있다.

5. Work Experience

자신의 경력을 기재한다. 지원하고자 하는 직종과 관련된 경력을 쓰는 것이 좋다. 대학을 막 졸업하여 관련 경력이 없는 경우 intern이나 part-time으로 일한 경험을 쓴다. 직장의 이름, 직위, 맡은 일, 근무기간 등을 간단히 기술한다. 경력이 많은 경우에는

Education보다 먼저 쓰는 것이 좋다.

6. Additional Information

컴퓨터 능력 및 기타 특이할 만한 능력, 외국어 능력, 수상경력, 자원봉사 경력, 스포츠나 취미 등을 기재한다. 필요에 따라 아래와 같은 별도의 항목으로 만들 수도 있다.

- (Computer) Skills
- Foreign Languages
- Honors and Awards
- Activities
- Interests
- Publications/Presentations[1)]

7. Reference

추천인 혹은 참고인의 이름, 주소, 연락처를 기재한다. 학생의 경우 교수, 직장인의 경우 상사를 기재한다. 요구하면 제공한다는 의미로 "Available upon request"라고 쓰는 경우도 있지만, 차라리 생략하는 것이 바람직하고, 추천인을 특별히 요구하는 경우에만 사용한다.

위의 항목들은 일반적인 resume에서 통상적으로 쓰이는 것들로 필요에 따라 생략하거나 다른 적절한 항목을 추가해서 작성하게 된다.

영문이력서 작성 시 주의할 점

1. Reverse Chronological Order

국문이력서의 경우 학력 및 경력을 과거부터 현재 순서로 작성하는 반면 영문이력서는 최근 정보부터 과거 순서로 작성한다. 예를 들어, 대학원을 졸업했으면 대학원 정보(졸업

1) 논문이나 저술 혹은 전문가 모임 등에서 발표한 것들을 기재한다. 교수나 연구원 등의 경우에 해당한다. 보통 별지 형식으로 작성한다.

일, 전공과목 등)을 나열한 후 학부 정보를 쓰는 순서이다. 경력 사항도 가장 최근 직장에 관한 정보를 시작으로 과거의 직장 순서로 작성한다.

2. Personal Information

이력서 작성자의 나이, 성별, 인종, 가족관계 등의 개인적인 사항은 국문이력서에는 필수적으로 들어가는 항목들이지만 영문 이력서에서는 특별히 요구하지 않는 한 기재하지 않는다. 이는 영문이력서를 요구하는 회사가 속해 있는 나라에서는 나이, 성별, 인종, 종교 등에 의해 지원자를 차별하는 것이 법으로 금지되어 있는 경우가 많기 때문이다. 그래서 미국계 회사의 경우 구인광고의 끝 부분에 "Equal opportunity employer"라고 밝혀서 개인신상에 의해 지원자를 차별하지 않는다는 것을 밝히고 있다.[2)] 이런 이유로 국문이력서에서는 필수사항인 지원자의 사진 역시 요구하지 않는 한 붙이지 않는다.

3. Power Words and Action Verbs

이력서를 읽는 상대방에게 긍정적이고 적극적인 인상을 줄 수 있는 단어를 선택한다. 예를 들면, 직장에서의 임무를 기술할 때, "Led a team of 5-10 managers to provide efficient and effective operation"과 같이 서술한다. Power words와 Action verbs는 342페이지 참조.

4. Length and Layout

영문이력서의 길이는 경력이나 학력 기타 특별한 skill이 많은 경우에는 여러 장이 될 수도 있지만 신입사원의 경우 한 장이면 충분하다. 그러나 한 장에 맞추려고 너무 빽빽하지 않도록 줄 간격, 폰트의 종류 및 크기 등도 적절하게 조절할 필요가 있다. 큰 항목들의 글씨들은 굵게 하여 구별을 확실하게 해주는 것이 좋고, 작성 후 철자와 문법을 확인하는 것은 필수적 이다. Resume의 출력은 고급용지를 사용하는 것이 좋은 인상을 남길 수 있다. 적절하게 컬러를 삽입하는 것은 바람직하지만 너무 요란스럽지 않게 해야 한다.

---

2) 이와 반대로 미국정부가 소수민족, 여성차별을 없애기 위해 법률에 의해서 대입, 일자리, 직업훈련에 흑인과 백인 또는 여성과 남성을 일정한 비율로 채용하도록 하는 인원 할당 조치를 affirmative action(약자우대조치)이라고 한다.

Jennifer Kim

Campus:
456 College Hall Chicago, IL
67890
111-222-3333
joykim@ilstu.edu

Permanent:
123 Seocho-dong Seocho-ku
Seoul, Republic of Korea
+822-777-888-9999
tracygraduate@hotmail.com

OBJECTIVE: Export Sales/Marketing position in the Celltopia systems

SUMMARY:
- Marketing internship with GE Electronics.
- Fluent in English and Spanish. Native speaker of Korean
- Proficient in MS Office, Power Point, Windows 8 and the Internet.

EDUCATION:

Master of Business Administration, May 2015
Illinois Institute of Technology, Chicago,
Illinois Major: International Business
Master's Thesis: "Overseas Market Penetration Strategies of Global Firms"

Bachelor of International Trade, February 2013
College of Business, Hankook University, Republic of Korea
Graduated a GPA of 3.8 on a 4.0 scale

Courses taken included:

Import/Export Documentations	International Business
Trade English (Writing)	International Marketing
Trade English (Conversation)	Promotion Management

EXPERIENCE:

Marketing Internship, May 2012 to August 2013
GE Electronics, Chicago, Illinois
- Served as Marketing Assistant to Overseas Sales team, including market penetration analysis.
- Assisted in the development of several new overseas markets.
- Tracked and reported all overseas marketing efforts using CRM software.

HONORS/ AWARDS
- Dean's List each semester while in IIT, 2014-2015
- Finalist at the Overseas Advertisement Competition, 2012

ACTIVITIES:
- President, International Marketing Club, 2011-2012
- Volunteering – volunteered as a crisis translator at the local church, working primarily with Latin American refugees, 2010-2011

PAUL FREDERIC

360 Park Avenue, Apt. 4-A
New York, NY 10010
e-mail: jill.smith@xxx.com
212-802-6682

EDUCATION:

BARUCH COLLEGE, Zicklin School of Business New York, NY
Master of Business Administration, June2005
Concentration in Industrial/Organizational Psychology

INDIANA UNIVERSITY **Bloomington, IN**
Bachelor of Science, May 1998
Concentration in Hospitality Management

- Dean's List
- Recipient of 1998 Distinguished Student Award

EXPERIENCE:

SONY CORPORATION **New York, NY**
Operations Manager *05/12 – 08/13*

- Managed operations including forecasting, inventory control, purchasing and quality assurance; maximized revenues through efficient staffing, labor cost controls, and promotions
- Designed and implemented employee incentive programs to improve employee morale and internal customer satisfaction; reduced union grievances by 40% while maintaining streamlined, profitable department
- Developed and delivered employee training on company policies and procedures to increase productivity

MARRIOTT INTERNATIONAL **New York, NY**
Assistant Manager *09/10 – 04/12*

- Increased internal customer ratings by 17% through cafeteria restructuring project, including opinion surveys, menu engineering, physical plant redesign, special events and quality controls
- Developed and implemented annual business plan
- Introduced intra- and interdepartmental meetings to improve processes and employee morale resulting in 25% reduction in absenteeism and tardiness and increased productivity and service quality in a multicultural union work environment

ADDITIONAL:

- Seminars: Train the Trainer, Core Management, Progressive Disciplining, Preventing Sexual Harassment, Managing Diversity
- Language Skills: Fluent in French, conversational Spanish
- Computer Skills: Proficient in MS Word, Excel, PowerPoint, Outlook, Lexis-Nexis and other research databases

Eugine Park

456 W. 78th Street, Apartment 12B, New York, NY 10023
(212) 456-7890, student@aol.com

Experience

The New York Stock Exchange New York, NY
Associate – Strategy and Planning Group: *(July 2012- Present)*

- Analyzed state of financial markets and how technological advances have created alternate trading platforms for purchase and sale of financial securities.
- Explored strategic initiatives for New York Stock Exchange in order to maintain Exchange's competitive advantage and reputation as world's premier equities market.

SoccerAge.com New York, NY
Business Analyst: *(January 2012-June 2012)*

- Researched, wrote and edited business plan for SoccerAge.com, the most comprehensive worldwide soccer site on the Internet.
- Provided support to CEO and CFO at presentations with Investment Bankers.
- Analyzed and evaluated investment banking engagement agreements.

Pershing Division of Donaldson, Lufkin & Jenrette Jersey City, NJ
Analyst - Energy Industry / Market Generalist: *(October 2000-December 2001)*

- Created and posted morning, noon, closing and weekend market summaries.
- Supported analysts and clients with equity, market and economic research.

Merrill Lynch Garden City, NY
Assistant To Team Of Financial Consultants: *(Summer 1999)*

- Researched and produced equity research report mailings for clients.
- Assembled monthly statistics on buy / sell / hold list of stocks.

Professional Licenses

* Series 7 and Series 63

Education

Baruch College, Zicklin School of Business New York, NY
*Master of Business Administration, June 2015

Washington University St. Louis, MO
* Bachelor of Arts, May 2000
* Major in Economics; Minor in Business

Activities

* Zeta Beta Tau Fraternity; *Executive Board* (Spring / Fall 2000)
* Special Olympics; Supervisor/Treasurer (Spring 2000-2001)

Power Words & Action Verbs

Accomplished
Accurately
Achieved
Acted as
Activated
Actively
Acquired
Adapted
Administered
Advanced
Advised
Allocated
Analyzed
Anticipated
Appointed
Arranged
Assigned
Assisted
Associated
Assured
Attended
Authored
Avoided
Awarded
Bargained
Began
Built
Carried out
Changed
Charged with
Chosen
Clarified
Collaborated
Combined
Commanded
Commended by
Communicated
Compiled
Completed
Completely
Composed
Conceived
Conciliated
Concluded
Condensed

Conducted
Confirmed
Consistently
Constantly
Consulted with
Contacted
Continually
Contributed
Controlled
Converted
Convinced
Coordinated
Correlated
Counseled
Counseled
Created
Cut costs
Cut time
Dealt with
Decreased
Defined
Demonstrated
Designed
Determined
Developed
Devised
Diplomatically
Directed
Discovered
Distributed
Doubled
Earned
Economically
Edited
Effected
Effectively
Efficiently
Efficiently
Elected
Elevated
Eliminated
Emphasized
Employed
Enabled
Enhanced

Encouraged
Established
Estimated
Evaluated
Exceeded
Executed
Expanded
Expedited
Experienced in
Expressed
Extended
Facilitated
Familiar with
Focused
Followed through
Formed
Formulated
Functioned as
Gained
Generated
Guided
Handled
Have ability to
Headed
Held
Helped
Hired
Honored by
Identified
Illustrated
Implemented
Improved
Improvised
Inaugurated
Incorporated
Increased
Independently
Indoctrinated
Influenced
Inherited
Initiated
Instituted
Installed
Instructed
Instrumental in

Insured
Interpreted
Invented
Investigated
Involved with
Isolated
Issued
Jointly
Justified
Knowledge of
Launched
Lectured
Led
Made
Maintained
Managed
Mapped
Marketed
Maximized
Met
Minimized
Modernized
Motivated
Negotiated
Nominated
Obtained
Operated
Organized
Oriented
Originated
Outlined
Overcame
Overhauled
Participated
Perfected
Performed
Persuaded
Pioneered
Planned
Played vital part
Practiced
Praised for
Predicted
Prepared
Presented

Prevented
Priced
Processed
Procured
Produced
Proficient in
Profitably
Projected
Promoted
Proposed
Proved
Proven record of
Provided
Published
Purchased
Put together
Qualified
Quickly
Raised
Ran
Rapidly
Realized

Received
Recognized
Recommended
Recruited
Reduced
Regularly
Regulated
Removed
Reorganized
Replaced
Reported
Required to
Researched
Resolved
Responsible for
Reversed
Revised
Rose from
Saved
Scheduled
Secured
Selected

Sent to
Served as
Serviced
Set up
Shared
Shortened
Simplified
Skillfully
Smashed
Smoothed
Sold
Solely
Solved
Specialized
Spoke
Started
Stimulated
Studied
Submitted
Substantially
Substantiated
Succeeded

Successfully
Summarized
Supervised
Surveyed
Synchronized
Tackled
Taught
Tested
Thoroughly
Took over
Toured
Traveled
Tripled
Up-dated
Used
Utilized
Won
Worked with
Wrote

Answers

Story I

Situation 1

1. (a) 2. (d) 3. (b) 4. (b)
5. (a) 6. (a) 7. (c) 8. (d)
9. (a) 10. (b)

1. Q-pointer II는 스마트폰을 이용하여 presentation할 때 쓸 수 있는 laser pointer이다.
2. off the street – 길거리로 내몰리지 않는
   on the street – 실직하여, 집 없는
   on the way – 다가오는
   on the road – 이동 중인
   on one's way – 오고 있는
4. street – 거리 양쪽에 건물이 줄지어 서 있는 도시의 도로
   road – 도시와 도시를 연결하는 도로, 시골 길
5. '연락을 취하다, 연락해 달라'는 의미의 contact은 동사로 쓰일 때 with 등의 전치사 없이 쓰인다.
6. 일반적인 무역거래는 circular letter, 광고, 인터넷포털 등에서 거래 상대방을 찾은 다음 inquiry를 보내서 제품에 대하여 문의를 하게 되고 offer와 counter offer, 그리고 acceptance의 과정을 거쳐서 sales contract을 맺게 된다.
7. 참석자들은 Carleton Ranch에서 event 때 평상복을 입어야 하고 그날은 금요일이다. 토요일 마지막 event 때 "Sales Reps of the Year" 상을 수여하게 되어 있다.
   HR(Human Resource; 인적자원)
10. 직원의 training 과정에 대한 문의를 하는 서신이다.

Situation 2

1. (c) 2. (b) 3. (d) 4. (d)
5. (d) 6. (a) 7. (b) 8. (c)
9. (a)

6. 본문 – 귀사의 2월 25일자 이메일을 보면 당사의 의도에 오해가 있었던 것으로 보입니다. 당사의 CEO가 2월 20일 귀사 방문 중 언급했던 것은 천연 가죽제품이 아닌 인조가죽이었으며 인조가죽에 대한 수요가 감소할 것이라고 예상하기 때문에 당사는 귀사의 새로운 색깔의 송아지 가죽 제품을 수입하는데 관심

이 높습니다. 그러나 실행가능성은 귀사로부터 도면과 명세서를 받은 후에 결정될 수 있습니다. 귀사가 가능한 빨리 이 자재를 공급해주길 바랍니다.

(a) 이전에 있었던 잘못된 의사소통을 바로잡기 위한 것

7. 본문 – 휴대용 선풍기에 관한 3월 2일자 귀사의 주문을 취소해달라는 편지를 5월 2일 받았습니다. 귀사가 이렇게 늦은 시점에 그러한 요청을 해야 한다는 것에 유감입니다. 당사는 고객의 니즈에 신속하게 충족하기 위해서 시즌 전에 미리 제조업자에게 주문을 해야 합니다. 수량예상에 있어서도 당사는 받아진 주문에 의존합니다. 당사는 정기적인 고객들로부터는 어떤 요청도 거절하고 싶지 않습니다. 하지만 이 경우는 어쩔 수 없이 거절할 수밖에 없습니다. 귀사의 것도 포함해서 모든 주문은 이미 만들어져 배송을 기다리고 있습니다. 만일 귀사의 요청을 좀 더 빨리 받았더라면 기꺼이 도와주었을 것입니다. (b) 3월 2일자 주문을 취소하겠다는 요청을 거절하는 것. considerable, large, big은 '대량의' initial order는 '처음 주문'

9. excuse는 '면제하다'

Situation 3

1. (d) 2. (c) 3. (b) 4. (a) 5. (a)
6. (a) 7. (b) 8. (a) 9. (c)
10. (d) 11. (b) 12. (a)

3. (b)의 "~ be obliged to + verb"는 "~해야만 한다"의 의미이다. 이를 다른 것들과 같은 의미로 바꾸려면, We are obliged for your introducing us to some reliable importers.가 된다.
4. allowance는 매도인의 과실에 대한 보상의 성격으로 가격을 할인해준다는 의미를 내포하고 있으므로 to compensate the damage가 정답이다.
9. 본문 – 귀사가 공급하고 있는 fax machine의 세부사항과 가격정보를 보내주십시오. 이 내용은 buyer가 inquiry하는 것이다.
(c) 거래조건과 함께 도매가격을 팩스로 보내주세요. 이 내용은 buyer에게 reply한 내용으로는 적합지 않다.
10. d) price list and catalog(가격표와 카탈로그) – artificial additives(인공첨가물) – second to none(무엇에도 뒤지지 않는)
11. a) 귀사가 문의한 내용은 동봉된 price list No.321를 참조하십시오.
b) 귀사의 정보를 위해서 일주일 이내에 price list No.321를 동봉해드리겠습니다.
c) 문의하신 가격과 자세한 내용은 동봉된 price list No.321에 있습니다.
d) 동봉된 price list No.321은 귀사가 문의했던 정보를 드릴 것입니다.
12. booth – 전시장의 부스
market share – 시장 점유율
competitive prices – 경쟁력 있는 가격, 저렴한 가격

Situation 4

1. (d) 2. (a) 3. (d) 4. (d)
5. (a) 6. (b) 7. (b) 8. (a)
9. (c) 10. (a) 11. (b) 12. (d)

4. "regret to inform ~" 다음에는 부정적 내용이 온다. (Situation 9 설명 참조)
7. "Qtopia systems"에 귀사의 이름과 주소를 신용조회처로 제공하는 것을 허락해 주시기 바랍니다."의 의미이므로 "허락을 구하는" (requesting a permission) 내용이다.
10. "The firms(a) print in the heading of this letter are those for"에서 print는 이 문장의 주어인 firms를 수식하는 과거분사 printed로 써야 한다.
11. Proposal의 목적은 다른 사람으로 하여금 자신의 idea를 받아들이고 실행할 수 있도록 설득하는 것이다. 1. Define the idea. proposal에는 자신의 실제 idea를 분명하게

언급해야 한다. proposal의 목적과 범위와 한계까지도 규정해야 한다. 2. Be persuasive. 자신의 idea에 대한 특정한 이유와 그로부터 얻어지는 이익과 이점을 제공해야 한다. 3. Anticipate objections. 질문 받기 전에 해답을 제공해야 한다. 관계자들의 자격, 비용과 지출의 타당성, 대안에 대한 논쟁들도 포함될 수 있다.

12. d) 이 문제를 재고하도록 하겠습니다. – 재고할 여지가 없습니다. 같은 의미가 아니다.

Situation 5

1. (c) 2. (a) 3. (d) 4. (d)
5. (b) 6. (c) 7. (a) 8. (b)
9. (d)

8. 본문 – 그 회사에 대한 재정 상태와 평판에 대한 정보를 알려주시면 고맙겠습니다. 귀사가 보내주는 어떤 정보도 극비로 취급될 것이며 비용은 청구서 받는 즉시 지급될 것입니다. 신속한 답장 주시면 감사하겠습니다.
   (b) 관련된 금액은 귀사의 서신에서 언급된 액수에 비하면 적습니다. 그리고 항상 연체가 되어 결제되고 있습니다. – 부정적
9. (d) Any further information you may give us will pay our careful attention. pay 대신에 draw를 써야 "귀사가 주는 어떤 정보도 당사의 관심을 끌게 될 것입니다."가 된다.

Situation 6

1. (d) 2. (b) 3. (c) 4. (b)
5. (c) 6. (c) 7. (a) 8. (a)
9. (d) 10. (b)

8. "enjoy(or command) a good reputation": "좋은 평판을 얻고 있다."
   "punctually meet its commitments" : "(부채상환 등의) 약속을 정확히 지킨다."
9. 본문 – 그 회사의 신용상태에 대한 정보를 보내주셔 감사합니다. 특히 그 회사가 귀사와 얼마나 오랫동안 거래를 하였는지 그리고 지불기한이 지난 부채가 있는지 알고자 합니다.
10. 본문 – Janoski 사는 책임을 흡족하게 이행하는데 어긋난 적이 없습니다. 그리고 그들이 발행한 어음 은 항상 어김없이 즉시 결제되었습니다. 그 회사는 믿을 만합니다.

Situation 7

1. (d) 2. (c) 3. (c) 4. (b)
5. (c) 6. (d) 7. (c) 8. (a)
9. (a) 10. (a) 11. (c) 12. (d) 13. (a)

4. (a) offeror가 언제든 취소할 수 있다. (없다)
   (b) offeree가 유효기간 안에 수락을 해야 한다.
   (c) offeror가 사전통보 없이 수정하거나 취소할 수 있다. (없다)
   (d) offeror의 동의하에 수락을 해야 한다. (동의가 필요 없다)
10. 본문 – 당사는 가격을 동결하고 귀사와의 거래를 진척시킬 서류작업을 시작합니다. 거래조건과 이 견적서의 가격은 남은 며칠 동안 보장됩니다.
11. 본문 – 귀사의 요청에 따라 당사의 offer를 첨부하여 보냅니다. 가격은 원자재 부족으로 지난달 말 이후로 가격이 소폭 상승하였습니다. 즉각 승낙하여 주시면 감사하겠습니다.
    (c) 총 경비(overhead cost)의 상승으로 가격이 상승되었습니다.
12. 본문 – 원자재 가격인상으로 당사는 상품공급가격을 인상할 수밖에 없습니다. 가격인상을 피하려고 노력했지만 더 이상은 안 되겠습니다. 11월 24일 변경되는 가격표를 동봉해드립니다. 지금부터 10월 30일까지의 Order는 낮은 가격으로 적용됩니다. 당사의

가격인상을 이해하여 주시길 바랍니다.
13. 지금부터 10월 30일까지 주문하면 오르기 전 가격에 드리겠습니다.

Situation 8

1. (b) 2. (c) 3. (b) 4. (c)
5. (b) 6. (a) 7. (c) 8. (d)
9. (c) 10. (d) 11. (c) 12. (d)
13. (a) 14. (a) 15. (a) 16. (a)
17. (b)

12. 본문 - offer에 대한 승낙의 의미를 갖지만 첨가, 제한, 다른 수정을 포함하는 답장은 counter offer(반대청약)이라고 한다.
13. 본문 - 당사가 어제 받았던 귀사의 offer No. T-301 고맙습니다. 귀사의 offer에 관심이 가지만 가격이 상당히 높습니다. 대량구매에 대한 귀사의 할인은 어떻게 됩니까?
14. 본문 - 귀사의 offer는 가격과 품질 면에서 당사의 요구조건을 충족시켜줍니다. 그러나 상품 선적이 늦어도 11월 말까지 되어야 합니다. 이는 counter offer이다.
15. 지난해 수입이 약간 하락하였다.
16. 본문 - 귀사는 상품의 인기를 강조하지만 당사는 지금 여기 시장에서 탁월한 평판을 가진 매우 강력한 경쟁자가 있음을 알려드립니다. 그 상품은 가격이 15% 낮고 디자인, 스타일은 훨씬 우수합니다. 당사 소매상의 보고에 따르면 귀사제품은 가격을 USD45로 낮추어야 경쟁할 수 있다고 합니다.
17. (a)~(c) L/C가 9월 15일 전(까지) 도착하면 주문을 받아들이겠습니다. (d) L/C가 9월 15일까지 도착하면 대금을 지급하겠습니다.

Situation 9

1. (d) 2. (b) 3. (a) 4. (c)
5. (c) 6. (c) 7. (c) 8. (c)
9. (d) 10. (d) 11. (b) 12. (c)
13. (a) 14. (c)

8. "establish a pleasant business connection with ~" 거래관계를 시작하다
(c) 거래관계를 종료하다
9. (a) these, (b) them, (c) them은 strawberry pink, (d) They는 deep orange
10. 본문 - 이 서한은 당사가 제공하는 (1) 조기결제 할인율에 관한 귀사의 문의에 대한 답장입니다. 당사의 할인율은 (2) 상품인도 후 10일 이내의 결제에 대해서는 송장금액의 2%입니다. (3) 이 할인율은 자의적인 결정이 아닌, 비용 및 간접비와 이익을 기준으로 산정되었습니다. 우리 모든 고객에게 이 할인율을 제공할 경우, 우리회사는 재정적으로 위태롭게 될 것이고 반면 일부 고객들에게 개별적으로 높은 할인율을 제공할 경우, 불공정하고 비윤리적인 현상을 초래합니다. 귀사는 당사가 제공하는 (4) 10%의 할인이 업계의 평균 수준이다는 것을 아시게 될 것입니다. (- 이 내용은 "Our established discount is 2%"의 본문의 내용과 다르다.) 당사는 귀사를 가장 귀중한 고객으로 생각하며 이점을 충분히 고려해 주시길 희망합니다.
11. 본문 - 5월 8일 Expert Seminar에 초대해 주셔서 감사합니다. 하지만 고객과의 중요한 미팅 때문에 행사에 참석할 수 없습니다.
(2) had had는 주절과 종속절의 시제 일치에 의하여 have이다.
12. 본문 - 당사 메트리스에 대한 offer를 요청하는 7월 5일 귀사의 fax 감사합니다. 당사는 귀사의 승낙이 7월 20일까지 도착하는 것을 조건으로 확정 offer를 다음과 같이 합니다.
(c) 당사에게 offer하라고 요청하는 귀사의 편지 감사합니다. 그래서 offer 하고자 합니다. 이 내용은 본문의 서신에 대한 reply로서 적합하지 않다.
13. 본문 - 하지만, 귀사가 동의하신 대로 우리의 이전 서신에서 논의되었던 최근의 정치적

변화는 우리 의 원래 계획의 전망을 완전히 바꾸어 놓았습니다. 결과적으로 당초의 희망은 변함이 없지만 잠정적인 구매계획 조차 세울 수 없습니다. 당사는 이후의 정치적 진전이 원래의 계획을 실현시킬 수 있도록 기회를 제공하길 기원합니다.

(a) 당사의 구매의사를 묻는 5월 8일 귀사의 메일은 충분히 검토되었습니다. 이 문장은 본문의 앞에 올 수 있는 가장 적합한 내용이다.

14. 본문 – 10월 선적 분부터 FOB가격을 3% 인상하는 것을 미뤄달라는 귀사의 긴급한 요청을 충분히 검토했습니다. 명백히, 최대의 시장점유율을 보장하기 위해서는 현 FOB가격을 유지해야 하고 그것이 상호 이익이 될 것입니다. (C) 하지만, 현행 가격구조를 유지하게 되면 당사는 적자를 보게 됩니다. 그렇게 되는 중요한 이유 중 하나는 당사의 신제품이 충분히 업그레이드되었기 때문입니다. 질적인 경쟁 우위로 경쟁업체를 이길 수 있다는 것과 추가 비용이 당사에게 초래된 것을 이해해 주십시오. 귀사의 충분한 이해와 신속한 승인을 해 주시면 대단히 감사하겠습니다.

Situation 10

1. (c) 2. (d) 3. (d)

3. A(buyer): 기본 입장을 분명히 하겠습니다. 귀사와 계약을 하고 싶습니다.
   B(seller): (d) 귀사가 매년 25,000units의 주문을 보장한다면 계약을 하지 않을 이유가 없지요.

Situation 11

1. (a) 2. (c) 3. (d)

3. 본문 – 당사와 공식적인 거래관계를 제안하는 귀사의 mail 고맙습니다. 당사는 기꺼이 귀사를 당사의 귀중한 고객으로 모시겠습니다. 다른 고객들과 거래하고 있는 가계약서를 동봉합니다. 물론 이것은 단지 가계약서이며 상호 동의하에 변경하는 것을 조건으로 합니다. 이에 대하여 자유롭게 말씀하셔주시고 있는 조항 그대로 수락하신다면 서명하셔서 원본은 보관하시고 부본을 보내주시기 바랍니다.
   (d) 상대방은 제안된 거래조건에 동의한다면 수출상에게 서명된 계약서 사본을 보낼 것이다.

Situation 12

1. (d) 2. (d) 3. (c) 4. (a)
5. (b) 6. (d) 7. (a)

3. (c) claim: buyer는 결제 전에 클레임을 제기해야 한다. 이 내용은 올바르지 않은 내용이다. buyer는 결제하기 전에는 claim을 제기하지 않기 때문이다. (entertain a claim: claim 제기에 대하여 수리하다.)
4. 본문 – Article 11. 만약 seller가 계약서에 명시된 기간 이내에 상품을 인도하지 못할 경우에 buyer는 상품지연 1주일에 손해보상으로 상품가격의 2%에 상당하는 금액을 차감하기로 한다. 그 차감한도는 10%까지이다. 한도에 다다르면 buyer는 계약을 종료할 수도 있다.
   (a) 만일 seller가 5주 이상 선적을 지연하면 buyer는 계약종료를 선언할 수 있다.
5. (b) 위험은 Sydney port에서 seller로부터 buyer에게로 이전된다. CFR Sydney port 조건에서 비용은 Sydney까지 부담하지만 위험은 선적항인 Korean port이다.
6. Remark: 만일 귀사가 선박 "Big Bear"에 선복을 확보하지 못하면 즉시 연락해주세요
   (d) 상품은 seller에 의해서 지정된 "Big Bear"호에 선적되어야 한다.
7. 본문 – 각 나라들은 타고난 생산요소가 다르

다. 인구밀도, 노동력, 기후, 원자재, 자본 등이다. 이러한 요소들은 비교적 다른 나라로 옮기기가 어려운 경향이 있다. 그래서 상품을 공급하는 능력도 나라마다 다르다.
(a) 상품을 생산하는 상대적 비용이 나라마다 다르다.

Situation 13

1. (c)	2. (d)	3. (d)	4. (b)
5. (a)	6. (b)	7. (a)	8. (b)
9. (a)	10. (a)	11. (d)	12. (d)
13. (a)	14. (c)	15. (b)	16. (b)

11. FAS: Production cost + Delivery Cost (from factory to port) + Export Clearance Fee = 203,000 FOB: FAS + Loading Fee = 205,000
CIF: FOB + Freight + Insurance Premium = 220,000
DDP: CIF + Main Carrier Unloading + Import Clearance Fee + Delivery Cost (from port to the seller's premise) = 225,000
13. 본문 - FOB basis: buyer는 선호하는 선박회사를 지정하고 선복을 예약해야 한다. seller는 상품명, 수량, 포장, 총중량, 선적항의 화물준비날짜 등의 선적 전의 정보를 buyer에게 알려야 한다.
14. FCA(Free Carrier)가격조건은 seller가 수출통관한 상품을 buyer가 지명한 운송인에게 인도하는 조건이다. 운임은 후불로 목적지에서 지급된다.
15. 본문 - 지난 5년 동안 ABC사는 당사 거래의 25%를 차지해서 이 계약의 상실은 영업수익(operating revenues)을 감소시킬 것이다. 이는 당사가 3명의 기술자와 2명의 컨설턴트를 인원 감축(lay off)해야 함을 의미한다.
(b) ABC사가 재정상의 문제와 사업모델 변경으로 당사와 재계약하지 않기로 했음을 발표하게 되어 유감입니다. - 이 문장의 내용이 본문의 앞에 올 내용이다.
16. 본문 - 지난번 메일에서 귀사는 "가택경비장치"에 대하여 언급했었습니다. (a) 하지만 좀 더 자세한 내용을 보내주세요. (b) Ms. Jane Smith는 홍보부에 근무하고 있지만, 그 경우를 대부분 잘 알고 있습니다.
당사는 귀사가 가장 관심을 가지는 가택경비장치의 모델에 대하여 알고 싶습니다. (c) 예를 들면 아파트의 경보시스템은 주택의 시스템과 다르며 당사는 간단히 door에 맞게 디자인된 home systems와 전체 가옥에 맞게 디자인된 home systems를 가지고 있습니다. (d) 당사 제품의 e-catalogue를 첨부파일로 보내며: 아마 귀사는 귀사의 필요에 꼭 맞는 품목을 선택하실 것입니다. - 여기에서 가장 어울리지 않는 문장은 (b)이다.

Situation 14

1. (c)	2. (b)	3. (a)	4. (c)
5. (b)	6. (a)	7. (a)	8. (d)
9. (a)	10. (d)		

5. (b)의 "wish that~"은 실현 불가능한 희망을 나타낼 때 사용하므로 이런 문장은 어색하다.
7. 본문 - 당사는 $100,000의 전자계산기 1,000개의 귀사의 주문을 받았음을 확인합니다. 요청하신대로 9월 말까지 선적을 준비할 것이며, 가능한 빨리 당사를 수익자로 하며 10월 20일까지 유효한 취소불능 신용장을 개설하기를 요청합니다. 귀사의 신용장을 받자마자 즉시 귀사의 주문을 선적하겠습니다.
(a) 주문의 확인
8. (B) Executive summary(사업계획 요약) 사업계획은 무엇이며 무엇이 포함될 것인지 1 page로 요약하시오. (D) Market opportunity(시장 잠재력) 회사나 사업계획이 무엇인지, 목표시장, 현지 상품과 서비스를 간단히 묘사하시오. (A) Financial

analysis(재무 분석) 사업성과와 현재의 재무 상태, 판매 예측 등을 자세히 하기(C) Implementation plan(실행계획)

9. 본문 – Justin's가 새롭게 오픈한 기념으로 Grand Opening Sale을 합니다. – 위의 Retail sales letters는 기업이 sale을 알리거나 단골고객을 확보하기 위하여 사용됩니다. retail sales letters는 TV, 라디오, 신문과 같은 다른 매체와는 달리 구매가 기대되는 the specific(특정 고객)들을 선택하여 목표로 할 수 있는 장점이 있습니다. 이렇게 함으로써 기업은 그 상품에 관하여 가장 확실한 욕구를 가진 고객에게 다가 가게 됩니다.
10. 본문 – 우리가 10월에 계획하고 있는 Intranet seminar에 대한 귀사의 승인을 얻고자 합니다. (a) 이것은 Intra2013의 Korean version을 소개하는 Kickoff seminar가 될 것입니다. (b) 우리의 목표 참석자 수는 200명입니다. (c) 예상 비용은 3백만 원입니다. (d) 소매점의 공간을 확보하기 위하여 새로운 마감기일 을 제안하겠습니다. – 이 문장의 내용은 위의 내용과 전혀 다르다.

Situation 15

1. (a)	2. (a)	3. (c)	4. (d)
5. (d)	6. (c)	7. (a)	8. (a)
9. (d)	10. (b)	11. (d)	12. (b)
13. (b)			

5. (A) 신용장에 명시한 모든 서류가 제시되었을 때
(B) 신용장에서 명시한 물품이 신용장 신청인에게 배달되었을 때
(C) 신용장의 모든 조건들이 지켜졌을 때
(D) 관련 서류가 정히 제시되고 신용장 신청인이 대금을 결제했을 때
(B)와 (D)는 신용장에 의거한 대금지급의 전제조건이 되지 않는다. Situation 16의 '신용장의 독립성과 추상성' 부분 설명 참조
7. 본문 – 거래상의 위험은 buyer가 상품을 받지 못하는 것과 같은 요인들로 발생한다. 이러한 commercial risk를 예방하기 위해서 은행은 seller를 수익자로 하는 신용장을 발행하게 된다.
8. We are very sorry for not sending you an email upon issuing the L/C. 전치사 for 다음에는 명사 상당 어구인 동명사가 와야 하며 또한 동명사를 부정하려면 not이 동명사 앞에 온다.
9. 본문 – 당사는 home theater systems 위탁판매품에 대하여 Eletron Co.를 수익자로한 신용장이 서울 신한은행에 개설되기 위하여 9월 30일까지 유효한 $12,000의 취소불능신용장 신청서를 작성하여 동봉합니다. 선적을 마친 후에는 신한은행 앞으로 30일 기한부 어음이 발행될 것입니다. 그 어음에는 선하증권, 송장, 보험증권이 첨부됩니다.
(d) 수출상은 서울에 있는 은행에게 취소불능 신용장을 개설하라는 지시 편지를 썼다.
10. (B) (buyer) 당사에게 귀사의 auto mobile tire에 대한 가장 최근의 catalogue와 가장 낮은 가격을 견적해주세요.
(A) (seller) 당사가 귀사의 firm order(확정주문)를 11월 15일에 받는 것을 조건으로 모든 모델은 1월 중순까지 공급될 수 있습니다. 만일 항공편으로 상품을 원하시면 extra charge(추가비용)가 부과됩니다.
(D) (seller) 우리의 계약에 따라서, 귀사의 주문은 선적준비가 되어 있습니다. 귀사가 주문품에 대한 L/C를 개설하시길 요청합니다.
(C) (seller) 당사는 어제 선적을 확인했습니다. 송장과 비유통성 B/L을 동봉합니다.
11. 본문 – We have a pleasure to enclose our order. We have instructed First Bank of America of New York, to issue a Confirmed and Irrevocable Letter of Credit in our favor. (당사는 기꺼이 주문서를 동봉합니다. 당사는 뉴욕의 First Bank of America 에게 당사를 수익자로 하는 확인, 취소불능 신용장을 개설하라고 지시했습니다. – (d) in our favor는 in your

favor로 되어야 한다.)
12. (b) will cable → will be cabled
13. 본문 - 귀사의 주문 No.XYZ-090721에 관하여 당사는 귀사로부터 신용장이 개설되었다는 통지를 받지 않았다고 알리게 되어 유감입니다.
regret to inform - 알리게 되어 유감이다.

Situation 16

1. (b)	2. (b)	3. (b)	4. (a)
5. (d)	6. (c)	7. (c)	8. (a)
9. (b)	10. (a)	11. (b)	12. (b)
13. (a)	14. (c)	15. (d)	16. (b)

2. latest shipment date: November 20, 2015
3. 신용장의 첫 부분에 "Without adding your confirmation, ~"을 보면 'your'는 (이 신용장을 개설은행으로부터 받아서 수출상에게 통지해 줄) '통지은행의'이고, 통지은행이 confirmation할 필요는 없다는 것을 명시하고 있다.
9. (Partial) shipments are permitted. (부분선적은 허용된다.) (Transshipment) is not permitted. (환적은 금지된다.)
All drafts, drawn hereunder must state the number, date, and name of establishing bank of this(credit)(이 신용장에 의거하여 발행된 모든 환어음은 발행 number, 날짜, 발행은행명을 명시해야 한다.)
10. 본문 - 화환 신용장은 사전결제, 청산계정, 화환추심과 비교해서 더 선호되는 대금결제방식이다. due to (a) comport provided by the independent undertaking of banks(은행의 독립된 지급확약이 제공되기 때문이다)
11. (a), (c), (d)는 수입업자가 신용장의 개설 혹은 통지를 수출업자에게 하는 내용인 반면, (b)는 수출업자 가 수입업자에게 신용장개설을 요청하는 내용이다.
12. (a) Water Valve의 선적에 관한 귀사의 fax 감사합니다.
(b) 한국에 있는 은행들은 인도네시아 은행에서 개설된 L/C를 인도네시아의 재정사정 때문에 매입하기 어렵다는 것을 알려 드립니다.
(c) 당사는 그들을 설득하려고 많은 노력을 다하였습니다. 그러나 어쩔 수 없었습니다.
(d) 당사는 귀사에게 개설은행을 국제적인 일류은행으로 바꾸거나 결제조건을 T/T 송금방식으로 바꾸기를 요청합니다.
13. (a) negotiation L/C: seller가 신용장에 의거하여 발행한 환어음을 매입(negotiation)하여 대금을 결제 받을 수 있는 신용장
14. 본문 - 당사는 귀사의 order No. ACE-2301을 선적했음을 알립니다. 선적 후 선적서류는 매입이 제한된 서울지점인 Woori Bank로 제출되겠습니다. 귀사의 대금결제에 감사드립니다.
(c) 대금결제에 대한 관심을 끌기 위해서
15. seller는 신용장의 수익자(beneficiary)가 되며 환어음의 발행인(drawer)이 된다.
16. (b) Restricted L/C: 어음매입을 특정은행에 한정시킨 매입제한 신용장이다.

Situation 17

1. (d)	2. (c)	3. (b)	4. (c)
5. (d)	6. (c)	7. (a)	8. (d)
9. (c)	10. (d)	11. (c)	12. (b)
13. (a)	14. (b)		

5. (B) 3월 15일 귀사의 email에 관하여 당사는 다음과 같이 알려드립니다.
(A) 당사는 mobile phone, 10,000set를 선적했으며 4월 15일 2시 인천국제공항을 출발 예정입니다. (D) 요청하신대로 항공화물수령증, 상업송장, 포장명세서가 선적하자마자 귀

사에게 보내집니다.

(C) 상품이 제시간에 도착되기를 바라며 도착 10일 이내에 귀사에게 도착했다는 것을 알려주시기 바랍니다.

6. 본문 – 신용장조건은 귀사(seller)가 London 은행을 지급인으로 하여 송장금액으로 일람 후 30일 출급 환어음을 발행하는 것입니다. 환어음을 인수하기 전에 은행은 귀사에게 선하증권, 보험증권, 원산지증 명서의 제출을 요구할 것입니다.

   (c) 화환신용장 통지

7. 본문 – PENTAX의 서류제출 지연은 당사의 엔지니어링 일정에 영향을 끼쳐 건설에 악영향을 줄 수 있습니다. 이러한 서류들이 제출될 수 있을 때 return fax로 알려주십시오.

   (a) PENTAX가 기한이 지난 서류를 보내도록 지시하기 위하여

8. 본문 – 당사는 귀사의 주문서 No.155가 선박 EverMore Asia에 3월 5일 선적되어 20일 후에 Jakarta에 도착예정임을 알립니다.

   (d) 선박은 3월 25일 Jakarta에 도착할 수 있습니다.

9. 본문 – 이 선적에 대하여 당사는 BMB Bank, London을 지급인으로 하여 금액 USD90,000인 일람출급 환어음을 신용장에 의거하여 ANA Bank, Seoul을 통하여 발행했습니다.

10. 본문 – 당사는 귀사의 주문품이 부산에서 홍콩으로 항해 예정인(due to sail) Venus 호에 선적되었음을 통지해드립니다.

12. (d) 귀사의 최근 주문을 받게 되어 기쁘며 그 주문은 30일 조건에 따라 즉각 선적될 것입니다. (c) 귀사의 향후 주문에 필요한 신용한도를 높이기 위해 신용정보를 보내주시겠습니까?

   (a) 귀사의 편의를 위해서 간략하게 정리된 재무제표를 동봉합니다.

   (b) 주문해주셔서 다시 한번 감사드립니다. 그리고 오랫동안 상호 만족스러운 거래관계가 되기를 바랍니다.

14. 본문 – 다음 프로젝트 그룹 회의는 5월 11일 사무실에서 개최됩니다. 계획된 제안서는 다음과 같습니다. (b) 귀사가 이 회의에 참석할 수 있는지를 최대한 빨리 확인해 주시면 감사하겠습니다.

Situation 18

1. (d)	2. (a)	3. (a)	4. (c)
5. (d)	6. (b)	7. (d)	8. (b)
9. (d)	10. (a)	11. (c)	12. (c)
13. (b)			

5. (d) 지시대로 배서되지 않았음.

10. "~ B/L made out to our order ~"에서 our는 Bank of America를 나타내므로(a) to order of Bank of America라고 B/L 상에 표시되어야 한다.

11. 보험평가서의 내용이다. 상품이 포장에 대한 사고사항이 기재된 선하증권에 따라 선적되었으므로 claim이 받아들어질 수 없다는 것이다. 그래서 '사고조항이 기재된'의 뜻인 claused이다.

12. 본문에서 – but also avoid giving a limp handshake because this may convey an impression of weakness. (연약한 악수는 무기력한 인상을 줄 수 있기 때문에 피해야 한다.)

13. (c) 미국에서 비즈니스를 할 때에는 악수(handshake)를 어떻게, 언제(how and when) 하느냐를 안다는 것은 중요한 기술(important skill)이다.

   (b) American의 handshake는 bowing과 같으며 처음 소개받을 때 뿐 아니라 이후의 만남에서도 이루어진다. Business people들은 business meeting 전후로 악수를 한다.

   (d) 미국에서는 처음 인사할 때 허리를 굽혀 인사하지 않지만 한국 사람들에게는 깨기 어려운 습관이기도 하다.

   (e) 일부 국가에서는 처음 소개할 때 남성이 여성의 손에 키스하는 것이 관습이라고 하

지만 미국에서는 상식이거나 적절한 것은 아니다.

Situation 19

1. (d) 2. (d) 3. (c) 4. (d)

3. (1) 이것은 송하인이 무고장 선하증권을 발급받기 위해서 선박회사에게 제출하는 선류이다. – Letter of indemnity(파손화물보상장)
(2) 이것은 상품의 명세서로 수량, 단가, 총금액, 수입상의 이름과 주소, 날짜 등을 보여주는 수출상에 의해서 발행되는 항목별로 구분된 리스트이다. – commercial invoice(상업송장)
(3) 이것은 수출국에 주재하고 있는 수입국의 영사가 수출상품에 대한 가격, 송하인, 수화인과 같은 정보를 증명해 주는 서류이다. – consular invoice(영사송장)
(4) 이것은 수출상이 수입상에게 주문을 유발하기 위해서 또는 수입상의 요청에 의해서 수입국의 정부가 수출허가를 내주거나 외환배정을 허용하기 위해서 매입한 물품에 대해서 작성한 서류이다. – pro-forma invoice(견적송장)
4. 본문에서 Chris의 연구조사를 위한 예산은 승인되었다.
d) Chris의 new research는 재정지원을 요구하지 않는다. 이는 본문과 다르다.

Situation 20

1. (c) 2. (c) 3. (b) 4. (b)
5. (a) 6. (c) 7. (c) 8. (b)
9. (b) 10. (a) 11. (b) 12. (b)
13. (a)

3. (b)에서 이 거래는 신용장에 의한 거래이므로 drawee는 수입상인 VP INTERCANADA, LTD가 아니고 신용장 개설은행인 Bank of Canada가 된다.
9. (b) The drawee of this BoE is Top Export. 신용장 결제에 의한 환어음의 지급인은 개설은행이 되므로 Top Export가 아니라 Bank of Seoul이어야 한다.
10. Payment: 환어음은 계약이 성립된 즉시 seller를 수익자로 하여 개설된 취소불능신용장에 의거하여 30일 기한부 어음으로 발행되기로 한다. 송장금액으로 발행되며 선하증권, 보험증권, 상업송장 등 기타 서류가 첨부된다.
The seller should draw a sight draft for payment. Sight를 usance로 바꿔야한다.
11. 본문 – Value received and(b) charge the same to account of Chicago Trading Co., Inc. (상기 금액은 수취되었으며 그 금액을 buyer인 Chicago Trading에게 청구하시기 바랍니다.)
– credit fifty thousand dollars to the account of Chicago Trading. 이 문장에서 credit을 debit(차변 기재하다)으로 바꿔야 한다.
12. (a) 신용장이 일람출급이 가능한 경우 일람으로 지급하는 것을 의미한다.
(b) 상환이 지정은행에 행해져야 할 은행영업일에 또는 그 이전에 수익자에게 대금을 선지급하거나 또는 선지급하기로 약정하는 것을 의미한다. – 이는 negotiation(매입)을 의미한다.
(c) 신용장이 어음인수가 가능한 경우 수익자가 발행한 환어음을 인수하고 만기일에 지급하는 것을 의미한다.
(d) 신용장이 연지급이 가능한 경우 연지급 확약을 지고 만기일에 지급하는 것을 의미한다.
13. Your draft was not honored, please negotiate for the matter with the(drawer) and let him/her(protest) it at once. 귀사의 어음이 지급되지 않는다면 수출상인 발행인으로 하여금 법적대응을 하게 한다.

Situation 21

1. (d) 2. (a) 3. (c) 4. (b)
5. (a) 6. (b) 7. (a) 8. (b)
9. (a) 10. (d) 11. (a)

4. "자동차 회사들은 우리가 연비와 안전의 관계를 충분히 이해하지 못하고 있다고 주장하고 있다." 사실에 대한 주장에 관한 내용이므로 insist 다음에 should를 쓰지 않았다.
5. 본문 – 이것은 $ 100,000의 드릴 머신 5세트에 대한 귀사의 결제가 현재 지불기한이 지났다는(overdue) 독촉장입니다. 실수로(by mistake) 간과(overlooked)했을 수도 있습니다.
   확인하시고 이달 말까지 결제대금을 송금(remit)하여 주시기 바랍니다.
6. 본문 – 12월 12일 서신에서 당사가 주문했던 상품이 도착되지 않았다고 설명했습니다.
   귀사의 편의를 위하여 서신의 사본을 첨부하겠습니다. 상품도 받지 못하고 이전 서신에 대한 답장도 받지 못하여 주문과 함께 송금했던 USD 3,000를 환불해주시길 요청합니다. 취소된 수표 사본을 첨부해 드립니다.
   (b) 인도되지 않는 상품에 대한 환불요구
8. 당사의 주문품 13245가 오늘까지 도착하지 않았습니다. 지난 주에 도착 예정이었습니다. 고객에게 11월 말까지 공급할 상품이 필요합니다. 만일 이번 주 내에 도착하지 않으면 당사는 고객을 잃을 상황입니다.
   (b) 선적상황과 인도 날짜를 알려 주세요.
9. (b) 우리의 기록에 의하면 귀사는 2013년 1월부터 미지불 잔고가 있습니다.
   (c) 귀사의 1월 송장금액은 $4405이었으며 우리는 이 금액을 아직까지 받지 못했습니다. 송장 사본을 동봉해드립니다.
   (a) 만일 이 금액이 지급되었으면 이 통지를 무시하십시오.
   (d) 그렇지 않으면 미지급금 전액을 3월 1일까지 보내주시기 바랍니다. 계약에 명시된 대로 30일 이상 지나면 모든 미지급금에 대하여 5%의 이자를 청구하겠습니다.
10. "– 하지만 매우 유감스럽게도, 우리의 미지급계정 전액에 대한 지급요청을 계속했음에도 아직까지 답도 없을 뿐 아니라 심지어 확인조차 없었습니다. – 만일 8월 20일까지 대금을 받지 못하게 된다면 우리는 좀 더 심각한 조치를 취할 수밖에 없습니다."
    (a) 우리는 귀사의 미지급이 귀사의 정책이 아닌 직원의 착오이길 바랍니다.
    (b) 우리의 법률팀은 이번 사건을 통지 받았으며 귀사를 상대로 조치를 취할 준비가 되어있습니다. (c) 오직 귀사의 신속한 조치만이 이 상황을 개선할 수 있는 유일한 방법임을 이해해주시기 바랍니다. (d) 우리 모두의 시간과 비용의 손실을 막기 위해서 더 이상의 논의와 협상을 중단해야 함을 유감스럽게 생각합니다. – 이 내용은 8월 20일 까지 결제함으로써 상황을 개선할 여지가 있다는 본문의 내용과 는 다르다.
11. 본문 – 귀사에게 당사의 송장 KEAA-1212 대금이 오늘까지 결제되지 않았음을 다시 알립니다. 귀사의 경리부에 상기 송금을 했는지 확인해 주시기 바랍니다. 그리고 언제 송금해주실지 통지바랍니다. (a) 만일 이 서신과 귀사의 송금이 거의 같은 시기에 이루어졌을 경우 이 서신을 무시해주시고 귀사가 신속한 확인을 해주시면 매우 감사하겠습니다.

Situation 22

1. (d) 2. (d) 3. (b) 4. (d)
5. (d) 6. (d) 7. (c) 8. (d)
9. (c)

5. 본문 – 당사는 지금 당장 귀사의 송장금액을 결제할 수 없어 매우 유감입니다. 보낸 상품은 아주 좋은 상태로 도착했는데 화물 도착 이틀 후 호우로 인하여 재고품이 손상을 입었습니다. 보험회사가 손해를 보상해 주는 대로

지불할 수 있도록 하겠습니다.
(d) 대금 결제 기일 연장요구

6. 본문 – 10월 19일자 서신 받았음을 확인합니다. 그리고 당사가 (a) 통제 불가능한 원인으로 인도기일을 지키지 못해 매우 죄송합니다. (b) 석탄과 원자재를 공급해 주는 최근의 철도 파업으로 5주 내지 7주 지연되었습니다. (c) 당사는 최대한 인도 날짜를 앞당기기 위해서 노력했지만 실패했습니다. 이런 상황에서 당사는 귀사의 주문 취소를 받아들일 수밖에 없습니다. 하지만 (d) 지연은 당사의 업무 소홀이 아니라는 점을 알아주시기 바랍니다.
7. 본문 – 동봉된 사본을 보시면 아시겠지만 사무실 이사와 회사에 익숙해지는데 시간이 필요한 새로운 직원 채용문제로 대금지급이 지연될 수도 있음을 알려드렸습니다. 당사는 지금 새로운 사무실에 입주 중이며 다음 달까지는 직원들도 훈련이 마무리됩니다. 결제로 20,000파운드 수표를 동봉하며 6월 결제는 며칠 내로 전액 보내겠습니다. – (c) 결제에 관한 귀사의 문의 감사합니다. 주문서에 언급한 것처럼 당사의 결제방식은 90일 어음인수서류인도조건(D/A)이어서 귀사의 어음은 2012년 11월 30일 지급될 것입니다.
– 본문은 이사문제로 결제가 늦어질 수 있다는 내용인데(c)의 내용은 결제방식 때문에 지급이 늦어진다는 것으로 내용이 맞지 않다.
8. (d) Morris씨는 사무실 사람들과 친해지기 위하여 informal party를 준비했다.
9. (c) 그는 manager는 분명한 권위의식을 보여줘야 한다고 믿었다. 이 내용은 본문에서의 Morris씨의 생각과 다르다.

Story II

Situation 1

1. (c)	2. (c)	3. (c)	4. (b)
5. (b)	6. (d)	7. (d)	8. (a)
9. (a)	10. (c)	11. (a)	12. (b)
13. (d)	14. (d)	15. (c)	16. (b)
17. (a)			

9. A: 귀사의 결제조건을 말해주시겠습니까?
B: 당사는 일람 후 30일 전액 지급조건입니다만, 현금 결제 시 8% 디스카운트해드립니다.
A: 전자의 결제조건을 선호합니다. 언제 지급해야 합니까?
B: 선적서류는 은행을 통해서 귀사에게 발송될 것입니다. 귀사는 서류를 받은 후 30일 이내에 송장금액을 당사에게 송금하셔야 합니다.
12. 당사는 일람 후 120일 지불 조건으로 발행된 USD35,800 환어음을 인수했으니 관련 선적서류를 정확히 받으실 것입니다. 환어음은 만기일에 당사에 의해서 지급될 것입니다.
– 이 내용은 지급조건이 D/A이다.
14. 본문 – 대금결제조건에 관하여 금융위기 후 당사의 보수적인 판매정책으로 귀사의 180일 어음인수서류인도조건 제안을 받아들일 수 없어 유감입니다. 귀사에게 180일 기한부 신용장 조건을 요청하고자 합니다.
(d) 이 서한은 짧은 신용기한 때문에 요구사항을 거절하는 것이다. – 이 내용은 분문의 사실과 다르다.
15. 본문 – 귀사의 최근 60일 신용조건에 대한 신청에 감사합니다만, 당사는 현재 귀사에게 신용을 허용할 만한 입장이 아닙니다.
(c) 요청된 지불조건을 거절하기 위한 것이다.
16. (A), (C), (D)는 그들이 원하는 목표가격을 받아들일 수 있다면 거래를 성사시킬 수 있다는 확신이 있어 가격에 대한 논의를 하고자 한다는 내용이다. (B) 8%의 수수료는 우

리의 비용을 커버하지 못하므로 적어도 10% 수수료를 원한다. 이 내용은 앞 내용과 논리적으로 맞지 않다.

17. call report: 판매사원이 제출하는 '판매 리포트'

Situation 2

1. (c) 2. (d) 3. (c) 4. (c)
5. (c) 6. (b) 7. (b) 8. (a)
9. (c) 10. (d) 11. (a) 12. (c)

1. (c) He is willing to reconsider the payment terms later.
7. (b) 귀사가 당사의 제안에 관심이 있으시다면, 당사는 귀사에게 송장금액 10%의 특별할인을 해드리겠습니다.
   (c) 귀사가 당사의 제안에 관심이 있으시다면, 귀사가 당사에게 송장금액 10%의 특별할인을 해주면 고맙겠습니다. – 할인해 주는 주체가 다르다.
8. 본문 – 당사에게는 귀사가 특별히 pharmacies를 위해 개발한 application으로부터 대단한 benefit를 본 고객이 있습니다. 귀사의 시스템은 당사고객의 문제를 해결해 주는 답이 될 것입니다. – networking을 사용할 사람은 BCD의 고객이다.
9. (c) networking operation을 참관하기 위해서 약속잡기를 요청한다.
10. 본문 – 저(Patric Johnson)는 Mr. Torrence씨가 결정을 위한 기초를 쌓는데 아주 중요한 역할을 했다고 확신합니다. 프로젝트를 위한 The Executive Committee가 5월 30일 Seoul에서 개최됩니다. 그때 Committee에서 당신의 firm commitment(확실한 참여)를 발표할 수 있기를 바랍니다.
    (d) new joint project에서 Mr. Torrence의 적극적인 개입을 요청하는 것이 목적이다.
11. 본문 – American manufacture(의류제조업체)는 the Saudi Arabian distributor(유통업체)와 계획했던 것보다 오래 걸렸지만 가격과 판매방식에 대한 합의에 만족했다.
    (a) 아메리칸 의류제조업체와 사우디아라비안 유통업체는 오랜 협상을 마무리했다.
12. 본문 – 귀사가 당사의 명세서에 따라서 정확히 제품공급을 보장할 수 있다면 당사는 즉시 시험주문을 할 준비가 되어있습니다. appointed는 '임명되다'의 의미여서 대체될 수 없다.

Situation 3

1. (a) 2. (c) 3. (d) 4. (c)
5. (a) 6. (c) 7. (a) 8. (c)

3. (d) Mr. Park wants(Mr. Gupta) to acknowledge the order. 오더에 대하여 확인해 주는 사람은 Mr. Gupta이다.
6. (c) 대금의 지급시기와 상관없이 대량주문을 유도하기 위하여 해주는 할인
8. 귀사의(수출상) 카탈로그와 가격표를 보내주셔서 감사합니다.
   (d) 당사의(Mackenzie Bros.의 agent) 본사인 Canada 온타리오의 Mackenzie Bros.(수입상)로부터 온 주문서(R1423)를 첨부했습니다. (principal: agent에 대한 본인)
   (c) Mackenzie는 당사에게 60세트의 그릇을 상자 한 개당 10세트씩 담아 6상자로 포장할 것을 귀사(수출 상)에게 지시하도록 요청했습니다.
   (a) Mackenzie는 지난주 전화로 협의한대로 신용장 결제에 합의했으며 이달 말이 되기 전에 인도해야 합니다.
   (b) 만일 Mackenzie가 선택한 색상이 재고가 없다면 디자인이 주문서에 명시된 것과 같다는 것을 조건으로 대안을 수락할 것입니다.
   (e) 선적과 대금결제에 관한 통신문은 Mackenzie Bros.로 직접 보내주십시오.

Situation 4

1. (c) 2. (c) 3. (d) 4. (b)
5. (d) 6. (c) 7. (c) 8. (c)

7. (C) 귀사의 7월 20일 서신 받았습니다. 당사의 기대에 맞는 샘플을 보내주셔서 고맙습니다.
   (A) 귀사의 샘플에 호의적인 인상을 받았지만 가격이 저렴하지 않아서 이번에는 주문할 수가 없습니다. (B) 지난번 서신에서 지적했듯이 이 종목에 대하여 당상의 요구사항이 많지만 경쟁도 아주 치열합니다. (E) 이런 상황에서 당사는 수요가 많은 Sample No. 10에 가장 경쟁적인(저렴한) 가격을 요청할 수밖에 없습니다.
   (D) 당사는 귀사가 가격을 수정하기 위해서 노력해줄 것으로 믿습니다.
8. (b) 귀사의 4월 22일 서신 감사합니다.
   (a) 당사는 귀사의 offer에 있는 다른 type에 관심이 있어 이달 말까지 도착할 수 있도록 기간 이내에 급송을 보장한다면 다음과 같이 trial order(시험주문)하기로 결정했습니다.
   (c) 주문 내용
   (d) 당사는 제품이 5월 31일까지 당사에 도착되도록 제때에 급송되어야 하며 이날 이후에는 인도를 거절하고 취소할 권리가 있다는 것을 확실하게 이해하는 것으로 이번 주문을 합니다.
   (e) 당사를 지급인으로 하고 일람 30일 지급 환어음 결제를 제안합니다. 귀사가 동의할 수 있는지 알려 주십시오.

Situation 5

1. (d) 2. (d) 3. (a) 4. (a)
5. (b) 6. (c) 7. (d) 8. (b)
9. (c) 10. (d) 11. (d)

8. 본문 – 4월 21일자 귀사의 문의 감사합니다. 5월 초 홍콩에서 부산가는 항해에 관한 자세한 내용을 동 봉합니다. 귀사는 당사의 첫 출항 선박이 5월 3일 출항예정인 the Sun Star임을 아시게 될 것입니다. – (b) 4월의 선적지시서를 보내주십시오. – 본문에서는 이미 5월 항해에 관한 내용을 동봉했으니 이 서신 이전의 내용으로는 적합지 않다.
9. (a), (b), (d)는 seller가 cotton goods를 선적하고 lowest rate(가정 저렴한 요율)로 해상보험에 들겠다는 내용이다.
   (c) 당사의 경쟁업체가 산정한 요율을 비교해 보시면 귀사는 당사(보험회사)가 offer한 요율이 낮다는 것을 아시게 될 것입니다. – 이 내용은 보험회사가 하는 말이다.
10. 본문 – 항공운송서류는 명칭에 관계없이 다음과 같아야 한다.
   (A) 운송인의 명칭을 표시하고 다음의 자에 의해서 서명이 되어 있어야 한다. 운송인, 또는 운송인을 대리하는 지정된 대리인 운송인 또는 대리인에 의한 모든 서명은 운송인 또는 대리인의 것이라는 것이 확인되어져야 한다. (must be identified)
   (d) 대리인에 의한 어떤 서명도 그 대리인이 운송인을 대리하여 서명하였음을 표시하여야 한다.
11. 본문 – 우리는 두 출판사의 union(합병)이 자랑스럽습니다.
   – Rothmore-Medico가 Payne-Wyatt group에 온 것을 환영합니다.–
(d) 합병을 발표하기 위한 것이다.

Situation 6

1. (d) 2. (a) 3. (a) 4. (d)
5. (a) 6. (d) 7. (d) 8. (d)
9. (d). 10. (a)

5. 본문 – 만약에 lay days(정박일)이 초과된다면, the charter(용선 계약자)는 demurrage (초과정박료)를 지급해야 한다.; 작업이 허용된 기간 이내에 끝난다면 계약자는 dispatch

money(채선료)를 받게 된다. – 이 문장에서 조건을 나타내는 if 절에 if가 생략되면서 조동사 should가 앞으로 오게된다.

6. (B) MV Pacific Ruby는 5월 4일부터 8일까지 1번 선착장에서 선적할 것입니다.
   (D) 그 다음 Golden rose는 5월 19일부터 23일까지 선착장 8번에서 선적할 것입니다.
   (C) 당사는 귀사의 200box를 이들 선박에 예약하게 되어 기쁘며 선적서류를 동봉하겠습니다.
   (A) 완성하시어 가능한 빨리 반환하여 주시기 바랍니다.
7. (a), (b), (c)는 기일 내 선적될 수 있기를 바라는 내용이다.
   (d) 당사는 귀사가 당장 상품을 인도해 주시기를 원합니다. – 위의 문장내용과 다르다.
8. 본문 – 당사(수출상)는 다음 달 초 London으로 소형 배와 그 설비를 선적하려고 합니다. – 다음 달 말 전에 런던으로 갈 수 있는 선박과 운임요율을 알려주십시오.
   (a) 당사(선박회사)의 첫 선박은 MV Orient이며 2월 2일부터 7일까지 화물을 받습니다.
   (b) 당사(선박회사)의 운임요율은 톤당 USD 191.00이며 선적지시서를 첨부합니다.
   (c) 당사(선박회사)의 관세표를 보시면 운임은 cubic meter(입방미터)로 산정되었으며, 정규 선적에는 상당한 리베이트를 제공한다는 것을 아시게 됩니다.
   (d) 당사(수출상)가 보낸 선적서류를 보시면 아시겠지만, 비유통 선하증권 사본 2통과 선적송장 사본 2통이 동봉됩니다. (seller가 선적 후 buyer에게 보내는 선적서류에 대한 내용으로 본문 seller의 letter에 대한 선박회사의 reply로서는 적합지 않다.)
9. 본문 – (A) 귀하의 업무는 2012년 4월 10일 9시에 시작됩니다. 8시 30분까지 오셔서 직원들에게 귀하를 소개할 수 있었으면 좋겠습니다.
   (B) 귀하의 고용조건은 employees' handbook에 자세한 설명이 있습니다만, 면접할 때 논의된 바와 같이 근무시간은 필요사항에 따릅니다. 초과수당은 없습니다.
   (C) 초봉은 USD16,000이며 처음 3년 동안은 연 9% 증액됩니다. 이후는 협상을 조건으로 합니다.
   (D) 열거된 부가 급부뿐만 아니라 총 급여의 8%에 해당하는 Non-Contributory Pension Scheme(비기여방식의 연금설계)와 의료보험, 직원할인혜택이 있습니다.
   Non-Contributory Pension Scheme: 가입자의 직접 기여 대신 전액 일반재정으로 재원을 조달하여 운영하는 연금제도.
   (d) 근로자는 의료보험료를 지급할 필요가 없다. – 본문의 내용과 일치한다.
10. 본문 – 신용등급 조사원을 채용하는 면접에 합격했다는 사실을 알립니다. (A) 이 내용은 본문 앞에 와야 한다.

Situation 7

1. (d) 2. (b) 3. (c) 4. (c)
5. (b) 6. (a) 7. (a) 8. (c)

2. (b) 선박이 실종되고 상당한 기간이 지났음에도 아무런 소식이 없을 때는 현실 전손(actual total loss)에 해당한다.

Situation 8

1. (c) 2. (a) 3. (c) 4. (b)
5. (b) 6. (c) 7. (d)

7. 본문 – 올해 보험료가 인상된 이유를 알기 위해 (a) on your insurance policy(보험 증권)을 검토했습니다. (b) a reasonable explanation(충분한 이유)가 있었습니다. 귀하는 올해에 지난해와 정확히 같은 보험요율로 지급하시는 겁니다. 보험료가 오른 이유는 귀하가 보상범위를 올렸기 때문입니다. 지난해 새 트럭을 구입했을 때 보험 증권에 (c) penalty coverage(과태료 보상범위)를 올렸

고 제3운전자를 추가했습니다. 간단하게 말하면 올해의 보험료는 귀하의 새 트럭이(d) 구트럭보다 상당한 가치가 있다는 것을 반영한 것입니다. – 이 문장이 적합하지 않다.
안심하시고 다른 질문이 있으면 사무실에 들려주세요.

Situation 9

1. (d) 2. (c) 3. (b) 4. (d)
5. (a) 6. (c) 7. (a) 8. (d)
9. (a) 10. (a)

6. 선적되는 날에 선적통지를 구매자의 구매부서로 보내주시기 바랍니다. 구매자가 허락하지 않는 한 예정보다 일찍 배달하지는 마시오.
10. 귀사의 주문 No.5는 3월 20일 경에 완료될 것이며 3월 30일 부산을 출항할 예정인 “Easters Quees”에 선적됩니다. 기간 이내에 선적될 수 있도록 신용장을 개설해 주십시오.

Situation 10

1. (b) 2. (c) 3. (b) 4. (c)
5. (c) 6. (a) 7. (b) 8. (d)
9. (d) 10. (a) 11. (c) 12. (a)

8. (a) She said to (b) He told me about (c) She said that
9. (d) We talked about
10. leave는 전치사 from이 필요 없는 타동사이다.
11. consign: 위탁하다. (위탁 판매하기 위하여) 발송하다.

Situation 11

1. (c) 2. (b) 3. (d) 4. (d)
5. (a) 6. (d) 7. (d) 8. (d)
9. (b)

6. 본문 – 12월 5일에 귀사에게 선적된 Photophone 720에 내장된 칩이 불량임이 판명되어 회수될 것을 말씀드리게 되어 매우 죄송합니다. 귀사 지역에 있는 유통센터에 보내주십시오. (d) 당사가 끼친 불편에 죄송하며 귀사에게 품질 좋은 전자제품을 공급할 것을 약속합니다.
7. 본문 – 귀사 제품의 수요는 지난 분기에 비하여 두 배 이상 올랐습니다. 그래서 비누 300백만 개를 추가 주문하고자 합니다. 당사는 증가하고 있는 수요를 감당하기 위해 1개월 안에 제품이 필요합니다. 한 달 안에 이 주문을 완성하는 것이 가능한가요?
   (d) 귀사 제품에 대한 수요가 증가해서 비누 300백만 개를 긴급 주문하고자 합니다. 이전에 비슷한 경우를 잘 처리해주어 가능하다는 것을 알고 있습니다. – 이 내용은 본문의 내용과 다르다.
8. 본문 – 당사는 거친 마루에 사용되는 floor coverings(마루 깔개)에 대한 문의를 많이 받았습니다. 당사에게 sample를 보내주시면 도움이 되겠습니다. –
   (d) 제조비용을 낮추기 위해서 되도록 많은 아울렛을 통한 유통경로로 매출을 늘려야 한다는 것을 이해하십시오. – 이 내용은 sample을 보내달라는 수입상의 서신에 대한 reply로는 적합하지 않다.
9. 본문 – 당사는 귀사의 광고를 보고 Alpha Rapid Bottler에 관심이 있으며 Spain에서 soft drink를 제조하는 작은 회사입니다. 지금은 Wesco Bottler를 사용하고 있는데 귀사의 equipment(지식, 능력)를 듣고자 합니다. 근일 저의 공장에 방문해주시면 고맙겠습니다. – 음료제조업체가 상품(Bottler)을 구매하기 위한 상담을 받고자 하는 메일.
   (b) a sales consultant(컨설팅 세일즈)

Situation 12

1. (b) 2. ⓒ 3. (d) 4. (d)
5. (b) 6. (a) 7. (b) 8. (d)
9. (d) 10. (d) 11. (a)

3. (d) Guard Against Damp - 습기주의
6. meet the target: 목표액에 이르다.
7. 본문 - 당사는 오늘 선적품을 받았습니다. 상자들은 손상되 보였고 외관상 젖어 있었으며 stained(얼룩져 있었으며) dented(눌린 자국이) 있었습니다. 사실, 박스를 열었을 때 대부분의 책이 침수되어 있었으며 어떤 책은 눌리고 뭉개져 있었습니다. 이 선적에는 당사가 채우고 싶었던 많은 back orders(이월 주문)가 들어있었습니다. 귀사가 얼마나 빨리 replaced(대체하다) 해 줄 수 있는지를 알려주셔서 당사의 고객 들에게 주문품을 받을 수 있는 날짜를 알려줄 수 있기를 바랍니다.
   The boxes look damaged, stained, dented에서처럼 과거분사가 와야 한다. you can have this shipment replaced. 이 문장에는
   have(사역동사) + 목적어(사물) + 목적보어(과거분사)로 구성되지만
   have(사역동사) + 목적어(사람) + 목적보어(원형)인 경우도 있다.
8. 본문 - 당사(수입상)가 주문했던 상품이 정확히 공급되지 않았습니다. 2012년 7월 20일 CD case 12,000를 주문했었습니다. 수화물이 어제 도착했는데 단지 1,200개 뿐이었습니다. 당사가 모든 고객들에게 신의를 다하기 위하여 긴급구매를 해야 했기 때문에 이번 실수는 당사를 어려운 처지로 놓이게 했습니 다. 즉시 부족분을 보충해 주시고 다시는 이런 일이 일어나지 않도록 확실히 해 주십시오.
   (d) 수입상은 가능한 한 빨리 문제가 바로 잡히길 요청했다.
9. 본문 - 당사의 주문품 중 4개의 case가 손상되었다는 걸 알려드립니다. case가 너무 부서지기 쉽고 포장 이 해상운송에 충분히 적합지 않아 상품이 판매될 수 없는 상태입니다. 손상이 부실한 포장의 결과라는 것을 보여주는 손해사정인의 보고서를 동봉합니다. 대체상품을 항공편으로 보내주든지 검사비 포함 손상된 상품의 결제로 USD980.00를 보내주세요.
   (d) 하지만, 포장은 국제해상운송기준에 따른 것이며 포장에 대한 명세서는 계약서에 귀사의 합의가 있었던 것입니다. 재차 확인이 필요하겠습니다. - reply로서 적합하다.
10. 본문 - 아침 전화가 끝난 후 당사는 귀사에게 보냈던 carrel panel과 아주 똑같은 것을 선적했습니다.
   귀사가 처음 선적에 대해 보고했던 손상은 트럭회사의 부주의 한 취급 결과라는 게 확실합니다. - 손상된 화물은 적재해 놓으시면 당사가 가져가겠습니다.
   (d) seller는 잘못된 선적을 대체하고 그 손상은 운송인 부주의에 의한 것이라고 본다.
11. 본문 - 전체적으로 중국의 무역흑자는 수입이 늘고 유럽에서 중국제품에 대한 수요의 약화로 2010년 USD183 billion에서 2011년 USD155 billion으로 줄었다. 경제성장 속도의 둔화에 대한 중국의 우려에도 불구하고 자본 분석가들은 중국의 수출은 올해 10% 증가할 것으로 예측한다. -
   (a) 중국의 경제성장은 지난해만큼은 못하지만 분석가들은 수출성장에 대해서는 긍정적이다.

Situation 13

1. (c) 2. (c) 3(c) 4. (d)
5. (a) 6. (b)

3. (c) dozen(not dozens), 1다스, 1타(打), 12(개)(略: doz., dz); '형용사적' 1다스의, 12(개)의. ★ 수사(數 詞) 또는 그 상당어(단, some은 제외)의 뒤에 형용사나 명사로 쓰일 때에는 보통 단수로만 쓰인 다. (12 dozen을 말하는 gross도 마찬가지로 쓰인다.) 그러나

several, many, hundreds, thousands 등과 같이 쓰여서 '많이'의 의미로 쓰일 때는 dozens로 복수형을 쓴다. 따라서 "thousands of dozens of cushion covers"로 쓴다면 "큐션 커버 수천 다스"를 말한다.

4. (a) 보험증권은 No. M-153이며 2월 14일 Portland를 출항한 선박 "Kennedy"에 선적된 상품은 나쁜 날씨로 인하여 운송 중에 파손되었습니다.

   (b) 당사는 귀사의 5월 25일자 서신을 받고 귀사의 지시에 따라 8월 20일 부산에서 런던으로 출항하는 선박 "NamDong"에 선적된 USD 6,000 상당의 컴퓨터 3대에 대하여 해상보험에 가입했습니다. 귀사에게 보험증권과 USD 2,000의 어음을 보내며, 당사에게 10월 15일까지 송금해주시길 바랍니다.

   (c) 당사는(보험회사) 해상보험으로 발생한 손실에 대하여 보상하려고 하며, 귀사가 당사에게 claim할 때 당사로부터 원하는 것이 무엇인지 알려주시길 바랍니다. 그리고 귀사에게 제출해야 할 필요한 서식을 알려주십시오.

   (d) 귀사의 주문에 감사하며 이 주문이 우리 두 회사의 오래 지속되는 관계의 시발점이 되리라 믿습니다.

5. 본문 – 귀사의 8월 11일자 메일에 의하면, 당사의 의도에 오해가 있는 것으로 보입니다. (C) 당사의 CEO인 Mr. Danish가 7월 25일 방문 중에 언급한 것은 수동모델이 아닌 귀사의 오토메틱 트랜스엑슬이었습니다. (B) 당사는 수동모델에 대한 수요가 줄어들 것이라 예상하기 때문에 귀사의 오토메틱 모델을 당사의 앞바퀴 굴림 차량에 사용하는데 관심이 있습니다. (D) 하지만 한국에서의 규제 때문에 실행 가능성은 귀사로부터 도면과 명세서를 받은 후에 결정될 수 있습니다. (A) 당사는 귀사가 이 자재를 가능한 한 빨리 공급해주기를 원하지만, 만일 귀사의 정책이 계약의 보상범위 없이 그러한 편의를 허용하지 않는다면, 당사는 계획을 재고해야 하겠습니다. 귀사가 빠른 답장을 주시면 감사하겠습니다.

6. 본문 – 이전의 거래로부터 귀사는 이런 문제가 꽤 이례적이라는 것을 아시겠지요. 어찌되었든 귀사에게 끼친 불편함에 미안합니다. 하지만, 이번 거래는 CIF이었기 때문에 (b) 당사가 보험료는 지급했지만 지정된 선박의 본선으로부터 선적에 대한 법적인 책임이 없습니다. 더구나 무사고 선화증권은 상품이 선적될 당시 정상이었다는 것을 보여줍니다.

저자 약력

■ 김 민 호

전북대학교 무역학과, 교수
전북대학교 본부, 국제협력처장
전북대학교 GTEP(Global Trade Expert incubating Program) 단장

한국무역학회, 부회장
한국산업경제학회, 상임이사
무역영어 검정시험 출제위원, 대한상공회의소
관세사 무역영어 출제위원, 관세청

Southern Illinois University at Carbondale, DBA
Baruch College, City University of New York, MBA
전북대학교 상과대학 무역학과, 상학사

■ 한 방 울 (Belle Han)

전북대학교 무역학과, 강의전담 교수
전북대학교 언어교육부 영어강사
서울 PAGODA, YBM 영어강사

전북대학교 상과대학 무역학과 박사
서울대학교 대학원 경영학 석사 MBA
George Mason University, School of Management, B.S., Marketing

무역영어 스토리

초판 1쇄 인쇄 —— 2019년 9월 1일
초판 1쇄 발행 —— 2019년 9월 5일
지은이 —— 김 민 호 · 한 방 울
펴낸이 —— 전 두 표
펴낸데 —— 도서출판 **두남**
서울시 강동구 성내로6길 34-16 두남빌딩
신 고 : 제25100-1988-9호
TEL : 02) 478-2065~7, 2311
FAX : 02) 478-2068
E-mail : dunam1@unitel.co.kr
http://www.dunam.co.kr

정가 26,000원

ISBN 978-89-6414-849-5 93320